Economics of Managerial Decision-making

G. P. Marshall and B. J. McCormick

Basil Blackwell

Copyright © G. P. Marshall and B. J. McCormick 1986

First published 1986

Basil Blackwell Ltd
108 Cowley Road, Oxford OX4 1JF, UK

Basil Blackwell Inc.
432 Park Avenue South, Suite 1503
New York, NY 10016, USA

British Library Cataloguing in Publication Data

Marshall, G. P.
   Economics of managerial decision-making.
   1. Decision-making
   I. Title   II. McCormick, B. J.
   658.4'03   HD30.23

   ISBN 0–631–13187–6
   ISBN 0–631–14312–2 Pbk

Library of Congress Cataloging in Publication Data

Marshall, G. P.
   Economics of managerial decision-making.

   Includes index.
   1. Managerial economics. 2. Decision-making.
I. McCormick, B. J. (Brian Joseph) II. Title.
HD30.22.M38 1986   658   86–3562
ISBN 0–631–13187–6
ISBN 0–631–14312–2 (pbk.)

Typeset in 10/11 pt Ehrhardt by Photo·Graphics, Honiton, Devon
Printed in Great Britain by T. J. Press Ltd, Padstow, Cornwall

Contents

Acknowledgements

We are grateful to Philip Allan for permission to reprint table 3.6 from J. Pickering and A. J. Cockerill (eds), *The Economic Management of the Firm*. An earlier version of the chapter on personnel management appeared in the Pickering and Cockerill volume. Our thanks are also due to Graham Ray and Joe Smith for permission to reprint figures 6.3–6.5 which originally appeared in *Hardy Heating Ltd*, and subsequently in a revised version in *Hardy Developments Ltd*. Arthur Francis and the editors of *Sociology* have allowed us to use figure 3.4, and the Syndic of Cambridge University Press gave permission for us to reprint figures 5.2–5.4 from A. D. Chandler's chapter in the *Cambridge Economic History of Europe*, Vol. 7, Part II. We are also grateful to the Oxford University Press for permission to reproduce the discussion of linear programming from P. W. Bell and M. P. Todaro, *Economic Theory*. We would like to thank the editors of the *Journal of Consumer Research* for permission to reproduce figure 8.9, the editor of the *Journal of Industrial Economics* for permission to reproduce figure 12.5, and Elsevier Science Publications for figures 15.1–15.3.

Our chief intellectual debts are to Harry Townsend and Jack Gilbert. We have benefited from discussing business history with John Mason. Our understanding of the Japanese economy (as well as our prowess at snooker) owes a great deal to the patience of D. W. Anthony and G. Healey of the Sheffield Centre for Japanese Studies. Our debt to Dan Hemmings will only be apparent to the Sheffield coterie of finance students.

Finally, we acknowledge the enormous debt we owe to Linda and Monica who have had to bear the brunt of the burden of preparing the manuscript.

1 Introduction

Neoclassical economics is a moving target and its continual recreation can be a source of confusion to both practitioners and critics alike. Hence, we begin with an explicit statement of our objective. We are interested in the economic management of firms in advanced economies. We draw therefore upon Lewis's distinction between the core and the periphery of an evolving world economy (Lewis, 1978). The firms we are interested in are those to be found in the core of the international economy in the last quarter of the twentieth century. However, even within the core there are differences. Some economies, such as the United States, are leaders – scratching away at the technological frontier. Others are followers: Japan, Britain, Germany and Sweden, for example. Some are catching up rapidly whereas others appear to be stagnating. Each country, although a member of the core, has a different cultural background which exerts a considerable influence upon the behaviour of firms in the international economy.

The firms of our core differ from those which Alfred Marshall discussed in his *Industry and Trade* (1923) because the passage of time has brought new issues and new countries into the core. Marshall was concerned with the weakening of Britain's industrial performance but saw hope in that independence of character which was the British characteristic. He noted the emphasis upon education in Germany, the stress upon individuality and artistic skills in France and the drive towards multiform standardization in the United States. Were he alive today, however, he would have noted the enlargement and bifurcation of the core and the increasing involvement of the periphery in the world economy. He would, perhaps, be inclined to stress the importance of job rotation and forms of industrial cooperation in Japan. He would have observed that the forces of industrialization and trade which had ignored national boundaries and achieved a peaceful conquest and integration of Europe in the nineteenth century had been checked by the bifurcation of Europe as well as other parts of the world economy, into a core of market economies and a core of planned economies, each with its attendant periphery.

Chapter 2 is about a very neoclassical theme: the theory of trade; but it is the exchange theory of an advanced economy, probably the United States, possibly Japan, Britain, West Germany, Sweden, France or Australia; it is not the nineteenth-century theory of trade of Walras or Pareto, although their ideas serve as a starting point. Instead, it deals with the more recent preoccupations of advanced economies. First there has been the persistent

(Keynesian) problem of whether an economy can maintain full employment of resources. Second there has been the question of whether the state has to finance and produce some goods and services. Arising out of these two issues has been the general question: how do buyers and sellers assess the qualities of goods? To determine prices it is first necessary to determine what the goods are. Hence in chapter 2 we draw upon the bourgeoning literature of informational economics. What this literature emphasizes is the importance of merchants and the institutions which make markets work. In the 1950s and 1960s economists completed the task of delineating the assumptions required for an economy characterized by certainty. In the 1970s and 1980s they have increasingly turned to uncertainty and in doing so they have come to a realization of what sociologists such as Dore (1983) have called 'relational contracting', the awareness that trade is not conducted by anonymous agents, by 'city men', but by individuals who operate in a cultural and social milieu which ensures a climate of trust.

Chapter 3 introduces the firm as a bundle of contracts between resource owners, which overcomes some of the disadvantages of using markets. The disadvantage to which special attention has been directed is the problem of the behaviour of workers. This raises the further issues of: What should be the nature of the contracts between resource owners? Does monitoring imply a hierarchical structure? What should be the goals of firms? What is the nature of entrepreneurship? Are the contractual relationships between resource owners the same in all countries within the core?

Chapter 4 looks at the problems of strategy as a firm moves through a life cycle of birth, maturity, decline and, possibly, death. The concept of a life cycle of a firm was introduced by Marshall in the context of a nineteenth-century world of family firms which went through a cycle of 'clogs to clogs in three generations'. In Marshall's industries some firms were struggling to obtain a foothold, others had reached maturity and some were declining. Because of the complex nature of an industry, the industry supply price was determined not by the marginal firm but by a representative firm which enjoyed the advantages of economies of scale. Hence Marshall could assume that the the size of the industry was given, even though the composition of its firms could be continually changing. Marshall's concept of a representative firm was subsequently criticized for its neglect of internal economies of scale and the possibilities of monopoly, both of which might emerge with limited liability and the growth of markets. (In *Industry and Trade* Marshall did show an awareness of these issues.) For later writers, such as Sraffa, Robinson and Chamberlin, the emphasis was to shift away from the industry and the representative firm and towards a more detailed, axiomatic, treatment of the firm; and with this shift, and the belief that markets were becoming more oligopolistic, there has been a revival of interest in Cournot. However, we defer consideration of Cournot until chapter 8 because we think that the life cycle remains a useful concept. Joint stock companies in the late twentieth century have undergone senility and decay.

Chapter 5 returns to the theme of chapter 2: what is the nature of the firm? What is its structure? Weber explored the problem of bureaucracy and most subsequent work has been an amplification or criticism of his ideas. Hence the first theme of chapter 5 deals with Weber and his critics. The second theme is the evolution of firms' structures in the economies of the evolving core. The two themes are linked because scientific management, Theory X, formed the leitmotiv of the core economies of the nineteenth and early twentieth centuries, whereas sociotechnical systems, job rotation, workers' cooperatives and Theories Y and Z have emerged in the late twentieth century and particularly with new core countries, such as Japan.

Chapter 6 is concerned with the usefulness of accounting information as a guide to decision-making. It begins with the problem of designing the firm's structure to elicit information and control the firm. It goes back, therefore, to some of the issues of the previous chapter and presents them in a cybernetic framework replete with feedback, filters and Ashby's law of requisite variety. From the insights gained the chapter goes on to consider the limitations of financial accounting information.

Chapters 7 to 11 deal with specific areas of management, with functional areas. Chapter 7 presents a brief introduction to the changing patterns of marketing. Chapter 8 deals with the central problems of marketing. What do consumers want? How do they set about satisfying their wants? How might consumers respond to various marketing inducements? Successful marketing depends upon a knowledge of marketing structures, and chapter 9 places the problems of consumer behaviour within the context of market structures involving different numbers of firms. In chapter 10 the emphasis is upon product policy. Finally, chapter 11 concludes the discussion of marketing with an examination of the channels of distribution (internal as well as external) and location policy.

In chapter 12 the emphasis is switched away from *what* to produce to a consideration of *how* to produce – to production management. It begins with a general statement of the optimal production plan as set out in neoclassical economics (or, as it is sometimes called, classical programming). All combinations of factors are technically feasible (the 'putty' assumption) and the choice of techniques is then dictated by relative factor prices. The alternative assumption of fixed factors is then considered. Classical programming and linear programming may be treated as one-period models; but a detailed analysis of the multi-period problem requires an examination of network analysis. From sequential programming we move on to consider inventory theory and queueing problems. To this point it has been assumed that there are no problems surrounding the quality of the product. In production management texts it is assumed that quality control can be ensured by statistical sampling; but this is a Western (scientific management) approach which assumes that workers cannot be trusted, and is contrasted with the Japanese Kanban method in which workers are induced to produce a high-quality product and inventories are minimized through the use of quality circles and job rotation. Although the Japanese had a reputation for poor quality in the 1950s, present-day Japanese methods reach quality standards which seem unattainable to their competitors.

Chapter 13 introduces personnel management problems with a discussion of the hiring of labour. The difficulties of transforming the abstract marginal productivity principle into an operational tool of decision-making are explored. The treatment of hiring policies is extended to such issues as assessing the efficiency of labour before employment, overtime and short-time working and shift working. But management also need to consider the possible response of workers to inducements, and the theory of labour supply is elaborated. In many advanced countries wages are determined by some form of collective bargaining, and the next issue to be examined is the behaviour of trade unions and their effects upon wages and productivity.

Chapter 14 concludes the detailed examination of specific or operational areas of management by looking at investment and financial management. The emphasis is not upon accounting procedures but upon the determination of asset prices in a general equilibrium framework. However, present values are determined in the financial markets of different core economies and there is a brief account of different financial markets. The initial problem is then considered to be the determination of forward rates as a guide to future spot rates for assets. The establishment of forward rates then leads in to the establishment of appropriate investment procedures, and investment management is then linked to marketing and production management. Having established criteria for investment appraisal the discussion then turns to appropriate methods of financing, and involves a consideration of debt and equity finance and dividend policy. Finally, the problems of cash management are outlined.

Chapters 15 to 17 deal with the problems of particular types of firms. Chapter 15 examines the problems of multinational corporations; chapter 16 briefly discusses workers' cooperatives; and chapter 17 analyses the problems of public enterprises. These chapters are necessarily shorter than the previous ones because they rely upon the analysis of earlier chapters.

Bibliography and references

Dore, R. P. (1983) 'Goodwill and the spirit of capitalism', *British Journal of Sociology*, 34, 459–62.
Lewis, W. A. (1978) *Growth and Fluctuations 1870–1913*. London: Allen and Unwin.
Marshall, A. (1923) *Industry and Trade*. London: Macmillan.

2 The Propensity to Truck, Barter and Exchange

Within the context of this book we look at *trade* because it represents an alternative method of allocation to that of *diktat*. A discussion of trading enables us to understand both why firms emerge as an organizational alternative to resources being allocated through markets, and why well-established firms continue to use the market mechanism for certain allocative tasks.

Economics is the study of trading relationships. Why do agents trade? The simple answer is: because trade confers mutual benefits upon the participants. Crusoe and Friday have populated many textbooks with their illustration of this proposition. Crusoe, alone, is dependent upon his own skills in applying a crude technology to the meagre resources available on the island for the production of those goods which will satisfy his basic wants. Assuming that Crusoe likes any sort of food we can simplify his problem to one of how much fish and how much fruit to produce. The solution to the problem lies in deriving his *production* possibilities curve, which traces out the maximum outputs permitted by his technology, skill, effort and time. Given the availability of fish and fruit on the island and the absence of trade, this curve confines his *consumption* possibilities.

Where in the set of consumption opportunities does Crusoe locate himself? Clearly we have no idea about this unless Crusoe tells us, or we have a model of his behaviour which offers a good approximation to how he makes consumption choices. We shall return to the question of *how* to model consumption behaviour in a later chapter; for the time being let us assume that we can represent his actions as determined by a 'preference map'. It might be thought that *economics* begins here – formerly we had Crusoe the *engineer* mapping out his production alternatives but now we have Crusoe the *economic agent* who has to make a choice in relating his consumption wants to production possibilities. This view of what constitutes economic behaviour is best illustrated in Lionel Robbins's famous definition of economics as a (human) science dealing with the relationship between various ends and the scarce means of obtaining them (Robbins, 1932). However, it might be argued also that if we model Crusoe's behaviour on the assumption of a given set of preferences, then the problem remains within the competence of the engineer, at least to the extent that he is an applied mathematician – the problem is reduced to one of optimizing or maximizing (a preference function) with given constraints.

This is an argument which has been well expressed by James M. Buchanan (1979).

Buchanan's argument is very persuasive. Economists do need some of the skills of the engineer and, in particular, to understand the analytics of optimizing behaviour in the face of constraints; but economics must go beyond this to find its own identity and its own contributions to the understanding of human behaviour. On the desert island the real *economics* (or the real *symbiotics*, if we follow Buchanan completely) emerges only when we consider the appearance of Friday, for only then does Crusoe form an association with someone else which is based on *exchange* or mutual *agreement*. The association is formed because it is to the mutual advantage of the parties in terms of their social needs and their material wants. It can be demonstrated quite simply through the Ricardian principle of comparative advantage that, as long as the parties to an exchange obtain commodities at relative prices which are cheaper than their respective marginal costs of production, then trade confers more mutual benefits than autarky.

Trade and 'Efficiency'

Of course the Ricardian principle does not mean that material gain explains the motivation behind all trade, nor does it suggest that benefits from trade will be distributed equally between trading partners. Real-world exchanges demonstrate very often that social and political motivations for trade are common, and that bargaining strength and skill can influence the rate of exchange between commodities, etc. However, the principle established relates to the *potential* gains, regardless of their relative amounts, inherent in exchange which is based on comparative (cost) advantage. While recognizing that relative gains from trade can differ it might nevertheless be argued that comparative cost trading is efficient in the sense that each participant becomes better off in material terms – either because the same quantity of goods as before can be consumed now at a lower outlay – or because the same outlay as before will buy more goods now. Thus, by opting for trade rather than autarky each participant chooses a more efficient method of satisfying material wants.

We should note here that 'efficiency' is not a term to be used without caution. Very often the term seems apt in the circumstances but, equally often, a closer inspection reveals a meaningless adjective. Consider, for example, two of the activities which we have assumed Crusoe to be concentrating on so far – production and trading. His production 'problem' was described in terms of deriving a production possibilities curve from available resources and technology and normally, therefore, this is considered as a 'technological' issue. To go further, 'technological efficiency' is usually believed to be achieved along the production possibilities curve, or 'transformation frontier', rather than inside it, since from any point inside the frontier it is possible always to move to another point on the frontier by raising the level of employment and without suffering the goods trade-off which is the cost of any movement *along* the frontier. Figure 2.1 summarizes for the case of increasing (marginal) opportunity cost.

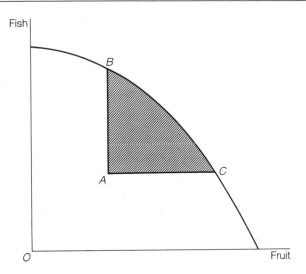

Figure 2.1 Marginal opportunity cost. A to B: more fish, no fruit trade-off; A to C: more fruit, no fish trade-off: B to C: more fruit, less fish; C to B: more fish, less fruit.

Figure 2.1 is the standard diagram of economics textbooks, showing that movements from *A* towards *B* or *C*, or towards anywhere in the shaded zone, are 'efficient'. On the face of it this looks an objective judgement, but this is not the case. As mere observers we cannot comment on the efficiency of such movements – only Crusoe can! Only Crusoe can say whether he prefers more to less, and until we have his preference function the production 'possibilities' shown in figure 2.1 are just that; they signal nothing whatsoever about efficiency. For example, if figure 2.1 relates only to what Crusoe could produce, regardless of whether he likes the commodities, producing more fish at no extra cost in terms of forgone fruit (e.g. from *A* to *B*) cannot be efficient if the very smell of fish makes Crusoe nauseous. In other words, without any knowledge of preferences, as mere observers, we are unable to tell whether or not one of the commodities (or both commodities) is a pollutant, an undesirable thing and, therefore, whether or not it would be 'efficient' to produce less of it rather than more.

Let us assume, then, that Crusoe does like both fish and fruit and does want to produce both these items for his own consumption. Can we not, then, discuss Crusoe's 'technological efficiency', that which relates to quantifiable outputs only, with subjective valuations not being a hindrance? Unfortunately this does not resolve the difficulty, because one of the inputs, indeed the most important one, is Crusoe himself (his skills, energy and effort). Suppose, for example, that Crusoe is a poor swimmer and is squeamish about killing fish. It might well be the case in these circumstances that he quite enjoys collecting fruit but hates catching fish; and it is not enough to say that these relative preferences for different productive activities will be reflected in Crusoe's relative productivities (e.g. a relatively flat curve in figure 2.1) for they may not be – Crusoe may possess very powerful self-control and be able to steel himself to become a very productive fisherman. The problem lies in the fact that Crusoe's distaste for fishing must be reflected somehow in the valuation of the output of fish; so how can we define 'technological' efficiency as something which relates to objectively quantifiable output?

Much the same difficulties would emerge if Crusoe were to be employed by someone else, and we shall have to face up to this in later chapters. As long as workers have different preferences for different modes of production it will not be possible to measure the relative efficiencies of alternative production processes unless this is taken into account. Very often account *is* taken of such differences when workers receive higher financial compensation for less attractive production methods, but this must be accounted for, then, in discussing the 'efficiency' of production methods. The way forward would seem to lie in letting our diagrams represent 'efficiency possibilities' as defined by the agent and not by the observer. In the case of self-sufficiency (or self-employment) this should present few difficulties. In the case of employer/employee relationships the likelihood of the employer defining 'efficiency', having regard for employees' preferences, will depend upon (a) his morality, (b) the likely effects of disregard upon employees' productivity, and (c) the bargaining strength of employees.

'Optimal' Resource Allocation

Given the qualifications and misgivings mentioned above, can we ever describe a whole economic system as being either 'efficient' or 'inefficient' ? Suppose, for example, that we consider both goods markets and factor markets working together – can we define 'efficiency' as being achieved in both simultaneously? In other words, is there some concept of 'social efficiency' which can be applied to an economic system as a whole, some means of deciding which allocation of resources can be described as 'the best'? In some societies the problem is 'solved' through either the charisma, or the power, of the leader – allocation pattern x is best because Adolph says so!' But in a democratic framework social 'rules' must be devised somehow. In particular, how can the economist offer any judgements about social welfare without reference to an accepted system of values? Much of the history of the foundation of theoretical welfare economics has been written in terms of a search for such a system and, in particular, for one which avoids value-judgements, and thereby bias. Of course the search is doomed from the outset – how is it possible to define an ethical rule which has no ethical content? The compromise has been to search for a rule which has a *minimum ethical content*, and at the present time economics still remains within that framework which, it is claimed, does have such a content – the Paretian ethical framework (after Vilfredo Pareto, 1848–1923) or what has become labelled as the 'new welfare economics'.

Despite being in the literature since around the turn of the century, the Paretian rule did not become entrenched until the late 1930s, or early 1940s. In fact its emergence followed the digestion by the economics profession of

Lionel Robbins's famous book *An Essay on the Nature and Significance of Economic Science* (1932), which did much to help destroy the last vestiges of utilitarianism inherited from the nineteenth century in the important works of A. C. Pigou at Cambridge.

Utilitarianism was based on the belief that the total welfare for society equals the sums of all the utilities (satisfaction) of the separate individuals within society, and that social welfare is improved when 'the greatest good is secured for the greatest number'. The problem with such a rule, of course, is that it necessitates a further value-judgement to be exercised when the greatest good for the greatest number can be achieved only at the expense of a minority; i.e. to judge a change in social welfare requires an interpersonal comparison to be made among the utilities of different members of society.

It was a distaste for such interpersonal comparisons which helped towards the emergence of the Paretian framework. The Paretian principle for comparing states of the world goes as follows: (i) weak form – social state A is better than state B if all individuals in the society prefer A to B; (ii) strong form – social state A is better than state B if one (or more) individual prefers A to B and the rest are indifferent between A and B. The strong form is the most often used by economists and it is usually worded – a *change* in the order of things is a Pareto improvement *if at least one person feels better off and none feels worse off*. The difference between this principle and utilitarianism should be clear. In terms of a simple society comprising two individuals, any change which increases the welfare of both is a Pareto improvement; any change which reduces the welfare of both is a Pareto regression; any change which increases the welfare of one but leaves the welfare of the other unchanged is a Pareto improvement, but any change which improves the welfare of one and harms the other *cannot be judged* within the confines of the Paretian framework since judgement involves an interpersonal comparison of utility. On the basis of the Paretian principle welfare economists have been able to make assessments about the desirability of alternative allocations of society's scarce resources on condition that the relative distributions of income are equally acceptable. Thus, returning to the production possibilities curve of our mythical island we can assume, now, two producer/traders, Crusoe and Friday, and define the conditions under which the curve is indeed some sort of efficiency locus. Figure 2.2 shows a box representing the constraints imposed on the island's economy by the available resources (say labour, L, and capital, K), technology, weather conditions, etc.

From the origin O^x is measured outputs of x (fish) while outputs of y (fruit) are measured from origin O^y; corresponding isoquant sets are introduced into the box as $x_1 \dots n$ and $y_1 \dots n$. The Pareto criterion requires that the locus of the best output combinations comprises points from which it is not possible for the economy to move without suffering a loss in output of one (or both) of the commodities (with a consequent loss in revenue for the corresponding producer). This locus is usually termed the (production) contract curve and it passes through the points of tangency between the two sets of isoquants, i.e. efficiency is satisfied when marginal technical rates of substitution are equalized, when $\mathrm{MRTS}^x_{LK} = \mathrm{MRTS}^y_{LK}$. This can be appreciated intuitively

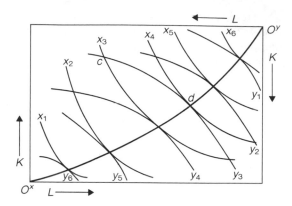

Figure 2.2

by seeing that for every point off the contract curve there is a superior point on it. For example, a reallocation of resources from point c to point d in figure 2.2 keeps output of y constant at y_3 but allows output of x to increase from x_3 to x_4.

By mapping from the tangency points in figure 2.2 we can now erect again the production possibilities curve as shown in figure 2.3. All points along the PP' curve are Pareto efficient, relating as they do to points of equality between marginal technical rates of substitution in figure 2.2. The slope of the curve PP' measures the marginal rate of transformation of x into y ($MRTxy$), i.e. it measures the ratio of the marginal costs of producing x and y, MC_y/MC_x.

Now, any point along the curve PP' in figure 2.3 represents a specific commodity output which can then be exchanged between Crusoe and Friday.

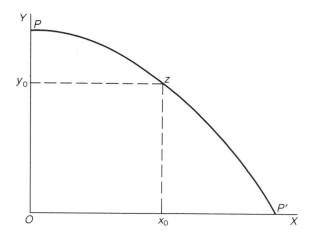

Figure 2.3

How is this output to be distributed in accordance with the Pareto criterion? Clearly, again, the best points (of consumption this time) will be those from which any movement must make at least one of the consumers worse off. Thus, again, we look to points of tangency – this time between indifference curves. In figure 2.4 the preference maps of both Crusoe and Friday ($a_1 \ldots n; b_1 \ldots n$) are introduced into the box formed by the constraints imposed by a given output of Oy_0 and Ox_0.

In figure 2.4 the efficient consumption points lie along the (exchange) contract curve y_0x_0 where marginal rates of substitution are equalized ($\text{MRS}^a_{xy} = \text{MRS}^b_{xy}$). Again, for any point off this contract curve (e.g. e) there is at least one superior point on it (e.g. f) where more of one commodity is enjoyed without any loss of the other. Note that the shape of the contract curve in figure 2.4 is drawn as a wavy line, to remind us of the difficulties of defining subjective preference maps.

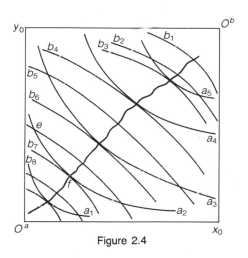

Figure 2.4

So, can we now devise some overall ruling, some 'grand optimum' condition from the Paretian framework? Such an optimum can indeed be defined as when the rate at which one good can be transformed into the other at the margin (MRT_{xy}) equals the consumers' marginal rate of substitution between the two goods ($\text{MRS}^a_{xy} = \text{MRS}^b_{xy}$). If, for example, the marginal social cost of $1x$ is $2y$ while consumers' preferences value $1x$ as $1y$ then the economy is producing too much x and too little y, according to consumers' preferences, and a Pareto improvement is possible.

Since Pareto optimality is about welfare (utility) maximization it is usual to map from 'output space' into 'utility space' to present a final view of the 'welfare frontier' or 'utility possibility frontier'. However, for present purposes there is nothing to gain from going so far; instead one can summarize, now, the conditions for a Pareto-optimal allocation of resources for a $2 \times 2 \times 2$ economy à la Crusoe (a) and Friday (b), where x and y are the goods produced by variable resources L and K.

(i) efficient production: $\mathrm{MRTS}^x_{LK} = \mathrm{MRTS}^y_{LK}$

(ii) efficient consumption: $\mathrm{MRS}^a_{xy} = \mathrm{MRS}^b_{xy}$

(iii) efficient mix: $\dfrac{\mathrm{MC}_y}{\mathrm{MC}_x} = \mathrm{MRS}_{xy}$ for both a and b.

Using the Paretian 'Yardstick'

The literature of welfare economics over the past three decades and more has been replete with articles and books which analyse real-world phenomena from the standpoint of these Paretian 'welfare conditions'. There is nothing within the Paretian framework to favour either a competitive market system or a wholly centrally planned economic order. To satisfy the rules of Pareto optimality, all that is required is that the ratios of marginal costs be equated with price ratios in all areas of production, and that these same price ratios be equated with marginal rates of substitution in all areas of consumption. These conditions are satisfied under perfect competition, but equally so under the dictates of a perfectly informed central planner. However, welfare economists in the mixed enterprise systems of the real world have regarded perfect competition as their blueprint and advocated policies to 'correct' real-world resource allocations when the latter do not result from marginal cost pricing.

Because of the acceptance of perfect competition's yardstick, perceived divergences from Pareto optimality have been discussed in terms of 'market breakdown'. Such breakdown results usually from two sources: monopoly power and so-called 'externalities'. When monopoly persists in any market, prices no longer truly reflect marginal costs and a Paretian welfare loss is incurred. Externalities persist when some costs and benefits have not been 'internalized', i.e. are either uncompensated or unrewarded. When this happens supply quantities can fail to accord with optimal requirements defined in Paretian terms.

It is not the intention at this stage to enter into a discussion of internalization processes and the debate over what should be the appropriate role of the state in the economic order. Such matters are left for chapter 17. It should be pointed out here, however, that our analysis does not set out to adhere, at all costs, to a view of the world as one populated by neutral economic agents engaged in a mathematical game in which outcomes are always predetermined. Rather, we prefer to believe that the nature of organizations and of 'social arrangements' makes adoption of welfare constructs like Pareto optimality a fruitless exercise in many respects. To continue with a view expressed earlier, and to echo Buchanan again, we are persuaded by the argument that the concept of a perfectly competitive general equilibrium squeezes out all the social content from individual behaviour in the market place. Furthermore, to model competition as a tool of 'social engineering', a device which stands as an alternative to centralized (governmental) resource allocation, is to misrepresent the true nature of the market process, which is about a network of relationships *evolving* from a process of trading, this evolution being reflected in markets *becoming* competitive (Buchanan, 1979).

The above remarks represent part of a statement of intent; it is difficult to remain consistent when the methodological framework of economics contains so many fractures while clinging, still, to the neoclassical paradigm. We shall be eclectic and shift our ground, perhaps too often for every reader's taste. Several of the issues raised so far will be discussed in more depth in chapter 17. In the meantime let us continue with more observations on market processes.

Money, Trading and Degrees of Ignorance

What happens when both the number of agents engaged in each market and the number of commodities available for trade increases from 2 to n? A major problem of information now arises, for although each trader *may* have perfect knowledge about the goods he is selling he will be much less knowledgeable about the qualities of other commodities. Since the acquisition of knowledge about other commodities is costly, then price differences for the same commodity can occur which will, in turn, offer incentives to specialist traders – dealers and middlemen. However, even the abilities of the middlemen can be easily outstripped by the continual growth in the number and variety of commodities available, and the outcome of the process is for one good to act as proxy for all others, to be accepted in lieu of all others in the process of exchange. Such a good is labelled *money*.

Money certainly facilitates trade but it does not remove all the problems relating to the acquisition of information. One problem that still remains is that of assessing the characteristics of commodities. Money prices may offer a reliable guide to quality but they can also mislead. In a world where every economic agent does not possess perfect knowledge there can be an asymmetry of information in the market place; either buyers or sellers, but not both, possess full knowledge (as far as this is possible) of the qualities of the goods offered for sale. In these circumstances a 'false equilibrium' might be established, in which the market clears but not at a price and quantity consistent with full knowledge on both sides of the market.

We can think of markets being characterized by four different combinations of knowledge and ignorance. The simple matrix of table 2.1 shows these combinations and suggests for each box an example from the real world.

Knowledgeable Buyers and Sellers: the Financial Market

Financial markets is the example used by economists wishing to demonstrate how the real world can be competitive and efficient and the characteristic which is underlined usually is that of 'information efficiency'.[1] Such markets are believed to be efficient in the sense that all information is contained in current prices and it is pointless, therefore, to analyse trends in prices in order

---

[1] For a clear and concise critique of the assumed efficiency characteristics of financial markets see Tobin (1984). Tobin's more accurate description of the information characteristic is that of 'information arbitrage efficiency'. We should note that this is not the only type of efficiency singled out by Tobin – there are three others.

Table 2.1

| | | BUYER | |
		Knowledgeable	Ignorant
SELLER	Knowledgeable	Financial market	Second-hand cars market
	Ignorant	Antiques market	Unemployment in the labour market

to gain a profit. In other words, 'outsiders' cannot make any gains, only 'insiders' can. This characteristic means in fact that an 'actively managed' portfolio of 'financial investments' cannot beat the market, or that 'prices are a random walk', in the sense that their correlations with past histories are too weak to be exploited profitably.[2]

Ignorant Buyers and Knowledgeable Sellers: Second-hand Cars

Owners of used cars may be presumed to know their strengths and weaknesses, and to have an estimate of the car's worth to them in terms of alternatives. In contrast, would-be purchasers of used cars may have great difficulty in judging their reliability prior to purchase. This ignorance on the buyers' side of the market will render potential buyers distrustful of sellers' claims and can be a factor which prevents an equilibrium from being established. For example, buyers' distrust may mean that sellers of good cars are unable to obtain prices which are a good deal better than the prices of poor cars, because buyers are unwilling to 'gamble' on relatively high prices being a signal of higher quality. On the other hand, buyers will be suspicious of prices which are 'too low' because these may signal very poor quality. Thus a range of prices will be the norm with good cars at the top and poor ones at the bottom. Suppose, now, that there is an excess supply of second-hand cars and prices begin to fall. This means that owners of good cars will withdraw them from the market as prices drop below owners' opportunity costs. At the same time demand may fall if buyers suspect that lower prices reduce their chances of obtaining a good second-hand buy. Thus the market may not move towards another equilibrium in the sense that the price mechanism will not be conveying the information necessary to bring together buyers and sellers of good cars.

One way round the problem is for sellers of second-hand cars to offer guarantees of reliability. Paradoxically, however, in the short run this might lead to the market becoming less perfect. As customers locate the reliable sellers the good reputation of the latter will spread and consumer loyalty to a small group of sellers will increase.

[2] Tobin (1984), p. 5; for a detailed analysis of this phenomenon see Cragg and Malkiel (1982).

Ignorant Sellers and Knowledgeable Buyers: Antiques Auctions

The antiques market is not characterized by wholesale ignorance on the selling side but it is a market in which the occasional knowledge advantage enjoyed by buyers can lead to the latter enjoying substantial gains. One method by which buyers have exploited their knowledge advantage at real-world auctions is the formation of auction 'rings'. An auction ring is an agreement among dealers not to bid against each other at a public auction on the understanding that once one of the members of the ring has bid successfully for an item, whose true value is well in excess of the amount of the successful bid, the ring will conduct a second auction among its members. The difference between the two prices – the one at public auction, the other at the 'knockout' – is shared, then, among the members of the ring.

Auction rings were declared illegal under the Auction Bidding Agreements Acts of 1927 and 1969. But should such rings be illegal? The problem is this: how can dealers who have invested in acquiring knowledge be assured of a return on their investment? A seller might be ignorant as to the properties of the good he wishes to sell but its value may be revealed to him by the bids of dealers. In effect the pricing system, the auction process, would aggregate and transmit the bits of disparate information possessed by knowledgeable buyers to the ignorant seller. Hence the seller would not have to invest in knowledge. This belief rests on two assumptions. First, there is freedom of entry to the auction – but that might depend upon the auctioneer correctly identifying the commodity. A Rembrandt would attract more wealthy buyers than a painting attributed to Bloggs. Second, that those buyers who have correctly identified the good would freely give their knowledge to the seller. Neither assumption seems plausible.

Credit Rationing

The existence of asymmetric information may also account for the existence of credit rationing and a fringe of unsatisfied borrowers. The problem is analogous to that of used cars. Banks and other financial institutions may not know whether borrowers may be able to repay their loans; and as interest rates fall the probability of bad borrowers entering the market may increase.

Buyer and Seller Ignorance: Unemployment

In elementary textbooks wages and employment are determined by the demand for, and supply of, labour. On the demand side, employers are guided by a law of diminishing marginal revenue productivity whereby successive additions to the labour force result in successively smaller additions to sales revenue. On the supply side, workers are influenced by the relative attractions of income and leisure. At some level of wages, equilibrium in the labour market is attained.

But how does the labour market respond to disturbances? The simplest market is an *auction market* or *casual market* in which wages are continuously adjusting to changes in demand and supply. In so far as unemployment occurs it is minimal; but where skill requirements are complex, and hiring and firing costs high, then workers will tend to be offered long-term contracts. In such *contract markets* wages and employment may not respond to short-run disturbances. An employer may be reluctant to hire an unemployed worker because the employer faces the problem of assessing the employee's abilities. Workers may not readily switch jobs because of the loss of income and costs of finding jobs. In such markets reductions in demand may be achieved through temporary layoffs. In such markets wages may not fall because employers fear that lower wages might attract less skilled workers. In such markets workers might not be readily dismissed, but once dismissed might find it difficult to get a new job.

Price and Quantity Uncertainty: Organized Futures Markets

Commodity uncertainty is the fundamental uncertainty, but there can also be price and quantity uncertainty. Even when the characteristics of goods are known – wheat or cotton, for example – there may still be problems arising from the fluctuations in price and quantity. Price stability may be capable of being achieved through the use of organized futures markets, but quantity uncertainty may require government intervention or even international governmental arrangements.

The standard argument for organized futures markets is that they enable a businessman to hedge against a price risk. The objection is that such markets may allow speculators to destabilize markets to the detriment of genuine traders and producers such as farmers. The truth may be that organized futures markets bring together dealers whose reputations are so well established that it is worth dealing with them – their word is their bond and their bond acts as if it were money; contracts become liquid assets which can be traded as if they were money. In other words, price uncertainty can only be dealt with if there is commodity certainty. What organized futures markets do is to underwrite transactions by establishing rules of trading, the terms of contracts, the methods of operating a market and the conditions of membership of the market. Like a multi-banking system with a clearing house the organized futures market has a central clearing system which reduces the need to check upon the worth of dealers.

The argument that a futures market is simply an insurance scheme runs up against the counter-argument that price risks could simply be countered by exchanging forward contracts. Consider the following problem. We may assume that current (spot) and future prices move in parallel. If they did not then gains and losses would occur. Thus suppose a merchant is holding wheat. If the spot price falls he will suffer a loss, and if it rises then he will profit; by selling a futures contract, equal in quantity to his inventory, then, he can eliminate price risk. Thus if the spot price falls then the futures price will fall by the same amount. Hence the loss on the inventory equals the gain on the futures contract and so the merchant breaks even. But is it necessary to have an organized futures market to achieve this result? Why not simply allow traders to arrange forward contracts? Why has there to be an elaborate institutional arrangement to conduct trading? The price insurance argument, as normally elaborated, does not address itself to this issue.

Will speculation in futures contracts bring about price stability? Must speculators destabilize prices in order to gain a profit and, in doing so, work against the interests of genuine producers, such as farmers? The standard argument for believing that speculators stabilize prices is that they will do so in order to maximize profits. Profits maximization achieves price stability. The thesis runs as follows. Assume that there is a belief in a long-run equilibrium price. If current prices then fall below the long-run price speculators will buy in the hope of making a profit when prices rise, and their act of buying now will cause the price fall to be less than it would have been in their absence. By similar reasoning price rises are damped down. Irrespective of the arguments and evidence as to the influence of speculation upon prices, however, there still remains the question: why is it that only certain goods are traded in organized futures markets? The answer to that question, we have suggested, lies in the demand for contracts which are liquid, saleable assets.

As a postscript we observe that farmers seldom engage in organized futures markets, whereas merchants do. The reason lies in the fact that the merchant can control the size of his inventory whereas the farmer may not know the size of his crop. Hence the need, often, for state intervention.

Screening, Signalling and Moral Hazard

Throughout our discussion of markets we have continually emphasized the problems raised by asymmetric information, by ignorance on the part of buyers or sellers, or both. Ignorance can, of course, lead to suspicion and could drive agents away from trade and towards self-sufficiency. Yet such are the potential gains from exchange that agents will attempt to overcome the obstacles to trading. One solution would be to use proxy variables as measures of the reliability of goods. Hence, traders may use *indicators* or *indices*. Indicators may be objective factors such as educational qualifications which might suggest to an employer that a person with a degree must be intelligent. Indices are rules of thumb such as: women are not in the labour market for the same length of time as men and, therefore, have not been as well graded or assessed as men; therefore, choose men rather than women! Another rule of thumb might be to use price as an indicator of quality – 'if it costs a lot, then it must be good'.

Educational qualifications may be used as screening or filtering devices by buyers. Alternatively, we may view them as *signals* or *guarantees* by sellers. Hence sellers may seek to acquire those indicators which they think the buyers are using. However, guarantees may be difficult to negotiate; thus buyers may not treat goods with due care and attention. Insurance claims may multiply if householders become disenchanted with their bathroom suites and 'accidentally' damage them in order to get replacements. Sellers may renege by arguing that buyers have not exercised due care and attention. *Moral hazard* is a concept used by insurance agents to express the possibility that insurers may not honour the spirit (as well as the letter) of a contract. Lawyers also emphasize the point that it is impossible to legislate for due performance.

Externalities and Indivisibilities

Information problems may give rise to market breakdown and the need to devise institutions to support or supplant the market. Other causes of market failure are *externalities* and *indivisibilities*.

An externality in consumption exists when the level of consumption of a good by one person has a direct effect upon the welfare of another person as opposed to an indirect effect through the price system. Thus one person may enjoy the beauty of another person's garden without having to pay for the privilege of viewing it. A production externality exists when the productive activity of one firm directly affects the productive activities of another firm. For example, a firm may discharge chemical waste into a river, and this may affect the fishing 'catch' of firms further downstream. Externalities therefore give consumers or firms something for which they do not pay. In some cases the things received are pleasant and lead to an increase in utility; in other instances they lead to a fall in utility.

Externalities may be due to indivisibilities. An indivisibility arises because there is a 'lumpiness' in consumption or production. A road or a railway coach may have to be a minimum size for technological efficiency; and if the road or railway coach is underutilized then it would be possible to allow others to consume their services without prior payment. This leads to the possibility of market failure. If, for example, A and B would both benefit from the construction of a road then A and B may attempt to conceal their preferences in the hope that the other would finance the project. The result could be that the road is not constructed. Alternatively, A could finance its construction but it would be underutilized because he demands from B a price equal to the average cost of its construction and usage despite the fact that once built its fixed cost is a byegone and the marginal cost of usage may be zero.

Externalities and indivisibilities may generate a demand for state financing and production in order to overcome market failure. In effect, households or firms may coerce themselves into payment of taxes in order to free themselves from the weaknesses of the market. However, the state may only be required to provide the financial arrangements, and production could be left in the hands of private producers. Thus the state may finance education and health care but leave production in private hands and supply citizens with vouchers which can be spent with private firms. Nor is it always necessary for externalities to give rise to state intervention. Coase (1960) has pointed to the use of the common law and the courts to settle some kinds of externality such as pollution and accidents. Nor need state intervention lead to the complete suppression of the market system. Pigou (1928) suggested that taxes and subsidies could be used to correct market prices. Thus, producers of pollutants could be taxed for their excessive production, and underprovision of medical care and education could be reduced through subsidies. Lange (1938) argued that a socialist economy could be decentralized through the use of accounting prices – themselves embodying the principle of taxes and subsidies – which could be raised and lowered in order to achieve efficient consumption and production.

Externalities may therefore generate demands for their regulation either by the state or through private arrangements, but whichever method is chosen this may not lead to their elimination. We need to distinguish between Pareto-relevant and Pareto non-relevant externalities. A Pareto-relevant externality is one in which the existence of a difference between benefits and costs will lead to pressures to make them equal through the use of taxes or subsidies. A Pareto non-relevant externality exists when there is no pressure to eliminate an externality. For example, the fact that there are road accidents does not mean that there will be an automatic pressure to eliminate them if the costs of road safety schemes will exceed their potential benefits.

Finally, we may note the connection between externalities, indivisibilities and information. Information, knowledge, may give rise to externalities. Once something is discovered it may become freely available to everyone. Hence there may be an underproduction of knowledge and perhaps the need for a patent system in order to protect the creators of knowledge. Even the firm may be an institution designed to protect the creators of knowledge – but that is to anticipate the contents of the next chapter.

Bibliography and References

Akerlof, G. A. (1970) 'The market for "lemons" : quality uncertainty and the market mechanism', *Quarterly Joural of Economics*, 84, 488–500.
Alchian, A. A. (1974) 'Why money?', *Journal of Money, Credit and Banking*, 9, 17–24; reprinted in Alchian, A. A. (1977) *Economic Forces at Work*. Indianapolis: Liberty Press.
Buchanan, J. M. (1979) *What Should Economists Do?* Indianapolis: Liberty Press.
Buchanan, J. M. and Stubblebine, W. (1962) 'Externality', *Economica*, 29, 371–84.
Coase, R. H. (1960) 'The problem of social cost', *Journal of Law and Economics*, 3, 1–44.
Cragg, J. C. and Malkiel, B. G. (1982) *Expectations and the Structure of Share Prices*. Chicago: Chicago University Press (a National Bureau of Economic Research Monograph).
Hayek, F. A. (1948) *Individualism and the Economic Order*. London: Routledge and Kegan Paul.
Lange, O. (1938) 'On the economic theory of socialism'. In B. E. Lippincott (ed.), *On the Economic Theory of Socialism*. Minneapolis: University of Minnesota Press.
McGuire, M. C. (1972) 'Private good clubs and public good clubs: economic models of group formation', *Swedish Journal of Economics*, 74, 84–99.
Pareto, V. (1972) *Manual of Political Economy*, translated by A. S. Schwier and A. N. Page. London: Macmillan.
Pigou, A. C. (1928) *The Economics of Welfare*. London: Macmillan.

Radford, A. (1945) 'The economics of a POW camp', *Economica*, 12, 189–207.
Robbins, L. C. (1932) *An Essay on the Nature and Significance of Economic Science.* London: Macmillan.
Salop, S. (1968) 'Parables of information transmission'. In A. Mitchell (ed.), *The Effect of Information on Consumer and Market Behavior.* Chicago: American Marketing Association, pp. 6–15.
Samuelson, P. A. (1969) 'Pure theory of public expenditure and taxation'. In J. Margolis and H. Guitton (eds), *Public Economics.* London: Macmillan, pp. 98–123.
Sen, A. K. (1975) 'The concept of efficiency'. In M. Parkin and A. R. Nobay (eds), *Contemporary Issues in Economics.* Manchester: Manchester University Press, pp. 196–210.
Tobin, J. (1984) 'The efficiency of the financial system', *Lloyds Bank Review*, 153, 1–15.

3 The Nature of the Firm

One of the themes developed in chapter 2 was that, no matter how strong the social preference for using the market mechanism as the main avenue by which resources are allocated in the economy, the more costly it is to use markets the less likely it is that markets will be used. It is this line of approach which led Coase (1937) to offer a rationale for the emergence of 'firms' : firms exist in order to reduce the number of contracts involved in the production of a commodity and, as a consequence, to reduce the 'transaction costs' involved. For each product to be produced through the market mechanism requires the negotiation and conclusion of a series of separate contracts including, indeed, a range of contracts between each and every resource owner, given that resources must combine in order to produce the finished article.

This is not to say that firms themselves eschew the market mechanism – as we shall see later firms may often rely upon transactions as part of their internal organizational structure (they may create internal labour markets and engage in internal subcontracting). But a feature which does help distinguish the firm from the market is that while the latter unconsciously allocates resources through agents transacting together, the former can achieve allocative ends through the exercise of command and/or conscious cooperative organization of resources within the framework of a prevailing technology. The picture is strikingly created in the imagery of Sir Dennis Robertson (1923), which depicts the market as an 'ocean of unconscious cooperation' and firms as 'islands of conscious power in this ocean'. The conscious coordinating authority does lie, of course, within the hands of 'the entrepreneur'.

In a nutshell Coase's firm emerges because of time and uncertainty – it takes time for exchanges to be effected and the longer the time, the more uncertain the outcome. It would seem, then, that firms exist, according to Coase, for the same basic reasons as the institution of money. However, to complete the picture, that is to explain the firm in terms of more than an organizing entrepreneur whose functions resemble those of a powerful middleman, Alchian and Demsetz (1972) have suggested that we look also to the nature of the production process where we can see that the non-separable nature of most production functions requires that resources be combined in some form of team arrangement. Each resource must be used *in combination* with other resources in order to produce anything, and this creates two problems which cannot be resolved through a market process: how to determine the size of reward appropriate to the productive contribution of every resource input, and how to monitor the productive effort applied by every resource input in the face of incentives to shirk.

The problems of shirking and reneging are solved, as in the political sphere, by the establishment of a contract whereby all resource owners assign to someone the task of supervising their activities and fixing rewards. As Rousseau observed, men put themselves in chains in order to be free. By the creation of a Leviathan all resource owners are released from the low output level resulting from shirking and evasion, and from the increased output there emerges a surplus which satisfies the resources owners for their increased efforts and pays the supervisor for his diligence. However, this contract theory leaves unanswered several questions. What meaning can be attached to the ownership of a firm? Do all resource owners own the firm? Why are the ownership rights of a firm always considered to belong the suppliers of physical and financial capital? And why does the supervisor tend to be identified with the suppliers of finance and physical capital? What, in short, accounts for the alleged superiority of the capitalist firm in which capital employs labour? To these questions Alchian and Demsetz have suggested that 'ownership' of the classical (capitalist) firm is defined in terms of a five-fold set of rights:

1   To be a residual claimant on returns to the activities of the enterprise.
2   To observe the behaviour of inputs.
3   To be the central party in all contracts involving inputs.
4   To measure the output contributions of the various inputs.
5   To sell all these rights to any other party.

Regarding the firm as an organization of 'team effort' helps towards an explanation of the continuity of firms' activities. Of course some firms may be formed to exist for one production period only: e.g. a university lecturer decides to 'build' his own house and to that end he hires a team of artisans and labourers, monitors production during his spare time and takes his residual in the form of outlay savings on what it would have cost him to purchase such a house from a building contractor. It is true also that some firms can be classified as 'casual' in that the demand for their outputs is sporadic. Thus a team of skilled artisans may organize themselves as a firm of jobbing builders and produce houses or act as 'property repairers' as and when there is a demand for a high-quality finish.

However, one would expect that, normally, a firm thrives on a continuity of production because this reduces costs. Frequency of transactions leads to continuous relationships among resource owners with the latter becoming increasingly skilled in conducting particular transactions and in carrying out market searches both for themselves and for other resource owners. In this way the members of a team obtain and maintain certain advantages over outsiders to the market, and these advantages help to bind them together.

The essence of the firm, i.e. team production, has been described in terms of (organized) cooperation. This view of how things are produced can be extended also to how firms expand their production arrangements through vertical and horizontal integration.

However, before proceeding to discuss in more detail the organization and activities of 'the firm' as distinct from 'the market' we should note that this separation of the two institutions, whilst useful in many respects, does obscure what happens often in reality and, to that extent, obstructs our comprehension of real-world phenomena. Firms in the real world rarely operate as islands in the full sense of that description, and it is the complex nature of economic activities which led Edwards and Townsend (1958) to propound a three-fold classification in terms of: integration by the market, integration by administration (the firm), and integration by cooperation (the information agreement, etc.)

Richardson (1972) has sought to explain the factors which may determine whether activities are integrated by administration or by cooperation by distinguishing between *similar* and *complementary* activities. Firms, he suggested, would find it expedient to concentrate on similar activities; that is, activities which made the same demands upon the same capabilities or resources. Where activities are also complementary or similar then coordination could be achieved within firms. However, if activities were dissimilar then they could be coordinated through the market or through cooperation. Where matching of an intermediate input with a final output needs to be closely coordinated then coordination may be through cooperation rather than the market. Richardson also stressed the need to use the triple classification cautiously, and instanced examples of activities which were coordinated by different institutional arrangements in different countries.

We should note also, before we proceed any further, that the view of the firm projected by the analysis so far stresses the mutual advantage of team production to all resource owners. However, the precise institutional arrangements characterizing firms have been the subject of dispute between neoclassical and radical economists. Williamson (1975, 1980, 1981), for example, has taken the view that vertical chains of command (hierarchies) are an essential feature of firms, and horizontal chains of command describe markets. Radical economists, such as Marglin (1974), have suggested that hierarchies are not necessary for efficiency but arise in order to permit capitalists to extract any surplus created by team production.

Williamson suggests that there are three principles of organizational design: (1) asset specificity, (2) externality, and (3) hierarchy. Asset specificity refers to those assets which are specialized in use and are not easily transferable to other uses and users; they correspond to Alchian and Demsetz's specific, durable capital assets. The externality problem arises from difficulties of assessing and quantifying goods and activities, and is related to Alchian and Demsetz's stress on interdependence of inputs. Finally, the hierarchy principle refers to the possibility of distinguishing between operating and strategic activities, between day-to-day decisions and long-range decisions, and that this differentiation by means of a vertical command structure leads to greater efficiency. This is the argument which Marglin has criticized. Furthermore, Putterman (1984) has questioned whether it is always necessary for efficiency for capital to employ labour. At this stage we shall merely note the existence of this dispute. It has an obvious bearing upon the merits of workers' cooperatives.

Clearly we might stand the Alchian and Demsetz argument on its head and argue that the owners of specific durable human capital should be the claimants on the residual income of a firm. This is an issue to which we shall return in chapter 5.

The Goals of the Firm

Most of the attention paid to the firm of the economics textbook, the 'neo-classical firm', has centred on the goal of profit maximization or the max-imization of the entrepreneur's residual reward. In order for the firm to be perceived as operating in this fashion it is necessary to assume further that information flows are perfectly efficient and that entrepreneurs operate with perfect knowledge and act on the basis of certain expectations. There may be occasional *ex post* surprises, as when an individual entrepreneur finds that he has not achieved an expected profit outcome because his original plan was formulated on the assumption that other firms in the market would 'stay put', would continue operating the status quo, while he went ahead with his plan, whereas in fact these other firms have not followed suit. But any uncertainties about product, prices, technology, availability of raw materials, etc., the stuff of real-world planning nightmares, are assumed away in the models of price/output behaviour under conditions of perfect knowledge.

Economists, of course, are aware of the shortcomings of approaches built on the certainty assumption, although they remain somewhat loath to relinquish the analytical tidiness that it permits. One way to 'remove' the uncertainty problem is for economists to adopt Debreu's (1959) concept of the 'contingent commodity economy', within which each commodity is distinguished not only by its physical and spatial characteristics and by the date at which it is delivered, but also by the state of the world in which it is delivered. By a 'state of the world' is meant the values which are assigned to the uncertain features of economic activity. Commodities are therefore defined as being contingent upon the occurrences of certain events, and a 'market system' comprises markets in all such contingent commodities.

Because a commodity's definition depends upon a state of the world – for example, an umbrella delivered on a sunny day is not the same thing as an umbrella delivered on a rainy day – traders on both sides of the market must take precautions against all contingencies, and the only certain method by which to protect themselves is to arrange that each commodity is delivered only if the relevant state of the world comes about. In other words, in such a world all trade is arranged in advance of any production and at a set of prices based upon 'conditional contracts'.

However, while Debreu's ideas provide us with an exciting analytical game, they do not approximate 'states of the real world'. No such economy exists – there is not a complete set of markets – nor could such an economy exist given that it requires perfect knowledge of technology on both sides of the market and perfect knowledge of all possible states of the world. In other words Debreu does not move us away from the neoclassical reliance on perfect information. So it is that it might be safe to conclude that firms do not aim to maximize anything, although they may enjoy a *maximum realized profit*. The attainment of realized profits is a much weaker assumption than the aim of profit maximization and it fits better with the fact of uncertainty. In terms of team production we can consider team members as realizing quasi-rents – once resource owners have entered into contracts of mutual employment then resources become temporarily immobilized and any earnings are determined by the nature of contracts and by prevailing demand conditions. In these circumstances the range of 'animal spirits', inertia, drive, sudden optimism etc., all play their part and a firm's survival may be the result of superior knowledge, but it can also be due to good luck. Survivors in such a world may well be characterized as cautious and inconspicuous, playing the 'safety-first' game. We shall return to some of these themes in later chapters.

Entrepreneurship

The notion that a firm is a team or club raises the question: what is an entrepreneur? Nineteenth-century usage has accustomed us to think of entrepreneurship as the prerogative of captains of industry, but this viewpoint stems from an age when it was customary to think of the firm as owner-managed, with the owner-manager making all the decisions and bearing all the risks. The development of the modern corporation and of economic analysis suggests that this approach needs to be reappraised.

Entrepreneurs are people who have the ability to do things differently, or to do different things. They may produce existing goods using new techniques of production, or they may produce new goods. They may create disequilibrium in markets, or they may promote equilibrium. Thus, Schumpeter's entrepreneur (1939) creates a gale of creative destruction, whereas Kirzner's entrepreneur (1979) seizes on the fact that price differences exist for the same good in different markets and, by buying cheap and selling dear, not only makes a gain for himself but also, by removing price disparities, increases the utilities of others.

Entrepreneurship is not synonymous with risk-taking. It is true that creating changes involves an element of uncertainty, but it is possible to have uncertainty without economic agents attempting to promote change. Farmers may use the same methods of production each year because they have proved efficient, but they can still be subject to risk from unanticipated changes in the weather (and merely walking out of the house exposes a person to risk). There can, therefore, be risk without entrepreneurship; it would be Pareto non-relevant risk in the sense that the costs of its removal would exceed any possible gains. Also there can be entrepreneurs who do not bear risks; what entrepreneurs are required to do is to create and cope with change by making decisions which will lead to an increase in wealth, and there may be others who are willing to bear the risks associated with entrepreneurship. Entrepreneurs are supposed to earn profits, and profits are a residual. Hence it would seem that workers are not entrepreneurs because they accept fixed payment systems. However, this overlooks the fact that many employment situations are characterized by continuity. It is possible, therefore, for workers to bargain for a share of profits when contracts are revised; past profits are not byegones, and managers will have to take into account the fact that workers may expect some share of profits.

The overlapping of the functions of owner, manager and entrepreneur are depicted in figure 3.1, a diagram well known to economists from a paper by Ng (1974) in which he explores the compatibility of 'utility maximization' with that of 'profit maximization' in the case of the owner-managed firm. The decision-making agent is the owner-manager whose relative preferences for leisure (measured along the horizontal axis) are reflected in the shape of the indifference curves, C_1, C_2 ... C_n, which constitute his well-defined and well-behaved preference map. The possible money income/leisure choices (or constraints) confronting the owner-manager are shown by AB, which represents what he could earn if he were to sell his managerial skills in the market place (the slope of AB measures the going rate for such services) and by DE which shows the amounts he can earn by managing his own firm, where these amounts comprise his imputed wage as a manager of the enterprise plus profit

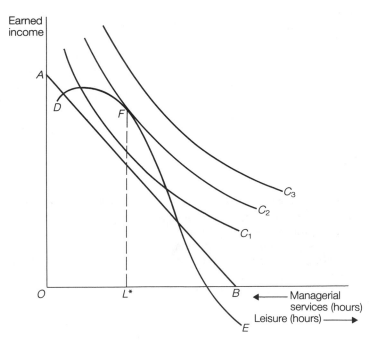

Figure 3.1 Optimum supply of managerial services where both money profit and subjective utility are maximized.

and which is constructed net of his outlays on other inputs. The line AB reflects a fixed return for the entrepreneur's services in the market (where he is a price-taker) while the shape of DE clearly exhibits diminishing returns to the application of the entrepreneur's managerial services in his own enterprise.

If the return offered by AB is a true measure of the opportunity cost of the entrepreneur's managerial services then the vertical distance between DE and AB can be considered as profit – this distance reaches a maximum at L^*. If the entrepreneur's preference map can be represented by the sample of indifference curves C_1, C_2 and C_3, then the optimum income/leisure position is shown at F, where DE is tangential to C_2 and where *both profit and subjective utility are maximized* as the entrepreneur consumes OL^* hours of leisure.

The picture can be varied by postulating different shapes for the preference map and considering the implications of this for the buying and selling of entrepreneurial services. Figure 3.2 shows an alternative in this respect. The figure shows alternative preference maps superimposed on the same set of constraints as depicted in figure 3.1. $A'B'$ is drawn parallel to AB and tangential to F to show the fact that when the entrepreneur reaches the maximum profit point he then faces a further choice between either selling more of his services to another enterprise, hence moving to the left of L^* (enjoying less leisure),

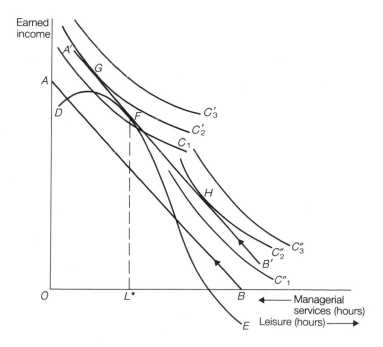

Figure 3.2 Optimizing behaviour where preferences and constraints combine to divorce maximum money profit from maximum utility.

or buying some additional managerial services from outside and moving to the right of L^* (enjoying more leisure). If the entrepreneur's preference map can be represented by the sample C'_1, C'_2 and C'_3, then point G represents the optimum point, reached by selling managerial services to the outside; buying managerial services from outside and consuming more leisure provide the optimum strategy at point H if the preference map can be represented by the sample C''_1, C''_2 and C''_3.

The Legal Structure of the Firm

So far we have assumed that firms are created in order to overcome some of the costs of using markets. We then sought to clarify the concepts of profit maximization and entrepreneurship. The purpose of firms is to attempt to maximize realized profits and the task of entrepreneurs is to select those policies which might lead to maximum realized profits. Now we are in a position to examine the nature of ownership rights in firms and the distribution of realized profits. From out of the myriad of possible forms of ownership rights we extract the following: (1) sole traders and partnerships, (2) joint stock companies, (3) the Japanese system of lifetime employment, (4) the West German system of codetermination, (5) not-for-profit firms.

Sole Traders, Partnerships and Limited Companies

The sole trader bears final responsibility for the running of a business and is the owner of any residual income that accrues from the activities of the enterprise. As the person ultimately responsible for the activities of the business, the sole trader faces *unlimited liability* for any debts incurred by the business. A partnership involves joint proprietorship of two or more persons, each of whom must accept unlimited liability for the debts of the enterprise and, to ensure a collective responsibility on this issue, can draw up contracts which are binding on other partners.

A limited company is a form of ownership which limits the liabilities of each 'owner' to the extent of that person's financial stake in the enterprise. Note that all three types of enterprise are described in terms of ownership and not in terms of responsibility beyond that, i.e. an owner may or may not play an active part in the decision-making process – he may choose to delegate this to a manager.

It might be interesting to consider the relative importance of these three membership systems. Table 3.1 reveals that most firms in the UK are small – some 66 per cent of all firms have taxable earnings of less than £10,000 p.a. However, as we can see from table 3.2, the numerical preponderance of small firms is offset by the greater earning power of large firms. In 1978 some 46 per cent of all income was earned by firms which had incomes over £1 million and the incidence of large firms increased appreciably between 1961 and 1978.

Table 3.1.   The number and relative size of commercial enterprises in the UK in terms of annual taxable income, 1960–78

Range of annual income		1960–1		1971		1978	
		No.	%	No.	%	No.	%
£0–£1000	Individuals	1326	82	1170	75	559.2	56.7
	Partnerships	130	8	91	6	92.3	9.4
	Companies	165	10	290	19	334.2	33.9
	Total	1621	100	1551	100	985.7	100
£1000–	Individuals	188	52	706	71	1059	75.6
£10,000	Partnerships	119	33	227	23	247.2	17.6
	Companies	52	14	68	7	95.4	6.8
	Total	359	100	1001	100	1401.6	100
£10,000–	Individuals	1	3	60	53	56.4	31.1
£100,000	Partnerships	5	21	22	20	83.7	46.1
	Companies	19	76	31	27	41.3	22.8
	Total	25	100	113	100	181.4	100
£100,000–	Partnerships	0.1	3	0.3	5	0.1	1.2
£1 million	Companies	3.4	97	6.1	95	8.9	98.8
	Total	3.5	100	6.4	100	9.0	100
Over £1 million	Companies	0.3	100	0.7	100	0.9	100
All sizes	Individuals	1515	81	1882	72	1674.6	64.9
	Partnerships	255	10	340	13	423.3	16.4
	Companies	239.7	10	396	15	481.6	18.7
	Total	2009.7	100	2618	100	2579.5	100

Source: Inland Revenue, Annual Statistics, various years.

Income Distribution

The classical theory of the firm, and the one which figures prominently in the analysis of Alchian and Demsetz's work (1972), tends to be based upon the three legal forms discussed in the previous section. It is assumed that the owners of finance capital are the risk bearers because they commit their resources to embodiment in durable specific physical capital and as a result they claim the residual income. In effect, the owners of finance capital hire the other resources which they pay fixed rewards. This view of economic activity was also embodied in the classical theory of income distribution which distinguished among labourers, landlords, financiers and merchants who received respectively: wages, rents, interest and profits. But economists have

Table 3.2. The distribution of annual taxable income of trading concerns of various sizes as a percentage of total income of all concerns, 1960–78

Range		1960–1	1971	1978
£0–£10,000	Individuals	20.9	18.8	15.3
	Partnerships	8.3	7.3	5.4
	Companies	4.8	2.7	1.5
£10,000–£1 million	Individuals	0.3	1.0	3.8
	Partnerships	2.6	5.0	9.3
	Companies	35.6	25.9	18.6
Over £1 million	Individuals	–	–	–
	Partnerships	–	–	–
	Companies	27.3	39.1	46.2
All sizes	Individuals	21.2	19.8	19.1
	Partnerships	10.9	12.3	14.7
	Companies	67.7	67.9	66.3

Source: Inland Revenue, Annual Statistics, various years.

long recognized that enterprising labourers can earn 'profits' and rents can be earned by any resource owner who supplies a service which is in elastic supply. The more updated version of factor pricing is shown in table 3.3.

The disentangling of rewards from specific social classes is closely connected with the emergence of complex business forms and with the fact that rewards to resource owners may depend upon the information available to them. Thus, financial shareholders may receive not a (possible) fluctuating reward but a fixed dividend which may only be adjusted at lengthy intervals. Indeed, workers may have more commitment to the firms in which they are employed, and may have more entitlement to be considered to be the ultimate risk bearers because shareholders may be able to liquidate their holdings costlessly in the stock market. Hence, we need to analyse more closely the nature of property rights and income distribution.

Table 3.3. Functional categories of income

	Necessary payment	Surplus or deficit
Current income receipts	Transfer price or opportunity cost	Rent
Current income receipts related to past investments	Interest	Profit or loss

Division or Divorce? The Problems of Ownership and Control

As it has been assumed that financial holders are the *de jure* owners of firms, considerable attention has been directed to the effect of the division of labour between finance owners and managers. Specifically, it has been suggested that while large numbers of shareholders are unable to combine easily to protect their rewards, managers are able to divert profits to their own use.

Implications of a Divorce

If a divorce of ownership from control has taken place, what modifications does it require economists to make to the standard (neoclassical) theory of the firm? A hint that such a divorce does require theoretical modifications to be made appeared in the earlier analysis borrowed from Ng. In the Ng model the owner-manager does indeed aim for profit first but then, in one instance at least, trades off against leisure by hiring the services of another manager. The reason that the manager does this is because, ultimately, he is a *utility maximizer* and utility depends upon leisure as well as monetary return in the form of profit. Now, when the manager is also the owner, any potential conflict of interest does not arise because profit/leisure decisions are resolved within the utility function – profit and utility may both be maximized simultaneously or maximum profits may help to purchase more leisure, depending upon the shape of the preference map. However, when ownership is divorced from control, conflicts of interest may well arise and managers may want to pursue other goals which do not suit the objectives of the owners – particularly if the market permits discretion to reside with the managers.

The problem has attracted the interests of several economists. As early as 1947 Reder was underlining the existence of 'organizational slack' – when firms aim for 'safe' rather than 'maximum' profit levels (Reder, 1947). A similar theme was developed some years later in the X-inefficiency model which featured in the work of Liebenstein (1979). Some economists have related power and prestige to firm size rather than profit levels. Both Baumol (1959) and Williamson (1970) have pursued this line in a static framework, while Marris (1964) has derived a dynamic model of firm's growth which reflects similar reasoning. Williamson's model has generated a lot of interest because it suggests a comprehensive set of variables which can appear in the managerial utility function, and his model has something to offer to each of the many areas of academic study of the enterprise. The variables divide into pecuniary (monetary) and non-pecuniary (status, prestige, power etc.) with the latter being rendered measurable by taking managerial spending as a proxy for the satisfaction gained from such expenditure – Williamson's concept of 'expense preference'.

Profit maximization does not disappear, however, and although it may have gone from the bridge it remains very much part of the engine room. Prestige, power etc. can only be pursued by managers if owners are somehow placated and a minimum profit constraint is the common feature among 'alternative' theories of firms' behaviour. The Baumol model shows this very clearly, and we consider it now in more detail in the (simpler) Baumol framework, although the main point applies equally to the Williamson model.

Baumol presents his model in both static and dynamic form. In each case managers, rather than owners, exercise their discretionary power in aiming to maximize sales revenue rather than profit. Bigger sales mean bigger companies which in turn means more power and prestige for managers who can then enjoy even more discretionary control; so runs the story. The static version of Baumol's model predicts behaviour for a single period during which sales revenues are maximized subject to a minimum profit constraint. Figure 3.3 depicts the firm's 'managerial equilibrium'.

Figure 3.3 adopts the conventional notation for total revenue and total cost and π refers to the total profit function. Profits are maximized at output Ox_1 (where $dTR = dTC$), and sales revenue is maximized at output Ox_2. The level of output, Ox_2, represents equilibrium for the firm if the maximum profit constraint is no greater than π_2 (e.g. π_1 is well within the requirements) but the output must be cut back if the constraint is greater (e.g. π_3). Thus, if the minimum profit constraint does not constrain the decision-maker, the sales maximizer will produce more than the profit maximizer.

Baumol's model has been introduced here as an example of a managerial alternative to simple profit maximization; it is not the intention to embark upon a detailed critique of the model, nor to discuss the detail of other alternative models. Suffice it to say that Baumol presented also a dynamic model in which managers attempt to maximize the growth of sales.

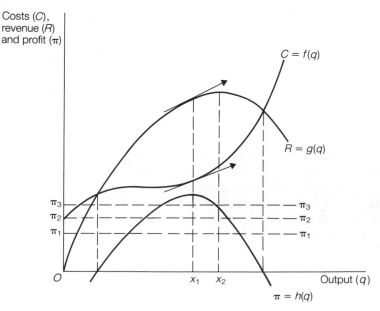

Figure 3.3   Baumol's sales maximizer (static version).

Evidence of a Divorce

Providing evidence of a divorce of ownership from control is not easy. There are problems of definition and problems associated with the periods of observation. Sargeant Florence (1947) found a tendency for managerial control to increase in Britain between 1936 and 1951; just under one-third of British firms were owner-controlled by the end of the period. However, Nyman and Silberston (1978) studied 276 large firms in 1975 and found that some 56 per cent were owner-controlled (see tables 3.4 and 3.5). There is also evidence of interlocking directorships, which suggests an even greater potential for control (Stanworth and Giddens, 1975).

However, to count the size of shareholdings is not enough. There will always be doubt as to what constitutes a controlling block of shares. Thus, if shares are widely dispersed, and their owners tend to vote randomly, a small block of votes cast in one particular direction may exert considerable influence; hence, *ad hoc* percentage rules of measurement may not reveal the existence of controlling groups. A more sophisticated way of measuring the dispersion

Table 3.4. Ownership control and industry

Industrial group	Total no. of companies in 'Top 250'	No. of companies owner-controlled
Food	15	12
Drink	7	4
Tobacco	3	1
Oil	5	2
Chemicals	12	3
Metal manufacturing	5	3
Mechanical engineering	15	8
Electrical engineering	13	8
Vehicles	8	5
Metal goods (NES)	9	3
Textiles	6	3
Building materials	12	4
Paper, printing and publishing	7	4
Other manufacturing	6	3
Construction	9	7
Transport	8	3
Retailing	17	13
Merchanting	17	11
Miscellaneous services	7	7
Conglomerates	24	11
Unclassified	19	11
Total	224	126

Source: Nyman and Silberston (1978).

Table 3.5. Ownership control of the UK 'Top 250' in 1975

Percentage of voting shares held by a single institution or by the board of directors and their families	Type of holder								Total
	I	F	D	C	G	M	O	N	
Unquoted company	3	..	8	1	1	..	..	3	16
Over 50%	4	..	15	1	1	..	1	..	22
40–50%	1	..	5	1	..	..	1	..	8
30–40%	1	..	8	1	1	..	..	..	11
20–30%	8	1	2	..	..	..	..	1	12
10–20%	5	4	17	..	..	..	..	..	26
Other holdings greater than 10%	..	..	2	..	..	4	..	..	6
5–10%	1	4	5	..	..	..	..	..	10
Total	23	9	62	4	3	4	2	4	111
Family chairman or MD (but less than 5% shareholding by individual or group)									15
Total owner-controlled									126
No known control									98
Total firms									224
Percentage owner-controlled									56.25

Notes:
Types of holder: I = another industrial company; F = financial institution; D = directors and their families; C = charitable trust; G = government or quasi-government agency; M = mixed control type; O = other control type; N = not classifiable due to lack of information.
Source: Nyman and Silberston (1978).

of share ownership is to use the Hirschman–Herfindahl index of concentration, which measures concentration in terms of the sum of the squares of the shares of each shareholder. Using this measure, Cubbin and Leech (1983) found a high degree of dispersion in 85 companies in the engineering, electrical/electronics, textiles/clothing and food industries in 1973, which suggested that the control shareholding might be quite small.

Stigler and Friedland (1983) have, however, cast doubt upon the Berle and Means' thesis (1932) that a divorce of ownership from control had emerged in the United States in the 1930s, by finding no significant differences in the returns of managerially controlled and owner-controlled firms during the interwar years. In Britain Radice (1971) found a tendency for owner-managed firms to have better profit rates than managerial firms; other observers, such as Silberston (1983) found no differences. Lack of conclusive evidence may stem from differences in periods of observation and a failure to allow for the influence of other variables. Williamson (1970) found evidence that, faced with falling profits, managers cut down on expenses and secretarial staff, but at a later date (1975) he suggested that the divorce of ownership from control may have been a temporary phenomenon which occurred before multi-divisional structures and effective methods of consolidating accounts were devised. Evidence that multi-divisional structures have been superior to unitary structures in large firms has been provided for the UK by Cable and Steer (1978) and Teece (1981). This raises the possibility that the different findings of Radice and Silberston arose because they were studying firms before and after changes in organizational structures occurred in Britain.

How Control is Exercised

Concentration upon the ownership of financial shares, and the ambiguous nature of the evidence of divorce of ownership from control, suggests that we need to consider all the channels through which control might be exercised. Although some controls exist to safeguard the interests of financial shareholders, those controls must not be considered in isolation from those available to other resource owners. In short, we need to examine how the internal and external markets of resource owners interact. We begin with the controls for safeguarding the interests of financial shareholders.

Finance: Company Law

The common view is that the modern corporation has its basis in company law. What company law does is to emphasize two ideas: corporate personality and limited liability; and, in addition, the protection of creditors and investors.

'Corporate personality' refers to the fact that a 'corporate legal person' is different from a 'human legal person' : 'it is invisible, immortal, and resides only in the intendment and consideration of the law' (Case of Sutton's Hospital, 1612, 10 Co. Rep. 1a 23a). Thus it follows from the concept of a legal corporate personality that the death of a financial shareholder or the sale of shares by a shareholder does not terminate a company's existence, as it would in the case of a sole trader or partnership. In a nutshell, there is a veil of incorporation through which the owners of a corporation cannot be perceived (*Salomon* v. *Salomon* & Co. Ltd 1897, A.C. 22); and though there have been some moves in the direction of lifting the veil of secrecy, the idea still retains validity.

The concept of limited liability refers to the fact that only the financial wealth expressly invested in the company can be held as security or for payment of company debts. Other assets of financial owners, therefore, cannot be legally attached for payment of liabilities.

The introduction of limited liability enabled firms to raise sufficient finance to cover spending on other resources, and to provide a bond to cover various commitments which might occur in the exploitation of economies of scale. However, the ability to divorce decision-making from financial risk-bearing was dependent upon the introduction of control systems which would prevent fraud, embezzlement and extravagance. Internally, control is exercised in a variety of ways. First, hierarchical management structures exert a check upon spending. Second, the divorce of decision-making from the provision of payments and the collection of receipts prevents decision-makers from issuing their own cheques. Third, the introduction of boards of directors responsible to shareholders and not concerned with day-to-day affairs introduces a control point to which appointments and dismissals of managers have to be finally referred. Directors are agents of the company and not employees; nor are they required to be members of the company in the sense of owning shares, but they are required to disclose financial interests in shares and debentures, not only of themselves but also of their families, and they may not make a secret profit. Furthermore, the fact that directors of one company may be directors of other companies provides a point of comparison with othe firms, and also the audit conducted by an external agency provides a further check upon efficiency. It is interesting to note that the audit was not something foisted upon companies by governments in search of tax receipts; rather, it was something which emerged as a voluntary response to the problems of control.

The Managerial Market

In an attempt to reduce risks, investors are likely to hold portfolios of shares which are diversified across the securities of many firms and, to the extent that an individual does hold shares in many firms, he is unlikely to have a particular interest in any one of them; he may lack commitment. Hence, we should not conclude that a divorce of ownership from control is inefficient; nor should we assume that it leads automatically to a redistribution of income from shareholders to managers and workers. The problems of efficiency and equity may depend to a large extent upon the nature of the competition for managers and other employees.

Managers compete both within and between firms, and all teams of resource owners are interested in acquiring efficient managers. Within the top firms managers compete amongst themselves, and junior managers compete for higher positions. Of course, it might be possible for managers to collude, but a group of managers are more likely to be better at selecting managers than a group of shareholders; the problem of collusion can be reduced by the possibilities of take-overs by other teams of managers. Teams of resource owners are, in fact, continually looking for managers, and can base their selection upon the salaries received by managers; pay can be an index of quality.

The Trade Union Challenge to Management Control

Information is given to outsiders by the procedures of financial accounting, the competition of managers, and by workers and their unions. Union wage claims may reveal something about the profits which firms have earned, and strikes may be a means of soliciting information. The emergence of trade unions has, in fact, led to a form of dual control in firms, the implications of which have not been fully resolved. In most Western economies unions stand to one side of the managerial control system and act as a check upon its operations. There have been attempts to move from this dual form by incorporating unions into the boards of management but, at least in Britain, there has been a reluctance to proceed along this road. Instead, unions have tended to exercise control through collective bargaining. Management may pursue any policy subject to meeting the demands of the unions. Thus, unions have tended to act as debenture holders. As we shall see, this dual system of decision-making stands in contrast to the more integrated system prevailing in Japan; and even within Western Europe, it is possible to detect differences in the manner in which property rights are exercised within firms.

Firms as Coalitions of Diverse Interests

Consideration of the interests of various resource owners has led economists to an increased recognition that firms do not concentrate upon a single, homogeneous goal but, rather, they are trying to aim for several targets which is a reflection of the team nature of the firm. Indeed, some writers have gone further and suggested that firms are clubs attempting to reconcile the interests of both resource owners and consumers. On the basis of this approach, the consumers of tinned beans are therefore regarded as members of the Heinz Beans Club (McGuire, 1972). And in some approaches the textbook distinction between consumption and production is swept aside by stressing the point that consumers may consume in factories as well as in the home. Hence, the fact that a manager may enjoy wall-to-wall carpeting in his office should not be taken as a sign that the divorce of ownership from control has led to a diversion of profits from shareholders to managers but a recognition that some managers may be prepared to accept a lower salary in return for a better office. The doctrine of 'net advantage' (the sum of monetary and non-monetary rewards) has long been enshrined in wage theory.

Table 3.6, which is borrowed from Pickering and Cockerill (1984), shows one view of the complex motivations and influences at work in an enterprise.

Whilst a table such as table 3.6 serves as a useful overview – and as a reminder that assuming a single motive, profit, can mislead the economist into adopting a simplistic view of firms' activities – it does offer an operational model. Indeed, to try to encompass all motivations within a multi-objective model is to render the theory of the firm too detailed and cumbersome a tool of analysis from which to produce testable hypotheses about firms' behaviour

Table 3.6. Interest groups and performance indicators

Interest group	Performance indicators
Owners	Profitability, growth, dividends, security, share price
Directors	Growth, market share, profitability, security
Managers	Growth, cash flow, discretionary expenditure, security
Employees	Earnings levels and growth, employment levels, security
Suppliers	Level, growth, variation and security of orders, payment period, prices
Customers	Prices, quality, after-sales, efficiency of distribution channels, new product development, credit terms
Investors	Share price, dividends, asset composition and growth, financing of assets, return on capital (profitability)
Competitors	Growth, profitability, market share, non-price behaviour, advertising, investment rate
Government	Corporate taxation contribution, potential employment level, growth and regional distribution of output and employment, trading practices, balance of payments contribution

Source: Pickering and Cockerill (1984), p. 4.

(Marris and Mueller, 1980). Instead, economists have tried to identify dominant influences on firms' behaviour.

Lingering Doubts

There are, in any case, doubts about the case for control of shareholders'
interests which we have described. What the development of 'efficient' capital
markets may have done is to create an exclusive preoccupation with short-run
profits. Because financial shareholders can flit from company to company with
comparative ease, they may lack commitment. Similarly, the greater mobility
of managers may cause them to concentrate upon short-run profits not merely
because their pay may be tied to profits but also because they can use their
existing pay levels as an indicator of their worth to other firms. Paradoxically,
therefore, increasing efficiency may have resulted in a lowering of the profit
horizons. And yet it may all be due to other factors. The ageing of populations
in Western economies may be the factor responsible for the emphasis upon
short-run profits and consumption rather than savings. But it is time to examine
the evolution of firms in Britain, Japan and West Germany.

The Evolution of Ownership of British Firms

Nyman and Silberston's evidence (1978), that ownership of financial claims
by institutional shareholders has been increasing, directs our attention to both

the changing nature of financial ownership and the persistence of family ownership. These themes have been explored by Francis (1980). In his analysis the development of large successful companies has been due to the influence of marginal groups, such as Nonconformists, Jews and, now, possibly Asians. Such groups have stood outside the normal pattern of British society. We should be careful, however, when accepting the notion of marginal groups. The Irish, the largest minority, do not seem to appear in the annals of the successful, and most minority groups tend to emphasize their successes and hide their failures. Indeed, it is possible that when the *Dictionary of Entrepreneurship* is completed we shall have a different view of the ethnic and religious origins of businessmen.

With this caveat in mind we can examine Francis's analysis. The success of the agrarian revolutions of the sixteenth and seventeenth centuries did not lead to a flow of financial capital into industry. Instead, it tended to flow into trade and the development of large trading companies. The subsequent development of the Empire also resulted in a flow of managerial talent into both trade and the foreign service, particularly the Indian Civil Service. Furthermore, the fortunes made in trade did not then flow into industry. There has been a suggestion that the financing of the Industrial Revolution owed a great deal to the profits from the slave trade (Williams, 1949). However, it would seem that the bulk of the profits from trade went into the creation of landed estates. Hence there was a closed circuit of finance and management linking agriculture with trade.

The effect of the interrelations of land, trade and Empire was three-fold. First, it was possible for merchants to become assimilated into the landed classes and for the values of the latter to be maintained. Unlike other European countries, Britain did not have a bourgeois revolution in which the nobility were pushed aside: it was not until after the passing of the Third Reform Act that the grip of the landed aristocracy upon society was loosened (Stone, 1984). Second, all the institutions for gathering and transmitting finance were geared to the needs of the Empire and not to domestic industry. Third, any financial capital which did flow from the City and other financial institutions tended to be loan capital than risk capital. Hence those who founded manufacturing firms had to provide their own capital – the classical model of the owner-manager. Of course there were some landowners who did engage in industry, but such activities tended to be regarded as offshoots of estate development – as in the case of coal mining.

According to Francis, the result of the preoccupation with land and the Empire was that industrial development became the product of two marginal groups: those who, for religious or racial reasons, were not members of the ruling class; and those who might be suitably termed 'gifted amateurs', who had an interest in things mechanical. It was the former group who tended to found large firms, and the latter groups only created large firms as a result of defensive mergers. When the marginal groups acquired wealth, they did not marry into the landed aristocracy; instead they built their own estates near the industrial towns and gave England both a landed and an industrial gentry.

Given the structure of society, it is not surprising that the divorce of ownership from control should not be so prevalent. Lack of access to capital markets meant that founders had to rely on their own resources; and even when limited liability was introduced it was a long time before it had any significant effects. Most British firms adopted the device of the private company which enabled joint stock to be combined with family control. In so far as marginal groups tended to lose control, it was as a result of two forces. First, there was the 'clogs-to-clogs' syndrome, whereby the loss of interest on the part of sons and grandsons, or the absence of sons, led to the employment of professional managers. But note: the fall-off in ability implied in the 'clogs-to-clogs' metaphor meant that it might be 60 years before family control weakened. Hence despite the introduction of limited liability in the middle of the nineteenth century most British firms were still family-owned and controlled at the turn of the century. Secondly, the loss of the Empire and the subsequent nationalization of British interests overseas has caused financial institutions to seek domestic outlets for capital and a desire for control. This movement towards institutional ownership has tended to be concentrated, because of a lack of expertise, on the large companies. Unlike Germany, small British firms still face the problems of raising finance from institutions whose headquarters are in London, and whose skills in assessing risks have been acquired in overseas markets. However, we should not overlook the pressures towards institutional ownership exerted by the tax system which, until recently, exempted life insurance from tax and by the nature of the rules of incorporation of many insurance companies and pensions funds which establish trustees and not shareholders. Hence we have a tendency towards the ownership of firms by firms.

The Irrelevance of Divorce: the Case of Japan

If British firms exhibit ownership by families and ownership by institutions, most large Japanese firms appear to be completely owned by other firms. The transformation was begun under the American occupation after the Second World War. Before the war most firms were supervised by directors on behalf of shareholders, who tended to be a few wealthy families, known as the zaibatsu. The workers tended to be organized into national trade unions. The alliance of the zaibatsu with the military led to attempts to reduce their influence; about 28 large holding companies, as well as some 300 other large firms, were dissolved and the members of the zaibatsu were allowed to drift into retirement. The dispersion of ownership was further accentuated by the 1950 commercial code, which prevented directors from holding shares in firms for which they were agents. After the Korean War (1952) there was some relaxation on the moves towards egalitarianism and some of the original zaibatsu – Mitsui, Mitsubishi and Sumitomo – were reassembled. In addition, three major groups – Fuji, Dai-ichi and Sanwa – emerged and centred on the banks. The two groupings may therefore be regarded as an evolution from the zaibatsu organizations of pre-war Japan in which collections of

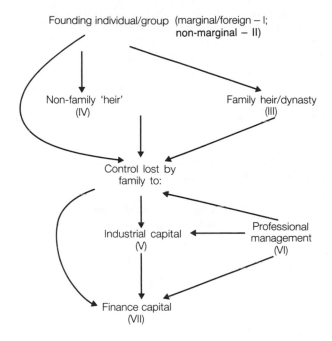

Figure 3.4   Stages in corporate control (after Francis, 1980).

manufacturing, trading and financial corporations were controlled by wealthy families under the umbrella of holding companies. Dispersion was given a further twist in the 1960s when, in an attempt to stave off possible American take-over bids, firms started to acquire each other's shares, with the result that it is often difficult to determine who owns which firm.

Not only have there been changes in financial ownership, there have also been changes in unionism. The American Administration tended to favour the introduction of plant-level agreements, as opposed to industry-wide agreements, and also the encouragement of company unionism. During the Korean War, and through the early fifties, the movement towards company unionism was accelerated by the hostility towards the national unions which tended to be left-wing-dominated. National unions also tended to become increasingly irrelevant because large firms were pursuing policies of internal recruitment and promotion, life-time employment, age-related wage scales, the payment of large bonuses and joint consultation (the ringi system). These factors are interdependent. Large firms tended to select new employees with a view to training and continual employment up to the age of 55. With guaranteed employment, companies could invest in the acquisition of skills by their employees. With age-related wage scales, each employee had an assured income. Of course, guaranteed employment would have produced extreme rigidity in operations, had it not been for the flexibility of the bonus scheme, and for the policy of rotating workers between jobs. However, the idea of profit-sharing might not have been accepted had it not been for the introduction of the shopfloor system (the ringi system) of worker participation in production scheduling. Hence Japanese firms exhibit capitalism to a high degree. Ownership is widely diffused, with all employees being encouraged to be entrepreneurs in their own firms but allowed to diversify some of their risks partly through investing savings in banks and insurance companies and partly through the small firm sector.

The German Two-tier System

British firms have tended to adopt a unitary control system with directors being required to wear two hats. German firms have adopted a double-decker system of management with the executive board (Vorstand) being distinguished from the supervisory board (Aufsichtsrat). The distinction was embodied in the 1937 Companies Act in response to abuses of the company law after the First World War. However, the distinction goes back, in fact, to the Handelsgesetzbuch of 1897 which, in turn, drew upon the legislation of 1884 and 1870. The function of the supervisory board is to provide an effective monitoring body which is independent of the shareholders' meeting and the directors. German firms prefer a collegiate system, with the team being appointed by the supervisory board, and employees have been fitted into the structure through the introduction of works councils in the 1920s and, later, through the system of Mitbestimmung (co-determination) in the 1950s. The Bullock Committee (1977) proposed a similar system of worker-directors for British firms in the 1970s, but it was rejected by the trade unions. A further proposal emanating from the EEC in 1983 has also been rejected by British employers and unions.

How can we explain these different patterns of monitoring property rights? Are they all equally efficient? The answer (or answers) lies partly in the cultural values residing in different societies, partly in the dates at which countries started to industrialize and partly in the part played by the state in economic development. Organizational theorists tend to speak of the culture of a firm as being created by the web of property rights which link the members together (Jones, 1983); but those property rights can be significantly affected by the system of property rights which society establishes, and the culture of a firm is shaped by the culture of the society in which it resides. Partly through employer resistance and partly through trade union rejection, workers were not formally incorporated into British firms. Both responses were probably no more than a shared reflection of cultural values which emphasized individualism: British unionism was descended from the guilds and it resisted mass unionism; the journeyman and his mate were a firm, and fitted into a society which emphasized individualism. Furthermore, the coincidence of the Industrial Revolution with the French Revolution brought about a confusion of trade unionism with sedition, with the result that trade unions were long outlawed. When trade unions came to be recognized, paradoxically, they insisted on being placed outside the law – their funds were to be protected against claims for damages arising out of strike action. In contrast, the United States and Australia started with universal manhood suffrage, which meant that workers were more prepared to use politics and the law to achieve their objectives (Phelps Brown, 1982).

Not-for-profit Firms

Joint stock companies permit the sale of property rights, but there are numerous firms which do not allow members to dispose of their assets. Thus, a trade union member cannot sell his membership. A donor to a charity has nothing to sell, and obtains nothing more than the joy of giving. Members of churches have no rights to sell assets. Such firms have communal property rights and are frequently called 'not-for-profit firms'. The preceding analysis suggests that monitoring of efficiency may be extremely difficult in such organizations, and that special measures may have to be taken in order to prevent shirking and malfeasance. Thus the existence of a celibate clergy may be a means of protecting communal property from dissipation in the Catholic Church, whereas the Anglican Church has to provide livings for its clergy. Trade union members may be reluctant to admit newcomers because there is no means of charging a fee for the benefits they obtain. Communal property rights firms are, of course, numerous in the public sector and their existence raises considerable problems. For example it is not obvious why we have public sector firms. Public goods could be produced by private firms and financed by the government; by such a procedure efficiency might be ensured by the market. Hence it is not obvious why we have government firms. Such issues take us into the analysis of later chapters, where we consider public enterprises and workers' cooperatives.

Bibliography and References

Alchian, A. A. (1950) 'Uncertainty, evolution and economic theory', *Journal of Political Economy*, 58, 211–21; reprinted in Alchian (1977).
Alchian, A. A. (1977) *Economic Forces at Work*. Indianapolis: Liberty Press.
Alchian, A. A. and Demsetz, H. (1972) 'Production, information costs and economic organization', *American Economic Review*, 62, 777–95; reprinted in Alchian (1977).
Baumol, W. J. (1959) *Business Behavior, Value and Growth*. New York: Macmillan.
Berle, A. A. and Means, G. (1932) *The Modern Corporation*. New York: Macmillan.
Bowles, S. (1984) 'The production process in a competitive economy', *American Economic Review*, 75, 16–36.
Bullock Committee (1977) *Report on Industrial Democracy* (Chairman: Lord Bullock). London: HMSO, Cmnd 6706.
Cable, J. R. and Dirrheimer, M. J. (1983) 'Markets and hierarchies: an empirical test of the multidivisional hypothesis in West Germany', *International Journal of Industrial Organization*, 1, 43–62.

Cable, J.R. and Steer, D. (1978) 'Internal organization and profit: an empirical analysis of large UK firms', *Economic Journal*, 27, 13–30.

Cheung, S. N. S. (1983) 'The contractual nature of the firm', *Journal of Law and Economics*, 26, 1–22.

Coase, R. H. (1937) 'The nature of the firm', *Economica*, 4, 386–405.

Cubbin, J. and Leech, D. (1983) 'The effect of shareholding dispersion in the degree of control in British companies: theory of measurement', *Economic Journal*, 93, 351–67.

Debreu, G. (1959) *The Theory of Value*. New York: Wiley.

Edwards, R. and Townsend, H. (1958) *Business Enterprise*. London: Macmillan.

Fama, E. F. (1980) 'Agency problems and the theory of the firm', *Journal of Political Economy*, 86, 288–307.

Francis, A. (1980) 'Families, finance and firms', *Sociology*, 14, 1–28.

Jones, G. (1983) 'Transactions costs, property rights and organizational culture: an exchange perspective', *Administrative Science Quarterly*, 28, 3–27.

Kirzner, M. (1979) *Perception, Opportunity and Profit*. Chicago: University of Chicago Press.

Liebenstein, H. (1979) *General X-Efficiency Theory and Economic Development*. Oxford: Oxford University Press.

McGuire, M. C. (1972) 'Private good clubs and public good clubs: economic models of group formation', *Swedish Journal of Economics*, 74, 84–99.

Machlup, F. (1967) 'Theories of the firm: marginalist, behavioural and managerial', *American Economic Review*, 57, 1–33.

Marglin, S.A. (1974) 'What do bosses do?', *Review of Radical Political Economics*, 6, 60–113.

Marris, R. (1964) *The Economic Theory of Managerial Capitalism*. London: Macmillan.

Marris, R. and Mueller, D. (1980) 'Industrial organization, corporate strategy and structure', *Journal of Economic Literature*, 18, 32–63.

Ng, Y.-K. (1974) 'Utility and profit maximization by an owner-managed firm: towards a general analysis', *Journal of Industrial Economics*, 23, 97–108.

Nyman, S. A. and Silberston, A. (1978) 'The ownership and control of industry',*Oxford Economic Papers*, 30, 74–101.

Phelps Brown, E. H. (1982) *The Origins of Trade Union Power*. Oxford: Oxford University Press.

Pickering, J. and Cockerill A. J. (eds) (1984) *The Economic Management of the Firm*. Deddington: Philip Allan.

Putterman, L. (1984) 'On some recent explanations of why capital employs labour', *Economic Inquiry*, 22, 171–87.

Radice, H. K. (1971) 'Control type, profitability and growth in large firms', *Economic Journal*, 81, 547–62.

Reder, M. W. (1947) 'A reconsideration of marginal productivity theory', *Journal of Political Economy*, 55, 450–8.

Richardson, G. B. (1972) 'The organization of industry', *Economic Journal*, 82, 883–97.

Robertson, Sir Dennis (1923) *The Control of Industry*. London: Nisbet.

Sargeant Florence, P. S. (1947) 'The statistical analysis of joint stock company control', *Journal of the Royal Statistical Society*, 110, 2–19.

Schumpeter, J. A. (1939) *The Theory of Economic Development*. Cambridge, Mass.: Harvard University Press.

Silberston, A. (1983) 'Factors in the growth of firms – theory and practice'. In D. Currie *et al.* (eds), *Microeconomic Analysis*. London: Croom Helm.

Stanworth, W. and Giddens, A. (1975) *The Modern Corporate Economy*. Cambridge: Cambridge University Press.
Stigler, G. J. and Friedland, C. (1983) 'The literature of economics: the case of Berle and Means', *Journal of Law and Economics*, 26, 237–89.
Stone, L. (1984) *An Open Elite?* Oxford: Clarendon Press.
Teece, D. J. (1981) 'Internal organization and economic performance: an empirical analysis of the profitability of principal firms', *Journal of Industrial Economics*, 30, 173–200.
Williams, E. (1949) *Capitalism and Slavery*. London: Deutsch.
Williamson, O. E. (1970) *Corporate Control and Business Behavior*. Englewood Cliffs, New Jersey: Prentice-Hall.
Williamson, O. E. (1975) *Markets and Hierarchies: Analysis and Anti-Trust Implications*. New York: Free Press.
Williamson, O. E. (1980) 'The organization of work: a comparative institutional assessment', *Journal of Economic Behavior and Organization*, 1, 5–38.
Williamson, O. F. (1981) 'The modern corporation: origin, evolution, attributes', *Journal of Economic Literature*, XIX, 1537–68.

4 Strategy: Birth, Growth and Death of Firms

We begin with some definitions.

1 *Strategic management* is concerned with the overall long-run policies of a firm: with determining what to produce, how to produce and for whom to produce – that is, with the central problems of economics.
2 *Operational management* refers to the day-to-day resolution and implementation of strategy.
3 *Control* refers to the means by which the performance of a firm is monitored and assessed against its goals. Control implies the use of feedback mechanisms to correct deviations from goals.
4 *Structure* is the framework through which strategy is transmitted and control exerted.

Strategy

Strategy is concerned with the long-run aims and policies of a firm and not the day-to-day minutiae of management; it involves a concentration on the overall nature of the business, on how it can adapt to changing circumstances or maintain the status quo. Although in the short run a firm is constrained by its available resources, in the long run strategy can overcome those constraints through the development of new processes and products and the opening up of new markets. Strategy, therefore, is the means by which a firm confronts its environment which may include considering the behaviour of rivals.

The Contextual Basis

Porter (1982) has attempted to illuminate a firm's problems by means of the Wheel of Competitive Strategy. In the hub of the wheel are the firm's goals, of which there are many possibilities. These goals may define the manner in which the firm is going to compete in markets. Radiating from the hub are the spokes which indicate the key operating policies by which the goals are to be achieved. If the policies (spokes) are not connected to the goals (hub) then the wheel will not roll.

The Contextual Basis of Strategy

The wheel of competitive strategy rolls along a path which is influenced by the nature of the industry and the markets in which the firm seeks to operate and which, in turn, are subject to broader social and political considerations. It is the nature of these external forces which serves to judge the fitness of the wheel.

The starting point for the discussion of strategy is the nature of the industry and the market. *Industry* is a supply-side concept; it represents the area within which a firm finds it relatively easy to expand; it is an area demarcated by specialist knowledge. *Markets* are regular networks of contact between buyers and sellers; they are defined in terms of both demand and supply; and although we shall pose the questions concerning industry and market in terms of an existing firm, even the management of a new entrant would like to know the answers to the following questions.

1   Is the industry growing or stagnating? Is it capable of absorbing the output of existing firms, or must some or all of them cut back output? If the industry is expanding, are the existing firms capable of meeting demands or will new firms be able to enter?

2   What is the degree of competition between existing firms? Is there competition or collusion? Are firms insulated from each other by product differentiation? How do existing firms respond to different forms of competition – to price, product or advertising competition?

3   Is there ease of entry to the industry? Are there economies of scale which preclude the entry of new firms? Is it possible for firms established in other industries to switch their resources into the firm's industry and market? Is it possible to deter potential entrants by product differentiation, low price policies, control of distribution channels and patents? What advantages accrue to the established firm? Is it worthwhile maintaining excess capacity as a threat to outsiders?

4   What is the nature of the market which the industry serves? Is it subject to product innovation and a proliferation of substitute products?

5   What is the nature of the firm's suppliers? Are supplying industries competitive or monopolistic? Are they dominated by trade unions? Are they nationalized industries?

6   What is the nature of the firm's buyers? Are purchases confined to a few buyers, such as government? Is there any danger of buyers engaging in vertical integration and becoming their own suppliers?

Alternative Strategies

In the light of the answers to the preceding questions management can choose between one of three strategies. It can either:

1   seek to dominate the industry by being the lowest cost firm; or
2   carve out a particular part of the market by product differentiation; or
3   focus on a particular part of the market in which it can supply a differentiated product at lowest cost.

Each strategy presupposes that the firm's policies with respect to other existing firms, possible entrants, and suppliers and buyers have been fully resolved; in particular, that it is possible to convert a competitive situation into a monopolistic situation where the firm has some control over its destiny. The main problem is, of course, to avoid conflicting strategies and attempting to straddle too many segments of the market with no clear cost advantages or superior product.

The Birth of Firms

Firms Entering Existing Industries

Imitation is the sincerest form of flattery, and denim is its usual garb. Most new firms start small and enter existing industries; their owners hope that markets will expand or that they can take customers away from existing firms. The advantages of imitation seem overwhelming. It seems relatively easy for a shop assistant to run a shop; thus bookshops are often set up by employees of other bookshops. In some industries, for example building and construction, the elaborate subdivision of work means that there is often a fine distinction between employer and employee. In some industries *franchising* can be practised. An individual purchases supplies of some good, receives training and obtains the sole right to sell the good in a particular locality, and the would-be businessman has the advantage of selling a tested product. Thus, Wimpey, Dyno-Rod, Colonel Saunders and Ziebart offer franchises.

The majority of new firms which open each year fall into this category, and may fail because those who create them have not faced up to the question of whether demand is expanding or whether they possess the abilities to attract customers from existing firms. Indeed, many firms are established in shrinking markets. Having been made redundant, many craftsmen set up small firms in the hope of gaining employment through the exploitation of segments of the market which large firms would find it costly to enter. In the US some 8 per cent of the labour force tended to be self-employed between 1950 and 1975, and there has been a rise to 10 per cent during the recession of the late 1970s and early 1980s. In Japan some 40 per cent of the labour force was self-employed in 1950 and there was a continuous decline to about 18 per cent in the early 1970s. As in the UK, there has been a slight rise in self-employment during the recent slump. The major differences in the importance of self-employment in the UK and Japan, however, reflect differences in the level of economic development. As countries industrialize, the numbers employed in agriculture (a stronghold of self-employment) decline, and even the numbers of self-employed in the service sector (e.g. retailing) undergo a contraction.

New Firms with New Ideas: the Gap in the Market

IBM was created by marketing men who were used to going out and selling cash registers; but the introduction of electric calculators and electronic computers led to imperceptible shifts in managerial strategy and a preoccupation with technology and mainframe computers. Apple started to produce because IBM had overlooked the domestic market. There may, of course, be deliberate decisions not to cover all the market, and the history of IBM is replete with examples of firms producing complementary components. In the 1960s rising real incomes led Marks and Spencer to produce high-class clothing but they overlooked the market for children's clothing and the gap was filled by Selim Zilkha who introduced Mothercare (now part of Habitat), which was based upon the success of Prenatal in France. These are just two of the many examples of market gaps being plugged by the products of new entrants.

Revolutionizing Existing Industries

Producing the same product as existing firms may be easy but may not guarantee the newcomer a firm foothold; hence the need to innovate if new products and processes are a means of eroding the preserve of a sleepy incumbent. Thus Smith's Potato Crisps were challenged by the many flavours of Walker's Crisps, and Bic circumvented patents of Biro.

New Firms and New Industries

In some instances new firms may create new industries. Thus, despite the existence of rayon it was the discovery of nylon by Du Pont which created the man-made fibres industry, by introducing a cheaper, more crease-resistant and more easy-to-launder cloth. In the field of household durables the list of products which created industries is endless; for example, vacuum cleaners and automatic washing machines. In the office the typewriter created an industry and revolutionized office procedures.

Most new firms tend to be small, with finance provided by the founders, and although technological change is supposed to favour large firms and to enable them to move into new industries, it is possible for small firms to exploit new technologies. Thus microcomputing and associated software seem to be new industries open to small firms; there are also the traditional industries, such as clothing, where small firms persist.

Growth of Firms

Firms grow for many reasons: expanding markets, new products, new processes, economies of scale, cheap resources and new channels of distribution may provide a stimulus to growth. Most of these reasons can and have been fitted into formal models, such as those of Baumol (1959), Bhagwati (1970), Marris (1964) and Williamson (1964). But growth does not fit easily into economic analysis because it involves decisions about intertemporal consumption and saving. As Professor Hyde (1962) observed, it is difficult to explain William Lever's obsession with work long after the need to secure a comfortable standard of living. Independence, persistence, the willingness to work extremely hard and for long hours, as well as interest, seem to be the qualities associated with success. In addition there is a willingness to take risks, to be ruthless and to inspire others. Personal qualities need not include high educational qualifications or scientific skills, although they are useful in science-based industries. Finally, there is chance and opportunism, the awareness of an opportunity, the capacity to exploit that opportunity and the ability to enlarge the bridgehead; growth and entrepreneurship may, therefore, go hand in hand.

Forms of Growth

Edwards and Townsend (1958) have distinguished seven forms of growth which can be achieved by internal growth or mergers.

1 *Increasing the output of existing products* is the simplest form of growth if the market expands and economies are obtainable. The most outstanding examples of this form of growth have been brewers and the oil companies.

2 *Producing varieties of the same product sold in similar markets* is a means of tapping different income levels and tastes in the same market. Thus car manufacturers may produce different models and some firms, such as confectioners and biscuit manufacturers, may find it profitable to produce a range of products because retailers and customers do not like buying each separate product from a separate seller; e.g. fruit gums from fruit gum sellers, fruit pastilles from fruit pastilles sellers. Moving 'up-market' by producing better-quality products has been successfully practised by Marks and Spencer.

3 *Using the same technological knowledge in different markets or acquiring new technologies to meet the same demand.* Electrical and electronics manufacturers and chemical firms have often found it advantageous to use their store of knowledge to produce a range of goods, such as washing machines, vacuum cleaners, toasters, electric irons, calculators and digital watches as well as a variety of drugs, textiles and paints. Other firms have gained from meeting the same basic demand (e.g. typewriters) by producing mechanical, electrical and electronic models.

4 *Producing goods in joint supply or joint demand.* Chemical and electrical firms can grow through diversification because their basic processes yield many by-products.

5 *Making what is bought or reaching forward to the final consumer.* Vertical integration may take place for reasons of security or because of a belief that there are monopoly profits to be exploited. Thus legal restrictions on the number of pubs resulted in brewers acquiring them in order to ensure retail outlets and, it is often claimed, in order to obtain economies of scale.

6 *Growth in all directions.* Sometimes firms grow in one direction and then in another. Chemical firms are obvious examples of diversity induced by the products of research and development; and diversity may be a means of spreading risks.

7 *Growth by purchase and amalgamation.* Instead of starting from scratch – buying plant and equipment, hiring labour, investing in know-how, developing an organization and finding markets – firms may buy existing businesses or parts of firms. Mergers are common but there have been notable merger waves. Thus there was a spate of amalgamations around the turn of the century, a rationalization movement in the 1920s and 1930s, and a merger boom in the 1960s.

Research and Development

The period from 1950 to 1970 was dominated by the growth of firms in particular industries – notably chemicals, man-made fibres, electronics and plastics. Bunching of economic growth in a few industries has occurred in the past. There was a concentration on textiles, coal and iron at the end of the eighteenth century and railways dominated the middle years of the nineteenth century. But what has been striking about the growth of firms in the third quarter of the twentieth century has been their domination by science-related technologies and by vast expenditures on research and development. Hence it might be interesting to pay some attention to the part played by research and development in a firm's growth strategy.

Determinants of Research and Development

Although invention may contain an element of luck the contribution of chance may be deemed slight. Beveridge (1957) studied many important discoveries, and came to the conclusion that success arose because researchers were looking for something specific. There are also many incentives to encourage research workers – Nobel prizes are available, the worth of a journal article can be measured in terms of salary advancement and career enlargement; and a new successful product promises huge bonuses for its discoverer. In other words, successful research pays off and the incentive to undertake research lies in the promise of such rewards.

However, in the pursuit of rewards research and development use scarce resources, and compete with existing activities. Hence there is a trade-off between carrying on with existing activities and using some of them to pioneer new activities. The recognition that research can be treated as an economic problem has led Becker (1971) to suggest the following optimal R and D spending rule:

Spend on R & D until the ratio of the marginal products of inputs before and after spending (MP_i/MP_i^0) is equal to the ratio of total expenditure on that factor ($p_i x_i$) and the marginal cost of improving its productivity (h_i).

$$\frac{MP_i}{MP_i^0} = \frac{p_i x_i}{h_i} \qquad\qquad (4.1)$$

Market Structure and Innovation

So far we have taken market structure as given, but if we assume that every firm knows how much its rivals spend on research and development then we tend to conclude that either all firms spend the same amount and converge on the pay-off at the same time, or that, knowing what others are spending, one firm spends slightly more than the others and wins the race. Neither outcome seems plausible. *Rather, it seems more realistic to postulate that there is an interaction between market structure and the pace and direction of technological change, that technological uncertainty generates market uncertainty and that the market structure cannot be taken as given* (Dasgupta and Stiglitz, 1980).

Technological uncertainty – uncertainty about the outcome of technological change – may be reduced by spending more. Thus management may begin by postulating a probability distribution of completion dates and choose the one which maximizes profits. The choice of which path to follow will depend upon what rivals are expected to do; however rivalry depends not only upon the number of firms in the industry but also upon the number of possible firms which can enter the market. Hence there may be a high level of R and D expenditure even though an industry is highly concentrated if the market can be contested by outsiders. In other words, high degrees of concentration are not by themselves evidence of lack of effective competition; a point which will meet with more analysis in chapter 9.

Bias in Research and Development

Does R and D exhibit a bias? Is it predominantly inclined towards labour-saving processes? A labour-saving invention is one which raises the marginal product of capital relative to labour, a capital-saving invention raises the marginal product of labour, and a neutral invention leaves the ratio of marginal products unchanged. Hicks (1963) drew a distinction between induced and autonomous inventions. He defined induced inventions as those which were promoted by change in relative factor prices, and autonomous inventions as those which occurred without any change in factor prices. He concluded that autonomous inventions were comparatively rare and that most induced inventions were labour-saving, prompted by the fact that capital accumulation tended to reduce the price of capital relative to labour.

The trouble with Hicks's analysis is that it fails to distinguish between inventions and factor substitutions within technology; that is, it ignores the distinction between shifts of isoquants and movements along an isoquant. Nor is it obvious why a management should search in a particular direction. Faced with an increase in costs, management will seek to reduce costs and may search in a variety of directions. There is no presumption to search for labour-saving inventions – although if labour is the largest component of costs there may be a presumption that labour costs offer more scope for saving.

Despite the agnosticism of theory empirical work does indicate the directions in which management searches. Thus, Rosenberg (1976) has drawn attention to the focusing and inducement mechanisms operating within firms. Bottlenecks and slack may constitute focusing points and inducements to invention and innovation. Thus the spate of inventions in spinning in the Industrial Revolution led to a rise in the demand for handloom weavers and the search for a power loom.

Patents

The issue of autonomous versus induced inventions has a bearing upon the desirability of patents as a means of promoting an increase in knowledge. If most advances are autonomous, the result of instinctive curiosity, then inducements may be unnecessary; but if inventions are induced then there is a problem of what is the appropriate inducement. Attempts to increase knowledge through the design of new processes and products raise difficulties for society because it is in the interest of society that new knowledge should be disseminated rapidly, whereas it is in the interest of the inventor that he gets an appropriate reward for his efforts. The purpose of the patent system, and the copyright system as applied to literature, is to attempt to give the inventor a guaranteed reward by creating a scarcity of processes and products which could not otherwise be maintained. They represent an attempt to devise new ways of attaining given ends through the guarantee of patent rights.

The objections to the patent system are that it may divert resources to patentable as opposed to non-patent activities, that it may create socially undesirable monopolies (as in the case of the Boulton–Watt patents which were granted for 25 years) and encourage the excessive use of resources to design around the periphery of a patent. There may be pre-emptive patenting of ideas. Hence it has been suggested that inventors should be guaranteed a reasonable reward subject to compulsory licensing of the patent to would-be users. Compulsory licensing plus a reasonable reward, it is argued, would satisfy society's desire for rapid dissemination of new knowledge plus guaranteeing the inventor a just reward.

Empirical evidence on the promotion and dissemination of knowledge reveals that the use of the patent system is not widespread. This may seem surprising. In the nineteenth century it might have been reasonable to suppose that the existence of the family firm provided a sufficient safeguard of know-how; members of a family might not be willing to divulge trade secrets to outsiders. But with the growth of joint stock companies it might be expected that firms would resort more and more to the use of patents and to legal measures to prevent employees moving from firm to firm disseminating ideas. Yet proliferation has not occurred. Leading firms may be able to recoup from employees by offering lower wages for instruction. In the fashion trades copying by the mass consumer firms occurs, but does not seem to have reduced the ranks of the fashion houses and their customers. Reverse engineering – the shopping down and copying of innovative products without any formal transaction with the innovating firm – is, however, commonly practised and is an important means by which technology transfer takes place between industrially advanced countries. In other industries there may be other effective methods of protection. Thus, Taylor and Silberston (1973) note that in the pharmaceutical industry it is possible to use patents because commodities can be well-defined and firms cannot rely on secret know-how until the expiry of the pay-off period. However, in basic chemicals they found that patents had a marginal effect, that economies of scale formed an effective barrier to imitators and that a licensing system might lead to a suppression of information. In mechanical engineering there was little use of patents because it was not an R and D field, and in electronics and man-made fibres there was also little use of patents because high entry barrier costs seemed to afford sufficient protection. They came to the conclusion that, although there is little use of patents, there is a slender case in favour of the use of the patent system as a stimulus to the discovery of new ideas.

The Direction of Evolution: the Chandler Thesis

Edwards's and Townsend's classification of forms of growth can be reduced to three possibilities: (1) expanding sales of the same product; (2) diversifying into related products; and (3) diversifying into unrelated products. Following on from this, Chandler and his associates (1962, 1977) have suggested that there is a natural line of evolution from unique production to diversified production, and that the strategy of what to produce determines the structure of how to produce it. Structure, therefore, follows strategy, and there is an evolution from unitary to multi-divisional structures.

Channon (1973) has adopted the Chandler thesis and demonstrated its relevance to British industry during the period 1950–70. During the 1950s there was little diversification according to Chandler; however, the dominance of single-product firms started to diminish in the 1960s as firms diversified both nationally and internationally. Firms which did diversify tended to pre-dominate in the food, drink and tobacco, oil, and power machinery industries. In the case of the brewers and tobacco manufacturers it was alleged that being family-owned firms there was a reluctance to diversify because of a possible loss of control to professional managers. In the 1970s, however, the effects of government anti-smoking campaigns were causing the tobacco manufacturers to widen their interests, and the fears of an energy crisis led to some oil companies investing in overseas coalfields and in coal-carrying vessels. However, the Chandler thesis must not be pushed too far. The amount of diversification by British firms is still very slight, and is usually into the production of related commodities. There has been little tendency to create conglomerate firms.

Formal Models of Growth

So far we have concentrated upon listing reasons and causes of growth. Now we shall outline some formal models of growth which attempt to incorporate some of the main reasons advanced for expansion.

The Lognormal Distribution of Firm Sizes

Our starting point for producing models of growth of firms is the observation that the distribution of firm sizes in many industries is typically skewed with a large number of small firms and a few large ones. However, if the data are transformed by taking the logarithms of sizes and not the actual sizes, then the resulting distribution tends to be normal, or rather lognormal. For example, in figure 4.1 the horizontal scale measures firm size in terms of sales and the resulting frequency distribution exhibits a skewed shape. However, if the data are transformed by taking the *logarithms* of sizes rather than the actual sizes, then the resulting distribution tends towards being lognormal, as shown by figure 4.2.

The fact that the shape of the distribution shown in figure 4.1 can be derived from a transformation of the shape shown in figure 4.2 suggests that the explanation of the latter does not rely solely upon the existence of economies of scale. A lognormal distribution results from the multiplicative (log-additive) interaction of a large number of independent forces, each of which exerts little influence. Table 4.1, derived from Prais (1975), shows how Gibrat's Law, which assumes that growth is independent of firm size, can give rise to

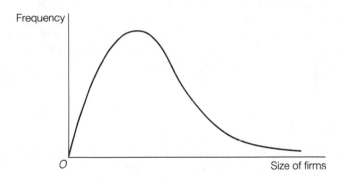

Figure 4.1

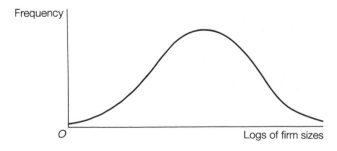

Figure 4.2

lognormal distribution. Initially there are 128 firms, each of equal size and each selling 100 units. In subsequent periods the firms are subject to a simple growth process whereby half the firms remain unchanged in size, a quarter increase their sales by 10 and a quarter lose 10 sales. Hence at the end of the first year the firms will no longer be of equal size. Furthermore, if the process is continued in the second year then the degree of dispersion will increase, and if the percentage of sales of the 10 largest firms is used as a measure of concentration then it will be seen to have risen from 7.81 per cent to 9.22 per cent in the third year.

In table 4.1 the growth rate is constant, but if it were increased or decreased then the rate of concentration would be increased or slowed down. If, instead of postulating that firms grow by the same absolute amount, we assume that they grow by the same percentage, then the rate of concentration would become more rapid and the 'law of proportionate growth' would destroy the symmetry of table 4.1 because large firms would now grow by greater absolute amounts than small firms.

The law of proportionate growth, Gibrat's Law, states that: (1) large, medium and small firms have the same average proportionate growth rate; (2) the dispersion (variance) around the average is the same for all firms; and (3) the relative dispersion of firm sizes increases over time. The example contained in table 4.1 also suggests some of the assumptions necessary for a lognormal distribution to emerge. First, births and deaths must be unimportant. If they occurred and were concentrated in particular class sizes then there would be a departure from lognormality. Secondly, mergers must also be unimportant because they could lead to deviations from the average growth rate. Thirdly, the rule for equiproportionate growth means that there must be no economies of scale which would enable large firms to grow at a faster rate than small ones.

Managerial Factors

The lognormal distribution raises two issues. First, to what extent are actual distributions lognormal? Second, can traditional factors, such as demand, economies of scale and management be incorporated into the stochastic explanation provided by the lognormal distribution? The answer to the first question

Table 4.1.   Size distribution of firms illustrated under the 'law of absolute growth'

	Size of firm (employees)					
	80	90	100	110	120	All
Year 1	–	–	128	–	–	128
Year 2	–	32	64	32	–	128
Year 3	8	32	48	32	8	128

Source: Prais (1975).

appears to be that actual distributions are positively skewed; there appear to be more large firms than would be predicted by the theory and one factor accounting for the departure from lognormality has been mergers. The answer to the second question is that traditional factors may be regarded as additional factors leading to a tendency for there to be many small firms and a few large firms. But note: that what the stochastic approach suggests is that there would be a tendency to concentration even in the absence of such factors as mergers and economies of scale. We can now turn to traditional explanations of variations in firms' sizes by examining the role of managerial factors (Marshall, 1920; Lucas, 1978; Caves and Rosen, 1982).

Suppose we consider the problem of how to allocate resources among managers so as to maximize total output. If all managers were of equal ability then we might observe firms of equal size; but firms do differ in size and as real incomes rise over time then demands will change and lead to a reallocation of resources over managers, so as to increase total output. In this process of reshuffling resources and managers, take-over bids and mergers will be methods by which talented managers will acquire more resources. Furthermore, in reallocating resources new organizational structures may have to be divided so as to enable scarce managerial talent to be effectively used.

Technology and Demand

Firms not only seek to grow but also to protect themselves from new entrants to their markets. Hence we need to analyse what strategies management can adopt to protect their markets. One particular strategy which attracted the attention of theorists in the 1960s was limit pricing. New entrants will be attracted by the presence of profits higher than can be obtained elsewhere, but may be deterred by economies of scale which require a new entrant to be of a particular size in order to compete effectively. However, the addition of extra capacity to the industry may necessitate a reduction in market price in order to absorb the extra output, and if the market demand curve has a low price elasticity then the fall in price may cause losses to the established firm and the new entrant. Hence the possibility of an entry-limiting price policy. If an established firm is prepared to maintain its output when a new firm enters the market then market price will fall. The prevailing market price set by the established firm would therefore be a limit price.

These points are illustrated in figure 4.3. The long-run average cost curve LAC is L-shaped, reflecting the fact that economies of scale arise when output increases from OQ to OQ_1 and thereafter costs tend to remain constant. Hence the smallest scale at which costs are minimized, the minimum efficient size, is OQ_1. Now suppose that in the light of the industry demand curve AR the established firm sets price OP and sells OQ_2. If a new entrant produces OQ_1 ($= Q_2Q_3$) then market price would have to fall to OP_1.

In figure 4.3 an established firm knowing the minimum efficient scale of entry and estimating market demand price elasticity could fix an entry-limiting price which would maintain its market share. But suppose that market demand was growing. The established firm would then have to estimate the growth of demand and the proportion of that increase it might expect to gain as compared

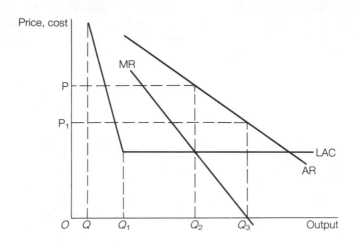

Figure 4.3

with a new entrant. It might also have to face the possibility that if it did lower its price then some of its loyal customers might switch to the new entrant because they felt that they had previously been 'ripped off'.

All the points raised in the two previous paragraphs have been summarized by Bhagwati (1970):

$$P_0 = P_c \left[1 + \frac{\bar{x} - k\lambda}{X_c \left\{ \epsilon/(N+1) + \epsilon \right\}} \right] \tag{4.2}$$

where P_0 is the entry-limiting price, P_c is the competitive price (equal to the minimum average cost of the potential entrant), X_c the industry demand at price P_c, N the number of existing firms, ϵ the elasticity with respect to the change in price of the current buyers' transfer of custom to the new entrant, $\bar{x}$ the minimum efficient scale of new entry, λ the possible growth of demand, and ξ the price elasticity of demand at P_c.

The Bhagwati model has the advantage of reconciling traditional factors, such as economies of scale, with changes in demand. But it does leave open the door for other strategies. For example, should an established firm acquiesce in the behaviour of a new entrant? Should it accept the new entrant's output as given and adjust its own output accordingly? Should it seek some form of joint profit maximization? Should it calculate the benefits from a war of attrition? Should it seek to deter the possible entrant by a visible and credible threat embodied in spare capacity? Might it not find it more advantageous to deter entry by advertising expenditures? At this point we merely note these questions and shall take them up in chapter 10.

Finance, Take-overs and Managerialism

In his book *The Economic Theory of Managerial Capitalism* Marris (1964) presented a model of corporate growth incorporating three elements: (1) differences in the goals of shareholders and managers; (2) a theory of the stock market valuation of firms; and (3) a theory of take-overs.

Marris's thesis assumes that shareholders wish to maximize the return on their investment whereas managers are interested in maximizing the growth rate of the firm's assets. Managers will be interested in the firm's growth because the main source of promotion is through the internal managerial market of the firm and their salaries, perks and prestige depend more on size than profitability. Managers are able to dictate policy because shareholders are dispersed and find it difficult to control managers.

The theory of the stock market valuation of a firm which Marris adopted is that a firm's current market value depends on the expected next dividend and the expected long-run growth of dividends, with the latter corresponding to the expected growth rate of market value or capital gain. In any period shareholders will trade off current dividends (distributed profits) against the firm's retentions (retained profit) which give rise to capital gains. Shareholders' preferences between current dividends and retentions will depend upon the expected return from any investment which the retained profits are used to finance. Thus, if the capital market were perfect and if firms were maximizing net wealth then shareholders will be indifferent between dividends and retentions because they can always realize capital gains by selling shares.

The final element in Marris's model is a theory of take-overs which is based upon differences in the value placed upon firms by the existing owners and potential owners should stock market valuations fall below the valuations of some outsiders. Whether a successful take-over takes place will depend upon the *market valuation ratio* of the firm, which is measured by the stock market value of the firm divided by the book value of its assets. The stock market value measures the stock market's assessment of the firm's future earning power, whereas the book value of its assets gives a rough measure of the value of the resources used in the firm. If the valuation ratio is low, then the value of the resources tied up in the firm may be greater than the stock market's valuation of the firm and a successful take-over might be possible.

The growth of a firm depends in part upon the availability of finance, and managers have three methods of raising finance: borrowing, new share issues or retaining profits. However, there are limits to the amounts of finance which can be raised by each of these routes. As the amount of borrowing increases, borrowers and lenders become subject to greater risks. Because the priority claims of debenture holders must be met managers may lose control if profits fall. New share issues could also lead to loss of control, and are only possible if the stock market takes a favourable view of the firm's investment programme. If retentions rise shareholders may become dissatisfied and dismiss the management or sell their shares. If they sell their shares then the market value of the firm could fall and take-over bids leading to the dismissal of the existing management could take place.

In its simplest form the Marris model assumes that expansion is financed through the use of internal funds only, and that there is a particular retention ratio which is consistent with security. If managers retain as much profit as they need to finance expansion, and if this maximum retention ratio is the same at all levels of profitability, then there will be a linear relationship between the availability of finance and the firm's profit rate, as is shown in figure 4.4. The supply curve of capital shows the maximum growth rates which can be financed at different profit rates. Below the curve are points at which the growth rate will depress the valuation ratio and invite a take-over. The demand growth curve in figure 4.4 reflects the factors which promote or inhibit the desire for growth by managers. Although managers can free themselves from the limited demand for particular products by diversification, there does come a point at which the costs of growth begin to increase. The rise in costs comes from increased spending on advertising to promote new goods, increased spending on research and development, and other administrative costs. Hence the inverted U-shaped demand growth curve as is shown in figure 4.4.

By bringing together the supply curve of capital and the demand growth curve figure 4.4 is able to depict feasible combinations of profit rates and growth – the shaded area. We now assume that the management decide upon a particular growth rate. In order to achieve this growth rate management will choose a set of key variables through which the firm can respond to markets. Thus if markets were assumed to exhibit no change then the firm will achieve a steady growth rate. In figure 4.4 L gives the maximum profit rate and M gives the maximum growth rate. Point L will be preferred by shareholders because it will, assuming a given retention ratio, give maximum dividends. But

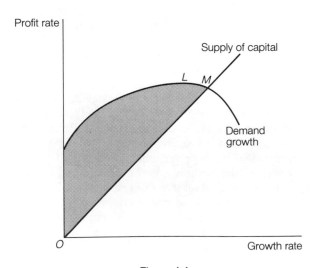

Figure 4.4

if the capital market were imperfect then shareholders would prefer to be to the right of L at a point which measures their trade-off between dividends and capital gains. In contrast, managers will prefer to be at M because that gives them maximum growth combined with security from take-overs as reflected in the slope of the capital supply curve; but, if managers were willing to take risks and work with lower valuation ratios then they might operate to the right of M (figure 4.4).

The possible trade-offs of shareholders and managers are summarized in their indifference curves in figure 4.5. Shareholders' utility is maximized by the combination of dividends and capital gains which would accrue if the firm operated at E, where the demand growth curve is tangent to one of their indifference curves. In figure 4.5 the valuation curve has been drawn to yield a maximum at the point where the stock market value of the firm will be a maximum if the shareholders' utility is maximized. The managers' indifference curves show their trade-off between growth and security (valuation ratio). Their utility is maximized at F. Hence there is a possible clash of interests between shareholders and managers.

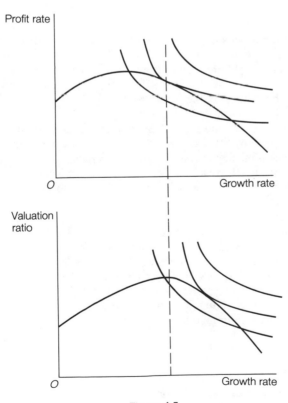

Figure 4.5

The Marris model attempted to capture the factors determining the growth of British and American firms in the 1960s and 1970s. With the development of financial institutions, the greater efficiency of capital markets, the increased mobility of managers and the prolonged recession of the 1970s and 1980s there has been a greater emphasis upon short-run profits. Conscious that mobility is dependent upon success, managers have been more prone to pursue short-term gains and to avoid speculative ventures in R and D, and their activities have been reinforced by the desire of investors for liquidity. In contrast the immobility of managers and the rarity of take-over bids have enabled Japanese firms to concentrate upon long-run developments (Dore, 1985).

Stagnation and Decline

Stagnation and decline may be due to a lack of managerial competence or market opportunities. The two causes are, of course, interrelated since opportunities depend upon perceptions; hence we begin with the human factor.

Life Cycle

The decline of family businesses used to be summed up in the adage: 'from clogs to clogs in three generations'. But what happens if there are no sons or daughters willing and able to take over the firm? Allen Lane created Penguin Books, tapped different markets with Pelicans, Puffins, Penguin Education, etc., educated the nation in the University of Paperbacks and saw his firm become part of the Establishment. But his daughters did not share his interests, and in later years he became disenchanted with his empire and incapable of nominating a successor. Struggles for the throne, the drying-up of paperback rights as hardback publishers produced their own paperbacks, and the financial difficulties of the 1970s resulted in the firm being absorbed by Pearson Longman. But the issue of leadership remained unresolved until an outsider was appointed.

Succession problems can also arise in joint stock companies, especially when the corporate structure has concealed a family control. Thus, IBM was managed by Tom Watson Senior, who was succeeded by his son; then the family succession ended and an outsider had to be found. At ITT on the death of Colonel Behn internal rivalry dictated his position had to be filled by an outsider; when Behn's successor, Genen, retired ITT appointed an internal candidate: 'one of the younger men on the rise, the kind who leave the corporation unless he continued to receive additional power and status' (Sobel, 1982).

Product Market Decline

Predicting the decline of a product or industry is extremely hazardous; short-run factors may mask long-term trends. Nevertheless there may be portents.

1   *Demographic* changes, such as the fall in the birth rate, may signal a reduction in the demands for prams and baby foods.

2   *Technological change* has replaced slide rules with calculators, and is revolutionizing office equipment.

3   *Needs and fashions* are a major source of change. Some commodities blaze brightly in the market place for a short time and then disappear (e.g. skateboards) while others seem to enjoy a periodical renaissance (e.g. berets and mini-skirts).

4   *Foreign competition* is also an important source of diminished demand. As industrialization spreads outwards from the core to the periphery of the world economy, industries in the core experience severe competition. In the 1920s and 1930s the UK textile industry had to contract in response to competition from Japan; in the 1950s and 1960s Japan's textile industry became exposed to the low-cost textile industries of new industrializing countries, such as Hong Kong, Singapore and the Philippines. Furthermore, the spread of industrialization appears to be accelerating as a result of the increased mobility of capital and know-how. In the nineteenth century Britain enjoyed some 60 years of supremacy in shipbuilding; after the Second World War Japan enjoyed some 20 years of dominance.

Exit Barriers

Even when decline is apparent, however, adjustment may be difficult. Plant and equipment may be highly specialized and have a low opportunity cost. What second-hand market exists for disused cooling towers? Even the labour force may have a low opportunity cost if substantial sums have to be paid in redundancy compensation, and governments may impede change if it is to be accompanied by prolonged unemployment. Pride may also be an obstacle to change; but in the end, all exit barriers are really entry barriers to something else.

Strategies for Decline

Faced with the need to accommodate a decline a firm can pursue one of seven strategies:

1   Change the leadership in the hope of finding someone to chart a new path. Thus, Peter Meyer's appointment at Penguin's brought an entrée to US paperback rights and cut through many obstacles to change.

2   Seek to dominate what remains of the industry.

3   Establish or create a niche in the market by, for example, catering for exclusive tastes.

4   Divest quickly may be the optimal solution.

5   Harvest whatever profits are available and pursue a policy of controlled disinvestment.

6 Seek protection.
7 Seek to expand overseas.

The UK Cutlery Industry

Some of the issues which we have raised in connection with the decline of firms can now be illustrated by reference to the postwar history of the UK (Sheffield) cutlery industry. The standard industrial classification of cutlery comprises knives, forks and spoons; scissors; penknives; surgical instruments; etc. The main contraction has taken place in the market for kitchen cutlery. In the 1950s the industry was characterized by a high degree of specialization and coordination through the market.

At the end of the 1950s some firms were experiencing competition from imports of Swedish satin-finished stainless-steel cutlery. However, this intrusion was largely ignored. Firms continued to produce traditional designs. Canteens of cutlery were an infrequent purchase – mainly for wedding presents – and purchasers still preferred the standard designs of long-bladed knives with 'bone' handles and a small cutting edge. There were also the bulk purchases of cheap cutlery by, for example, Woolworths and the holiday camps. There was also an export of knives with horn handles to North America. But Swedish cutlery was regarded as something catering for minority tastes.

Competition intensified in the sixties and seventies as a result of imports of cheap stainless-steel cutlery from the Far East. There was an attempt to limit imports through tariffs but the trade association split when one of the major firms, Viners, decided that the correct policy for survival was to import 'blanks' for finishing. Other firms sought to cater for specialist segments of the market. However, the contraction of the market as a result of foreign competition continued, and was not alleviated by the removal of minimum wage legislation in the seventies.

Despite the contraction of demand there was no parallel contraction of supply. Excess capacity was still prevalent in the early eighties; there were still too many firms producing too small an output to be efficient. The condition of excess capacity was that which was analysed by Chamberlin in *The Theory of Monopolistic Competition* (1933), and which could be observed in the cotton industry in the interwar years and to the 1950s. Many firms are family-owned and may find it much easier than managerial firms to accept a lower than market rate of return on their capital. Indeed, family-owned firms may appear to be 'successful survivors' when compared with managerial firms, because of the willingness to accept a lower reward. There is also the point that in industries with large numbers of independent producers it may be difficult to get agreement on a reduction of capacity. Each firms hopes that its rivals will quit the industry and allow it to make a profit. What is required is some means of coercing firms to rationalize production, by permitting survivors to compensate those who leave the industry. But given the existence of free entry the numbers of firms with which to reach agreement is unlimited. Potential entrants are, in effect, free riders on any domestic agreement not backed up by some form of protection to survivors. In the absence of such an agreement liquidation rather than migration becomes the norm. Excess capacity and liquidation are therefore analogous to involuntary unemployment of labour, and arise for the same reason: the presence of an externality created by lack of information. It is this externality which constitutes the barrier to exit.

Divorce and Death: Sell-outs and Buy-outs and Privatization

The deaths of firms seldom involve the physical destruction of assets. The usual practice is for the assets of one firm to be acquired by other firms. Indeed, during the merger waves of the 1960s and 1970s suicide (a willingness to merge) was a common cause of death with many firms waiting to be taken over. Although most deaths, as well as births, involve small firms there is also considerable interest in amputation, the disposal of some, but not all, of the assets of firms. Thus, during the period 1970–78 divested subsidiaries accounted for more than one-fifth of the companies acquired by non-financial firms (Chiplin and Wright, 1982). Most divestors and acquirers were in the food, drink and tobacco, miscellaneous services and property sectors of the economy, and the reasons for disinvestment were as follows:

1 *To correct a mistake.* In 1980 Associated Biscuit Manufacturers sold the unprofitable subsidiary Dickman, which it had taken over in 1978.
2 *Financial difficulties.* Alfred Herbert sold Herbert Sigma Instruments in 1980 despite the latter's profitability.
3 *Strategic reasons connected with markets and technological change.* In 1980 Thorn acquired EMI and proceeded to dispose of the leisure industry assets to Trust House Forte, the hotels and restaurants to Scottish and Newcastle Breweries, and the electronic scanner business to General Electric and Omni Medical.

An interesting method of asset disposal is the buy-out, in which the previous management and employees purchase the assets of an ailing firm. This is a possible method of forming a worker cooperative but its success may depend upon whether the assets can be bought at a discount, whether the buyers possess information (asymmetrical information) which is not available to outsiders, and whether the buyers can generate a socio-psychological atmosphere which will generate greater efficiency. When the buyers are the former employees there is a difficult problem of determining the value of the firm, and in America independent agencies have been developed to determine valuations.

Finally, *privatization*, the disposal of public assets, has begun to emerge in recent years. Thus Amersham International, a wholly owned subsidiary of the United Kingdom Atomic Energy Authority, was sold in 1982 and the National Freight Corporation was sold to its former employees. The reasons for denationalization include the belief that nationalization is inefficient, that asset disposal is preferable to raising taxes, and that profitable activities should be run by private enterprise whilst only cases of market failure should be subsidized by the state. There is also the fear that strong trade unions in unprofitable industries should be prevented from obtaining subsidies from the taxpayer or other profitable public corporations. A more comprehensive discussion of these issues is presented in a later chapter.

Bibliography and References

Baumol, W. J. (1959) *Business Behavior, Value and Growth*. New York: Harcourt Brace.
Becker, G. S. (1971) *Economic Theory*. New York: Alfred Knopf.
Beveridge, W. J. (1957) *The Art of Scientific Investigation*. London: Heinemann.
Bhagwati, J. (1970) 'Oligopoly theory, entry prevention and growth', *Oxford Economic Papers*, 22, 297–310.
Caves, R. E. and Rosen, J. B. (1982) 'Uncertainty, transactions costs and the size distribution of rival firms; theory and evidence from the women's outerwear industry', *Quarterly Review of Economics and Business*, 22, 6–22.
Chamberlin, E. H. (1933) *The Theory of Monopolistic Competition*. Cambridge, Mass.: Harvard University Press.
Chandler, A. D. (1962) *Strategy and Structure*. Cambridge, Mass.: Harvard University Press.
Chandler, A. D. (1977) *The Visible Hand*. Cambridge, Mass.: Harvard University Press.
Chandler, A. D. (1980) 'The growth of the transnational industrial firm in the United States and the United Kingdom: a comparative analysis', *Economic History Review*, 2nd series, 33, 396–410.
Chandler, A. D. and Daems, H. (eds) (1962) *Managerial Hierarchies*. Cambridge, Mass.: Harvard University Press.
Channon, D. F. (1973) *Strategy and Structure of British Enterprise*. London: Macmillan.
Chiplin, B. and Wright, M. (1982) 'Disinvestment and structural change in UK industry', *National Westiminister Bank Review*, 65, 42–51.
Clay, H. (1948) 'The Monopolies Act', *Lloyds Bank Review*, 15, 1–13.
Dasgupta, P. and Stiglitz, J. (1980) 'Industrial structure and the nature of innovative activity', *Economic Journal*, 90, 266–93.
Dore, R. P. (1985) 'Financial structures and the long-term view', *Policy Studies*, 10, 10–28.
Edwards, R. and Townsend, H. (1958) *Business Enterprises*. London: Macmillan.
Freeman, C. (1974) *The Economics of Industrial Innovation*. London: Penguin Books.
Hicks, J. R. (1963) *The Theory of Wages*, 2nd edn. London: Macmillan.
Hyde, F. (1962) 'Business behaviour and profit maximization'. In K. A. Tucker (ed.), *Studies in Business History*. London: Frank Cass.
Lloyd Jones, R. and Le Roux, A. A. (1984) 'The birth and death of firms: the growth and death of firms in the early nineteenth century cotton industry', *Business History*, 24, 141–55.
Lucas, R. E. (1978) 'On the size distribution of business firms', *Bell Journal of Economics*, 9, 508–23.
Marris, R. (1964) *The Economic Theory of Managerial Capitalism*. London: Macmillan.
Marshall, A. (1920) *Principles of Economics*, 8th edition, London: Macmillan.
Morpurgo, J. M. (1980) *Allen Lane*. London: Hutchinson.
Porter, M. E. (1982) *The Competitive Strategy*. New York: Free Press.
Porter, M. E. (1985) *The Competitive Advantage*. New York: Free Press.
Prais, S. J. (1975) *The Evolution of Giant Firms*. Oxford: Oxford University Press.

Rosenberg, N. (1976) *Perspectives on Technology*. Cambridge: Cambridge University Press.

Sobel, R. (1981) *IBM*. New York: Times Books.

Sobel, R. (1982) *ITT*. London: Sidgwick & Jackson.

Taylor, C. T. and Silberston, Z. A. (1973) *The Economic Impact of the Patent System*. Cambridge: Cambridge University Press.

Williamson, O. E. (1964) *The Economics of Discretionary Behavior*. New York, Prentice-Hall.

5 Structure

Introduction

'Structure follows strategy' was the conclusion which Chandler (1962) drew from his study of the evolution of American firms. Strategy dictates answers to the following organizational questions. Should jobs be broken down so as to yield narrow areas of work and responsibility, in order to obtain the benefits of specialization? Should the structure of a firm be elongated with many levels of management, or should it make use of very wide spans of control? Should jobs and departments be organized along functional lines or should they be organized on a product, or geographical, basis? What kinds of incentives should be used to integrate activities? What structural requirements are posed by the demands of changing processes and products? These are the questions which managers pose when they think of organizational design.

Chandler sought answers to some of these questions, but his analysis tended to be critical of the invisible hand and of economics, and was preoccupied with the long-run to the neglect of the possible short-run effects of structure upon strategy (Alford, 1976). Hence we begin our investigation of the determinants of organizational structure from a different vantage point. As figure 5.1 indicates, most studies of organizational structure can be regarded as reactions to Weber's theory of bureaucracy. Thus Chandler's work can be regarded as a contingency theory with structure being dependent upon time and circumstances. In the first part of this chapter, therefore, we discuss the contributions of sociologists, psychologists and political scientists to the analysis of the determinants of structure. We attempt then to synthesize those discussions in an economic theory of bureaucracy. In the second part we move from the study of individual plants to the broad sweep of history and discuss the Chandler thesis in terms of developments in various countries with especial reference to the period since 1945.

Weber on Bureaucracy

Weber's work on bureaucracy was a by-product of his investigations of the interactions of religion and the rise of capitalism and his reaction to Marx. Marx had suggested that it was the substructure of exchange relationships which determined the superstructure of ideas, and that bureaucracy was an

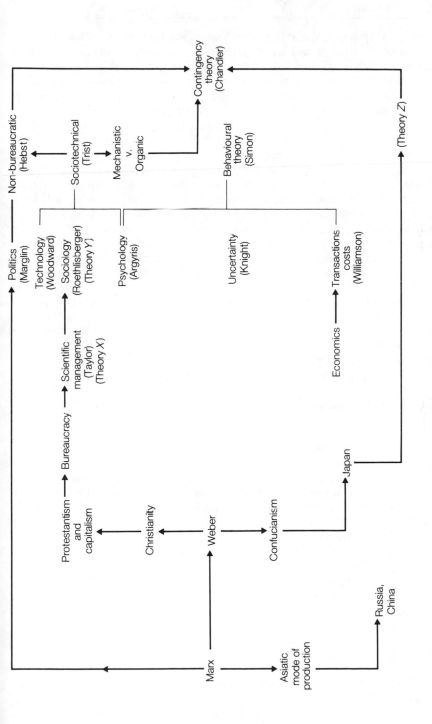

Figure 5.1 Theorizing about organization and behaviour.

instrument by which the ruling class controlled and ensured that decisions were implemented. It was noted also by Marx that the manner in which exchange relationships took place in a capitalist society could lead to alienation. What Weber attempted to do was to stand the Marxian view on its head by permitting the superstructure to influence the substructure, and by taking the view that bureaucrats might be neutral in their political behaviour.

In Weber's view organizations seem to require some concept of authority – of A being conscious that his actions are being influenced by B's decisions – and Weber distinguished between the 'charismatic', the 'traditional' and the 'rational' types of authority. Rational authority rests upon an impersonal legally established order and within the rational bureaucracy each person has a well-defined sphere of competence, with deference being given not to the individual but to the office he holds. Weber traced the emergence of rational authority and bureaucracy, as embodied in capitalism, to the emergence and evolution of that strand of Protestantism known as Puritanism.

Weber's analysis of the interrelations of religion and capitalism has attracted considerable attention, and its detailed study lies outside our competence as well as interest. However, we may note that some writers have suggested that the antecedents of capitalism may be found in Catholicism, most notably in the body of thinking known as Erastianism (Trevor-Roper, 1972). We may observe also that what has been called the Asiatic mode of production, with its emphasis upon charismatic or traditional authority, may have been the result of the need for collective ownership and production of public works, such as irrigation schemes, and that the success of Japanese industry may have been due to the evolution of Japanese Confucianism into a form of Oriental Puritanism (Morishima, 1982).

Scientific Management

If we accept Weber's delineation of bureaucracy then we may observe also that scientific management, as practised and preached by Taylor, Emerson and Gilbreth, and the theories of management put forward by Fayol (1949) and Follett (1941) can be regarded as a fleshing-out of Weber's bureaucratic model. Thus, Taylor (1915) emphasized the importance of centralizing all the items of information relating to work practices and then eliminating from them all inefficient operations. Fayol set out the tasks of managers and the principles by which they must execute those tasks. In his writings he stressed the importance of authority and responsibility, unity of command, good order, *esprit de corps*, etc.

Sociological Factors

Although Weber's work was sophisticated and complex, it was a simplified version of his ideas which came to be accepted as the essence of his thinking, and it was this summary which came to be criticized. The simplified theory of bureaucracy postulates an efficient machine in which orders give rise to anticipated consequences. But why should human beings obey orders? Might they not pursue goals other than those promulgated by their superiors? And why should the structure be hierarchical? These questions have formed the basis or outcome of research carried out by sociologists, psychologists and political scientists from the 1920s onwards. Some issues, such as the effect of the division of labour and de-skilling of the labour process, had, of course, been raised by Adam Smith but, as a result of their activities, sociologists, psychologists and political scientists anticipated the later work of economists on property rights, trade and incentives. They also introduced a new element: trust.

Although there are many strands in post-Weberian thinking it is useful to begin with the findings of the famous Hawthorne Experiments carried out at the Hawthorne plant of General Electric in the 1920s (Roethlisberger and Dickson, 1964). The starting point for the research was an attempt to establish the effects on output and productivity of changes in the physical working conditions and methods of payment. As such the research could be regarded as an elaboration of the views of the scientific management school, and the work carried out in British munitions factories during the First World War. To analyse the effects of changes in working conditions the research workers established control groups in the relay assembly room and the bank wiring room, and these experiments suggested (especially those in the relay assembly room) that productivity continued to rise despite changes in working conditions. This was attributed to the development of social relationships between members of the work group which lay outside the formal bureaucratic relationships. These social relationships came to be embodied within the concept of the *informal group*. Interactions between members led to networks of trading and the development of sentiments between members (Homans, 1950).

However, some adverse effects were also observed. For example, while the relay assembly room experiments pointed to the development of a high trust relationship among employees at different levels, the bank wiring room experiments pointed to the obstacles in the way of the development of trust. Further case studies by Merton (1940), Selznick (1949) and Gouldner (1954) also demonstrated the possibility of unanticipated adverse effect of bureaucratic systems. In Gouldner's study of the operations of a gypsum mine an initial high-trust system developed into one of low trust when product market conditions deteriorated. A demand for greater efficiency and control over the work situation severed the previously friendly and informal relationships. The result was that there was a defence of established patterns of behaviour, conflict and a strike.

Psychological Factors

The work of sociologists, such as Gouldner, overlaps and complements the work of social psychologists such as Argyris (1964), who were concerned with the impact of organizational rules upon the individual. Thus, budgets which are too tight or too slack might defeat the objects of management. If budgets are too tight then workers might fail to respond to the incentive scheme; they would insist upon revisions of budgets. But if budgets are too slack then they might not reveal the laxity of the standards. These studies have received confirmation from the work of accountants and indicate the shaky foundations upon which accounting standards are based.

Of course the fact that sociologists and psychologists have reached similar conclusions should not obscure the differences in methodology. In the work of the psychologists there is a greater emphasis upon perception, attitudes and learning experiences. However, perception, the view that individuals have of situations, may be conditioned by factors which sociologists stress, such as group influence.

Theory *X* and Theory *Y*

The work of sociologists and psychologists led McGregor (1960) to distinguish between theory *X*, which he associated with the scientific management school, and theory *Y*, which he attributed to the human relations school. The distinction between these two theories is summarized in Table 5.1.

Table 5.1.

Theory X	
1	The average human being has an inherent dislike of work, and will avoid it if he can.
2	Because of this human characteristic of dislike of work, most people must be coerced, directed, threatened with punishment, to get them to put forth adequate effort towards the achievement of organizational objectives.
3	The average human being prefers to be directed, wishes to avoid responsibility, has relatively little ambition and wants security above all.
Theory Y	
1	The expenditure of physical and mental effort in work is as natural as play or rest.
2	External control and the threat of punishment are not the only means for bringing about effort towards organizational objectives. Man will exercise self-direction and self-control in the service of objectives to which he is committed.
3	Commitment to objectives is a function of the rewards associated with their achievements.
4	The average human being learns, under proper conditions, not only to accept but to seek responsibility.
5	The capacity to exercise a relatively high degree of imagination, ingenuity and creativity in the solution of organizational problems is widely, not narrowly, distributed in the population.
6	Under the conditions of modern industrial life the intellectual potentialities of the average being are only partially utilized.

Technical Factors

Should organizational structures be flat or tall? Tall structures with long chains of command and many levels of management offer workers long-term career prospects and progression. They enable higher management to create internal labour markets. Tall structures lead to possibilities of communication distortion, and to the temptation to bypass some managerial levels in order to get quick decisions. Foremen frequently find themselves bypassed by shop stewards who think they can make agreements with higher management. In the case of nationalized industries there is a temptation to bypass the commercial management and seek a 'beer and sandwiches solution' with the political management at No. 10.

The optimal organizational design – tall or flat – would seem to be a question of benefits and costs. Economists would seek to discover whether the market offered a more efficient alternative to long internal chains of command. The competence of managers would also have to be assessed and the types of incentives that could be used would need to be appraised. One attempt to cut through these complex questions was proposed by Woodward (1958). The Hawthorne Experiments suggested that different technologies may have been a contributory factor in accounting for the different patterns of behaviour in the relay assembly room and the bank wiring room. Woodward pursued this theme with respect to formal theories of organization. Her work suggested that continuous process industries, such as chemicals, tend to have tall organizational structures, whereas jobbing factories tend to have flat structures. Her classification ran into difficulties, however, with firms having intermediate technologies, and it did not take into account the uncertainties present in product markets and production processes.

Socio-technical Factors

Socio-psychological theories and technological theories tended to coalesce in the socio-technical theory put forward by Trist and associates (Trist et al., 1963). In their studies of coal mining systems Trist and his colleagues showed that different mining technologies gave rise to different worker responses. Thus, the traditional hand-got system was an all-in system in the sense that all members of the small work group performed all the operations of getting and transporting the coal, as well as advancing the coal face, within a shift. Although the pace of work was relatively slow there was a high level of group satisfaction.

The hand-got system began to be replaced in the 1920s by the machine-got/hand-filled system, which persisted until the 1960s. Under this system the coal was undercut by a machine and then blown down with explosives. The coal was then hand-filled onto a mechanized conveyor belt. However, there were features of the procedure which gave rise to a considerable amount of social discord. The three main tasks of coal-cutting, hand-filling and advancing the coal face were conducted by three different shifts, which not only produced a new division of labour but required tight supervision and control to achieve efficiency. Unfortunately, geological conditions made it difficult to simulate factory conditions and there were often problems in getting workers on one shift to complete work left over from a previous shift because of, for example, roof falls, faults or absenteeism. When adverse conditions were encountered it was difficult to maintain the efficiency of incentive payment schemes. Trist and his colleagues argued that with a higher level of technology – the power loading system of machine-cutting and loading of coal – it would be possible to achieve the high level of worker satisfaction of the old hand-got system because all tasks would have to be performed within the shift and the excessive division of labour would be abolished. What the studies by Trist and his associates ignored, however, was that the power loading system, plus a time rate method of wage payment, such as was introduced in the 1970s, could permit higher management a greater degree of control over the work team (McCormick, 1979).

Mechanistic versus Organic Structures

The work of Trist and his associates emphasized the uncertainties in the production process which could disrupt the workings of an 'ideal' bureaucracy, and this theme can be found in Burns and Stalker's (1966) distinction between mechanistic and organic firms. Mechanistic firms have organizational structures which tend to conform to the principles of an ideal bureaucracy, whereas organic firms have more flexible, more diffused structures. The main features of mechanistic and organic firms are set out in table 5.2.

The differences between the two types of firm lie in the nature of their environments. Mechanistic firms tend to have stable environments with few uncertainties in the production processes, whereas organic firms are confronted by unstable environments. Burns and Stalker (1966) also drew attention to the ways in which a typical bureaucratic organization responds to a disturbance by methods which attempt to maintain the bureaucracy. Thus, in their studies they found that it was common to set up committees as a kind of superman, or to add more branches to the organization, or to send for an outside specialist, a management consultant. In a later study of the BBC, Burns (1977) pointed to the advantages of an organic structure in permitting spontaneous coordination to occur.

Uncertainty and Bounded Rationality

Trist and his associates, and Burns and Stalker, emphasized uncertainties in the production processes, but these can also emerge in product and factor markets. Hence we need to look at the work on uncertainty. Knight (1921) drew a distinction between measurable risk and immeasurable risk, and this distinction leads on to Simon's concept of bounded rationality (Simon, 1982).

Table 5.2.   Characteristics of mechanistic and organic systems

Mechanistic systems (for stable environments)	Organic systems (for changing conditions)
1 Specialized differentiation of functional tasks into which the problems and tasks facing the concern as a whole are broken down.	1 Contributive nature of special knowledge and experience to the common task of the concern.
2 The abstract nature of each individual task is pursued with techniques and purposes different from those of the concern as a whole.	2 The realistic nature of the individual task is seen and set by the total situation of the concern.
3 The reconciliation for each level in the hierarchy of these distinct performances by the immediate superiors.	3 The adjustment and continual redefinition of individual tasks through the interaction with others.
4 The precise definition of rights and obligations and technical methods attached to each functional role.	4 The shedding of responsibility as a limited field of rights, obligations and methods. Problems may not be avoided as someone else's responsibility.
5 The translation of rights and obligations and methods into the responsibilities of a functional position.	5 The spread of commitment to the concern beyond any technical definition.
6 A hierarchic structure of control, authority and communication.	6 A network of control, authority and communication. Sanctions derive from presumed community of interest with the rest of the firm.
7 A reinforcement of the hierarchic structure by the location of knowledge of actualities exclusively at the top of the hierarchy.	7 Knowledge about the technical or commercial nature of the task may be located anywhere. This location becomes the ad hoc centre of authority and communication.
8 Tendency for interaction between members of the firm to be vertical.	8 Lateral direction of communication through the firm resembling communication rather than command.
9 Tendency for operations and working behaviour to be governed by the instructions and decisions issued by superiors.	9 A content of communication which consists of information and advice rather than instructions and decisions.
10 Insistence on loyalty to the firm and obedience to superiors as a condition of membership.	10 Commitment to the firm's tasks and to the technological ethos of expansion and progress are more highly valued than loyalty and obedience.
11 Greater importance and prestige attaching to local rather than cosmopolitan knowledge, experience and skill.	11 Importance and prestige attach to affiliations and expertise valid in the industrial, technical and commercial environment of the firm.

Source: adapted from Burns and Stalker (1966).

Simon's work on administrative behaviour derived from Barnard (1938) the concept of 'organizational equilibrium' as a situation in which the benefits to members of an organization are equal to their contributions – a view of equilibrium which is analogous to the economist's equalization of marginal revenue and marginal cost or wage and marginal product. However, Simon observed that the future cannot be fully foreseen, and that individuals have only a limited capacity for digesting all the information with which their environments confront them. For some problems which are repetitive and routine they will adopt standard operating procedures but for non-routine, novel problems they may be forced back upon judgement, intuition, rules of thumb and selecting as managers those who have a good 'track record' in solving unusual problems. Thus production manuals may suggest the use of a square root formula for inventory control but in practice the complex factors operating on purchases and sales may dictate a rule-of-thumb policy.

Political Factors

The most sustained attack on the need for hierarchies has been conducted by Marglin (1974). Economists such as Williamson (1975) have tended to argue that organizational structures arise because of transactions costs. Hence changes in the production system from, for example, the domestic system, arose because the steam engine enabled a centralized system, the factory, to replace the more expensive putting-out system.

Knowledge is power, however, and an alternative reason for hierarchies has been put forward by Marglin, who argues that the factory system was a means by which the potential gains from technological innovation were realized by capitalists and entrepreneurs. In other words, technological inventions required organizational inventions for their benefits to be realized. In the guild system knowledge was collectively owned by the guild, whose members were enjoined not to reveal the 'mysteries' to outsiders. However, the decline of serfdom and the guilds, and the growth of individualism, threatened the collective ownership of knowledge, for, by its very nature, knowledge is a public good; once revealed it is available to all at zero cost. It may be possible to protect some forms of knowledge through the use of patents, but such a method of protection is often costly and easy to evade. Moreover, patents do not protect the knowledge associated with using an invention; that is, knowledge of the gains from innovation. In the period after the French Revolution, when men were set free, it became increasingly difficult to stop the movement of workers who had acquired that knowledge from their former employers.

The capitalist's solution to the problem of protecting knowledge was to transfer work to factories and to subdivide jobs within the factories. Transfer of production to factories meant that materials and machines could be more easily protected, and minute subdivision of work meant that it was much more difficult for workers to acquire a knowledge of all the tasks involved in a particular manufacture. Knowledge, and therefore control, rested in the hands of the capitalist.

Marglin reinforces his argument by pointing out that Adam Smith's discussion of pin manufacture assumed away the problem of control by taking it as axiomatic that there was only one method of manufacture. In Smith's description each worker performs a single specialist task, such as drawing wire, making a point or head, etc. However, Marglin argues that it would have been possible to rotate workers between jobs so that after a year or two they would have obtained a knowledge of all jobs. Alternatively, pin manufacture could have been organized as a worker cooperative. What the elaborate division of labour in the factory system did, therefore, was to remove the bargaining power which the worker and his family possessed under the domestic system. When the merchant put out his materials he surrendered knowledge and power to the household; if he attempted to beat down wages then he might risk the worker adulterating his materials.

On the basis of Marglin's critique, therefore, it is possible to view all subsequent changes in managerial structures as stemming from a desire to increase the capitalist's share of total revenue rather than a desire to increase efficiency. Thus the introduction of line and staff, and Taylorism, could be regarded as further attempts to subdivide labour processes and to concentrate knowledge. Similarly the shift to multi-divisional structures could be regarded as further attempts to increase efficiency; and even though the use of socio-technical systems could be regarded as a step in the other direction, they still retain hierarchies.

An Economic Theory of Bureaucracy

Can a synthesis be produced from the various strands of thinking which we have outlined in figure 5.1 and discussed in previous sections? Economics is a study of exchange relationships, but such exchanges are viewed as giving rise to horizontal structures. Thus workers hire foremen and foremen hire workers and both, in turn, are hired by and hire managing directors. There is a pattern of trading and, through exchanges, property rights are traded. In this approach hierarchies are illusions, mere veils, behind which a pattern of horizontal trading relationships takes place. It is true that the trading model, which exploits the principle of comparative advantage, assumes complete divisibility of activities, but that divisibility is guaranteed by the mobility of workers, foreman and managing directors.

But are these property rights protected by law? The answer is: not in every case! Many are difficult to enforce by legal processes. Inventions can be protected by patents but many aspects of organizational conduct cannot be embraced by the law. It is impossible to make rules to govern specific performance. Fox (1974) has forcibly argued that it may be impossible to establish contracts which cover all contingencies, and that attempts to do so lead to the emergence of low-trust relationships; workers will feel that they are not to be trusted and will act in a defensive, aggressive manner.

Investment in trust can take place when trade is expected to be permanent. Notions of fairness and trust, social relationships which are embodied in the concept of an informal group, then begin to envelop the formal group. Investment in trust will take two forms. First, there will be a filtering of trading partners. No society can exist solely on a diet of self-interest and the cash nexus and will develop, in addition, non-monetary values and introduce social conditioning, in order to cohere. Indicators of such social conditioning will be race, religion, sex, age, and education, and these will form a basis for the selection of trading partners. Secondly, once trading partners have been selected, further investment will develop those interactions and sentiments which lower trading costs and form the characteristics of trading groups.

Of course, trading in information is not perfect. There are technical, physical, problems in transmitting information. The mathematical theory of information pioneered by Shannon (1949) cannot capture all the nuances and subtleties of intonation and emphasis in written and verbal communication. Both forms of communication may suffer in transmission from abbreviation, simplification, condensation and loss of detail, best highlighted by the transformation of the message: 'Send reinforcements we're going to advance' into 'Send three and fourpence we're going to a dance'.

Natural loss of information makes it difficult to assess the efficiency of an organization. Trading patterns may possess a degree of discretion which permits partners either to advance the interests of others or to pursue only their own ambitions. In practice, goal displacement may occur; directors may pursue their own goals and foremen may not implement orders for fear of disturbing trading relationships. Such discretion may be reduced by tighter control or by invoking competition for posts; but it may be possible also to reduce inefficiency by promoting trust.

In the description of bureaucracy presented in previous paragraphs the distinction between authority and power became a difference between competitive and monopoly trading. In competitive trading individuals trade on the basis of comparative advantage, and authority is largely irrelevant. Hierarchies are simply means of decomposing complex situations into manageable or stable subsystems. What hierarchies do, therefore, is to allocate individuals to particular subsystems on the basis of comparative advantage. But if trading situations contain monopoly elements then power, monopoly power, can emerge to alter the distribution of gains from trading.

It is, of course, somewhat pretentious to refer to the analysis outlined in this section as an economic theory of bureaucracy when it so obviously derives so much from other disciplines. It owes as much to Weber and Durkheim as it does to economists. But it owes perhaps even more to *The Theory of Moral Sentiments* which the founding father of economics, Adam Smith, wrote before embarking on *The Wealth of Nations*.

The Chandler Thesis

So far we have concentrated upon micro-issues, upon the ideas drawn from case studies by sociologists and psychologists. Now we shall return to the broad sweep of history. Weber saw the problem of authority and organizational structure in terms of the needs of different societies and the changes in societies. Thus there were charismatic, traditional and bureaucratic leaders and the latter emerged as Protestantism and challenged Catholicism. With Chandler we return to the analysis of organizational change over time and across countries.

The United States

Before 1840

According to Chandler it was the railways which brought about a shift towards formal, functional management structures. In the pre-railway era, from Independence to the 1840s, trading was mainly conducted through the market with merchants occupying a pivotal role, and as settlement moved westwards and the market expanded the division of labour increased. The country was an agricultural economy based upon family units – even in the South where there was a system of commercial cotton production. The activities of producers were therefore tied together by the merchant who supplied them with raw materials and household goods and marketed their products. Typically resident in an East Coast port, the merchant engaged in exporting and importing and he often had extensive commercial and family connections with the Old World.

The expansion of the cotton trade gave a large impetus to specialization among merchants and financiers, and the personal world of the all-purpose merchant began to decline. The first factories of any importance were established in the cotton industry but there was no significant impact upon managerial organization. The main requirement was for working capital to cover the raw material, cotton, and to pay wages, and the remaining items of expenditure were lumped together with an allowance for depreciation. Usually it was the practice to cover depreciation in good years. Thus there was no need for an elaborate accounting system.

1840–1920

The railways were not only the first large-scale businesses, but because they opened up markets they stimulated the development of large-scale firms in other industries. Because all the problems of financing and administering large firms had to be met by the railways, railway executives were thus forced to become pioneers of modern management techniques. The large sums of money involved in financing railway construction meant that there had to be developments in monetary and financial institutions. In the typical textile mill only one employee might handle money – paying wages – but on a railroad money was being received by conductors, station agents, freight and passenger clerks, and all the monies received had to be accounted for. Furthermore, the railroads handled not one commodity but thousands (journeys) and prices had to be set for those goods. Fixed costs were also important and railroad executives were forced to pioneer cost accounting. Finally there were the problems of coping with large numbers of employees, passengers and goods. Large numbers of employees meant personnel management; large numbers of passengers and goods meant the need for time-tables and safety inspectors; and all these activities had to be coordinated.

In the 1850s the basic management problem was solved by making a distinction between line and staff responsibilities. Each railroad president delegated authority to the general superintendent and through him to the manager in charge of each of the divisions of transportation, who were given the title of 'divisional superintendent'. Each line manager was responsible for the movement of passengers and goods. The executives in other functional departments, such as maintenance of the way, equipment and finance, were made staff officers who set standards but could not give orders concerning the movement of passengers and freight. Thus, line managers handled men, and staff officers handled things (figure 5.2). With the expansion of business into new regions, new goods and new groups of passengers, more levels of

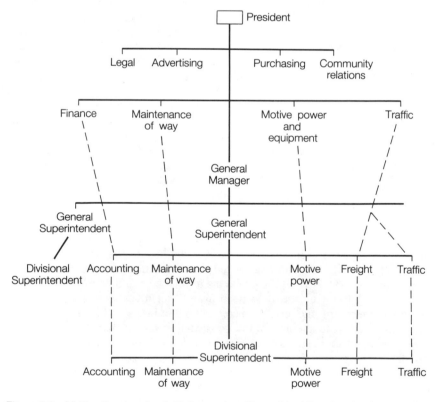

Figure 5.2   Multi-unit enterprise (with line and staff) used by US railroads after the 1870s and in modified form by airlines and bus and truck companies in the twentieth century (after Chandler in Mathias and Postan, 1978).

management were inserted on to the line, and at each level there were created associated staffs (figure 5.3). General managers were responsible for regions as opposed to districts, and this led to the distinction between strategic and operational management.

The railways enlarged markets and permitted the emergence of mass production techniques, especially in the metal-using and metal-working industries. In the 1890s managers in these industries began to analyse and rationalize production operations and, by time-and-motion study, began to establish standard times for tasks, to create incentive payment schemes for the achievement of norms and to attempt a system of factory production control through the establishment of functional foremen responding to the dictates of planning departments. Such was the essence of *scientific management* pioneered by Frederick W. Taylor of the Midvale Steel Company. Taylor's goal of extreme specialization was seldom achieved. Foremen tended to remain generalists because Taylor's proposal failed to pinpoint authority on the shopfloor and clarify the line of command from president to general manager and down to the shopfloor. His ideas represented a response to the problems posed by absorbing large numbers of mid-European immigrants with little command of the English language into the mass production industries – but they met with resistance from the Anglo-Saxon-dominated craft unions.

During the 1880s and 1890s mass production coalesced with mass marketing and a relatively small number of large multi-functional firms began to dominate many American industries. The impetus came from two directions. First, there were the firms who found that the existing distribution networks were unable to cope with their buying and selling requirements. Second, there were the firms which found the existing networks satisfactory but grew bigger through

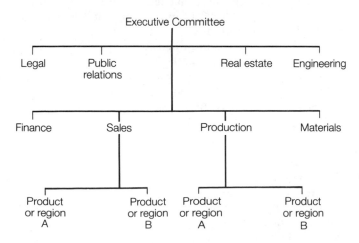

Figure 5.3 Multi-unit, multi-functional enterprise used by integrated manufacturing corporations from the 1890s onwards (after Chandler in Mathias and Postan, 1978).

cartels and mergers which were later rationalized into trusts or holding companies with each of the constituent companies centralized under the control of a single manufacturing department.

Firms which took the second route comprised three groups:

1   Makers of semi-perishable, low-priced goods produced by continuous process machinery; for example, cigarettes, canned goods, soap.
2   Makers of new types of machinery which required specialized marketing services such as sewing machines, typewriters and agricultural machinery.
3   Firms which relied upon the introduction of new technology for mass distribution rather than for mass production; for example, refrigerated meat.

Firms which took the second route did so because of temporary over-capacity to which they responded through the formation of cartels and, later, trusts. Thus Standard Oil, after consolidating its refining, bought suppliers of raw materials and marketing outlets.

Space does not permit a detailed discussion of all the developments in marketing, but some comment upon the activities of the McCormick Company are required because its policies were later followed by the automobile companies. What McCormick did was to use the nineteenth-century network of merchants as the basis for the sale and servicing of his reaper and, more importantly, as a means of coping with the problems of production scheduling. McCormick's lead was followed by Ford because the main buyers of cars were prosperous farmers and because the firm's mass production techniques required a marketing strategy; hence Ford's development of exclusive franchises to merchants coupled with high-pressure sales techniques. In contrast, General Motors sought to meet the challenge of Ford's policy of one model and 'any colour as long as it is black', by introducing a full-line product policy of numerous models. Because product differentiation meant frequent model changes, General Motors thus required detailed demand and sales forecasts, and therefore established a uniform marketing system.

But if Ford followed McCormick in creating a network of exclusive franchises to merchants, his pioneering of the assembly line represented a unique contribution to scientific management and one singularly fitted to the exploitation of the internal combustion engine.

1920–80

During the 1920s a new stage in the development of organizational structures began. Many large firms – especially chemical, electrical and automobile firms – began to diversify, and most of the firms adopted a new decentralized structure to meet the demands of the new strategies. The new structure was first perfected by du Pont with the introduction of semi-autonomous divisions. Each division was defined by the markets which it served, and its internal structure was similar to that of the large integrated multi-functional firm. Thus divisions continued to integrate production and distribution but their semi-autonomous nature released head office to concentrate even more on long-term planning and avoid the conflicts between functional managers. So was created the multi-divisional firm.

At the end of the Second World War, therefore, large American firms had pioneered all those structural and strategic characteristics which Galbraith (1971) has described so vividly. There was a technostructure of professional managers who, freed from day-to-day details and conflicts between functionaries, concentrated on long-run objectives. There was an emphasis upon research and development and multi-divisional structure seemed capable of indefinite expansion both domestically and internationally. Hence, the typical *multinational* structure of figure 5.4. However, it would be wrong to think that the long production and distribution chains integrated by administration meant the demise of the market. Indeed, the price signals at the ends of the columns became even more crucial; and faced with change such organizations might develop *matrix organizations* which cut across the boundaries of products and functions. Matrix organizations became common in the aerospace industry (figure 5.5).

Missing from Chandler's discussions, however, are the more recent shop-floor developments of the 1950s. During the Cold War phase immediately following the Second World War trade unions were identified with Communism and anti-trade unionism tended to weaken their influence. But unionism would not have stagnated if, in a prolonged boom period, employers had held wages and conditions of employment down. What happened, especially in the firms in the new technologies, was that many of the ideas from the

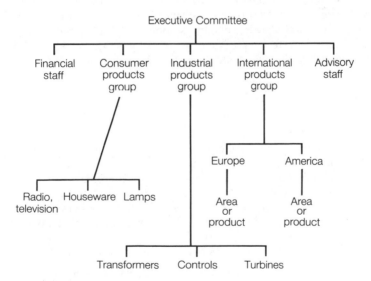

Figure 5.4. Multi-unit, multi-functional, multi-industrial, multinational enterprise (after Chandler in Mathias and Postan, 1978).

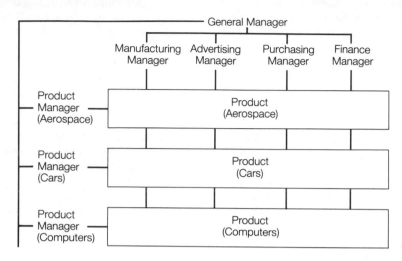

Figure 5.5   Matrix organizational structure.

Hawthorne Experiments (and their aftermath) came to be incorporated into workshops. Careful selection of employees, the offer of permanent employment and job rotation provided for both the economic and socio-psychological needs of workers. There was a greater emphasis upon managerial policies at shopfloor level. These ideas were adopted and adapted by the Japanese, and we shall therefore discuss their main features in the later section on Japan.

Britain

Chandler's analysis poses many questions concerning the lack of impact of British railways upon management structures. Why was there a failure to anticipate American methods? Why did American firms combine successive stages of production and distribution – vertical integration – supervised by managers with long-term strategies? The questions have to be posed because in the pre-railway era there was no substantial difference between British and American production and distribution systems; merchants were important and accounting was rudimentary (Pollard, 1965).

In his *The Railway Economy* (1850) Dionysios Lardner stated that:

The organization of the administrative machinery necessary for the conduct of the practical business of a railway, or a system of railways, brought under a common direction and management, includes the following four principal departments or services, more or less distinct and independent of each other; these are:

1 The services of the way and works
2 The service of draft
3 The service of carriage
4 The service of the stations

Each of these departments has its separate staff, machinery and stock.

But Lardner's book is essentially a textbook rather than a history. With the exception of a study of the famous railway manager, Mark Huish, by Gourvish (1972) we have no studies of railways which concentrate upon management. What Gourvish's study suggests is that it was extremely difficult for a general manager to initiate a strategy when his directors were intent upon draining away funds in order to pay dividends. Furthermore, the creation of a railway clearing house to clear inter-company indebtedness may have removed the need for individual companies to establish elaborate accounting procedures, and also inhibited mergers of numerous companies with short lines and continually engaged in transferring passengers and goods from one line to another. Nor did the heavy costs involved in raising finance – which may have created some pressure to introduce limited liability as a means of widening sources of supply – have much influence upon British industry.

Most British firms tended to be family-owned, and remained so despite the introduction of limited liability. There was, in fact, no great pressure from industrialists for limited liability. Indeed, the reaction was a typical compromise – *the private company* – which combined limited liability with private ownership. The demand for external finance might have been forthcoming had market expansion prompted it, but the peculiarity of British economic expansion was that it led to further division of labour. There was a further complicating factor. British firms did not serve a homogeneous market but an Empire of heterogeneous tastes in which merchants played the vital role of linking consumers to firms. Even in the domestic market there was an emphasis upon craftsmanship and individuality. Of course, individualism may have been a response to the slower growth of the domestic market in the second half of the nineteenth century, and the necessity to indulge in price and quality discrimination in order to squeeze every bit of profit out of the market.

There were mergers at the turn of the century but there was little attempt at rationalization. Thus the early days of the Calico Printers' Association, formed in 1899 by the amalgamation of 59 firms, were characterized as 'chaotic as a board of directors of 84 members, of whom 8 were managing directors, struggling to form a coherent policy' (Payne, 1974).

It was the nature of British markets which led to the structure of British firms and industries, and this point must be set against the criticisms: that Britain failed to respond to new developments, that there was entrepreneurial failure in the third quarter of the nineteenth century, that there was a failure to move quickly into the newer industries, such as chemicals and electrical engineering, and a persistence with older industries, such as shipbuilding.

The Chandler thesis is that structure follows strategy, whilst the contrary thesis that strategy is dictated by structure seems to be applicable to Britain in the nineteenth century. If we take shipbuilding as an example then it is possible to be impressed by the fact that the industry was extremely fragmented, that all firms were family firms, that educational attainments were ignored, labour-intensive methods were used and the trade unions were exceedingly militant. Yet the British shipbuilding industry dominated the world in the last quarter of the nineteenth century. Its fragmentation could be defended on the grounds that it was primarily an assembly industry, and its failure to employ engineers with high educational attainments could be defended on the ground that the industry did not use a high-level technology while the low capital intensity reflected the cyclical character of demand (Pollard and Robertson, 1979). The steel industry was also accused of backwardness by Burn (1940), but McCloskey (1973) has put up a spirited defence. On cost grounds there was no incentive to switch to the phosphatic ores of Lincolnshire because scrap was available and acid steels were in high demand. Hence while the Gilchrist–Thomas process and the open hearth were not taken up, the Talbot tilting furnace was quickly adopted. Yet the defence appears too convincing. It assumes that businessmen are programmed to respond to given prices; but entrepreneurship is about coping with introducing novelty, of transcending the obvious. In the end the defence may simply be that British society was trapped in a comparative advantage of using unskilled labour to produce coal and textiles.

It is possible, however, to argue that structure inhibited strategy in the inter-war years, that the excessive specialization of British industries and firms prevented adjustment to depressed demand conditions. Thus Clay (1931), in his brilliant analysis of the cotton industry, observed that the multiplicity of units and freedom of entry to the industry prevented any agreement being reached to remove excess capacity. Even if some firms had agreed to buy up excess capacity and remove it from the market there was no guarantee that they would benefit from such a venture. Visible evidence of profits would have encouraged new entrants and prompted foreign imports. Industries characterized by freedom of entry can therefore have excess capacity in the long run; there are too many firms, each too small to be efficient, and there are too many to reach agreement (Chamberlin, 1948).

Until the 1960s most British firms and industries seemed to remain immune to change. The cartels formed in the 1930s introduced collective resale price maintenance and reduced competition. War-time planning controls persisted until the mid-1950s. Even those firms which had been created by mergers in the 1890s, or the rationalization measures of the inter-war years, tended to remain holding companies; that is, beneath an outer shell, the old companies survived in a loose federal structure.

The structure and degree of concentration of British industry began to change dramatically during the sixties and seventies. Anti-monopoly legislation in the fifties had resulted in the outlawing of restrictive practices including resale price maintenance. The result was a push towards increased competition which was intensified by: (a) the loss of former colonial markets which had been protected by Imperial Preference, (b) the decision to join the European Common Market and (c) the 1966 Kennedy Round of tariff reductions. There was also the impact of American investment in Britain. The response to these disturbances was an attempt to stabilize markets by promoting mergers as substitutes for cartel firms. Mergers were justified on the grounds that British firms had to achieve economies of scale comparable to those of their foreign rivals; but many of these mergers had disappointing results – many were defensive and few achieved a rationalization of production. As in the nineteenth century, many mergers were merely federations.

Mergers sometimes led to diversification. Thus, in the industries characterized by a high rate of research and development, such as electronics, chemicals and pharmaceuticals and engineering, it was possible to apply certain innovations to a wide variety of products. A second group, comprising food, textiles, newspapers and publishing, diversified in an attempt to offset low growth rates. Finally there was a group which did not diversify, but which sought mergers within their own field of activity; this group, spanning drink, tobacco, oil, and power machinery were often family firms, major producers in their own field and with low growth rates.

It was the changes of the sixties which led to a shift towards multi-divisional structures.

Other Countries: Problems and Solutions

So far we have discussed changes in structures of British and American firms. This makes sense when tracing the evolution of organizational structures from the eighteenth century. It accords with the importance of Britain in the world economy and the growing importance of the United States. But other countries have since become important in the world economy, especially since the end of the Second World War. Specifically we have to consider West Germany, to a lesser extent France, more importantly Japan and, finally, we have to recognize the planned economies of Eastern Europe and China. There are, in fact, interesting parallels amongst these countries; the Americans imposed industrial reforms on West Germany and Japan, and Russia re-modelled the economies of East Germany, Poland, Hungary, Czechoslovakia and Rumania at the end of the Second World War. For captive countries their subsequent evolution has been, in part, an escape from those administrative measures and the assertion of older values and structures. In the case of Yugoslavia there was a distinct attempt to establish decentralized socialism with semi-autonomous producers' cooperatives. In the case of Britain, France and Italy there was a tendency to succumb to American methods, partly through trade, but increasingly, in the sixties, through investment as a result of the over-valuation of the dollar and the spread of multinational companies. Hence the Chandler thesis needs to be set in the context of widely differing politico-economic organizations with disparate cultural values.

Germany

If American business produced the vertically integrated firm and the line and staff principles of organization, Germany promoted the cartel and the investment bank.

German industrialization went through three phases. The first, running from about 1720 to about 1790, involved the recruitment by the state of a small group of competent businessmen as managers for industries in which the government had a special interest. The second, from about 1790 to about 1840, saw the state – primarily the Prussian state – providing its own industrial experts for a select range of strategic industries. The third phase, from 1840 to 1914, saw the rise of the private industrialist and financier, more or less independent of government interest or intervention. Significantly, it was only this final entrepreneurial phase, accompanied by pronounced social and economic readjustments, which produced an extensive form of industrial activity in Germany (Trebilcock, 1981).

Whereas British banks had tended to engage in short-term lending, German banks often indulged in long-term lending and were concerned with reducing risk. Hence they encouraged the formation of cartels. Economists have been prone to view monopoly practices with suspicion because of their tendency to restrict output and stifle entrepreneurial initiative; but when Britain passed the Monopolies and Restrictive Practices Act in 1948, Clay (1948) pointed to the advantages conferred by German cartels and, earlier, in his *Industry and Trade*, Marshall had pointed to the high rate of technological advance achieved by German industry. What German cartels did was to impose uniform manufacturing conditions and eliminate obsolete plants; also they made available new ideas which were implemented by the college graduates emerging from the *technical high schools*.

Much has been made of the merits of the German educational system, but what has often been overlooked is that German success lay less in fundamental science and more in the exploitation of foreign discoveries.

> Aniline dyes, the generation and conveyance of electric power, the Gilchrist–Thomas process for iron manufacture – each basic to Germany's late-nineteenth century pre-eminence – were French and British, not German discoveries. The essential connection between foreign invention and domestic innovation was the German research team (Trebilcock, 1981).

In effect the German economy was a command economy well endowed with managers and sparsely endowed with entrepreneurs. In its exploitation of foreign ideas and its dualistic industry with 'heavy layers of very small and very large concerns and its very thin layer in the middle', it anticipated Japanese dualism. The small firms provided a buffer to accommodate fluctuations in demand and a field for experimentation.

At the end of the Second World War German productive capacity was roughly equal to that of 1938; it was the overrunning of factories by Allied troops, not the 'thousand-bomber raids', which caused production to cease in 1944. In the early postwar period there was a movement to free trade and a non-interventionist political system. The changes were dramatic when viewed against the politico-economic system of Nazi Germany, but should be regarded as a return to nineteenth-century patterns of behaviour. The Allied controllers attempted to break up the politico-economic structure by introducing anti-monopoly measures and attempting to disperse concentrations of power in the iron, steel, engineering and chemical industries. But the Americans pursued only a lukewarm competition policy and nothing was attempted in the British and French zones. IG Farben was split into three firms but no buyers could be found for units in the Steel Trust. In the mid-fifties, pre-war levels of concentration obtained but, as was noted earlier, hostility to cartels was not a prevalent attitude in Germany.

Integration and diversification began to acquire momentum in the 1960s. In the 1950s single-product firms formed 34 per cent of the top 100 firms; by 1970 they formed only 22 per cent. Firms which had diversified into unrelated industries formed $7\frac{1}{2}$ per cent of the top 100 in 1950; by 1970 they had risen to 18 per cent. Firms which had diversified into related trades increased by 6 per cent, from 32 to 38 per cent. In 1950 only 5 per cent of large firms had a divisional structure; in 1970 the number had risen to 50 per cent (Dyas and Thanheiser, 1976).

Growth and diversification led to changes in managerial structures. German company law distinguished between the supervisory board (Aufsichtstrat) and the executive board (Vorstand). The supervisory board was elected by the shareholders, who also had the power to revoke its mandate. In turn the supervisory board appointed the executive board, which was responsible to it collectively for the management of the firm. As a result of the introduction of codetermination (Mitbestimmung) a labour representative was appointed to the Vorstand in the coal and iron and steel industries.

The top-level executives who dominated the Vorstand were known as Unternehmer, and they carried much more authority and power than their counterparts in British and American industry; even their social origins tended to be much wider. According to Hartmann (1959):

> He [the Unternehmer] usually traces his authority to value systems or charismatic endowment. For instance, top management may claim the obedience of its subordinates because the individual Unternehmer considers himself as (1) trustee of private property, (2) 'called' to his position by a divine or otherwise transcendent force, (3) a member of a social elite, or (4) an individual of extraordinary powers.

Within the German firm the distinction between management and labour was usually drawn at a much higher level than in British or American firms. But within the Vorstand the Unternehmer exercised a collegiate form of management and growth, and diversification increased the degree of specialization within the Vorstand and pushed some layers of decision-making to an intermediate level, creating, in the process, a more diffused managerial structure for operational decisions. However, although some German firms did introduce

multi-divisional structures, there is evidence that they were not always successful, and that German company law and Mitbestimmung cut across the lines
of authority which multi-divisional firms sought to achieve.

The Planned Economies of Eastern Europe and China

Regulation, rather than personal initiative, has long been a characteristic of
the Russian economy. It was prevalent under the Czars, intensified under
Stalin, ameliorated under Khrushchev, was restored by Breshnev and Kosygin,
and reconsidered by Gorbachev; it was observed by Marx and Weber in their
discussions of the Asiatic mode of production which was thought to be a
characteristic of semi-arid areas, where land was a free good and irrigation
schemes required public works programmes. It was, of course, not confined
to Asia and was present in Moorish Spain and pre-Hispanic America.

Central planning, or 'directive planning' as Kosygin preferred to call it, has
to be distinguished from indicative planning as practised in France. Under
indicative planning firms are expected to supply estimates of their output
targets to the planners, who then seek to reconcile them (Meade, 1971). Under
directive planning the targets are set by the Party, which is the entrepreneur.
However, because there is an inevitable exchange of ideas based upon knowledge of time and circumstance, and an attempt to reconcile grasp and reach,
the difference between indicative planning and directive planning can be one
of degree with rather more planning from above and less response to consumers' wants in the Soviet System than in that of the French.

The case for directive planning in Russia after the Revolution rested upon
the drive for industrialization and the need to build up heavy industry in order
to catch up with the capitalist economies. It rested also upon the assumption
that consumers' wants are relatively simple, and unemployment does not exist
in a socialist economy. In a planned economy undergoing change these goals
and assumptions came to be incompatible. The need to switch resources to
heavy industry implied a reduction of consumption, and the desire to catch
the capitalist economies implied the need for incentives, especially necessary
in an economy which guarantees full employment and does not use the stick
of unemployment. Hence the importation by Lenin of Taylor's ideas on
scientific management and, in particular, the use of incentive wage schemes.
Socialism was to be compatible with equality in some directions but not in
others.

However, the use of wage incentives implies a possible lack of control over
consumer demand and the use of resources, and incompatibilities arose. To
maintain full employment aggregate money demand was kept at high levels. To
assist production incentives were introduced. To control resources rationing of
consumer goods was introduced. The combination of these factors led to
suppressed inflation. Able to get jobs but unable to get goods workers sought
other utilities – high labour turnover signified the search for more interesting
but not necessarily more lucrative jobs. High absenteeism indicated that
domestic leisure was preferred to low-paid factory work, and loafing on the
job was preferred to working in the factory.

Some of these side-effects might have been tolerated in Russia but their extension to countries such as Czechoslovakia, led to periodic crises. In Yugoslavia the system was rejected in favour of workers' cooperatives which permitted some autonomy. After the death of Stalin there was some experimentation with the use of the market by some countries, notably Hungary and Czechoslovakia; but following the Czechoslovak, Hungarian and Polish periods of political unrest there was a noticeable return to directive planning.

China tended to follow the Russian pattern until Mao Tse Tung initiated his ideological breakthrough. There then followed the Great Leap Forward and the Cultural Revolution. The Great Leap Forward was an attempt to outdo Stalin's drive for industrialization. It collapsed due to problems with harvests but it was notable for its serious attempt to replace material incentives with socio-political incentives which, had they been successful, would have resolved the problem of giving priority to the production of capital goods. In more recent years there has been an emphasis upon devolution and giving communes greater autonomy. This suggests a move towards the Yugoslav pattern and runs the risk of widening income and wealth differentials.

Japan

Firms may grow by addition or by subdivision. In the nineteenth century British firms grew by subdivision; they observed Adam Smith's dictum that 'the division of labour is limited by the extent of the market'. As markets grew firms divested themselves of uneconomic operations. In contrast American firms tended to grow by addition. In the second half of the nineteenth century vertical integration by administration was characteristic of American firms; they were stimulated and prompted by the railways and mass markets. In the twentieth century American firms grew by diversification; they became conglomerates and achieved, by administration, the integration of diverse activities. But Japanese firms had already introduced the conglomerate firm in the nineteenth century.

Gerschenkron (1962) has emphasized that the more backward an economy the more diversified are the areas over which it has to start industrializing simultaneously. Japanese industrialization started late in the nineteenth century after the opening up of her markets to Western trade. The government gave a lead in this respect through the development of transport and communications, and the establishment of pilot plants endowed with Western technology which were later sold to private owners. Finally there was the emergence of an entrepreneurial class, the zaibatsu, families whose origins lay partly among the merchants and partly among the declassed feudal groups.

Given the need to industrialize over a broad front, the requirement of large plants to achieve Western economies of scale and the limited numbers of entrepreneurs, there emerged large, diversified firms. In the last decade of the nineteenth century many of them, such as Mitsui and Mitsubishi, began to wrestle with the problems of controlling different activities. Mitsui organized each enterprise as an independent unit and tried to control them by establishing a strong headquarters staff. In contrast, Mitsubishi allowed each business to operate as a separate unit under the control of a single management. The centralization/decentralization moves of Mitsui and Mitsubishi, therefore, anticipated the similar strategies of General Motors and Du Pont in the 1920s.

However, it is not the distant past but the spectacular growth of the Japanese economy since the Second World War which has attracted attention, for several reasons. First, Japan has been considered to be the last major economy to take off into industrialization and growth by using the market. Second, its dual industrial structure has been felt to contain unique advantages for growth and development. Third, cultural values appear to have played a conspicuous part in Japan's economic growth (Dore, 1973; 1984; 1985).

A feature of the Japanese economy which has attracted much interest and comment is its dual industrial structure, comprising a sector of large firms and a sector of small firms. Entry to the large firm sector is by rigorous selection and, once admitted, employees are guaranteed permanent employment until the age of 55. At 55 workers are retired, but may be assisted or found employment in the small firm sector. During their permanent employment workers proceed up a job hierarchy, and may be rotated from job to job, from department to department, and even between subsidiaries of the same firm. Other notable features of the permanent employment system are the use of wage structures based upon age, the system of large bonuses (deferred wages) and the fact that company unionism or enterprise unionism is practised with some 25 per cent of all company directors having been union officials.

Now some of these features are not unique to Japan. Most countries have dual industrial structures consisting of large and small firms, and most countries were able to offer permanent employment to most workers during the full employment years 1940–70. For example, a British schoolboy who avoided going into coal mining, textiles or the gas industry in 1940 could have obtained permanent employment. Moreover, closer examination of employment patterns in large firms reveals that only some 30 per cent of employees had implicit (and not legal) lifetime contracts, and after the oil price rises many firms, especially in the man-made fibres industry, engaged in extensive redundancy programmes. Similarly, the practice of basing wages upon age can be considered to be partly a crude measure of productivity which has been increasingly abandoned in the 1970s and partly as a means of coping with the life cycle problems of family responsibilities and retirement in a period when the Welfare State was not in existence. However, Koike (1984) has pointed out that Japanese age–wage profiles are not dissimilar from those occurring in Britain, France and the USA.

Indeed, once these characteristics are set aside we observe that large firms have practices and procedures which are similar to those prevailing in other advanced economies. For example, job rotation, job hierarchies and the absence of craft unions were characteristics of the British coal and iron and steel industries in the nineteenth century. What is significant, however, is that in some of the newer industries of the twentieth century, such as car manufacture, craft unionism was able to obtain a foothold and prevent the emergence of job hierarchies and job rotation (Turner, 1962). Likewise in America, large firms, such as IBM, have long practised job rotation and lifetime employment, and Ouchi (1979) has dubbed such a system the 'clan system' because its tight-knit organization is capable of generating intense loyalty and efficiency. Indeed, many of the features of the Japanese firms stemmed from the findings of the human relations school and were introduced into large firms following the anti-union legislation of the 1950s. However, they were not so noticeable as in Japan, partly because they were not so widely adopted in industries such as iron and steel and car manufacture, where traditional unionism prevailed, although the form of unionism practised was a form of company unionism, being based on the plants. What the Japanese did was to adopt these practices over a wider range of industries. In pursuing this policy, managers were assisted by the rejection by workers of craft unionism and by the collapse of independent, often left wing, unions, in the Cold War years of the 1950s. Before the Second World War craft unionism was prevalent in Japan and, had it continued, a union structure similar to that in Britain might have emerged. Two interesting and unresolved questions remain, therefore. First, why did the Japanese workers reject craft unionism. Second, why did they persist with company unionism after the passing of the Cold War? A partial answer to the second question is to note that in all countries unionism, especially independent unionism, tends to stagnate in prolonged boom periods. For example, British trade unionism stagnated in the 1960s.

A system of permanent employment, however, even when offered to a few workers, may require either wage flexibility or job adaptability. In permanent employment systems, such as those in the USA, flexibility is achieved by 'bumping'. In a recession junior workers are dismissed and senior workers may take over their jobs through a process of job enlargement. In the Japanese system wage flexibility tends to be achieved through variations in the bonuses, and through the fact that increases in basic rates in all firms tend to be concentrated in a relatively short period in the spring, the Shunto or 'Spring Offensive'. This compression of the negotiating period overcomes the disadvantages of decentralized bargaining systems (McCormick, 1985).

The bonus and permanent employment schemes also offer other advantages by permitting the firms to use their employees as the financial risk-bearers, or equity shareholders. Because of the underdeveloped financial system and the comparative absence of a Welfare State most savings tend to be channelled into the banks, and savings tend to form a large proportion of income, partly because bonuses are regarded as transitory income and partly because of the underdeveloped social security system. Because the banks tend to offer finance only at fixed interest rates, the workers are required to act as equity holders.

The willingness of the employees to act as equity shareholders has been assisted by other factors. First, the ringi system of consultation enables workers on the shop floor to have some control over decision-making. Second, the traditional wealthy families, the zaibatsu, who were associated with pre-war Japanese imperialism, were deposed during the US occupation and Japan has experienced a period of comparative egalitarianism. Third, during the 1960s, Japanese firms became frightened of American take-over bids and began to acquire each other's shares with the result that it is extremely difficult to say who owns Japanese firms (Aoki, 1983). These three factors have been responsible for the emergence of a form of workers' capitalism, or labour-managed firms, or Japanese socialism, which has had distinct advantages over the practices in other countries.

The projected slow growth rates of the 1980s, however, raise the question: can the Japanese system persist? With low growth rates the numbers of workers who can be given permanent employment might have to be reduced, and it may prove difficult to establish an *esprit de corps* amongst larger numbers of temporary workers through the use of wage incentives. If morale is to be maintained through the payment of higher fixed wages might not such wage contracts reduce the flexibility of the economy? In addition, there is the problem of a slowing down in population growth – with fewer younger workers there has been pressure to raise the retirement age to 60. Raising the retirement age to 60, however, means loss of promotion prospects to younger workers, and could saddle firms with increasing wage burdens due to the use of age-wage scales. The cost effectiveness of the Japanese system therefore needs to be critically reappraised – it is possible that Japanese management practices will converge on European and American practices in the late 1980s.

All of this raises the intriguing question: which form of organizational structure will China adopt in its pursuit of economic growth and industrialization? Organizational structures have tended to be fashioned to meet the needs of the new industries thrown up in each successive long wave. In the early nineteenth century they were influenced by the British experiments in textiles and coal. American ideas came to dominate the railways and iron and steel in the last quarter of the nineteenth century and in the automobile industry in the early twentieth century. But the spread of organizational developments through Europe and the USA were strongly influenced by the underlying belief about human nature – the importance of original sin. How else can we explain the preoccupation with shirking and monitoring? How else can we explain the attempt to build an economics in which original vices conjure up universal benevolence? The rise of the Japanese economy has introduced an alternative assumption – original virtue – with its concomitant stress upon harmony and collaboration.

Now Chinese Confucianism has been considered by Morishima (1982) following Weber, to be a counterpart to Japanese 'Protestantism'. The economic reformation of China could therefore proceed by imbibing 'Protestant' cultures from both Western and Eastern advanced economies – from American, British, German and Japanese firms which have been called in to develop China. Perhaps we should not end by speculating about China's future but instead go on to consider India and the Weberian themes of authority and the world's religions. For, as Sen (1976) observed, no factory can be run on a diet of material incentives.

Bibliography and References

Alford, B. W. E. (1976) 'The Chandler thesis – some general observations'. In L. Hannah (ed.), *Management Strategy and Economic Development*. London: Macmillan.

Aoki, M. (ed.) (1983) *The Economic Analysis of the Japanese Firm*. Amsterdam: North Holland.

Argyris, C. (1964) *Integrating the Individual and the Organization*. Illinois: Irwin.

Barnard, C. I. (1938) *The Functions of the Executive*. Cambridge, Mass.: Harvard University Press.

Burn, D. (1940) *Economic History of the Steel Industry*. Cambridge: Cambridge University Press.

Burns, T. (ed.) (1969) *Industrial Man*. London: Penguin Books.

Burns, T. (1977) *BBC: Public Institution and Private World*. London: Macmillan.

Burns, T. and Stalker, G. M. (1966) *The Management of Innovation*. London: Tavistock.

Caves, R. E. (1980) 'Corporate strategy and structure', *Journal of Economic Literature*, 18, 64–92.

Chamberlin, E. H. (1948) *The Theory of Monopolistic Competition*, 6th edn. Cambridge, Mass.: Harvard University Press.

Chandler, A. D. (1962) *Strategy and Structure*. Cambridge Mass.: MIT Press.

Chandler, A. D. (1966) *The Visible Hand*, Cambridge, Mass.: Harvard University Press.

Chandler, A. D. (1980) 'The growth of the transnational industrial firm in the United States and the United Kingdom: a cross-national study', *Economic History Review*, 33, 396–410.

Chandler, A. D. (1984) 'The emergence of managerial capitalism', *Business History Review*, 58, 473–503.

Chandler, A. D. and Daems, H. (eds) (1980) *Managerial Hierarchies*. Cambridge, Mass.: Harvard University Press.

Channon, D. F. (1973) *The Strategy and Structure of British Enterprise*. London: Macmillan.

Clay, H. (1931) *Report on the Position of the Cotton Industry*. London: Securities Management Trust.

Dore, R. P. (1973) *British Factory – Japanese Factory*, London: Allen and Unwin.

Dore, R. P. (1983) 'Goodwill and the spirit of capitalism', *British Journal of Sociology*, 34, 459–62.

Dore, R. P. (1984) *Authority and benevolence: the Confucian recipe for industrial success*, Pembroke College, Oxford: mimeo.

Dyas, G. P. and Thanheiser, H. T. (1976) *The Emerging European Enterprise*. London: Macmillan.

Fayol, H. (1949) *General and Industrial Management*. London: Pitman.

Floud, R. and McCloskey, D. (1981) *The Economic History of Britain since 1700*, 2 vols. Cambridge: Cambridge University Press.

Follett, M. P. (1941) 'The giving of orders'. In H. C. Metcalf and L. Urwick (eds), *Dynamic Administration*. New York: Harper.

Fox, A. (1974) *Beyond Contract*. London: Faber.

Fox, A. (1983) 'British management and industrial relations; the social origins of a system', in M. J. Earl (ed.), *Perspectives on Management*. Oxford: Oxford University Press.

Galbraith, J. K. (1971) *The New Industrial State*. London: Deutsch.

Gerschenkron, A. (1962) *Economic Backwardness in Historical Perspective*. Cambridge, Mass.: Harvard University Press.

Gouldner, A. (1954) *Patterns of Industrial Bureaucracy*. New York: Free Press.

Gourvish, T. (1972) *Captain Mark Huish and the London and Northwestern Railways*. Leicester: Leicester University Press.

Habakkuk, H. J. (1968) *Industrial Organization since the Industrial Revolution*. Southampton: University of Southampton.

Hartman, H. (1979) 'Co-determination: today and tomorrow', *British Journal of Industrial Relations*, 13, 54–64.

Homans, G. (1950) *The Human Group*. New York: Harper.

Hyde, F. 'Business behaviour and profit maximization'. In K. A. Tucker (ed.), *Studies in Business History*. London, Frank Cass.

Internal Conference on Business History. University of Tokyo Press, 1981.
   Vol. 1: *Strategy and Structure of Big Business*, ed. K. Nakagawa.
   Vol. 2: *Social Order and Entrepreneurship*, ed. K. Nakagawa.
   Vol. 3: *Marketing and Finance in the Course of Industrialization*, ed. K. Nakagawa.
   Vol. 4: *Labor and Management*, ed. K. Nakagawa.
   Vol. 5: *Government and Business*, ed. K. Nakagawa.
   Vol. 6: *Development and Diffusion of Technology*, eds A. Okochi and H. Uchida.
   Vol. 7: *Development of Mass Marketing*, eds. A. Okochi and K. Shimokawa.
   Vol. 10: *Family Business in the Era of Industrial Growth*, eds A. Okochi and S. Yasuoka.

Kelly, J. E. (1978) 'A reappraisal of sociotechnical systems theory', *Human Relations*, 31, 1069–99.

Knight, F. H. (1921) *Risk, Uncertainty and Profit*. Chicago: Haffner.

Koike, K. (1984) 'Skill formation systems in the US and Japan: a comparative study'. In Aoki, M. (ed.), *The Economic Analysis of the Japanese Firm*. Amsterdam: North Holland.

Kondratieff, N. (1935) 'The long waves in economic life', *Review of Economics and Statistics*, 17, 105–15.

Lardner, D. (1968) *The Railway Economy*. New York: Augustus M. Kelly, reprint of 1850 edition.

McCloskey, D. (1973) *Economic Maturity and Entrepreneurial Decline, 1870–1913*. Cambridge, Mass.: Harvard University Press.

McCormick, B. J. (1979) *Industrial Relations in the Coal Industry*. London: Macmillan.

McCormick, B. J. (1985) *The Cause of Low Unemployment in Japan*. Buckingham: University of Buckingham Press.

McGregor, D. (1960) *The Human Side of Enterprise*. New York: McGraw-Hill.

Marglin, S. A. (1974) 'What do bosses do? ', *Review of Radical Political Economics*, 6, 60–113.

Mathias, P. and Postan, M. M. (eds) (1978) *Cambridge Economic History of Europe*, vol. 7. Cambridge: Cambridge University Press.
   Part I: Fohlen, C., 'France in the nineteenth century' ; Kocka, J., 'Entrepreneurs and managers in German industrialization' ; Payne, P. L., 'Industrial entrepreneurship and managers in Great Britain'.
   Part II: Chandler, A. D., 'The United States: the evolution of enterprise' ; Kaser, M. C., 'Russian entrepreneurship' ; Yamamura, K., 'Entrepreneurship, ownership and management in Japan'.

Meade, J. E. (1971) *The Theory of Indicative Planning*. Manchester: Manchester University Press.

Merton, R. (1940) 'Bureaucratic structure and personality', *Social Forces*, 18, 560–8.

Morishima, M. (1982) *Why Has Japan 'Succeeded'?* Cambridge: Cambridge University Press.

Ouchi, W. G. (1979) 'The design of organizational control mechanisms', *Management Science*, 25, 833–48.

Payne, P. (1974) *British Entrepreneurship in the Nineteenth Century*. London: Macmillan.

Pollard, S. (1965) *The Genesis of Modern Management*. London: Penguin Books.

Pollard, S. and Robertson, P. (1979) *The British Shipbuilding Industry 1870–1914*. Cambridge, Mass.: Harvard University Press.

Roethlisberger, F. and Dickson, W. J. (1964) *Management and the Worker*. Cambridge, Mass.: Harvard University Press.

Selznick, P. (1949) *TVA and Grass Roots*. Berkeley, Calif.: University of California Press.

Sen, A. K. (1976) 'Rational fools: a critique of the behavioural foundations of economic theory', *Philosophy and Public Affairs*, 6, 317–44.

Shannon, C. (1949) *Mathematical Theory of Communication*. Illinois: University of Illinois Press.

Simon, H. A. (1982) *Models of Bounded Rationality*. Cambridge, Mass.: MIT Press.
Vol. 1: *Economic Analysis and Public Policy*.
Vol. 2: *Behavioral Economics and Business Organization*.

Taylor, F. W. (1915) *Scientific Management*. New York: Harper and Row.

Trebilcock, C. J. (1981) *The Industrialization of the Great Powers*. London: Longman.

Trevor-Roper, H. R. (1972) *Religion, The Reformation and Social Change*, 2nd edn. London: Macmillan.

Trist, E. L. et al. (1963) *Organizational Choice*. London: Tavistock.

Turner, H. A. (1962) *Trade Union Growth, Structure and Policy*. London: Allen & Unwin.

Weber, M. (1946) *Essays in Sociology*, translated and edited by H. H. Gerth and C. Wright Mills. New York: Oxford University Press.

Weber, M. (1947) *The Theory of Social and Economic Organization*, translated and edited by Talcott Parsons and A. M. Henderson. New York: Free Press.

Weber, M. (1968) *Economy and Society*, translated and edited by Guenther Roth and Claus Wittich. New York: Bedminster Press.

Williamson, O. E. (1970) *Corporate Control and Business Behavior*, Englewood Cliffs, New Jersey: Prentice Hall.

Williamson, O. E. (1975) *Markets and Hierarchies*. New York: Collier Macmillan.

Williamson, O. E. (1980) 'The organization of work: a comparative institutional analysis', *Journal of Economic Behavior and Organization*, 1, 1–35.

Woodward, J. (1958) *Management and Technology*. London: HMSO.

Woodward, J. (1965) *Industrial Organization: Theory and Practice*. Oxford: Oxford University Press.

6 Control and Performance

Control is the means by which management ensures that goals have been attempted and deviations from norms are corrected. Control therefore requires that goals be specified, that information be provided about attainment or failure to attain those goals, and that a structure be provided through which information can flow and authority be exerted. In chapter 3 we looked at the problem of specifying goals and in chapter 15 we shall return to the issue when we consider the public sector. In this chapter we shall begin by looking at the problem from the point of view of systems engineering or cybernetics. We shall then move on to consider the nature and value of information and, finally, examine the usefulness of accounting information.

A Cybernetic Approach to Control

A general approach to control is offered by cybernetics, which may be defined as the study of automatic communication and control in living bodies and mechanical and electrical systems. For example, a production process may be viewed as a 'black box' within which inputs are transformed into output. The expression 'black box' refers to the fact that we do not know the nature of the qualitative transformation which takes place within the box; we can only make inferences from the behaviour of inputs and output. From the black box there emerges a stream of output which is sold on the market. The resulting sales figures are then compared with the firm's sales target and any discrepancies can be corrected through a feedback mechanism which may be positive or negative. In the case of a negative feedback the difference between target and achievement is reversed and transmitted to the system. Thus a rise in wages would signal a cut-back in the firm's labour force. A positive feedback would, however, directly transmit the difference between plans and outcome. Hence a negative feedback would have a stabilizing effect and a positive feedback would have a destabilizing effect upon a firm.

Types of Control

Proportional Control

The simplest type of feedback involves a proportional control which aims to adjust a variable, say output, by some proportion of the amount by which it deviates from the target level. However, a proportional control runs into two difficulties. The first, common to all controls, is that if it operates with a time lag then it may accentuate deviations. Thus, if sales oscillate and the control operates when sales rise, but is only effective when sales are falling, then stocks may be forced above their target levels. The second problem is that, lags apart, if any disturbance signals a new and permanent change in the state of the world then a proportional control designed to react to a discrepancy between current and target sales would cause target sales to persistently deviate from possible sales.

Integral Control

What the previous problem suggests is the need for a system in which management learns from experience and gradually adjusts its policies until the disturbance is brought under control. This requires the keeping of detailed records of all deviations, and output adjustments to be made on the basis of the sum of past deficits and surpluses; that is, to introduce some form of integral control.

Derivative control
Further refinement of the control mechanism could be achieved by measuring the rate of change of deviations: that is, whether a surplus or deficit is growing quickly or slowly.

Variety
Our description of the control mechanism has suggested that there are only two possible states of the world which have to be considered. In reality there may be thousands of possible states of world. Thus demand may be influenced by both market and environmental uncertainties. To take an example from Meade (1971) a manufacturer of umbrellas and sunshades may have to consider whether it will be wet or fine, and how many umbrellas will be bought if it is wet. Furthermore the production decisions for 'tomorrow' may influence the production possibilities for subsequent 'days'. There may be a decision tree in which expectations as to whether it will be wet or fine in the next period will lead to considerations as to whether it will be wet or fine in subsequent periods. In short, there may be a number of possible market states or outcomes: there may be *variety*.

The analytic chart of complexity
Lawrence and Dyer (1983) have used the concept of variety to examine how a firm or industry adapts to information complexity and resource scarcity:

1   Information complexity refers to the variety in a firm's environment which directly influences its choice of which goods and services to supply.
2   Resource scarcity refers to the degree of difficulty an organization experiences in securing the resources it needs to survive and grow.

Figure 6.1 illustrates the *analytic framework of adaptation* which firms may go through. Labelled 1 to 9 are nine industrial areas which summarize the environmental conditions faced by firms. The diagram can be used also to chart the paths of firms and industries as they experience changes in their environments and changes in the means by which they cope with those changes. Thus, US car firms went from intermediate information complexity and a low degree of resource scarcity, as indicated by high profit margins, in the 1920s to a crisis of resource scarcity and increasing information complexity in the 1980s. Lawrence and Dyer argue that their dichotomy between resource scarcity and information complexity enables them to draw upon and synthesize the contributions of economists, who are interested in resource allocation, and sociologists, psychologists and biologists, who are interested in perception, learning, motivation and adaptation by organizations.

The law of requisite variety
The solution to variety is to increase variety. As Ashby (1952, 1956) put it: 'Only variety can destroy variety.' Thus a retail store may increase the number of assistants in order to cope with possible demands and to avoid queues and loss of goodwill through customers going elsewhere. But Ashby's dictum

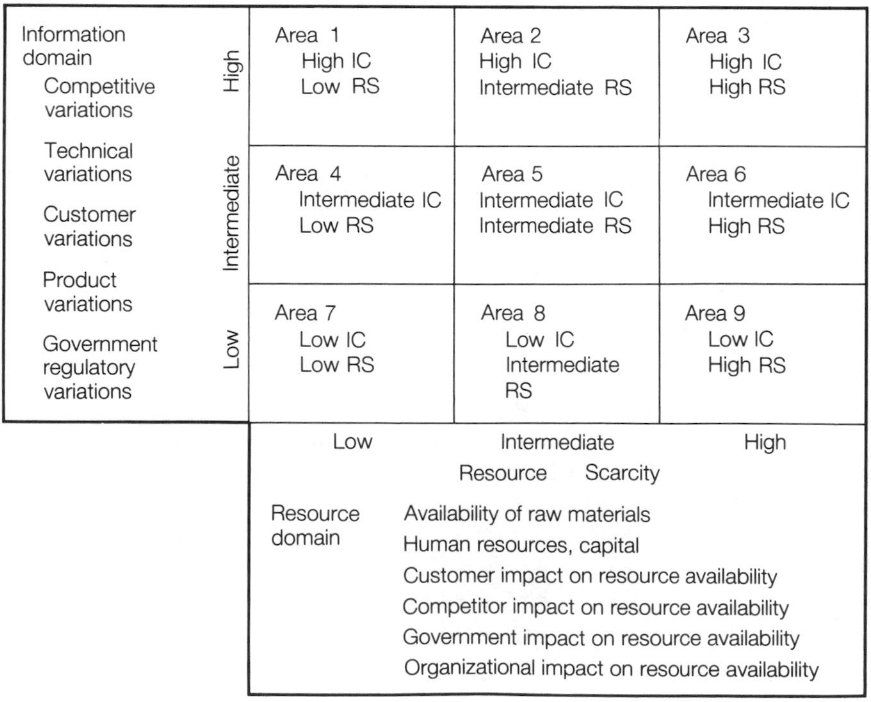

Information domain	High	Area 1 High IC Low RS	Area 2 High IC Intermediate RS	Area 3 High IC High RS
Competitive variations				
Technical variations	Intermediate	Area 4 Intermediate IC Low RS	Area 5 Intermediate IC Intermediate RS	Area 6 Intermediate IC High RS
Customer variations				
Product variations	Low	Area 7 Low IC Low RS	Area 8 Low IC Intermediate RS	Area 9 Low IC High RS
Government regulatory variations				
		Low	Intermediate Resource Scarcity	High
		Resource domain	Availability of raw materials Human resources, capital Customer impact on resource availability Competitor impact on resource availability Government impact on resource availability Organizational impact on resource availability	

Figure 6.1   Informational complexity and resource scarcity. (*Source*: Lawrence and Dyer, 1983.)

contains a drawback. The potential variety facing a firm may be large and costly to absorb. A firm will therefore only extend its variety as long as it can expect benefits from doing so. However, the reaping of benefits can be shrouded in uncertainty and there may be *residual uncertainty*. Management will therefore operate within an area of 'bounded rationality', to use Simon's expression for management's problem of coping with complexity (Simon, 1982).

Control and structure: an extension
Figure 6.2 takes into account the points raised in the previous section. The impact of the firm's environment, its market and environmental uncertainties, is shown by an undulating path. On the basis of the information available to it, management will introduce some variety into the firm's structure which will reduce uncertainty but not eliminate it entirely; the residual uncertainty will lie outside the bounds of managerial competence.

The firm's appraisal of its environment requires the use of scanning devices, such as salesmen, and the use of filters to sift the economically useful information from the 'noise' present in the signals which firms receive from the market. For example, statistical techniques can be used to decompose time series into trends, cycles and residuals. In addition there are the control mechanisms which embody *comparators* such as financial ratios.

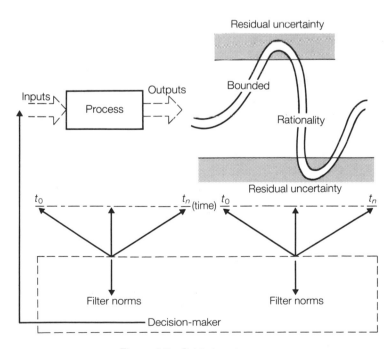

Figure 6.2   Control system.

Levels and Types of Control

In figure 6.2 we have drawn one loop between the firm and its environment. In practice there will be several loops. Thus most firms will attempt to distinguish disturbances in kind from disturbances in degree. Disturbances in degree, such as a 2 per cent increase in demand, will tend to be handled in a primary feedback loop within the context of extant rules. In other words there will be operating decisions embodied in the primary loop. Disturbances in kind, such as the collapse of the market, will involve longer-run adjustments in which new rules for disinvestment and investment in some new market will be developed in a secondary (or strategic) loop. The ability of a firm to decompose systems into subsystems which deal with disturbances of different frequency, and the establishment of effective links between the subsystems, greatly enhances the adaptability and survival of the firm. As we noted in the previous chapter, hierarchical systems represent attempts to cope with complexity.

Accounting Information for a System of Control

So far we have been concerned with the basic requirements of an optimal information and control system and their relationship to organizational structures. What we shall do now is examine the usefulness of accounting information as a basis of control. In short, is accounting information of value to the decision-maker? What are its limitations? In any firm the accountant is responsible for the supply of certain kinds of information both within the firm and also to outsiders. Within the firm the accountant is responsible to management and, through the directors, he is responsible to the shareholders, the Inland Revenue, the Registrar of Companies and, in the case of the public corporations, to ministers of state and Parliament. In recent years there have been attempts to widen the scope of the information provided by accountants in order to provide financial details of possible mergers, redundancies and liquidations, as well as the financial prospects of firms to trade unionists in order to assist them in collective bargaining. There have also been pressures for firms to include some form of social accounting or social audit which measures the general impact of a firm upon its environment.

Financial Accounting

Traditionally, accounting has been divided into financial and management accounting. Financial accounting is mainly concerned with reporting historical information to interested parties outside the firm. In the case of the small privately owned firm the interested party would be the owner-manager, but with the spread of limited liability and share ownership many, if not most, of the interested people may not be involved in the day-to-day affairs of the company. The information which is reported is governed by accounting principles which are intended to give an honest and fair reflection of the financial affairs of the firm and the main documents which are used to supply this information are the balance sheet, the profit and loss account, the flow of funds statement and the directors' report.

The legal requirements for company accounts are contained in the Companies Acts of 1948 and 1967 as amended by the 1976 Act. The 1981 Act introduced some slight changes, but the main Acts are those of 1948 and 1967. The Acts require companies to keep records, but do not prescribe the manner of presenting information. The accounting principles or standards are not contained in the legislation but represent a generally agreed way of presenting information. Recommendations from the professional bodies of accountants are not binding on members but are mere guidelines, and there may be a number of acceptable ways of presenting information. Finally, the auditors of a company act as 'watchdogs' to ensure that the information provided gives an honest and true picture of the financial affairs of the firm.

Interrelations of Management, Accounting and External Agents

Figure 6.3 shows the interrelations between management, the accountant and the external agents. On the left-hand side is the cycle of planning and control set by management. Management decides a strategy, determines how it is to be carried out and sets the standards of performance to be embodied in its yardsticks or comparators. The implementation of policy leads to outcomes which have to be evaluated and the assessment of outcomes leads, by feedback, to the confirmation or revision of strategy. Thus the left-hand side contains the structure of control which we discussed in the first section.

The central column reveals the role of the accountant. Management planning is expressed by the accountant in budgets which embody the possible costs associated with standards. Budgets lead to actions which yield information which, in turn, is embodied in performance reports. Performance reports are evaluated and may lead to a revision of strategies. In addition, the information which is collected and processed is incorporated in the annual report and is available for analysis by external agents.

The Balance Sheet

In order to indicate the type of information contained in a company's reports and accounts we shall refer to the published report of Unilever for 1982. The Unilever group of companies consists of two parent firms: Unilever PLC, London, and Unilever NV, Rotterdam. The companies have identical boards of directors and are linked by agreements, one of which equalizes the dividends payable on the ordinary capital of the two parent companies. Hence the combined affairs of the two companies are of more importance to financial shareholders than those of the separate companies.

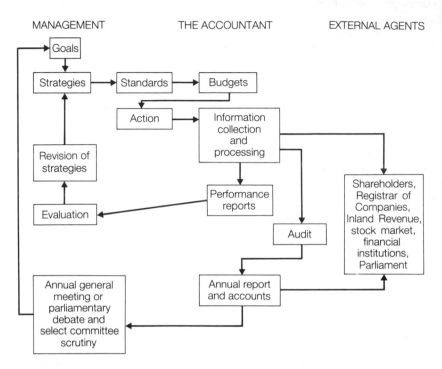

Figure 6.3   Interrelations of management, the accountant and external agents. (*Source*: BBC, 1969.)

Unilever is a multinational, multi-divisional firm whose products include foodstuffs, detergents and toilet preparations, chemicals, paper, and plastics; it has plantations in numerous countries. Furthermore, from the point of view of the business economist its history has been well documented by Charles Wilson (1954).

Figure 6.4 shows the interrelations between the balance sheet and the profit and loss account of a firm, and it can be used as a basis for an examination of Unilever's accounts. The balance sheet can be considered in two parts. On the one hand there are the assets employed by the firm; on the other hand there are the methods of financing those assets, the liabilities. Traditionally, assets and liabilities were set down side by side in the balance sheet but Unilever follow the modern practice of displaying the balance sheet in a vertical form. This has the merit that funds for day-to-day activities, such as working capital, are kept distinct from the funds used to finance fixed assets (table 6.1).

Long-term external finance takes the form of: ordinary shares (2), loan capital (4) and deferred liabilities (5). Preference share capital (1) is a form of equity capital but carries the proviso that no dividend on the common or

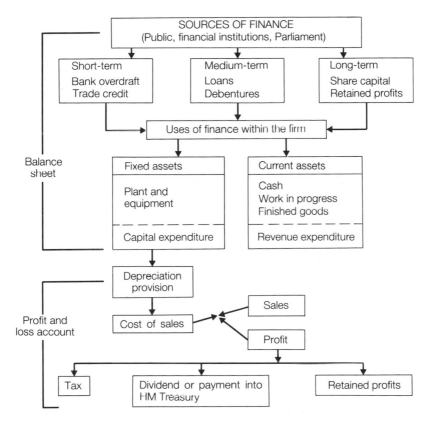

Figure 6.4 Interrelations between balance sheet, profit and loss (income) and funds flow items. (*Source*: BBC, 1969.)

ordinary equity capital may be paid until after the preferred dividend has been paid. A major item is the finance provided by ordinary shareholders in the form of retained profits (table 6.2).

The uses to which those funds are put is indicated by the fixed assets (b) which are mainly plant and equipment, investment in associated companies, listed shares and other firms.

Short-term borrowings comprise bank loans and overdrafts as well as future taxation.

Turning to the asset side of the balance sheet we can observe a distinction between fixed and current assets. The appropriate mix between them will be determined by technology, factor prices and management's views about its cash flows of payments and receipts over time. Thus current assets (working capital) cover an important cycle within the firm, which is vital both for profitability and liquidity (the ease of meeting its debtors). In this operating

Table 6.1. Consolidated balance sheets, Unilever, 1982 (£ million)

Capital employed

1	Preference share capital	67.8
2	Ordinary shareholders' equity	2901.1
3	Outside interest in subsidiaries	163.5
4	Loan capital	739.1
5	Deferred liabilities	924.0
		4795.5

Employment of capital

6	Fixed assets	3289.7
7	Associated companies	197.7
8	Trade investment	47.4
9	Other long-term assets	170.7
10	Working capital	1909.1
11	Provision for taxation	(220.2)
12	Dividends	(88.0)
13	Net liquid funds	389.1
		4795.5

Table 6.2. Consolidated sources and use of funds, Unilever, 1982 (£ million)

Funds generated from operations	
Profit before tax	725.4
Elimination of items not involving flow of funds before tax less dividends and interest	(42.8)
Depreciation	272.6
Unfunded retirement benefits	64.3
Others	10.8
Funds from other sources	2.6
	1027.7
Tax payments during the year	(257.8)
Capital expenditures less disposals	(430.6)
Purchase/Sale of subsidiaries	(75.7)
Purchase/Sale of associated companies/trade investment	(0.5)
Additional working capital	(23.6)
Dividends paid during the year	(137.2)
Other uses	(30.5)
Total uses	(955.9)
Increase/decrease in net liquid funds	71.8

cycle there is a cash flow out of the firm for raw materials, wages, etc., up to and including the point where the customer takes delivery of the finished goods; when the customer pays, cash flows back into the firm and the goods yield a profit and the value of current assets increases. The frequency with which a firm turns over its current assets is an important factor determining the profitability of the firm. Current assets will increase all the time in a profitable company subject to periodic withdrawals or payments on fixed assets, tax payments, dividend payments and investments outside the company.

Profit and Loss Account

What the owners of a firm are interested in is the profit or income of the firm. Income may be defined as that which the owners could consume whilst maintaining capital intact. Hence the firm is envisaged as being a going concern, and the definition of income excludes income or profit which might be obtained from the sale of assets. But even when the sale of assets has been eliminated from the definition of income there is still the problem of depreciation. Plant and equipment wear out, and allowances (depreciation allowances) must be set aside to replace machines. The accountant employs various methods of calculating depreciation allowances. For example, a machine may be presumed to have a life of n years and to wear out at the rate $1/n$ per year – this is the method of straight-line depreciation. However, such methods are essentially subjective, although no more open to that criticism than the economist's concept of *user cost*, which may be defined as expected benefits from using equipment 'today' as opposed to 'tomorrow'. In addition to the problem of measuring depreciation there is the difficulty caused by changes in the general level of prices (inflation and deflation).

The profit and loss account of Unilever (table 6.3) gives several definitions of profit available as income. Thus there is operating profit or gross profit,

Table 6.3. Consolidated profit and loss account, Unilever, 1982 (£ million)

Sales to third parties	13,215.7
Costs	(12,509.4)
Operating profit	706.3
Concern share of associated companies before tax	54.8
Income before trade investments	4.6
Interest	(40.3)
Profit before taxation	725.4
Taxation on profit of the year	(333.0)
Tax adjustments previous year	13.4
Profit after tax	405.8
Outside interests and preference dividends	(32.6)
Profit attributable to ordinary capital	373.2
Dividends on ordinary and deferred capital	(136.6)
Profit of the year retained	236.6

which is the difference between sales revenue minus the cost of goods sold; whilst profit before taxation is the surplus remaining after charging against gross profit all expenses including depreciation properly attributable to the normal activities of the business. After the removal of taxation management has to decide how much of net profit should be paid out as dividends and how much should be retained for future operations.

Assessing Managerial Performance

Using the information contained in the balance sheet and profit and loss accounts it is possible to gain some insight into a firm's performance – at least when judged against the performance of other firms operating in similar markets. The procedure used to assess performance is known as *ratio analysis*. Figure 6.5 indicates a pyramid of ratios. At the top is a measure of profitability defined as the return on capital, and which in Unilever in 1982 was 9.3 per cent. From this ratio can be derived other ratios, and some of the relevant values for Unilever are shown, although it must be borne in mind that it is not always possible to get detailed estimates of all ratios from company reports.

Profitability is, however, not the only concern of management, and there is a potential conflict between the pursuit of profit and the desire for liquidity. Liquidity refers to the ease with which an asset can be converted into money in order to meet the demands of creditors. Money is obviously the most liquid asset because it is universally accepted as a medium of exchange and other assets can be said to possess degrees of liquidity by virtue of their nearness to money. Thus Treasury Bills may be considered to be highly liquid because they are redeemable in 3 months, whereas plant and machinery may be illiquid.

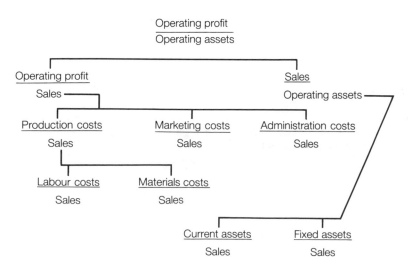

Figure 6.5   A pyramid of ratios. (*Source*: BBC, 1969.)

The clash between profitability and liquidity arises because investment in plant and machinery may yield a higher return than money left in the bank.

Money, the most liquid asset, is especially required to finance the demand for working capital, a demand that arises primarily from the fact that the process of purchasing raw materials or goods, converting them through various stages of production into finished goods, selling those goods and collecting the sales revenue, takes time. During that time payments must be made to resource owners; hence the need constantly to appraise liquidity ratios.

The best-known indicator of short-term liquidity is the *current ratio* which is expressed as:

$$\frac{\text{Current assets}}{\text{Current liabilities}}$$

This ratio is a measure of the ability of a firm to meet its current obligations, and is based on the assumption that current assets are easily converted into cash which can be used to meet current liabilities. In 1982 the current ratio for Unilever was 1.8 per cent; but a note of caution must be entered. Many of the current assets, such as stocks of raw materials, are not converted into cash except over a lengthy period. Hence creditors may be more interested in the *acid test ratio* or *quick ratio* of cash inflows to cash outflows:

$$\frac{\text{Current assets} - \text{inventories}}{\text{Current liabilities}}$$

Current Cost Accounting

The accounts which we have so far examined have been based upon historical costs, and in a period of price changes it becomes important to obtain a more realistic measure of a firm's performance. Unfortunately the task of preparing a 'realistic set of accounts' is not only difficult but is also controversial. What shareholders want is a measure of the income available for consumption; that is, money income deflated by an index of consumer (retail) prices.

However, if a firm is defined as an entity with a corporate personality distinct from its shareholders, then a more relevant measure may be assets deflated by an index of assets prices. In table 6.4 we show the current cost balance sheet for Unilever. The data in the tables have been prepared on the basis of the UK Statement of Standard Accounting Practice number 16, which suggests the procedure which might be used to prepare current cost accounts.

The Disclosure of Information

The information contained in company reports is primarily designed for shareholders, the Inland Revenue and potential investors – it is an account of financial stewardship; but it may not be the information which other groups within the firm and within society may want. Thus employees and trade unions may want to know something about the long-term prospects of firms, their

Table 6.4.   Consolidated current cost balance sheet, Unilever, 1982 (£ million)

Capital employed	
Preference share capital	67.8
Ordinary shareholders' equity	5345.7
Outside interest in subsidiaries	242.9
Loan capital	739.1
Deferred liabilities	536.2
	6921.7
Employment of capital	
Fixed assets	4354.6
Associated companies	333.3
Trade investments	73.1
Other long-term assets	170.7
Working capital	1909.1
Provision for taxation	(220.2)
Dividends	(88.0)
Net liquid funds	389.1
	6921.7

manpower plans, their redundancy programmes. It may, of course, be argued that a union should be able to make some assessment of a firm's prospects through the process of collective bargaining, but it may also be argued that a strike is a costly method of extracting information. In addition to the claims of employees there are the demands of groups, such as environmentalists, who argue that managers should pursue other goals as well as profits. Opposed to these claims also is the assertion that the task of managers is to maximize profits within the guidelines laid down by the state on the grounds that the pursuit of other goals may be an excuse for managerial inefficiency. The trouble with this latter point of view is that it may encourage everyone to do as little as possible and not act as social pioneers.

Management Accounting

Financial accounting is backward-looking; it is concerned with the past performance of the firm. Management accounting is forward-looking; it involves long-term strategies and day-to-day operations; therefore the material collected for finance accounting is not always suitable for management accounting. Thus the cost data which form the basis of financial accounting are concerned with actual outlays, with *ex-post* costs, whereas management accounting is preoccupied with *ex-ante* costs. It follows therefore that management accounting must of necessity make use of economic analysis and in that sense the material in the remaining chapters of this book is devoted to issues of management accounting; for example, the chapter on costs and costing.

Management accounting is concerned with the design of management information systems which will reflect the firm's goals, and although profit and the return on capital are the basic objectives, it necessarily follows that in the pursuit of those objectives all aspects of policy, such as product development, pricing, advertising, personnel management and investment will need to be considered. The technique which is used in planning, controlling, coordinating and motivating is known as *budgetary control*. A budget is a plan expressed in quantitative terms which permits of control because it allows actual performance to be measured against a performance standard, motivates because of the incentives built into the performance standard, and coordinates because the various aspects of the firm's policy are brought together within the budget's constraints.

To imply that there is only one budget is misleading, however; there will be operations budgets, finance budgets and capital expenditure budgets. Thus

1 *Operations budgets* will be based upon:
   (a) the 'sales budget', which will deal with the output to be sold and at what price;
   (b) the 'production budget', which will deal with the resources needed to produce that output and at what cost; this will be based upon departmental budgets.
2 *Financial budgets* will involve:
   (a) 'cash budget', which translates the operating budget into cash inflows and outflows in order to minimize the cost of idle cash and safeguard the liquidity position;
   (b) a 'funds flow budget', dealing with sources of finance and their uses.
3 *Capital expenditure budgets* deal with long-term policy.

The great virtue of the budget is that it imposes a discipline. Its weakness is that, being an annual or cyclical activity, it tends to emphasize the short run at the expense of the long run, and it is difficult to administer in times of rapid technological change and innovation.

However, behind the budgets lie decisions concerning investment, production, marketing and the use of labour, and on these issues economic analysis provides not only analytical tools but also the link between accounting and business policy making.

Behavioural Accounting

The major problem with budgeting is the fact that budgets are imposed upon people who are also expected to provide the information for the construction of budgets. If budget standards are set too tight then employees may refuse to attempt them, whilst if they are too slack then workers conceal how easily they have been attained. There is therefore a problem of creating demand-revealing mechanisms, of creating incentives for employees to reveal information. Hence in recent years some accountants have become preoccupied with the behavioural aspects of accounting, of how individuals react to accounting information (Hopwood, 1973).

Bibliography and References

Ashby, W. R. (1952) *Design for a Brain*. London: Chapman & Hall.
Ashby, W. R. (1956) *Introduction to Cybernetics*. London: Chapman & Hall.
BBC (1969) *Hardy Heating Ltd*. London: BBC Publications.
Hopwood, A. (1973) *An Accounting System and Managerial Behaviour*. London: Saxon House.
Lawrence, P. R. and Dyer, P. (1983) *Renewing American Industry*. New York: Free Press.
Meade, J. E. (1971) *The Controlled Economy*. London: Allen & Unwin.
Ouchi, W. G. (1979) 'The design of organizational control mechanisms', *Management Science*, 25, 833–48.
Schoderbeck, P., Kefalas, A. and Schoderbeck, G. (1975) *Management Systems*. Dallas: Business Systems.
Simon, H. A. (1982) *Models of Bounded Rationality*. Cambridge, Mass.: MIT Press.
    Vol. I: *Economic Analysis and Public Policy*.
    Vol. II: *Behavioral Economics and Business Organization*.
Wilson, C. H. (1954) *Unilever*, 2 vols. Oxford: Oxford University Press.

7 Changing Patterns of Marketing

We can distinguish four areas of activity, undertaken by an enterprise, which might be labelled 'operational'. Inevitably these areas overlap and the dividing lines are often very blurred; nevertheless for analytical purposes we can separate these areas into: marketing, finance, production and personnel. Each area has to be 'managed' and the firm's success or failure depends upon the quality of such management. We shall study each of these areas in turn, commencing with that area of activity which concerns the relationships between the single enterprise as seller, its customers as buyers, and those other enterprises which either threaten rivalry or offer cooperation. This area of activity we are labelling 'marketing management', adopting a wide and comprehensive interpretation of its sphere of influence. Marketing management is concerned with carving a segment or market from an otherwise amorphous mass of potential buyers who may be households or other firms. The goods traded may be 'non-produced' goods, such as antiques, or goods which have emerged from a long planning process. Marketing therefore has links with production, and via purchasing and producing there are links with finance and personnel management. Above all, marketing involves entrepreneurial skills to reconcile demands and supplies. To get a 'feel' of the areas which we are to explore let us briefly review some patterns observed in the UK during the postwar period.

Retailing

From the 1950s to the 1970s in the UK there was a dramatic rise in real incomes which not only allowed the satisfaction of existing wants but also permitted the emergence of new wants and speculation as to the extent to which those new wants were the creation of 'advertising men'. Full employment resulted in labour shortages and a narrowing of wage differentials as employers attempted to compete for the available sources of workers amongst young people and married women. The baby booms of the late 1940s and early 1950s, coupled with the narrowing of wage differentials, produced the phenomenon of a 'teenage market' in the 1950s and 1960s. The increase in the numbers of married women in employment led to a reduction in the time available for housework and a rise in the demand for convenience foods and the emergence of one-stop shopping centres. 'Multiples' (multi-plant retail shops) and departmental stores, which had emerged in the interwar years, increased in importance and pushed out independents. Supermarkets and even hypermarkets became fashionable, and car ownership permitted an increase in shopping in town centres and forced a reduction in corner shops. Planning legislation also assisted the growth of large retail stores.

The tendency of retail shopping to become geographically concentrated enabled 'the multiples' to attain economies of scale, but these could only be achieved if they could lower prices, and prices could only be lowered if the big retailers could break the collective retail price maintenance practised and enforced by manufacturers. This was achieved by the countervailing power of the big retailers. Price competition therefore started to emerge in the 1960s, and was associated with increasing concern over product liability. Under resale price maintenance manufacturers had sought to control the quality of their goods through standardization, branding and after-sales service guarantees and to prevent the use of their goods being used as loss-leaders by the insistence upon no price-cutting. Retailers were prepared to accept collective regulation provided the number of retail outlets was controlled. The abandonment of resale price maintenance therefore raised the question of who was to provide guarantees of product quality and after-sales service. In part the problem was resolved by the emergence of independent product repairers; in part it was resolved by the big retailers guaranteeing the reliability of products. But in granting guarantees it was obviously easier to guarantee one's own goods, and 'own brands' began to emerge – although they tend to be confined initially to a few products, such as soap, cereals and tea. Of course all guarantees have to be paid for, and it is possible that as real incomes rose consumers became more willing to pay for such guarantees. However not all problems of product liability were solved by the market, and there was pressure for legislation to protect the consumer.

Vertical Integration

The traditional pattern of moving goods from manufacturers to final consumers provided two intermediaries – wholesalers and retailers. The functions of retailers are to buy, sell and store goods; to break bulk; to engage in risk sharing; display goods; provide information and credit and, above all, to provide a collection of heterogeneous goods in small lots in anticipation of demand. The functions of wholesalers are to break bulk and economize in the costs of moving goods. If there were m manufacturers and r retailers then there would be $m \times r$ transactions with each manufacturer sending a small shipment to each retailer and not being able to obtain any economies in transactions costs. What the wholesaler does is to collect large shipments of homogeneous goods from each manufacturer, break them down and re-assemble them into large shipments of heterogeneous goods to each retailer with the result that there are $m + r$ transactions; the functions of the wholesaler are thus similar to the functions of money. Of course there had always been instances of direct selling but the usual pattern had four links – manufacturers, wholesalers, retailers and households. This pattern began to be disrupted at the turn of the century and wholesaling came to be undertaken by big retailers and manufacturers who integrated forwards into retailing. The process was accelerated in the 1950s and 1960s. Vertical integration and horizontal integration (as in the case of the multiples) became more pronounced.

International Marketing

Changing patterns of integration occurred internationally as well as nationally, and have offered a challenge to international trade theorists. According to established theory an international equalization of product and factor prices results from the free movement among countries of goods and resources. In the absence of tariffs and transport costs, and with no differences in technologies, trade might be expected to take place on the basis of comparative advantage with relative strengths of demand determining the terms of trade. Following the tariff reductions of the 1960s and 1970s the concept of import penetration came to play an increasing role in marketing strategy and industrial organization (Caves, 1985); but some tariffs still exist and, in the presence of tariffs and no restrictions on factor mobility, then factors move as compensatory adjustments, to the effects of less mobile products. However, there is a qualification to this: the product cycle thesis suggests that a pioneering firm in an advanced economy, such as the USA, might initially produce a good at home and then export it. At a later stage it would look around for a cheaper location and commence manufacturing abroad. However, licensing to others is an alternative to own-production abroad, and the rise of multinational corporations, of firms which produce in more than one country, has therefore to be explained in terms other than tariffs and transport costs. An explanation must encompass such things as the desire to protect know-how. The problem therefore is as much a problem of industrial marketing as it is of retail marketing.

Industrial Marketing

Industrial marketing tends to occupy a shadowy place in the literature, possibly because it is not so dramatically observable as are the changing patterns of wholesale and retail distribution towards final consumers. There is also the point that industrial buyers are presumed to be more knowledgeable than households, and therefore problems of advertising are less acute. Furthermore, the changing patterns of vertical and horizontal integration of firms have tended to transform external marketing into internal marketing; but transfer pricing is no less a problem of marketing and is increasingly important given the complexity of industry.

Government Intervention of Markets

There are some products whose markets have been severely affected by government intervention. Thus, in an endeavour to stabilize farm incomes governments and international agencies established farm price support schemes which led to marketing boards buying up supplies in periods of glut and releasing them in periods of dearth. Unfortunately the presence of someone willing to buy unlimited supplies has seemed often to persuade producers to produce increasing mountains of farm goods, as in the experience of the EEC. In other instances attempts at stabilization of primary producers' incomes has led to nationalization.

The Long Recession of the 1970s and 1980s

One effect of the harsher economic climate of the 1970s and 1980s has been to cause firms to revise their marketing strategies, and this has led to changes in structure with a consequent reduction in the autonomy of marketing management and a closer integration of marketing, finance and production. Financial performance, measured crudely by return on net worth, can be increased through varying profit margins, sales and the structure of debt. During the 1950s expanding markets led to an emphasis upon increasing the volume of sales by acquiring new buyers, and the stress upon increasing sales by expanding the market was associated with a functional management structure with specialist marketing, personnel, finance and production departments. Functionalism encouraged efficiency through specialization but was ill-suited to market penetration, to changing products and markets, and came to be replaced in the 1960s by multi-divisional structures which released top management to cope with the overall problems of strategy, innovation and adaptation. Multidivisional structures did not solve all problems however, and led often to interdivisional conflict and the search for alternative structures. The search became increasingly important in the 1970s and 1980s when stagnant markets prevented sales expansion and market penetration could result in quick responses from rivals. Hence there emerged an emphasis upon improving productivity, of cost reduction, improving the sales mix and price competition. Above all there has been an emphasis upon the financial implications of marketing decisions, of variations in the sales mix leading to variations in fixed and variable costs, and long- and short-term debt financing. Emphasis upon the interrelations of finance, marketing and production has reduced the autonomy of marketing departments and led to the creation of matrix forms of organization.

Given the preceding description of changes in marketing arrangements since 1945 we can now set out the analytical structure of the section on marketing management as follows:

1 Consumer behaviour: marketing management needs some idea of what consumers want and how they behave in the face of changing

relative price structures and changing household incomes. Empirical knowledge of such matters is extremely difficult to acquire and theoretical guidance is essential. Economists have produced theories of consumer behaviour but they have not received the acclaim of marketing analysts – some exploration of such theories should prove to be interesting and the next chapter attempts a brief explanation of the theory of consumer behaviour as a background to the practical problems of marketing management.

2   Whatever the guidance from theories of consumer behaviour, management must make decisions concerning prices and/or quantities in the light of both prevailing and anticipated market structures for a given product; concerning the nature of the product or products offered for sale by the enterprise; concerning the ways in which consumers can be informed about a product or range of products; and concerning the models and locations through which the consumers acquire products. Consequently the links between the next chapter and the remaining chapters of the section can be represented as follows:

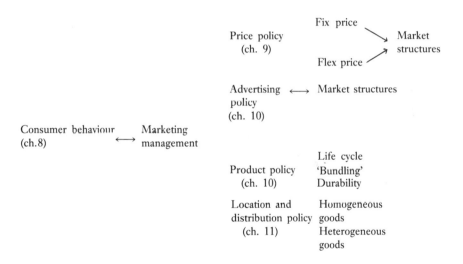

Reference

Caves, R. E. (1985) 'International trade and industrial organization', *European Economic Review*, 28, 377–95.

8 Consumer Behaviour

What questions confront the 'marketing manager' in relation to an existing product? Any list is bound to include *Who?* (who buys it?) *How?* (how do they buy it?) *When?* (when do they buy it?) and *Where?* (where do they buy it?) In other words, the manager 'identifies the market' – identifies both the characteristics of his consumers and the characteristics of their consumption. By constantly updating the information on these questions the manager is able to vary his supplies in order to match the preceived demands.

The above view of the marketing manager's problem reflects the neoclassical approach to economics or, at least, to pricing. The neoclassical economist regards price as being determined by the combined forces of demand and supply, and it would seem that in this framework the role of marketing becomes preoccupied with the demand side of the problem. However, not all economists would label themselves as 'neoclassical'; indeed many economists, particularly those characterized as 'Post-Keynesian' (a very misleading description since most economists writing after Keynes have been 'neoclassical' in their thinking) regard price as being supply (i.e. cost) determined with marketing problems being concerned as much with trying to account for rivals' actions and reactions as with the behaviour of consumers. The approach adopted in this chapter avoids preoccupation with only one side of the market in order to throw light on all aspects of the marketing problem. Because of this the approach might be dismissed as being too eclectic, but the current state of economics would seem to require eclecticism.

The Economic Approach to Consumer Behaviour

At the outset it must be emphasized that there is one concept which is fundamental to an understanding of consumer behaviour – the *hierarchy of wants* (Georgescu-Roegen, 1966, 1968). This concept was to the forefront in classical writings but it became obscured by later economists' emphasis upon 'wants' rather than 'needs' – where the latter usage was maintained, as in psychology, the fundamental nature of the hierarchy continued to be stressed (Maslow, 1954).

The hierarchy of wants recognizes that consumers have specific wants which are subject to dialectical laws. The most important law is that wants are arranged in a hierarchy with three distinct layers – biological wants, with the same hierarchy for all human beings; social wants, with the same hierarchy for all members of the same society; and personal wants, with no uniform hierarchy. The fact that biological and social wants have the same hierarchy means that interpersonal comparisons may be drawn. Hence it is possible to postulate that taking a pound from a rich man and giving it to a poor man may make society better off with reference to basic or social wants, and that satisfying basic wants may require public financing (involving taxation and income redistribution) and, perhaps, may require public production as opposed to private production, i.e. central planning rather than the use of markets. Finally, the proposition that there is not a general want but a hierarchy of specific wants leads to the recognition that: (1) a good satisfying one want may not be a substitute for a good satisfying another want; (2) some goods may be substitutes in satisfying a particular want; and that (3) a good possessing many attributes may satisfy more than one want.

Indifference Curve Analysis

Since the end of the 1930s (Hicks and Allen, 1934; Hicks, 1956) the dominant approach to the analysis of consumer (or household) behaviour in economics textbooks has been that of the indifference curve. Within this approach consumers are assumed to behave as if they have a well-defined system of preferences, which can be mapped for observation. The characteristics of such a mapping reflect a set of assumptions about the nature of measurement of behaviour and about the nature of the behaviour itself:

1   The consumer is *rational*, i.e. in the face of all relevant information the consumer is capable of making choices which will best further his aims.

2   The aim of consumption is to maximize satisfaction or 'utility', and in the case of desirable goods this means that the consumer prefers more to less. (In the case of undesirable goods, e.g. pollution, he prefers less to more.)

3   The consumer can measure the satisfactions derived from different bundles of goods, but only in an ordinal fashion. Thus bundles can be ranked in order of satisfactions derived from them, but numerical weights cannot be attached to the rankings. A is better than B, i.e. is ranked higher than B, but it is impossible to say by how much.

4   The preference mapping reflects 'indifference', i.e. for any given bundle of goods, yielding a given level of satisfaction, there is an infinite range of substitute bundles which would yield an equivalent level of satisfaction and among which the consumer would be 'indifferent'. Thus along any indifference curve the loss of any one bundle of goods can be compensated by the gain of any other. However, such compensation is not one-for-one at all points; rather the surrender of successive units of one good can be compensated only by successive increases in the amount consumed of the other good. This condition

is defined as a *diminishing marginal rate of substitution*, and is measured by the slope of the indifference curve.

5   The consumer chooses among bundles of goods in a manner which is both *consistent* and *transitive*. Thus, if bundle A is chosen over bundle B at any time then bundle A will be chosen over bundle B at all other times when both bundles are available. Further, if at any time bundle B is chosen over bundle C then bundle C must always be rejected in favour of bundle A when A is available (A > B > C), hence no indifference curve ever crosses any other one.

Mapping under Given Circumstances

Given this set of conditions the mapping becomes clear: each indifference curve is convex to the origin and the degree of slope reflects the consumer's relative tastes for the commodities; moving in a north-easterly direction, the consumer experiences higher indifferences curves and his well-being improves. Clearly, then, the consumer's objective is to reach the highest possible indifference curve compatible with the constraints under which he operates. To the economist the two major constraints are the consumer's available money income and the relative prices of the two commodities referred to by the mapping. For a given money income (spending power) of Z and price Py for any good Y his potential real income in terms of commodity Y is Z/Py. Thus, returning to a mapping, say between goods Y and X, we can impose a linear constraint on the consumer's activities in the form of a 'budget line' AB, the slope of which measures the ratio of the relative prices of Y and X:

$$\frac{Z/Py}{Z/Px} = \frac{Px}{Py}$$

Figure 8.1 shows the resulting picture.

Point E in figure 8.1 is termed the point of *consumer equilibrium*, it represents the best point for the consumer to choose, given all the circumstances in which he finds himself – he is unable to reach an indifference curve higher than IC_3 given his current constraints and any point on either side of E, along AB, lies on a lower indifference curve. Point E is characterized by the fact that the slope of AB equals the slope of IC_3 at that point, i.e. the marginal rate of substitution between Y and X equals the ratio of the relative prices of the same two goods, at the point of consumer equilibrium.

Mapping when Circumstances Change

What happens when money income or prices change? Clearly this upsets the state of balance defined for point E, and the consumer will attempt to re-establish equilibrium in the light of his changed circumstances. When prices remain unchanged but money income rises, this means that real income rises also, and the resulting change in the consumer's pattern of expenditure is

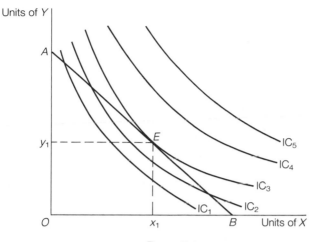

Figure 8.1

described as being due to an *income effect*. When relative prices change, however, the effect is more difficult to map because of the simultaneous change in real income – e.g. if the price of X falls and everything else remains the same, including money income, then the consumer experiences a potential increase in real income. Thus to discover the effect of the relative price change *only*, a compensating adjusting in money income is assumed so that real income remains the same. The resulting alteration in consumption pattern is described as being due to a *substitution effect* – units of one good (the one now relatively cheaper) are substituted for units of the other (the one now relatively more expensive) in magnitudes which keep real income unchanged. Thus a (real) income effect shifts the consumer onto another indifference curve, while a substitution effect moves him along the same curve.

Income and substitution effects differ not only in their relative effects on the level of consumer satisfaction, but also in the relative *directions* of change in the consumer's expenditure pattern. The substitution effect is unambiguous – if the relative price of X falls, more X (less Y) is bought; if the relative price of Y falls, more Y (less X) is bought. In other words, when the relative price of a commodity falls the *substitution effect on quantity* is positive. However, the income effect is less clear-cut since a rise in real income can be reflected in more of one commodity being bought but either more or less of the other – the real income effect of a fall in the price of X might result in either more X or less X being bought. In other words the *income effect on quantity* can be either positive or negative.

Analysing the indifference map, then, enables us to understand how the combined operation of income and substitution effects serves to determine the outcome of a change in the consumer's circumstances. When the substitution effect dominates the income effect, a fall in the relative price of a commodity will result in *more* of that commodity being purchased, even if the income effect is negative; when the income effect dominates the substitution effect and the former is negative, a fall in the relative price of a commodity will result in *less* of that commodity being purchased. Figure 8.2 summarizes three types of adjustment to a change in relative price. In each case the price of X falls while the price of Y remains unaltered, and money income is also fixed; AB is the original budget line and AC the budget line after the change in relative prices; $A'B'$ shows the 'compensated budget line', i.e. the constraint facing the consumer when the increase in real income, caused by the fall in the price of X, has been offset by an imagined reduction in money income of a sufficient magnitude to enable the consumer to enjoy his original level of real income and no more − in this way the substitution effect can be isolated from the income effect and each are clearly identified. In each case, then, a represents the original equilibrium position, c presents the new equilibrium after the change in relative prices, a to b results from the operation of the substitution effect and b to c results from the operation of the income effect.

As far as the present discussion is concerned it is important to note that which one of three situations depicted in figure 8.2 will prevail, in the experience of any one consumer, depends upon his tastes or preferences. Since the constraints are identical in each of the three cases, it is the indifference curve shapes which determine the relative outcomes. Hence, as the curves flatten in moving from figure 8.2(a) to figure 8.2(c) the consumer's relative preference for Y over X at any point is becoming stronger, and the substitution effect intensifies. However, this by itself is not sufficient to explain case 8.2(c) which is the famous example of the Giffen Good. Clearly the likelihood of the Giffen case increases with increases in the size of the income effect relative to that of the substitution effect. In other words, the Giffen case may appear when a good accounts for a large proportion of the consumer's expenditure (income) but will not do so when the good accounts for only a small proportion of consumer spending. This is one conclusion from indifference curve analysis which is challenged by a later development in consumer theory which we shall be discussing presently.

Critique

The initial excitement at the emergence of indifference curve analysis was based on the belief that its ordinal approach avoided the pitfalls experienced in the analysis of consumer behaviour based on the assumption of cardinally measurable utility and the axiom of diminishing marginal utility. This latter approach, emerging in the latter part of the nineteenth century, had been formalized in the works of Alfred Marshall, and therefore had become part of the accepted textbook methodology of the early twentieth century. However, growing dissatisfaction with the assumption that utility can be objectively measured, and the conceptual difficulties caused by the assumption of a constant marginal utility of the measuring rod of money, provided the spur to find a more acceptable approach. Indifference curve analysis was believed to be the answer.

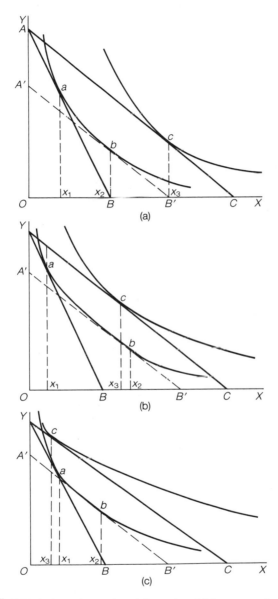

Figure 8.2   Adjustments to a change in relative price. (a) Income and substitution effects operate in same direction and more x is bought as its relative price falls. (b) Income and substitution effects operate in opposite directions – substitution effect dominates and more x is bought as its relative price falls. (c) Income and substitution effects operate in opposite directions – income effect dominates and less x is bought as its relative price falls.

But was it? Despite the appeal of the less restrictive assumption of ordinalism the indifference approach remains subjective and strong traces of a marginal utility approach can be found in the assumption of a diminishing marginal rate of substitution. Another serious defect is that, within the context of a hierarchy of wants, the approach may be applied perhaps at each point or layer in the hierarchy but not to analyse choices which span several layers. For example, how many motor cars would compensate an individual for being homeless? Furthermore, even at a given level of the hierarchy there may be no substitution possible – how many loaves of bread would compensate a thirsty consumer for being refused a glass of water? The way round the problem is to limit application of the indifference concept to commodities which satisfy a common want, i.e. to genuine commodity substitutes, but this clearly restricts the usefulness of the approach.

Does the approach have anything to offer the analysis of marketing problems? On the surface one would expect a positive answer to such a question since, after all, the *raison d'être* of both the marginal utility and the indifference curve approaches is to 'explain' demand, and in the process the theory has been described as one of 'consumer choice'. But does the consumer, or the household, as depicted in the indifference curve model, really choose? Is there any real purchasing decision to be made? It can be argued that the model depicts consumer behaviour as being no different from that of a programmed robot. Preferences are known and clearly defined in a convenient mathematical fashions, 'behaviour' is subjected to clearly defined constraints; there is no uncertainty of any kind; no 'dithering' is possible; no decisions have to be made; there is only one point that the consumer will ever 'choose' – the equilibrium point of tangency between the budget line and an indifference curve. In other words the concept of choice becomes a problem in applied mathematics and is easily solved. The model would seem to offer no insight into consumer choice processes (Buchanan, 1979) and to that extent is a disappointment to the marketing analyst.

On the question of explaining demand the indifference approach may have something to offer. Indifference curve analysis clearly shows the importance of substitution effects in relation to, and separate from, income effects and in consequence is able to help in the defining of substitute and complementary commodities. However, this itself is something of a mixed blessing. Earlier approaches to this particular problem had relied upon the cross-price elasticity of demand between any two commodities, a positive elasticity signifying substitutes and a negative elasticity signifying complements. Clearly, if such a measure includes the whole quantity effect as being the result of a price change then a misleading classification of commodities can occur unless income effects are always insignificant. For example, halving the price of cat meat is likely to lead to some increase in both purchases of cat meat and, say, sausage, thus suggesting that cat meat and sausages are complementary goods. By underlining the importance of the separate income effect, indifference analysis *in theory* avoids such results. Unfortunately, as a practical aid, compensating for real income changes is impossible without knowledge of preference maps and, therefore, marketing management is offered no real help.

Alternative Approaches

The fundamental drawback to a reliance on indifference curves as a means of explaining household behaviour is *subjectivity* – it requires economists to make assumptions about what goes on inside consumers' heads. As we shall see, this problem continues to dog alternative approaches despite their attempts to avoid it. It would seem that although the theory of consumer behaviour lies at the heart of microeconomics it offers also a very soft underbelly.

Revealed Preference

An early attempt at objectivity was offered by the revealed preference approach (Samuelson, 1938). The rationale of this approach has great appeal given the above comments about indifference curves – since we cannot explain acts of consumption, e.g. because an act does not indicate to us whether the motivation really is utility maximization rather than say, duty, or commitment, or apathetic habit, why not abandon the attempt to explain? The main purpose of the theory is to help us predict how a consumer will react to changes in circumstances, so why be concerned about the motivation? Why not predict from observations of what consumers do, from how they reveal their preferences?

The assumptions of the revealed preference approach are as outlined for the indifference curve approach except that preference revelation is substituted for the subjectivity of the diminishing marginal rate of substitution. Hence the approach simplifies into a comparison of choice sets determined by price/income constraints and all that we require to formulate predictions is an assumed starting point, i.e. that the consumer reveals a preference for a specific bundle of goods. Using two goods Y and X, figure 8.3 shows a

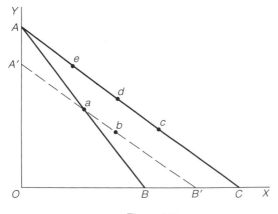

Figure 8.3

graphical representation of the approach and the consumer's decision stages are described below.

1   At the original level of money income and related prices of the two goods Y and X the budget line is AB and the consumer's opportunity set is OAB. Assume that the consumer chooses the bundle of goods represented by point a, i.e. of all the bundles available within the set OAB he reveals a preference for a.

2   A fall in the price of X, other things remaining unchanged, yields a new budget line AC and a new opportunity set OAC. The consumption 'frontier' in this new set is again the budget line, and the consumer will locate himself somewhere along AC. But where? The answer, again depends on the relative strength of income and substitution effects.

3   To isolate the substitution effect we eliminate the income effect. As before the budget line derived from a fall in the price of X, but with a compensating reduction in money income to enable no more than the original level of real income to be enjoyed, is shown by $A'B'$. This compensated budget line passes through the original bundle of goods at a and forms the boundary to a consumption opportunities set of $OA'B'$. Since the consumer has already revealed a preference for a he will not choose any other bundle in the area $OA'ab$ which diminishes his effective new opportunities set to BaB' and, given the assumption of consistency, will choose either a again or some point between a and B' as a result of the substitution effect. Suppose that he chooses b.

4   Returning the imagined reduction in income places the consumer somewhere along AC. If he chooses a bundle such as at c or d then the substitution effect is dominating the income effect but the latter is dominant if a point such as e is chosen.

Critique

At first sight the revealed preference approach would appear to be a real improvement on the indifference curve model, but to some extent it flatters to deceive. Certainly, as derived above, we seem to have the means of predicting reaction to a change in relative prices without the awkwardness of assumption about consumer psychology. To this extent the approach lends itself readily to econometric analysis of data on incomes and prices. But does it really advance our understanding of consumer behaviour? Observation alone does not help us to understand anything about motivation, and just because a consumer reacts to a set of circumstances in a certain way nine times out of ten does not permit an observer to predict that the action will repeat itself the eleventh time. Furthermore, and perhaps more crucial from the viewpoint of marketing management, observation can actually mislead when consumer tastes are changing. For example, in figure 8.3, how do we know that a revealed preference for bundle c has not resulted from a change in tastes as well as a change in relative prices? To the extent that consumers do not reveal their motivations, assuming that we can predict behaviour without adopting any hypothesis regarding such motivations may actually hinder our understanding of consumer behaviour.

The 'Household Production Function' Approach

Another attempt to liberate consumer theory from the pitfalls of subjectivity is the approach advanced and developed by Gary Becker (1965). Becker maintains the ultimate rationale of household behaviour to be that of max- imizing utility but the activities of the household are geared towards *production*, not consumption; i.e. towards producing the range of goods and services from which the household is able to derive its utility. Market goods and services, then, are not bought as consumption items but as inputs into a production process which produces 'final commodities', e.g. meals, (comfortable) accom- modation, 'cultural evenings' and children(!), all of which offer utility to the household members. The other important input into the production process, one which has received great emphasis from Becker, is that of *time*; the time put into producing 'final commodities' by household members.

The model can be set out as follows:

$$U = U(Z_1 \ldots Z_n) \tag{8.1}$$

$$Z_i = Z(x_1 \ldots x_n ; t_1 \ldots t_n ; R) \tag{8.2}$$

(8.1) tells us that household utility (U) depends on household consumption of 'final commodities' $Z_1 \ldots Z_n$; (8.2) tells us that production of final com- modities depends on market commodities, $x_1 \ldots x_n$, time spent on producing final commodities, $t_1 \ldots t_n$, and other variables, R. Equations (8.3) to (8.6) now spell out the constraints. To take a specific example, the production of a meal may require inputs of meat, vegetables, etc., shopping time, preparation time, a table and chairs, and so on. The constraints operating upon the production function are: household income, matched against the prices of market goods and the opportunity cost of household time (the wage available for market work). Thus, it is possible to write:

$$Y^m = \sum_{i=1}^{n} p_i x_i \tag{8.3}$$

which equates money income to expenditures on market goods and services. Total time, T, may be divided between market work, t_w, and other pursuits, $t_1 \ldots t_n$. Any time not spent at work (including time sleeping) is treated as an input into the production of some final commodity. Hence

$$T = \sum_{i=1}^{n} t_i + t_w \tag{8.4}$$

Time spent on market work is transformed into money returns through the wage rate, w, and combines with other sources of money income, such as rents, dividends and interest V to make up total money income:

$$Y^m = w \cdot t_w + V = \sum_{t=1}^{n} p_i x_i \tag{8.5}$$

Thus, (8.3) summarizes all the constraints operating upon the household's choice of market purchases – the amount of potential expenditure on market goods and services is limited by the sum of the money value of time spent at work and the total money value of other forms of income. If the value of time devoted to collecting and processing goods bought is now added to the monetary constraints summarized in (8.5), an expression can be found to represent final or 'full' income Y^f. The final expression is

$$Y^f = \sum_{i=1}^{n} p_i X_i + \sum_{i=1}^{n} w \cdot t_i = w \cdot t_w + V \tag{8.6}$$

Equation (8.6) summarizes some of the points made earlier – final income is 'spent' partly on market goods and services and partly on time devoted to household production financed by forgone earnings.

Given the model in this form, the household's aim is to maximize (8.1) subject to the constraints as summarized in (8.6) which results in

$$\frac{MUZ_i}{MUZ_j} = \frac{MCZ_i}{MCZ_j}$$

a familiar result.[1]

The expression for 'full income' in (8.6) summarizes the main point of Becker's approach – full income is spent partly on market goods and services and partly on time devoted to household production (financed by forgone

---

[1] Maximizing (8.1) subject to (8.2) via the Lagrangean multiplier technique yields:

$$L = U(Z_1 \ldots n) - \lambda \left[\left(\sum_{i=1}^{n} p_i \cdot x_i + \Sigma w t_w \right) - Y^f \right] \tag{8.7}$$

$$\frac{MUZ_i}{MUZ_i} = \frac{W \cdot \frac{dt_i}{dZ_i} + P_i \frac{dn_i}{dZ_i}}{W \cdot \frac{dt_j}{dZ_j} + p_i \frac{dx_j}{dZ_j}} = \frac{MCZ_i}{MCZ_j} \tag{8.8}$$

(8.8) tells us that the ratio of the marginal utilities of any two commodities Z_i and Z_j must equal the ratio of their marginal costs and the derivatives are the marginal 'input/output coefficients'. In other words the marginal cost of any Z is its 'shadow price', i.e. it is determined by the prices of market goods and time *and* by the productivity of these market goods and time in producing the Z.

earnings). By separating the goods and time components (8.6) and (8.8) indicate some of the likely trade-offs in household decision-making. For example, an increase in the relative price of Z_i would reduce the amount consumed by the household and, if the increased cost of Z_i results from a rise in the wage rate, then a relatively higher proportion of the increased cost would fall on those 'final goods' which rely relatively heavily on time inputs into the production function. The Becker prediction in this case would run as follows: an increase in the wage rate (compensated by a decline in property income) would not affect *total* household opportunities but would produce two substitution effects – (a) *goods* would be substituted for *time* in the production of 'final commodities', and (b) goods – intensive 'commodities' – would be substituted for time-intensive commodities in consumption.

The immediate appeal of Becker's approach is apparent. By a reorientation of approach away from consumption towards production the economic approach to household behaviour becomes much more operational, and its predictive capabilities depend largely on identifying, from the data, two clearly defined substitution effects. However, the attractions of the approach have proved to be much greater than this to many economists, not least among them Becker himself, because of its very wide applications. Through his definition of 'full income' Becker has attempted to explain household behaviour in terms of an all-embracing time constraint which would seem to some observers to break down the traditional demarcation lines between economics and other disciplines – all aspects of social behaviour are, in one sense at least, a response to the problem of allocating scarce time among competing ends. Two areas of social inquiry where Becker's approach has had a major impact and has spawned considerable debate are criminology (Becker, 1976) and marriage and family formation (Becker, 1976; Schultz, 1974; Liebenstein, 1976).

However, we are not yet at the end of the possibilities. An approach which is aiming to explain and predict objectively is uncomfortable with the presence of 'undefinables' such as 'tastes'. Tastes, more often than not, are assumed as given in microeconomics; they are represented by a symbol tucked away towards the end of a list of parameters in the demand function. If ever this parameter changes then the whole model is upset and often in an unpredictable manner – 'there is no accounting for tastes' has a double meaning for the economists. Obviously Becker's approach has a much weakened predictive potential if tastes are allowed to exert an independent, parametric influence, and in a later work (Stigler and Becker, 1977) an attempt was made to resolve this problem of tastes.

Any approach to consumer theory which avoids reference to tastes is bound to have consequences for marketing management, and we should pursue this matter further at this point. Bluntly, the Stigler/Becker position is that tastes do not change, nor do they differ significantly among people! They reach this position by adopting the production function approach to household behaviour so that any changes in such behaviour for a given household, or any differences in such behaviour among households, are explained solely in terms of relative prices and incomes. Their view of *consumption* is one of investment, or life cycle, and they adopt this as a challenge to the conventional view that tastes change as a result of consuming 'addictive' goods, for example, cigarette smoking, drinking alcohol, 'shooting' heroin, or close contact with people or things. Such activities lead to 'addiction' which, according to the conventional wisdom, is explained by saying that marginal utility rises over time because tastes shift in favour of the things being consumed; according to Marshall the more good music a man hears the stronger is his taste for it likely to become.

The Stigler/Becker explanation of, say, an individual's increased demand for music lies in the individual's accumulation of 'consumption capital', i.e. by 'investing' more time and attention in the 'production' of music appreciation an individual will eventually reap the returns of a heightened appreciation of music. The model suggests the following. The individual's preference function is unchanging over time and it contains music as a basic component. Music appreciation *now* is produced by current inputs of market goods (records, hi-fi equipment, etc.) and *time* and music appreciation in the *future* is, in part, produced by the current period's investment in music appreciation and in time spent on current consumption. Hence, over the life cycle, productivity increases mean that the 'price' of enjoying music falls but that the time spent in enjoying music will not necessarily rise, because increased consumption capital raises 'appreciation productivity'. In contrast with the traditional view, then, the time spent in enjoying music is more likely to rise (i.e. enjoyment becomes 'addictive') *the more elastic is the demand for music*. There is no need to resort to an assumption that tastes or preferences have shifted. (In the case of harmful addictions, such as those resulting from drug abuse, the model works in a similar fashion, albeit with negative signs.)

Critique

Starting with the Stigler/Becker developments, the model seems to be over-extended. Common sense seems to suggest that an increasing familiarity with a certain type of music may lead to a heightened appreciation of that type of music; it suggests also that no amount of exposure to a certain type of music is going to produce anything but increased loathing of it by the individual! What the model does not tell us, however, is *why* some individuals *want* to invest time and other inputs into the 'production' of appreciation of certain types of music. Within the Stigler/Becker framework there is no room for qualitative shifts in appreciation.

Another criticism of this approach is that, like much of capital theory, it collapses inter-temporal choice problems into the calculus of present values. To this extent, therefore, it fails to observe the changing nature of the individual as he passes through the life cycle. As Buchanan (1979) has emphasized, man has a view of himself, he not only knows what he is now but he has a vision of himself for the future, he knows the type of person he wants to become and this, more than anything else, distinguishes him from the animals. This view of man sees him as choosing his image and moving towards it, i.e. *changing*! The dream may or may not be fulfilled through time but *ex post* he cannot go *ex ante* (back) and change the dream – he becomes a different individual with, by definition, *different preferences*. This harks back to comments made earlier in this chapter regarding theories of consumer behaviour – there are many influences upon the ways in which individuals develop into the beings that they originally perceived themselves as becoming in the future – good manners, codes of conduct, commitment to causes, morals, etc.

Returning now to the seminal model and its treatment of time, we can echo comments made in chapter 2 on the valuation of output. Becker's theory of the allocation of household time does not distinguish between the utility obtained from doing things and the utility obtained from consuming things. Thus an individual who enjoys baking is assumed to derive satisfaction only from the bread he eats, not from the bread he makes. Of course this argument might be countered by introducing the concept of *net advantages* which is employed in labour economics. The person who likes baking will then be prepared to put a different price on his units of labour from the individual who dislikes baking but likes bread. Whilst this defence takes care of some doubts it does not remove them all. Once the production process is looked upon in the same way as the production processes of firms, and once labour is admitted as an input, then we are forced to recognize other peculiarities of labour. Unlike goods, labour services cannot be stored. Moreover, some activities can only be performed at certain times of the day, week or year. In other words production processes, because they are often sequential, tend to be time-specific; that is, operations can only be carried out at a certain times. Thus, children go to school in the day and not at night and, as shiftworkers soon discover, there are few places of entertainment open during the day.

In Becker's model the fundamental problem is not to allocate time but to allocate labour services, and the impression is given that activities can be performed in any units of time. This sleight of hand seems to arise because time is transformed into income which can be spent at any time, and goods are available which can also be consumed in any time period. However, even when we ignore the interrelationship between time and uncertainty and assume foreseeable events, such as night and day, we cannot ignore the fact that activities are atemporal.

Goods Characteristics

Another 'modern' approach to the theory of consumer behaviour, and again one which adopts a production methodology, is that developed by Kelvin Lancaster (1966). This model is critical of the utility/indifference approach from the viewpoints of both construction and practical significance – the utility/indifference approach looks at choices among commodities, whereas consumers, according to Lancaster, are interested really in the *characteristics* of commodities. In order to predict the market impact of a new commodity from its effect on the choices of a representative consumer the utility/indifference approach requires that a set of new preference maps be drawn up in order to compare the new commodity with the existing range of commodities which appear in the consumer's preference function. Lancaster's model aims to correct these drawbacks and we can demonstrate how it works by the following examples:

Example 1: Two characteristics/two goods
The analysis begins with a very simple model of two goods, each possessing the same two clearly defined characteristics, but in differing proportions. Let us suppose the two commodities to be household disinfectants which offer to rid premises of germs (characteristic G) while giving off a pleasant scent (characteristic S) in the process. Product A ('Alpine') offers the characteristics in the ratio of $1G$ to $5S$ while B ('Beatgerm') offers $1S$ to $5G$. We assume also that the amounts of these characteristics enjoyed by any consumer are directly proportional to the quantities consumed of A and B, and that characteristics are additive.

Now consider figure 8.4, which shows the choices facing a representative consumer. The consumer is assumed to allocate £4 per month to the purchase of disinfectants and the prices of A and B (per bottle) are 50p and 40p respectively. The first question to ask is what are the various combinations of *characteristics* that the consumer can obtain from his budget allocation of £4?

In figure 8.4 points along the ray OA represent combinations of characteristics G and S in the ratio $1S : 5G$. Therefore distance along the ray OA is determined by the amount of good A purchased. By spending £4 per month on commodity A the consumer can purchase 8 bottles which will yield him 40 units of characteristics G and 8 units of S – he is at point A'. Points along the ray OB show combinations of G and S in the ratio $1G : 5S$ and distance along the ray is determined by the amount of B purchased. By spending £4 (per month) on B the consumer is able to purchase 10 bottles, which will yield him 10 units of characteristic G and 50 units of S – he is at point B'.

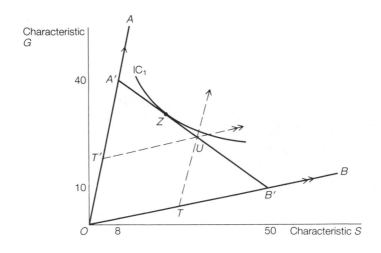

Figure 8.4

The rays OA and OB show bundles of characteristics which could be obtained if only one or the other commodity were to be purchased. However, by allocating his expenditures between both commodities the consumer faces a wider variety of combinations of characteristics. These possibilities lie along the line $A'B'$ which is derived from the consumer travelling along one characteristics ray (buying quantities of one good only) and then turning and travelling parallel to the other ray (buying quantities of the other good). For example, point U is reached by moving along OB until point T is reached, *halfway* along OB, and then moving from T, parallel to OA, i.e. the dotted line through U from T is parallel to OA and the dotted line from T' through U is parallel to OB. It should be clear that U is reached by spending £2 on each commodity: £2 spent on A buys 4 bottles, offering 20 units of G and 4 of S; while £2 spent on B buys 5 bottles, offering 5 units of G and 25 units of S.

Thus $A'B'$ represents a consumption possibilities frontier or *budget line for characteristics*. If the consumer's budget allocation rises, with unchanged prices, then this budget line shifts outwards, parallel to its original position (inwards for a reduced allocation), and if relative prices change then the *slope* of the budget line alters. Note, however, that it is the object of choice (characteristics) and not the mode of choice which differentiates this approach from traditional analysis. *The consumer must still choose.* In figure 8.4 an indifference curve, IC_1, the slope of which represents the marginal rate of substitution between characteristics, is tangential to $A'B'$ at point Z which represents, therefore, the best combination of characteristics which can be obtained with the available budget allocation.

Example 2: Two characteristics/three goods
Suppose now that a rival commodity C (' Clean-Glow') appears on the market in potential competition with A and B. The new commodity possesses the same characteristics as the existing ones, but in different proportions to both, i.e. $3G : 5S$. However, it is not the relative characteristics proportions which determine C's position in the consumer's budget allocation, rather it is the price of C relative to the prices of competing goods. Suppose, for example, that good C is offered initially at a price of 80p per bottle – figure 8.5 shows the consequences for such a marketing strategy.

In figure 8.5 the ray of OC plots combinations of G and S in the ratio of $3 : 5$ and shows the potential technical competition between C and the existing products (OC lying between OA and OB). However, at the initial price of 80p per bottle, a consumer's budget allocation of £4 (per month) purchases 5 bottles and a consequent characteristics combination of $15G$ and $25S$, i.e. point C'''! Clearly the consumer would not choose such an inefficient point since the same £4 spent on either A or B, or on some combination of A and B, enables the budget line $A'B'$ to be reached, and more of both characteristics to be consumed, e.g. point C''. It might be added that since all consumers face the same relative prices, albeit with different budget allocations, they face the same budget *slopes*, and therefore C''' must lie inside C'' for all consumers – at a price of 80p per bottle the producer of C *would have no buyers*.

Suppose now that the price of C is lowered to 50p per bottle. This permits the consumer to buy 5 bottles of C, at point C' and to enjoy a combination of

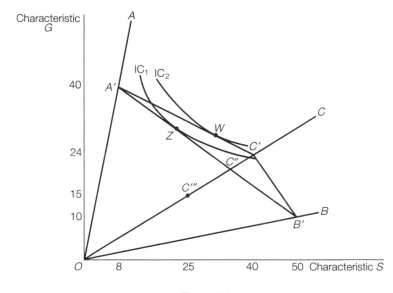

Figure 8.5

24 units of G and 40 units of S, if his £4 allocation is spent entirely on C. Thus, C'' is now inefficient since it lies inside any budget line linking C' to either $A(A'C')$ or B $(C'B')$. The full range of new possibilities lies along $A'C'B'$. Given his preference map, the consumer chooses point W which is on a higher indifference curve than Z (note that a 'corner solution' at C' would be possible with some other set of preferences).

The analysis we have discussed has been extended by Lipsey and Rosenbluth (1971) to the cases of inferior and Giffen goods with surprising results. They suggest that, far from being curiosum, Giffen goods may be common, and may occur when a small (and not large) percentage of income is devoted to a good. However, no empirical evidence to support their conclusions has been offered.

Critique

The drawback to the characteristics approach is that, since the consumer still has to choose, the predictions of consumer behaviour from the model still depend upon a preference map (for characteristics). However, in some respects the characteristics approach would seem to have more to offer the marketing analyst than the traditional approach, particularly in a world of rapidly changing consumer technology. The traditional approach requires a redefinition of the consumer's preference ordering each time a new product appears on the market, but defining preference maps in terms of characteristics avoids this problem and enables management to realize quickly the consequences of aiming to market a product with similar characteristics to a commodity (or commodities) already available to consumers. It is fairly clear from the above analysis that products offering the same characteristics are substitute goods – there is no need to try and *deduce* this by a roundabout method of measuring cross-elasticities of demand and imputing a substitute relationship for the commodities within the consumer's preference map – and that the closer are two goods in a technical (characteristics) sense, the more likely it is that one of them will be an inferior good.

As a final note it is interesting to see the links between the approaches of Becker and Lancaster. One example where this link is clear is the market for convenience goods. Over time there has been a substantial rise in demand for convenience foods despite also a rise in the price of such foods relative to the price of fresh foodstuffs. This trend is exactly what would be predicted by the Becker/Lancaster approach, in the following way.

Over time there has been a rise in the (real) market wage rate which has meant that the opportunity cost of 'non-market' activities has also been rising. This rise in the shadow price of non-market, i.e. household, activities has meant a related increase in the price of time-intensive commodities relative to the price of goods-intensive commodities. As a result households have experienced a substitution effect, away from time-intensive final commodities and towards goods-intensive ones – 'home cooking' has become more time-expensive than reconstitution of frozen or dehydrated foods. What has this to do with Lancaster? The link lies in the fact that commodities which differ in their time-intensities are likely to differ also in their other characteristics. Thus the choice between goods-intensive and time-intensive meals may involve a choice between market goods which offer characteristics like flavour and convenience in different proportions. Figure 8.6 shows the results. *AC* represents the original budget line with the consumer located at *a*. A rise in the

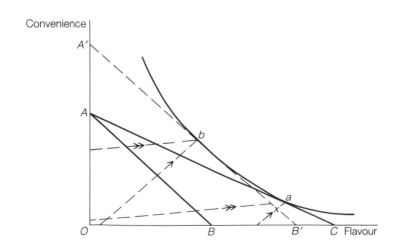

Figure 8.6

market wage rate cause the 'full' price of the flavour-intensive commodities to rise and the new budget line becomes *AB*. The substitution effect of the change in relative prices induces a switch towards convenience characteristics and away from flavour – from *a* to *b*.

Summary of Becker/Lancaster

By way of summary we suggest four ways at which the Becker/Lancaster approach offers new insights into consumer behaviour which are of importance to the marketing manager:

1 Relative prices have no effect on choice unless they are large enough to cause a brand switch, although it might be possible to obtain some small changes by combining brands.
2 Commodity 'bundling' can be performed either by firms or house-holds, depending upon the opportunity cost of time. This is especially relevant when attention is focused on married people who attempt to combine 'housework' and market work. A switch to convenience foods may result from a different method of commodity bundling by households rather than a change in tastes.
3 It is possible to incorporate some uncertainty into the analysis of consumer behaviour by assuming it to be reflected in certain charac-teristics, e.g. 'reliability', 'availability', etc.
4 Emphasizing characteristics is a constant reminder of the underlying importance of the hierarchy of wants.

The Demand for Durable Goods

The analogy between household and firm can be carried a little further by recognition of the existence of durable household goods. In the theory of the firm it is customary to assume that firms purchase durable capital goods, the flow of services from which is entirely within the control of management, and labour services which are subject to both managers' and workers' attitudes to production. Of course, as we shall see later, the existence of long-term contracts does permit managers some degree of control over the fund of labour services, but there is still the problem that the personality of the worker accompanies his fund of services. We can also assume that households pur-chase durable capital goods, the services of which can be varied, the major distinction between household and firm in this respect seeming to lie in the relative unimportance of the budget constraint for the firm.

The introduction of a demand for durable consumer goods does, however, raise difficult and complex issues both for households and suppliers of those goods.

1 Durability introduces a distinction beween purchases and consump-tion. Purchase is at a point of time, whereas consumption is a flow

over time. It may be assumed that consumption is proportional to the stock of the good but that is only one assumption about depreciation.

2   In addition to depreciation, decisions to purchase can be influenced by obsolescence (changes of fashion and technical change).
3   Durability means that current decisions can be influenced by past decisions.
4   Long-run price and income expectations may be important determinants of purchase.
5   Purchases may be volatile if households use transitory income to purchase goods which yield long-run permanent income and consumption.
6   Durable goods may incorporate complex technologies, and knowledge about them may take time to spread through the market.
7   Volatility of purchases may give rise to shortages and gluts which may not be alleviated by price changes but by rationing and stockpiling.
8   Durability can give rise to the coexistence of new and second-hand markets, and the latter may not be well developed, with the consequence that consumers have to be wary of 'lemons' (Akerlof, 1970); that is, goods whose defects cannot be discovered until after purchase (see chapter 2).

The consumer's problem may be viewed as one of minimizing the cost per unit of service provided by a durable good and this involves seeking a compromise between: (1) the price per unit of a durable good per unit of time; and (2) the maintenance or operating cost per service unit per unit of time. One method of calculating the price per service unit would be to take the loan repayment per unit on a bank loan or hire purchase agreement. If such agreements do cover maintenance then the consumers' problems are somewhat easy to resolve: the marginal utility per unit of service would be equated with the loan repayment per time unit.

Uncertainty

So far we have ignored the problems posed by uncertainty. We have tended *pace* Buchanan to assume that the consumer knows what he wants, and that the benefits which may accrue instantly or over time are known with certainty. Yet except in the case of goods habitually purchased, there is an element of uncertainty as to the benefits which will be obtained. Uncertainty stems from the difficulty of knowing whether a commodity will yield the benefits expected, and culminates in the problem of whether the best quality has been obtained at the lowest price. Hence we need to consider whether the problem posed by uncertainty can be incorporated into utility theory, and how a consumer might reduce uncertainty by acquiring more information about the qualities of goods through a search procedure incorporating the use of a scarce commodity, time, or whether uncertainty can be reduced by purchasing insurance.

Expected Utility Theory

The most widely used model of decision-making under uncertainty embodies what is known as the *expected utility theorem*. The essence of the theorem is that an individual will estimate the utility he will obtain from each possible outcome or state of the world, and the probability that each will occur. The utility associated with each outcome is then multiplied by the probability that it will occur, and the expected utility is the sum of these probability-weighted utilities:

$$EU = p \, . \, U(A) + (1 - p) \, U(B) \qquad (8.9)$$

where EU is the expected utility, A and B are the states of the world, p is the probability of A occurring and $(1-p)$ is the probability of B occurring.

Thus, to take an example, suppose that an individual bets £10 at odds of 5 to 1 that a particular team will win the FA Cup, and that the probability of such a win is 1/15. The expected utility of the gamble is calculated by finding the gambler's wealth in the event of the team winning or losing. The expected utility is:

$$EU = 1/15 \, . \, U(W_0 + 50) + 14/15(W_0 - 10) \qquad (8.10)$$

The first term on the right-hand side of the equation is composed of the probability of winning (1/15) and the utility associated with the final wealth ($W_0 + 50$); that is, the initial wealth plus the winnings. The second term gives the probability of losing the bet $(1 - 1/15)$ and the utility associated with initial wealth being reduced by £10. Now most individuals are *risk-averse*, and will only undertake a gamble if the expected utility from the gamble exceeds the utility that might be expected from the initial wealth. In the case we have been considering the gamble would be rejected because the expected gain in actuarial terms is negative.

$$50 \, . \, 1/15 - 10 \, . \, 14/15 < 0 \qquad (8.11)$$

Only an individual who derived utility from gambling *per se* would undertake such odds.

Although we have taken a gamble with only two outcomes, the approach can be generalized to handle any number of possible states of the world provided that they are all mutually exclusive. Hence we can write expected utility as

$$EU = \sum_{i=1}^{n} \pi U_i \qquad (8.12)$$

where π is the probability of outcome i and U_i is the utility attaching to that outcome.

Searching for the Lowest Price and the Best Quality

We can now apply the expected utility approach to considering an individual faced with finding the lowest price for a commodity. The simplest procedure would be to sample prices until the expected marginal utility from search is equal to the marginal cost of search. In figure 8.7 the consumer assumes that the prices of a good are normally distributed with a mean of £10. Suppose, then, that the consumer obtains a price quotation of £8. One-quarter of all prices lie below £8 and the average of all these lower prices is £7.60. If the customer shopped at another store the probability is three-quarters that a higher price would be found, and one-quarter that a lower price would be found, with a difference of £0.40. If we then assume that the consumer values the expected benefit from searching another shop at £0.11 then she will search if the extra cost is less than £0.11. If the search costs exceed £0.11 then she will accept the offer of £8.

In the above example we have assumed that the commodity being bought was a once-for-all purchase and that it was not an everyday item, such as food. This assumption rules out any benefits from finding the cheapest place to shop, which could then be used a store of information for future purchases. We also assumed that prices would not change after they were sampled. We could, of course, have modified the analysis by assuming that the probability distribution was based upon past experience and television and press adverts but there is the additional problem of whether the prices would still be prevailing and the goods would still be available when the consumer visits the shop.

The problem of finding the best quality is much more difficult to analyse, and depends upon how quality is to be assessed. Thus, if quality could be assessed before purchase by simple inspection, then the search process would be similar to that for finding the lowest price. If however, quality can be assessed only after purchase then the costs of consumption can be considerably increased and a consumer might decide to take out some form of insurance.

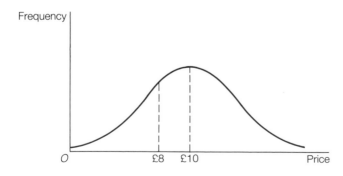

Figure 8.7

Insurance

In figure 8.8 we measure the incomes or benefits associated with two states of the world, S_a and S_b, along the axes of the diagram and the indifference curves indicate the individual's preference for the income associated with various combinations of S_a and S_b. The slope of the budget line AB measures the rate of exchange between income in states a and b – in other words, the cost of insurance. Now if a consumer were offered the prospect given by P she could raise her utility by trading along AB until she reached T. That is, she could trade some of the income in state b for more income in state a.

Insurance policies can take a variety of forms. The simplest would be where a consumer judges quality by price and is willing to pay a higher price in order to avoid a possible defective commodity; in this example the cost of insurance is obvious. Another strategy might be to wait until the good has been tested by other consumers – a form of consulting the experts. Alternatively, a consumer might prefer advertised and branded goods because she believes that firms which repeatedly advertise are indicating by their investment in advertising that they sell good-quality goods. The methods of obtaining insurance are, in fact endless, and are deeply rooted in the socialization processes by which society ensures its survival.

Expected Utility Theory: a Critique

The fact that there are different insurance procedures serves to draw attention to the various criticisms that have been brought against the concept of expected utility, and they raise the question: are there different kinds of uncertainty (just as there are different kinds of wants) which may require different procedures for their resolution?

The expected utility theorem assumes that people form prior probabilities, act upon the basis of these probabilities, and then they may revise those

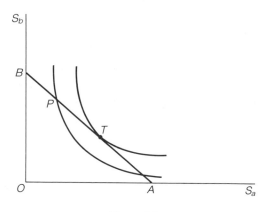

Figure 8.8

probabilities if they find that they are wrong. The question therefore arises: do people structure problems in the manner suggested by the theory? Laboratory studies have suggested that people may ignore evidence even when it can be used to form prior probabilities. For example, Kahneman (1982) found that respondents who were given a description of a person as being quiet and meticulous concluded that he must be a librarian, despite being told that librarians formed only a small percentage of the labour force. Of course it may be argued that laboratory experiments are unrealistic. Yet they do have the merit of focusing attention upon important issues, and remove much of the extraneous material and noise present in the real world. Furthermore there is the argument that, although people do not explicitly form probabilities, they act as if they do so. However, there now exist a considerable number of cases or examples which suggest that the theory should be modified or abandoned (Schoemaker, 1982).

Alternative Approaches and Some Conclusions

Given the limitations of the economist's approach to consumer behaviour it may be pertinent to consider the contributions which other disciplines can make. During the 1950s and 1960s marketeers turned increasingly to psychologists and sociologists for help in unravelling consumers' wants. One good reason for this apparent rejection of economics was that the long and sustained rise in real incomes forced attention upon the nature of new wants which consumers might be striving to meet and to articulate, and that economic analysis tended to ignore income effects and concentrated upon substitution effects associated with different goods which might satisfy the same want. A defence, or revival, of economic analysis in the 1980s might be due to the much slower growth of real incomes forcing consumers and marketeers to concentrate upon 'value for money' and substitution effects. Rather than concluding our discussion on that note we shall attempt to review the contributions of other disciplines and consider two questions. First, what is the nature of their contributions? Second, are their contributions complementary to those of economists? In pursuing these lines of inquiry we shall make use of three sources of information. First, we shall refer to the relative frequency of specific major topics in marketing journals over a 30-year period. Second, we shall consider a model of consumer behaviour, the Howard–Sheth model, which is widely cited in marketing textbooks. Third, we shall include in the discussion some references to textbooks such as that of Kotler (1984).

Figure 8.9 reveals the frequency of occurrence of specific major topics in consumer behaviour between 1950 and 1981. The topics are classified under four headings: (1) forces internal to the consumer; (2) external factors which impinge upon and shape consumers' behaviour; (3) factors influencing the purchasing decision; and (4) a miscellaneous category. We shall ignore the miscellaneous group, partly because it raises issues, such as consumerism, which lie outside the scope of the present chapter, and partly because some of the other topics mentioned might be considered within the scope of the first three groups.

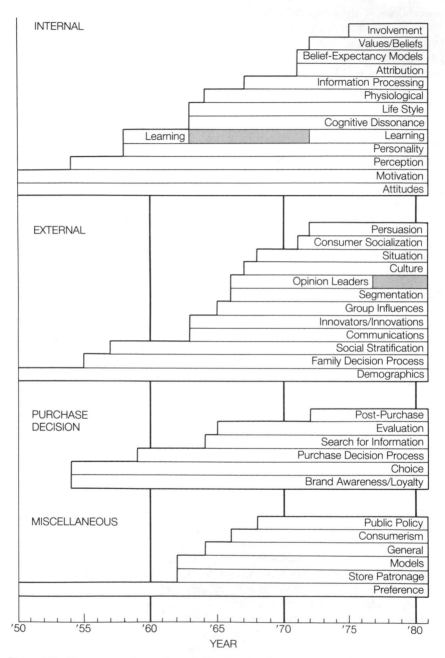

Figure 8.9 Occurrence of specific major topics over time. (*Source*: Helgeson, J.G., Law, E.A., Kluge, J., Mager, J., and Taylor, C. (1984) 'Trends in consumer behavior: content analysis', *Journal of Consumer Research*, 10, 449–54.)

Confining our attention to the first three categories, we may begin by observing that the internal factors raise in a very sharp way the theories of consumer behaviour provided by different disciplines. Thus economists, as we have noted, emphasize the rationality of consumer behaviour, whereas psychologists have sometimes drawn attention to what economists might regard as irrational behaviour. Kotler (1965), for example, in his study of behavioural models for analysing buyers, has distinguished between five models of how buyers translate buying influences into purchasing decisions. Thus, Freudian man's choices are influenced strongly by motives and fantasies which take place deep within his private world. Veblenian man acts in a way which is shaped largely by past and present social groups. Pavlovian man behaves in a largely habitual (rather than thoughtful) way and certain configurations of 'cues' will set off the same behaviour because of rewarded learning in the past. Hobbesian man seeks to reconcile individual gain with organizational gain. Only Marshallian man is concerned chiefly with economic cues, such as prices and income.

Now preferences and motives may be shaped by motives and fantasies which take place within the private world of the individual, and some economists might concede that the formation of preferences is not a subject for economists. However, irrational behaviour may have economic consequences and what, from the point of view of the economists, may appear to be irrational behaviour might, from the point of view of the psychologist, be predictable. Thus consider the problem of *cognitive dissonance* which appears in the first category. Most people consider themselves to be 'smart, nice people' and feel uncomfortable in maintaining two seemingly contradictory ideas. In other words they attempt to avoid cognitive dissonance, a technical term which refers to post-purchase anxiety or doubt which the buyer of a product, especially an expensive product, sometimes develops. This doubt may be a partial carry-over from the pre-purchase period when the buyer had trouble making a choice. Thus if the product was a car with attractive and unattractive features then the consumer may, after consideration, choose a particular car in the belief that its attractive features outweigh its unattractive features. Once the car is in his possession, however, the less attractive features may start to bother him, and doubts set in.

Cognitive dissonance is usually put forward as a reason for manufacturers maintaining post-purchase advertising in order to reassure the buyer that the product he has bought is the one for him. We should, however, note two points in connection with cognitive dissonance. First, it is reasonable to assume that buyers will sometimes make mistakes. Second, in the case of goods which are frequently purchased, such as foodstuffs, it is unlikely that doubts will set in. To take another problem, it is possible that an individual may be irrational in the sense of not maintaining a consistent ranking of alternatives. Nevertheless it is possible that some forms of irrational behaviour will be forced to conform to the constraints imposed by the budget line (Becker, 1962).

There are, however, other topics in the first category upon which the economist can comment. Thus what in psychology is referred to as 'motivation theory' is called by the economist 'utility theory'. Psychologists and economists share a common belief in the concept of a hierarchy of wants. Furthermore, we may note that many psychologists, such as Ward Edwards (1967), have found utility theory of immense usefulness in the study of decision-making. In economics learning theory or learning effects are discussed usually in production theory in terms of inputs of resources and resulting output – but this approach can be applied to consumer theory also.

In the second category the most obvious topic for consideration is the influence exerted by the family and friends. Now it is possible to modify the utility function to incorporate external effects. Thus A's utility may be a function of the goods he consumes and the utility enjoyed by others. This approach has been applied in the theory of charitable behaviour. Furthermore, the behaviour of others may, as we have observed earlier, be a means by which an individual overcomes uncertainty. Where the economist might diverge from the psychologist and the sociologist is in his more comprehensive study of life-cycle decisions on consumption and production. Thus the Joneses with whom an individual wishes to keep up may not be the Joneses with whom he currently interacts, but some peer group whose company he wishes to join at some later date. Hence his employment decisions, as well as his consumption and savings decisions, may be influenced by his notions as to his desired permanent income and consumption.

The Howard–Sheth Model of Consumer Behaviour (1969)

That the contributions of economics and other social sciences to the study of consumer behaviour may be complementary can be reinforced by an examination of the Howard–Sheth model which is illustrated in figure 8.10. The model has four principal components: stimulus variables (inputs), response variables, hypothetical constructs, and exogenous variables. On the left-hand side of the diagram are the stimulus variables, and on the right-hand side are the response variables. In the central area of this consumption function are the response variables which offset the state of the consumer: these comprise perception, learning and motivation, which are the information and decision-making processes. Surmounting the flow chart are exogenous factors which intervene between stimulus and response: these variables are such things as personality, social class and culture, which in the economic analysis would be 'locked into' the state of technology of the consumption function.

Howard and Sheth distinguish between *significative* variables, which are communicated directly by actual brand products in the form of price, quality, etc., and *symbolic* variables, which are communicated indirectly by salesmen and advertising. The mix of significative and symbolic variables is, of course, influenced by management's views on the efficiency of various marketing variables (and these will be examined from the point of view of management in succeeding chapters).

Response to stimuli are seen to depend upon the following factors:

1   attention – the sensitivity of the consumer to the stimulus,

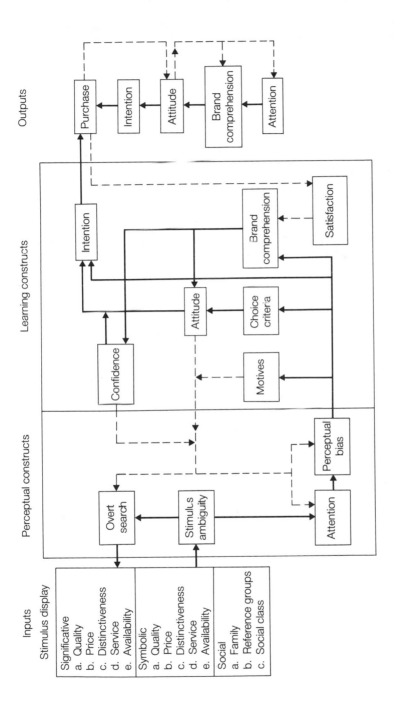

Figure 8.10 Howard–Sheth model of consumer behaviour.

2   comprehension – the amount of knowledge which a consumer poss-
    esses about a good,
3   attitude – the buyer's assessment of a good's potential to satisfy his
    needs,
4   intention – the predisposition to buy a good,
5   purchase behaviour – the act of purchase which confirms intention.

From the responses arise feedbacks which influence subsequent buying
decisions and which may or may not lead to repeat buying.

In addition to the Howard–Sheth model there are others, with similarities,
put forward by Engall et al. (1978), Nicosia (1966) and Andraesen (1965).
However, the Howard–Sheth model illustrates many of the basic features of
these models and their complementarity with economic analysis. Thus motivation theory may be interpreted in terms of utility theory and, following Becker,
social class and race (culture) may be quantified in terms of their effect upon
income. Many of the other features of the flow diagram will be appreciated
after we have examined managerial decisions about price, nature of product
and advertising expenditures.

Bibliography and References

Akerlof, G. A. (1970) 'The market for "lemons" : quality uncertainty and the market-
    mechanism', *Quarterly Journal of Economics*, 84, 488–500.
Andraesen, A. R. (1965) 'Attitudes and customer behaviour: a decision model', in L.
    E. Preston (ed.) *New Research in Marketing*. Berkeley, Calif.: University of California
    Press.
Becker, G. S. (1962) 'Irrational behaviour and economic theory', *Journal of Political
    Economic Theory*, 70, 1–13.
Becker, G. S. (1965) 'A theory of the allocation of time', *Economic Journal*, 75, 493–
    517.
Becker, G. S. (1971) *Economic Theory*. New York: Alfred Knopf.
Becker, G. S. (1976) *The Economic Approach to Human Behavior*. Chicago: University
    of Chicago Press.
Buchanan, J. M. (1979) *What Should Economists Do?* Indianapolis: Liberty Press.
Deaton, A. and Muellbauer, J. (1980) *Economics and Consumer Behaviour*. Cambridge:
    Cambridge University Press.
Edwards, Ward and Tversky, A. (1967) *Decision Making*. London: Penguin Books.
Engall, J. F. Kellak, J. and Blackwell, T. (1978) *Consumer Behavior*, 4th edn. London:
    Dryden.
Georgescu-Roegen, N. (1966) *Analytical Economics*. Cambridge, Mass.: Harvard Uni-
    versity Press.
Georgescu-Roegen, N. (1968) 'Utility'. In D. S. Shils (ed.), *Encyclopedia of Social
    Sciences*. London: Collier-Macmillan.
Ghez, G. R. and Becker, G. S. (1975) *The Allocation of Time and Goods over the Life
    Cycle*. New York: Columbia University Press.
Green, H. A. J. (1971) *Consumer Theory*. London: Penguin Books.
Hey, J. D. and McKenna, C. J. (1981) 'Consumer search with uncertain product
    quality', *Journal of Political Economy*, 89, 54–66.
Hicks, J. R. (1956) *A Revision of Demand Theory*. Oxford: Oxford University Press.

Hicks, J. R. and Allen, R. G. D. (1934) 'A reconsideration of the theory of value', *Economica*, new series, 1, 52–76.

Howard, R. A. and Sheth, J. N. (1969) *The Theory of Buyer Behavior*. New York: Wiley.

Kahneman, D. (1982) *Judgement under Uncertainty*. Cambridge: Cambridge University Press.

Kotler, P. (1984) *Marketing Management*, 5th edn. New York: Prentice Hall.

Lancaster, K. J. (1966) 'A new approach to consumer theory', *Journal of Political Economy*, 74, 132–57.

Leibenstein, H. (1976) *Beyond Economic Man*. New York: Oxford University Press.

Lipsey, R. G. and Rosenbluth, G. (1971) 'A contribution to the new theory of demand', *Canadian Journal of Economics*, 4, 131–63.

Marshall, A. (1920) *Principles of Economics*, 8th edn. London: Macmillan.

Maslow, A. H. (1954) *Motivation and Personality*. New York: Harper and Row.

Nicosia, F. M. (1966) *Consumer Decision Processes*. New York: Prentice Hall.

Rothschild, M. (1979) 'Searching for the lowest price when the distribution of prices is unknown', *Journal of Political economy*, 67, 1328–46.

Samuelson, P. A. (1938) 'New foundation for the pure theory of consumer's behaviour', *Economica*, 5, 61–71.

Schoemaker, P. J. H. (1983) 'The expected utility model: its variants, purposes, evidence and limitations', *Journal of Economic Literature*, 20, 529–63.

Schultz, T. W. (1974) *The Economics of the Family*. Chicago: University of Chicago Press.

Stigler, G. J. (1962) 'Information in the labor market', *Journal of Political Economy*, 70, 94–105.

Stigler, G. J. and Becker, G. S. (1977) 'De gustibus non est disputandem', *American Economic Review*, 67, 76–90.

9 Pricing Policy and Market Structure

Flex-price and Fix-price Markets

Markets can be classified into flex-price and fix-price markets. In flex-price markets the available stock of the commodity is 'thrown' on to the market in order to obtain the best price. In fix-price markets goods are placed on the market with a price tag and there is a presumption that buyers will be able to buy the good at the stipulated price over a period of time. Flex-price markets tend to be associated with primary products and foodstuffs and with developing countries, whereas fix-price markets tend to be associated with manufactured goods and developed economies. The rationale for the distinction is two-fold. First, many primary products cannot be stored and their perishable nature means that they must be sold within a limited period. Second, consumers in advanced economies have high incomes, their opportunity cost of searching is high, and they are presumed to value the convenience of standardized, branded goods which are readily available at a given price. The arguments, however, do not constitute a complete analysis. It would be possible for people on high incomes to employ specialists to locate goods at the lowest price; and flex-price markets can be found in advanced economies. Thus antiques, plots for oilfields and government contracts are frequently sold in flex-price markets.

Markets can be classified also according to the prevailing degree of competition. This is not to say that there is a one-to-one relationship between, say, perfect competition and flex-price markets and, say, monopoly and fix-price markets. However, these market structures do possess characteristics which foster differing degrees of price flexibility. To the extent that perfect competition is characterized by primary (and homogeneous) products, low transactions costs and firms' inability to influence market price through relative output shares, it is likely that market prices will be flexible. To the extent that monopoly is characterized by manufactured (and differentiated) products, high transactions costs and a firm's output being able to affect market price, it is likely that product prices will exhibit a degree of fixity.

Of course, it is difficult to define precisely the degree of competition in a market since a given range of price flexibility (or rigidity) cannot provide a sufficient condition for defining a market as 'monopolistic' or 'competitive'. One way round this problem is to identify markets according to demand elasticities; this suggestion is explored later in this chapter. Assuming, then, that it *is* possible to classify market structures, it could be expected that the possibility of a horizontal marginal cost curve, or at least a marginal cost curve with a horizontal section in it, is likely to be a feature of monopoly, where market power permits long output runs and the consequent economies of large-scale production. As we shall see later, built-in flexibility of productive capacity permits a range of outputs to be produced at one price, whereas the constraints of a U-shaped marginal cost curve, as faced by the perfectly competitive firm, require price to change with output in order to maintain the firm's profit-maximizing equilibrium. Much of this chapter is taken up with further discussion of these issues and also with other implications of monopoly for the behaviour of firms' managers. However, first, to set the scene, we explore the nature of the auction process by which many goods are valued in the market place.

Auction Markets

At the risk of oversimplification, we may adopt a simple classification of auction markets as follows:

1 Open auctions
   (a) English auction
   (b) Dutch auction
2 Sealed-bid auctions
3 Waiting-line (fix-price) auctions.

In open auctions every bidder is able to observe his rivals' bids, whereas in sealed-bid auctions, information on rivals' bids is not available. Waiting-line auctions are similar to sealed-bid auctions in that the values underlying bids are not observable.

In an English auction, or ascending-bid system, the individual who makes the highest bid obtains the commodity being offered for sale. The price of any article sold will therefore be the next price above the greatest price which the second most eager buyer is prepared to offer. Price is therefore not determined by the highest price which the successful bidder might pay, but by the price offer of the second most eager buyer. Hence the importance of analysing what determines that reserve price. In a Dutch auction, or descending-bid system, the auctioneer starts the bidding at a high price and then lowers the price by stages until he finds a buyer willing to make a bid. In sealed-bid auctions the successful bid will either be the highest or lowest depending upon the commodity which is offered for sale. Thus in the case of offshore oil leases the highest bid will usually be accepted, whereas in defence or construction contracts successful bids will tend to be low bids.

Auctions are characterized by a single seller (buyer) confronting numerous buyers (sellers) and the question arises: what is the optimal auction strategy to pursue in order to maximize profit (or minimize cost)? Should the optimal strategy be to conduct an open or sealed-bid auction? If an open auction should it be an English or Dutch auction? Under what conditions might the various systems give equivalent results? Consider the case of sealed-bid auctions. It might be supposed that sealed-bid auctions, by not enabling bidders to observe rivals' bids, might force bidders to reveal their reservation prices and enable the highest (lowest) price to be obtained. However, such a result would depend upon whether the bidders are risk-averse or risk-neutral. In a nutshell, bidders' strategies need to be considered. Thus one policy may be for bidders to take their rivals' potential bids as given – but that would assume that bidders never learn from their mistakes. Indeed it seems more plausible to assume that collusion will be attempted, and what is possible in sealed-bid auctions may also be true of open auctions. If the value of the commodity is uncertain (as, for example, in the case of antiques and oil leases) and bidders differ in their expertise and skills in the evaluation of goods, they will seek to conceal their knowledge. The dilemma is that bids may reveal to the auctioneer the highest value and reduce the bidders' profit; hence collusion may occur.

Waiting-line auctions have similarities to sealed-bid auctions. Choosing a time to arrive in a queue is comparable with deciding what money bid to make. The simplest assumption is that waiting time has an opportunity cost, and that poor people will have a lower opportunity cost than rich people; but if the value of a prize is an increasing function of time then rich people may be found in a queue.

Futures Markets

Auction markets may be concerned not only with current (often called 'spot') prices, but also with future prices. For example, a farmer may seek to sell some of his crop before it is harvested in order to ensure a minimum income for himself. He cannot sell all his crop in advance because the amount eventually harvested will be influenced by climatic factors outside his control. Hence he will be hedging his bets with part of the revenue from his crop being determined by a futures contract, and part being determined by a gamble with Nature and market demand when the crop is harvested. Futures markets have long been established for primary commodities (farm crops and minerals), and for foreign exchange and various options markets have recently been created for financial securities. Hence the workings of futures markets pose three questions. First, what are the factors determining the futures price? Second, what is the relationship between the futures price and the expected spot price? Third, how efficient are futures markets?

The simplest approach to the first question is to assume that the available supply of a commodity is currently available, that the commodity can be stored, and that there are no unanticipated changes in demand. Given these assumptions futures price will be determined by the actual spot price, the rate of interest on a risk-free asset, such as government bonds, and the cost of storing the commodity:

$$p_t^f \leq N = P^s (1 + r)^t + K_t \tag{9.1}$$

where p_t^f is the futures price for a commodity at time t, p^s is the current spot price, r is the risk-free interest rate and K is the carrying cost. Thus, if the futures price is likely to rise above the actual spot price by more than the carrying cost and the risk-free interest rate, then it will be profitable to engage in futures contracts and store more of the available supply.

The second question raises a much more difficult issue: what is the relationship between the futures price and the expected spot price at time t? On the assumption that economic agents use all the information available to them, and that they combine that information with the best economic theory which relates those facts and processes to outcomes, then we should expect the futures price to be an unbiased predictor of the expected spot price

$$p_t^f = exp\ (p^s)\ (9.2)$$

Thus if speculators think that the futures price is below the expected spot price then they will increase their purchases of futures and so drive the futures price to equality with the expected spot price, and in doing so obtain a profit greater than they could expect to earn on risk-free interest-bearing bonds.

This so-called 'rational expectations' hypothesis is not the only one put forward to explain the relationship between the futures price and the expected spot price. A second view, associated with Keynes (1936) and Hicks (1939), is that the two prices are unequal, and that hedgers must pay a risk premium to speculators in the form of a futures price below the expected spot price; this amount is called 'backwardation'. On the basis of this hypothesis the futures price might be expected to rise as the date towards contract maturity (i.e. availability of future supplies) draws nearer. In contrast is the hypothesis which asserts that the futures price will be above the expected spot price. Thus suppose a manufacturer wishes to obtain delivery of a raw material at a future date – he may find it inconvenient to purchase immediately because he lacks storage space, and hence he may try to induce a storage company to agree a futures contract which assures delivery at a future date. In this third case the futures price falls towards maturity. Finally there is the possibility that hedging strategies may vary over the length of the agricultural cycle. Thus immediately after the harvest, when the crop is large and inventories are considered too high, farmers may offer a large premium to entice speculators to take up futures contracts, but when the inventories fall towards the date of the next harvest, then they may offer small premiums.

The four hypotheses that we have outlined suggest two possible links between futures prices and expected spot prices; either the futures price is an unbiased predictor of the spot price or there is a systematic bias resulting from the existence of a risk premium. The possibilities of bias would seem to stem from imbalances in future sales and purchases stemming from differences in the expectations of buyers and sellers. Thus both buyers and sellers may act upon the basis of the best information available to them and use the best economic theory linking the available facts. However, the facts and theories may be different. Farmers are faced with different risks from those confronting merchants who store the good, or from those faced by manufacturers, and even from those which speculators have to consider. In a nutshell, there may be asymmetries in the information available to different economic agents. One implication of this conclusion is that the analyses of speculator behaviour in financial markets, which concentrate on the relationship between the risk and return on assets in terms of a capital asset pricing model, may run the danger of ignoring interrelations between the real and financial aspects of futures prices. This is an issue to which we shall return when we consider aspects of financial management in chapter 14.

Efficient Markets

This brings us to the third question: are futures markets efficient? The enormous expansion of futures trading since the end of the Second World War might suggest an unequivocal answer – London, as a centre of futures trading, has expanded to include potatoes, nickel, aluminium, crude oil, gold and silver, and a range of financial instruments, and new futures trading centres have been established in Sydney, Hong Kong and Singapore. However, such expansion has resulted from the activities of speculators, which prompts the question: is speculation destabilizing? To answer the question there is a prior function of futures markets which needs to be stressed; they create prices, they provide price signals and they collect, process and disseminate information. Speculators may play an important part in this process, by seeking to maximize their profits and therefore helping to smooth price movements. When prices are rising above the expected spot price speculators can release stocks and make a profit, and when prices are falling below the expected spot price they can make a profit by buying. Hence as long as speculators attempt to maximize profits they must stabilize profits. Against this thesis can be set the alternative view that prices are distorted by amateurs who climb on to the bandwagon without their behaviour being corrected by the speculators. Instead, speculators find it easier to profit at the expense of the amateurs rather than from assessing the underlying conditions of supply and demand. Now, if such destabilizing behaviour were common then it would be expected to leave a trace in price movements. However, the available evidence suggests that prices tend to follow a 'random walk' in which successive prices are unrelated to each other. Other studies have attempted to compare futures prices with eventual prices but the results have been mixed, suggesting that the interaction of real and financial factors varies from market to market. Finally there have been attempts to compare the forecasts implicit in futures prices with those derived from econometrically based forecasts. The results suggest that futures markets produce better forecasts than those derived from econometric forecasts (Yamey, 1984).

Fix-price Markets

Fix-price markets, in which prices are fixed for a considerable period of time during which demand may exhibit considerable fluctuations, seem to be a product of industrialization and high levels of consumers' incomes. Fixed prices started to become prevalent in England in the 1890s, and Marshall in his *Industry and Trade* (1923) observed that the French called them 'English prices'. They were associated with branding and standardization, and with a relative decline in agriculture (Jefferys, 1950). By the 1890s the value of UK agricultural output was some 15 per cent of the value of manufacturing output and Britain was tending to become a fix-price economy. In Germany and France the same relative decline in the importance of agriculture was not reached until the 1950s, and in Japan it was not attained until the 1970s.

Full Cost or Normal Cost Pricing: Businessmen's Vocabulary and Economic Analysis

Because of an apparent insensitivity of price to changes in demand fix prices were called 'full cost prices' by Hall and Hitch (1939) in their classic survey of businessmen's pricing policies. The pricing thesis offered by Hall and Hitch is one of firms attempting to cover cost *plus* a mark-up for profit. Clearly such a view of pricing differs from the more market-influenced pricing of neoclassical economics. However, the calculation of the mark-up was not investigated fully by Hall and Hitch (1939) and over the years there have been modifications. Machlup (1952) demonstrated that the mark-up cannot be divorced from market influences, and that full cost pricing remains closely linked to the more neoclassical approach to pricing. Steps along the way have been provided by Andrews (1949) and Brunner (1952), who have preferred the term 'normal cost prices' to denote the fact that businessmen calculate prices on the basis of long-run costs which are assumed to be constant or slightly falling, and on the basis of long-run demand. Latterly, Godley and Nordhaus (1972) have suggested that price is based upon the trend of wage costs, with the latter being used as a proxy for direct costs, and upon the general level of demand across the boom and slump of a business cycle.

These various amplifications of the original full cost thesis allow us to relate the businessman's vocabulary to the jargon of economic analysis. First, the businessman is assumed to fix price by adding a mark-up to direct costs:

$$p = avc + \% \tag{9.3}$$

where p is product price, avc represents average variable cost (direct cost) and $\%$ is the percentage mark-up for profit. Assuming direct costs to be constant (for simplicity) we can substitute marginal cost (mc) for average variable cost:

$$p = mc + \% \tag{9.4}$$

Now, if we assume that the firm is trying to maximize profits we can substitute marginal revenue (mr) for marginal cost since the firm will aim to equate the two:

$$p = mr + \% \tag{9.5}$$

However, marginal revenue is determined by price elasticity of demand ($mr = p + p/e$) so that in the case of a downward-sloping demand curve we can write:

$$p = p - p/e + \% \tag{9.6}$$

which simplifies to

$$p/e = \% \tag{9.7}$$

The mark-up therefore depends upon the price elasticity of demand; as price elasticity of demand approaches zero, as the model approaches pure monopoly, then price will approach infinity, but as price elasticity approaches infinity price approaches marginal revenue (equals marginal cost to maximize profits).

Finally, does the demand curve relate to the short run or to the long run? According to Andrews and Brunner (1976) it is long-run demand which is relevant to pricing, and since the long-run demand curve is expected to be highly elastic – reflecting the potential competition from new entrants, especially from those firms in other industries which can switch easily from one market to another – it follows that cross-entry from one market to another by firms is a major determinant of the mark-up.

Full Cost Pricing, Savings and Investments

Despite the possibilities of a reconciliation of economic analysis with business behaviour presented in the previous section, it is important to realize that a substantial group of economists known as post-Keynesian economists (e.g. Kaldor, 1960; Davidson, 1972) do not believe that the mark-up can be invested with the precision implied by the concept of the elasticity of demand. For them the mark-up is determined by the need to generate sufficient internal funds to finance investment. Businessmen tend to avoid external financing because it can lead to loss of control, and in considering the savings required out of profits it is alleged that capital projects are frequently unique, and that probability analysis cannot be applied. Investment decisions therefore arise out of the 'animal spirits' of businessmen, out of the urge to do something rather than nothing.

Fix Prices, Futures Markets and Goodwill

How long should a businessman maintain a particular price? Two factors would seem to dictate the answer. First there is the possibility of competition from rivals. Second there is the nature of consumer demand. Setting inter-firm competition aside, we shall confine our attention to consumer demand. In setting a fix price a firm is indicating that the current (spot) price is an accurate predictor of the future spot price. Current prices are future prices, and customers are assured that repeat purchases can be made at current prices. Hence there is an attempt to create goodwill. In addition to old customers, however, there may be new customers. The fix price will therefore be maintained as long as it is expected that the revenue from maintaining that price will exceed the costs of maintaining that price. The fix price is therefore a reservation price, analogous to the reservation price of the consumer search-ing for the lowest price or the reservation wage of the unemployed worker seeking a job.

Fix prices are future prices and, in order to safeguard themselves against unforeseen contingencies, fix-price firms will have to conduct hedging oper-ations. For example, a firm will need to hold an inventory to satisfy consumer demand. Even though it adopts a fix-price policy, however, it may be pur-chasing raw materials and labour in flex-price markets, and inputs may have been bought at different times and at different prices. Hence the firm must establish a 'hedging department' which is separate from the production depart-ment in order to cope with the profits and losses which accompany purchases and sales.

Break-even Charts Accounting Practice and Economic Analysis

Normal cost pricing is sometimes illustrated by means of break-even charts. In figure 9.1 variable costs are assumed to be a linear function of output, and when combined with fixed costs result in a total cost curve which is also a linear function of output. If it is also assumed that the firm can sell as much as it wants, then there is a linear total revenue curve. The resulting intersection of total revenue and total costs yields a break-even chart. The break-even point is at output OA. When the average revenue and average and marginal cost curves are derived from figure 9.1 we obtain figure 9.2, which reveals marginal cost below average cost. In order to cover costs the firm charges OP and produces OB.

Now the economist does not say that the businessman should charge a price equal to marginal cost; that is an outcome which obtains only under competitive

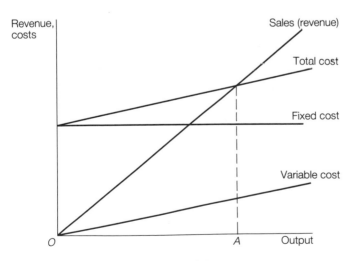

Figure 9.1

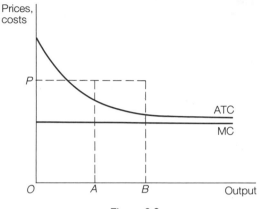

Figure 9.2

conditions. If pressed an accountant might admit that sales could vary with the price charged so that there was not one sales line, as in figure 9.1, but several, as in figure 9.3. He might concede also that at each price there would be a maximum amount of sales so that a total revenue locus could be derived from which the economist's downward-sloping average and marginal revenue curves could be obtained. Furthermore, the accountant might also concede that costs might only be constant over a given range of output. Hence we can construct a diagram (figure 9.4) with which an economist can feel some affinity – where direct costs are constant over the range *AB*.

Market Structures

The dependence of the mark-up on the elasticity of demand suggests a convenient classification of pricing policies by *market strategies*. We can also classify pricing policies by *market structures* (by numbers of buyers and sellers, ease of entry, etc.), and because strategy and structure are interrelated we can infer strategy from structure and vice-versa.

The strategy approach rests upon three concepts of price elasticity of demand:

1   *Own-price elasticity of demand* measures the proportionate change in the demand for one's own product following a proportionate change in one's own price. Symbolically, it is

$$\eta = \frac{dq}{q} \Big/ \frac{dp}{p} = \frac{dq}{dp} \cdot \frac{p}{q} \qquad (9.8)$$

where p is price, q is quantity sold and d denotes a small change.

2   *Cross-price elasticity of demand* measures the proportionate change in the demand for commodity A as a result of a change in the price of B.

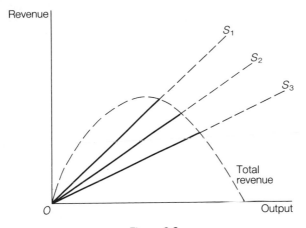

Figure 9.3

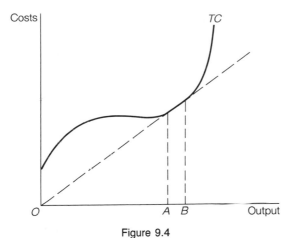

Figure 9.4

$$\frac{dq^A}{q^A} \bigg/ \frac{dp}{p^B} = \frac{dq^A}{dp^B} \cdot \frac{p^B}{q^A} \tag{9.9}$$

3   *Conjectural price elasticity* measures the expected proportionate change in a rival's price resulting from a proportionate change in one's own price.

$$\frac{dp^I}{p^I} \bigg/ \frac{dp^{II}}{p^{II}} = \frac{dp^I}{dp^{II}} \cdot \frac{P^{II}}{p^I} \tag{9.10}$$

Where I and II are the two firms.

Now the conjectural price elasticity of demand can be linked to market structure as follows. Suppose a firm offers a secret price cut Pn and the probability of attracting a customer is proportional to the firm's share of the market (S_i) then the variance of the firm's share of sales to new customers will be $PnS_i(1 + S_i)$ and the aggregate for the industry will be

$$C = Pn \sum_{i=1}^{n} S_i (1 + S_i)$$

for N firms. This expression equals $Pn(1 - HHI)$, where

$$HHI = \sum_{i=1}^{n} S_i^2$$

that is, the Herfindahl index of industrial concentration (Stigler, 1964).

This link between strategy and structure has enabled Cowling and Waterson (1976), Clarke and Davies (1982) and Lyons (1981) to extend the original mark-up equation to take into account possible rivals' reactions as suggested by the degree of market concentration and by import penetration, viz:

$$\frac{p - \sum_i MC_i \, (x_i/x)}{p} = \frac{H(1 + \mu)}{\eta} \qquad \text{(Cowling and Waterson) (9.11)}$$

$$p - \Sigma_i MC_i \, (x_i/x) = \qquad (9.12)$$

$$pD - \Sigma_i MC_i \, (D_i + x_i) D_i = \frac{H(1 + \lambda + \theta)}{\eta} \cdot \frac{D}{D \cdot M} \qquad \text{(Lyons) (9.13)}$$

where p is price, MC_i is the marginal cost of the ith firm, x_i is the output of the ith firm, H is the Herfindahl index of industrial concentration, η is the price elasticity of demand, μ is a weighted average of output conjectures of n domestic firms, α is a constant proportional output conjectural variation, λ is a conjecture about domestic production, θ is a conjecture about imports and D and M refer to domestic production for the domestic market and imports respectively. In the Cowling and Waterson model different conjectures about rivals' outputs exert an influence on price–cost margins of firms. In the Clarke and Davies model the variation of α between 1 and 0 permits firm behaviour to be classified between collusion and a situation where each firm takes the outputs of other firms as given. As will become apparent later, these formulae represent extensions of the Cournot model of duopoly, but for practical purposes they do assume a clear identification of markets which may be very difficult when cross-entry from one industry to another is possible.

Table 9.1. Market structures based on price and demand elasticities

	Own-price elasticity	Cross-price elasticity	Conjectural price elasticity
Perfect competition	Infinite	Infinite	Zero
Oligopoly	Large for increase, low for decrease	Large	Large
Monopoly	Greater than unity	Low	Zero

Table 9.1 presents a classification based upon demand price elasticities which will now form the basis for a discussion of pricing policies in the market situations of perfect competition, monopoly and oligopoly. Given the classification contained in table 9.1 we shall now examine the pricing policies pursued in the market situations of perfect competition, monopoly and oligopoly.

Perfect Competition

The essence of the competitive model is that the individual firm perceives that, at the prevailing price, its own price elasticity of demand is infinite, and that rivals will not follow its actions (the conjectural price elasticity of demand is zero).

Flex-price Competition

In analysing the behaviour of a competitive firm it is customary to assume a flex-price world, and that a firm responds to changes in demand through short-run adjustments in the rate of output from given equipment and in the long run through adjustments in the amount of its equipment. In order to maximize profits such a firm will, as a necessary condition, equate marginal cost with price, and as a sufficient condition attempt to cover total costs with total revenue. In the short run, if demand is depressed, then the firm may continue in operations as long as it can cover its running costs, but in the long run it must seek to cover total costs.

If market demand increases then the firm would increase output, and in doing so it would be guided by its marginal cost curve. However, the marginal cost curve of the firm would assume that factor prices remain constant. This seems unlikely as the rise in price will attract new firms into the market. Hence the firm's *ex-post* marginal cost curve would lie to the left of its *ex-ante* (planning) marginal cost curve unless the expansion of the industry led to external economies of scale.

Fix-price Competition

In markets characterized by expected fluctuations in demand firms will build in plant flexibility. Such flexibility is not costless. The costs of producing a given output will be higher, but the costs of producing a range of outputs will be lower than in a plant optimally designed to produce a given output. As a result of built-in flexibility marginal and average costs, as well as price, tend to remain constant over a range of outputs (Stigler, 1939).

Monopoly

The price policy of a monopolist can also be analysed in terms of whether there is constant or variable demand. Thus the monopolist will attempt to equate marginal cost with marginal revenue (with price being higher than marginal revenue because of the falling demand curve); but if demand increases then the monopolist may or may not raise price depending upon whether built-in spare capacity exists.

X-inefficiency

In the absence of economies of scale the pricing policy of a monopolist will produce an output which is lower and a price which is higher than that obtaining in a competitive industry. However, it is sometimes suggested that monopolists may also experience 'X-inefficiency' as well as allocational inefficiency. Defining X-efficiency is extremely difficult, however, although it would seem to relate somehow to a failure on the part of managers to maximize the productive potential of all labour inputs (including their own). In some discussions it is suggested that monopoly situations reduce the impact of market forces upon employees and enables them to increase their rewards. This could mean that workers, for example, are able to increase their wages at the expense of shareholders; but that would be merely income redistribution. In other instances it is suggested that employees are able to increase their rewards but take them in a non-pecuniary form because that is the easiest way to prevent outsiders monitoring the rewards of employees. The difficulty with this argument is that non-monetary rewards are compatible with competitive situations; thus wage theory has always acknowledged such forms of remuneration and embalmed them in the concept of 'net advantages'. Although X-inefficiency may exist, and may be of relevance for public policy, its impact upon marketing policy is difficult to assess.

The Coexistence of Fix and Flex Prices

Fix and flex prices for the same good may exist. In one market prices are unresponsive to demand changes whilst in the other market prices fluctuate with changes in demand and supply. The coexistence of the two markets may arise because of the existence of two sets of shoppers whose behaviour is determined by the opportunity cost of shoppers' time. Searching for the lowest price is time-consuming, and may be only worthwhile for those whose opportunity cost, as measured by the wage they can obtain, is low. High income earners will therefore tend to shop in fix-price shops where they may be given a guarantee of stocks being available, and they will be willing to pay for the privilege of being able to get goods easily. In the long run, prices might tend to equality between the markets if shoppers can switch markets and high income earners hire specialist buyers to search for them in flex-price markets.

Bargains and Rip-offs

The tendency for the same price to prevail in the long run depends upon the willingness of buyers to seek out low-price firms, and it is possible for prices to persistently diverge. Thus the cost curve may be identical for all firms but some firms charge a higher price than others. The high-price firms are able to charge a high price by catering to snob appeal through expensive packaging and sales price dispersion, whilst low-price firms cater for the mass market. Despite strong similarities of the goods the two markets never coalesce because the customers in the high-price markets consider the costs of search will outweigh any possible benefit.

Price Dispersion

Price dispersion can occur because of search costs and because information is continually being disrupted by the entry and exit of firms and customers. Thus, in large cities price dispersion can persist because of a continually changing flow of tourists.

Price Discrimination

Two firms may charge a different price for the same product because of the existence of two markets. It is also possible for one firm to charge different prices for its product because of the existence of isolated markets. Thus Pigou (1928) distinguished three degrees of price discrimination:

1   *First-degree price discrimination*, in which a different price is charged for each unit of a commodity sold with the result that all consumers' surplus is extracted.
2   *Second-degree price discrimination*, in which a monopolist sets n separate prices so that all units of a commodity with a demand price greater than x are sold at price x, all with a price less than x and greater than y are sold at price y and so on.
3   *Third-degree price discrimination*, in which a monopolist distinguishes groups of customers, separated by costs of moving from one group to another, and charges a different price to each group.

Because of the costs involved in detecting the price which should be charged for each unit Pigou felt that only third-degree price discrimination might be practicable.

Figure 9.5 illustrates the case of a firm faced by two separate markets A and B, and it is assumed to be impossible for goods sold in one market to be re-sold in the other market. The firm equates marginal cost with marginal revenue, the horizontal sum of the marginal revenues, MR_A and MR_B. The monopolist equates marginal revenues in each market because if marginal revenue were greater in market A than in market B it would pay to switch goods from B to A. If marginal revenues are equal, profits are maximized and the firm charges price OP_A in market A and OP_B in market B. Price OP_A is higher than OP_B, reflecting the more inelastic demand in A.

Dumping

During slumps foreign firms are often accused by domestic firms of dumping; that is, of charging prices below costs. Thus during the world recession of the 1970s and 1980s Japanese steel producers were accused of dumping steel in Europe and America. There were also allegations that dumping was being assisted by government subsidies. What constitutes charging prices below costs is, of course, a difficult knot to unravel. In the short run when demand is depressed then firms might be expected either (1) on the basis of full cost theory to cut back output whilst trying to maintain prices, or (2) on the basis of flex-price theory to cut prices as long as average variable costs were being covered.

One possible explanation of dumping is that variable costs do differ between countries because of differences in employment contracts. Thus Japanese workers in large firms enjoy a form of lifetime employment contract or profit-sharing whereby employment is guaranteed but income may be variable. Since the costs of terminating employment may be extremely high, and workers may be prepared to accept a fall in income, the marginal costs of steel production

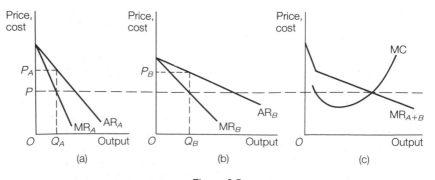

Figure 9.5

can, if necessary, become extremely low. In contrast, American and British workers may not value employment security so highly because of the existence of state unemployment benefits, and because such benefits set a floor to wage-cutting the marginal cost of steel may be relatively high.

Predatory Pricing

'Predatory pricing' is a phrase usually applied to a multi-product firm which prices a product below cost in order to eliminate a rival. The policy does, of course, rest upon the assumptions that one firm has greater financial strength than another, and that the successful firm can subsequently raise prices to recoup its losses and erect entry barriers to prevent outsiders coming into the market attracted by the higher profits. In an economy with an efficient capital market there is no obvious gain to shareholders from such diversification because they can always diversify their portfolios by buying and selling shares.

Sales

Price discrimination may be difficult to achieve because consumers could eventually discover that the same commodity is being sold at different prices; and even if it were difficult to switch from buying in the high-price market to buying in the low-price market because of transport costs, the fact that low prices exist could cause resentment. However, price discrimination may be practised over time. If a firm has a 'sale' in a week when other firms do not, then it can capture some of the informed shoppers as well as the uninformed shoppers, and where all firms have a 'seasonal sale' they can split the market over time by allowing the high-income buyers to be 'in fashion' at the beginning of the season and allow low-income customers to buy at the end of the season.

Loss Leaders

A loss leader is a product which is sold below cost in the hope of enticing consumers to purchase other goods which carry high profit margins. 'Loss leader' is therefore a misleading term, since such goods might be more realistically termed profit leaders; they attempt to lead to a situation where the firm makes a greater profit on its total sales. Loss leadership is therefore a policy which may be practised by multi-product firms whose products are interrelated or complementary in demand. Although multi-product pricing will receive more intensive analysis later, it is appropriate to consider loss leaders at this point as an aspect of retail pricing. (It may be assumed that industrial buyers might be less tempted and more discriminatory in their purchases.)

Figure 9.6 relates to a firm selling two products (and more) labelled A and B (curves relating to A are excluded from the diagram). The firm sells product B at price OP_1 as determined by the intersection of the marginal revenue and marginal cost curves, MR_B and MC_B, respectively. Now let us assume that product A has a relatively inelastic demand and that A and B are complementary because the firm (a retail shop) sells both, and there is a strong probability

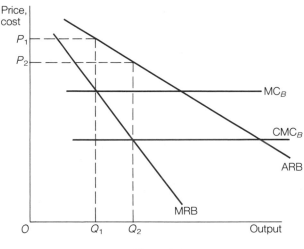

Figure 9.6

that if consumers enter the shop to buy A then they will also buy B. If the firm lowers the price of B, which is in relatively elastic demand, it may increase its overall profits. The curve CMC_B is the marginal cost curve of B minus the profits on A. In figure 9.6 the firm is able to lower the price of B to OP_2 and sell OQ_2. Successful leadership will therefore involve the ability to discriminate among the prices of product lines and to pursue such price discrimination on the basis of complementaries in demand; but loss leader policies may be disliked by manufacturers who may attempt to fix retail prices.

Resale Price Maintenance

Resale price maintenance is a marketing practice by which a manufacturer requires subsequent resellers (retailers) to offer them at minimum or stipulated prices. Resale price maintenance may be carried out by an individual or group of firms. Collective resale price maintenance is, however, usually considered to be illegal.

At first sight resale price maintenance is not an obvious strategy, because a monopolistic firm can obtain maximum profits from its monopoly power whilst a competitive firm is powerless to impose conditions on others. However, two hypotheses can be advanced as explanations of its occurrence. First is the 'outlets hypothesis' which postulates that profits are a function not merely of price but also of the number of selling outlets. Second, profits are a function not only of price and the number of outlets, but also of the quality of the product. Specifically, quality is considered as embracing advice to customers and after-sales service.

If sales and profits are a function of the number of retail outlets then the market demand curve shifts to the right as the number of outlets increases, although the extent of the shift falls as the number of outlets increases due to diminishing returns. The reason why sales increase may be due to the greater convenience to shoppers of a larger number of retail outlets. In order to induce an increase in retail outlets, however, a firm may have to increase the size of the retail margin; that is, the difference between production cost and retail price.

The second hypothesis is concerned with the fact that if retailers do not offer service and after-sales service then a manufacturer's profit may be affected. Thus some retailers may buy a manufacturer's product and lower the price by not offering after-sales service. In effect they become free riders who ride upon the reputation of the manufacturer. 'Unfair competition', it is alleged, arises between those retailers who do offer after-sales service and those who do not. Viewed from this perspective resale price maintenance is an alternative to the strategy of a firm owning retail outlets; it is a selling outlay designed to induce retailers to protect the quality of the product and the reputation of the producer. However, all firms are now required by law to give some guarantee of quality, and many large retailers are now offering their own guarantee as a more convenient substitute to that of the manufacturer, and some manufacturers operate their own after-sales service. Is there then no case for resale price maintenance? The case for its adoption may hinge upon the relative pull of variety as measured by the number of retail outlets and concentration as measured by the economies of scale to large retail outlets. Thus supermarkets may derive economies from risk reduction, large turnover, etc. ; but the geographical concentration of outlets may tend to reduce the sales of some goods. The problem for a manufacturer, therefore, is that an unregulated market of retailers may lower his profits if economies of scale reduce the number of outlets. He is faced with the alternatives of (a) licensing retailers to sell his goods and ensuring that the appropriate number of outlets and quality safeguards are made available through the retail margin he offers them; or (b) establishing his own retail outlets; or (c) allowing large retailers to develop with or without after-sales service – in the latter case he may supply after-sales service.

Multi-product Pricing

So far we have concentrated on the problem of a firm selling the same product in different markets. Now we must consider the case of a firm selling different products (Coase, 1946). These products may or may not be related on the cost side (e.g. mutton and wool) and may or may not be related on the demand side (e.g. bread and butter); we shall analyse some of the issues of cost and demand interrelationships.

Pricing of products with interrelated costs
For simplicity we shall consider the case of a monopolist producing two products whose costs are interrelated but whose demands are interdependent. In other words, the demand curves for each product remain unchanged whatever the price of the other product. Hence profits are maximized when marginal revenue and marginal cost are equated in each market.

$$MR_A = MC_A \tag{9.14}$$

$$MR_B = MC_B \tag{9.15}$$

Complications can arise when the marginal cost curves are interdependent in the sense that the marginal cost of A depends upon the outputs of A and B; and similarly for the marginal cost of B. In figure 9.7(a) the demand curve for A is DD and the firm charges price OP_A at which price OQ_A is demanded. But given the output of A which is demanded, the marginal cost of B, which is dependent upon the outputs of A and B, is also determined. Suppose the marginal cost of B is MC_B, given the output of A, then given the marginal revenue curve for B is MR_B the price the firm should charge for B is OP_B in figure 9.7(b).

There are, however, two possible effects of a change in the price of A upon the price of B. If a fall in the price of A and an increase in the output of A leads to a fall in the marginal cost curve of B then the price of B which would maximize profits must fall as the price of A falls; this is the case of *complementary production* and is traced out in figure 9.7(c). The second effect occurs when a

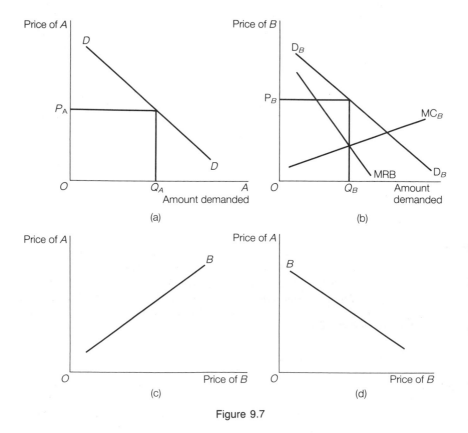

(a)

(b)

(c)

(d)

Figure 9.7

fall in the price of A leads to a rise in the marginal cost of B, and means that the price of B must rise in order to maximize profits; this case in known as *rival production* and is illustrated in figure 9.7(d).

So far we have determined the price of B on the assumption that the price of A is given. Of course, it would be possible to reverse the procedure and derive the price of A on the assumption that the price of B is given. Hence it is possible to determine the prices which would be charged for both A and B.

What we have done in figure 9.7 is to determine the appropriate pricing policies for two products which are jointly produced without specific reference to the problem of covering overheads. Instead of requiring each product to contribute a given amount of revenue, say 50 per cent, to cover overheads, we have required each product to be produced to the point at which maximum profits can be obtained from its sale. Thus there is no injunction to departmental managers that each product must carry a particular mark-up. Instead each manager is told to vary price, and hence sales, until he obtains maximum profits. Out of the maximum profits from the sale of all products it should be possible to cover overheads; of course pursuit of such maximum profits does require the firm to be willing to vary its mix of products, and it does require departmental managers to reveal their marginal costs.

Interrelated demands and cost
We shall now assume that the demand curves for the two goods are interrelated but costs are not. Hence the demand for A depends upon the prices of A and B. Given the price of A it is possible to obtain the demand curve for B, but this does not lead to a simple determination of the price of B because every change in the price of B will change the demand for A, even though the price of A is given. If A and B are complements then a fall in the price of B will increase the demand for A; but if A and B are substitutes then a fall in the price of B will lower the demand for A. Hence any decision about the price of B must take into account the demand for A. Figure 9.8 illustrates the effects upon the demand for A of changes in the price of B. The curve DD is the demand curve for A, given particular prices of B. If the price of B falls then the demand curve for A with a firm price of OP shifts the demand curve to D_1D_1 and the change in net revenue $LMNR$. Any change in revenue from product A must be added to the difference between marginal cost and marginal revenue if they are negative, in order to discover the price of B which, given the price of A, will maximize the firm's profits.

If A and B are complements then as the price of B falls the demand for A will rise. The effect of this rise in the demand for A upon the price of A will depend upon the marginal cost curve of A and the elasticity of the new demand curve as compared with the old one. There is also another factor to be taken into account – the price for A, with a given price for B, will also depend upon the extent of shift in the demand for B at different prices of B. The change in net revenue may rise or fall as the price of B is lowered with a consequential effect on the price the firm would wish to charge for A. By search, therefore, the firm will attempt to find the point of intersection of the price lines for A and B.

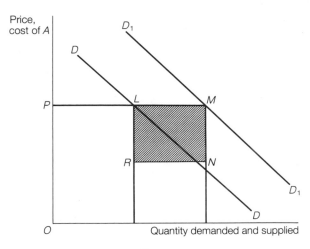

Figure 9.8

Joint costs and joint demands
Although seemingly intractable, the solution to this case will be solved by analysing the change in the firm's total costs. Thus if the price is given then the demand for A is given and a marginal revenue can be derived. If demands and costs are complementary then a change in the price of A will have an effect on the output of B and lower the marginal cost of A. If demands and costs are rivals then the effect of a fall in the price of A will, via its effect on the output of B, lower the costs of A. But if demands are competitive and production is rival, then a fall in the price of A will raise the marginal cost of A.

Two-part Tariffs for Single- and Multi-product Firms

Amusement arcades and pleasure parks offer a variety of 'amusements'. Polaroid cameras can be used only with Polaroid films. Gas and electricity boards may sell domestic and industrial appliances which use gas and electricity. We have, in these examples, cases of multi-product firms. But should they sell their products by charging prices equal to marginal costs; that is, along the lines suggested in the previous section? The answer depends upon whether the firms can tap the consumer surplus which accrues to each buyer. When a single uniform price is charged then that price will tend to be set so as to measure the marginal utility derived by consumers. Since the same price is charged for all units then on some units bought utility derived will be greater than price. It may therefore be possible for a monopolist to tap the consumer surplus by setting a lump sum 'entrance fee' and then charging a unit price for all units of the commodity purchased. This is a variation on price discrimination.

In the case of the amusement park, the owner has a choice between setting a single price for an 'all-day ticket', which enables the purchaser to use any of the facilities available, or fixing an entrance fee and then charging a price for each leisure facility used. A gas board could set a lump sum fee for the installation of the gas pipes and their maintenance and then charge a price per unit for the gas consumed. It may even charge a separate gas price according to the appliance used or the time of day that gas is consumed. The price policy pursued will therefore depend upon the extent of complementarity and substitutability between the various products sold and the extent to which it is possible for the firm to tap the consumer surplus (Scott and Morrell, 1985).

Exhaustible Resources: Pricing and Market Structure

Commodities such as oil, coal and metals present special pricing and production problems for their owners because they are non-renewable resources. If a machine wears out then it can be replaced, but when an oil well is exhausted it cannot be replaced. A well-owner has to face a choice between seeing his well intact or seeing its contents transformed into something else. Which policy he will pursue depends upon the expected rate of change of the price of oil and the rate of interest. If the rate of interest is, say, 10 per cent, and the price of oil is expected to rise by 5 per cent, then it will be more profitable to sell the oil and buy securities rather than leave it in the ground. If, however, the interest rate is 5 per cent and the expected price change is 10 per cent then it would be more profitable to keep the oil and sell it later. Hence the marketing decision treats the oil as a capital good which gives rise to a stream of income and which may or may not be greater than that of another capital good the income from which is measured by the market rate of interest. Hence, the marketing decision turns on

$$\dot{p} \gtrless r \tag{9.16}$$

where $\dot{p}$ is the expected price change and r is the rate of interest. The optimal rate of selling (and hence extraction) can also be expressed as the inter-temporal equalization of prices:

$$P_0^C = \frac{P_1^C}{(1 + r)} = \frac{P_2^C}{(1 + r)^2} = \ldots = \frac{P_n^C}{(1 + r)^n} \tag{9.17}$$

where P^C is the competitive price.

However, if production is monopolistically controlled then the relevant revenue criterion is not price but marginal revenue. Hence sales will be dictated by the attempt to equalize inter-temporal marginal revenues.

$$MR_0^M = \frac{MR_1^M}{(1 + r)} = \frac{MR_2^M}{(1 + r)^2} = \ldots = \frac{MR_n^M}{(1 + r)^n} \tag{9.18}$$

Since any divergence between price and marginal revenue is determined by the price elasticity of demand, $MR = P(1 + 1/\eta)$ then the monopolist's rate of sales can be expressed as:

$$P_0^M (1 + 1/\eta) = P_1^M \frac{(1 + 1/\eta)}{(1 + r)} = \ldots = P_n^M \frac{(1 + 1/\eta)}{(1 + r)^n} \qquad (9.19)$$

In figure 9.9 the length of the horizontal axis measures the total amount of the exhaustible resource, the left-hand vertical axis measures the present price and the right-hand vertical axis measures the present value of 'tomorrow's price'. In a competitive situation the amounts extracted in the two periods would be given by the intersection of the two demand curves, D and D_1. In a monopolistic situation the rates of extraction would be given by the intersection of the two corresponding marginal revenue curves and their intersection would depend upon the slopes of the demand curves. If the demand elasticities remain constant and increase at the same rate as the rate of interest, then the monopolist's rate of sales would be the same as that of a competitive industry. Of course these conclusions rest upon the assumptions that there are no extraction costs or economies of scale, and the results may not generalize to more than two periods.

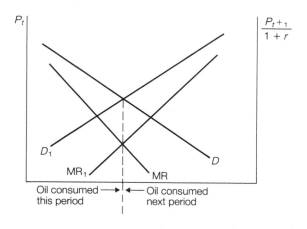

Figure 9.9

Monopolistic Competition and Excess Capacity

In discussing the models of perfect competition and 'pure' monopoly we tended to assume that everyone was knowledgeable about the market, and that all sectors could respond easily to changes in demand. The price/output 'decision' was a foregone conclusion in each market situation; it required each firm to equate marginal cost with marginal revenue. Despite the attractions of their predictive capabilities these models have nothing interesting to say about how a firm might reach its price/output decision when surrounded by uncertainty. In particular, what does a firm do when confronted by rival producers of very close, but not perfect, substitutes? In the 1930s there developed theories of both large-group and small-group behaviour to explain firms' reactions to such situations – theories of monopolistic competition and oligopoly.

The theory of monopolistic competition is something of a mixed blessing for the students of firms' behaviour; its critics would argue that the theory permits no predictions which could not readily be obtained from the theories of perfect competition and pure monopoly; its advocates would argue that the theory offers at least a starting point for modelling the behaviour of the ignorant seller and for introducing and integrating aspects of non-price competition with price competition. Let us consider both sides in turn.

A critical view suggests that monopolistic competition, as advanced by Chamberlin (1933), contains two essential ingredients: (a) the firm's product enjoys a degree of monopoly (e.g. through branding) in the market place and, therefore, the firm's decision-makers face a downward sloping demand curve; and (b) the abundance of close substitutes for each product means that in the longer run the firm's monopoly power is illusory and each firm is dominated by market forces. The critique continues by asking two questions: (a) how does a firm which enjoys a degree of monopoly power maximize profits in the short run? and (b) how does any firm maximize profits over the longer run when the market forces it to operate as a price-taker? The answer to both these questions, as predicted from the theories of firms' behaviour with perfect knowledge, is that firms equate marginal revenue with marginal cost, but in the long run this will mean earning no more than normal profits (i.e just covering costs). In other words the predictions of the price-taker's and the price-maker's behaviour under conditions of perfect knowledge detail the outcome of the essential ingredients of monopolistic competition theory. 'So what's new?' cry the critics, such as Stigler (1949) and Friedman (1953).

Three things are new, it is claimed by the advocates of monopolistic competition theory. First, the outcome of long-run adjustments is that each firm operates with excess capacity. Second, Chamberlin's analysis of the adjustment process offers a model of myopic behaviour and provides a useful starting point for understanding pricing behaviour under conditions of uncertainty about rivals' activities. Third, the model deals with non-price competition. For the moment we shall put this third issue on one side and note that the support for the model arises out of the degree of price competition both from within any group of firms and without that same group of firms. The effects of both types of competition are shown in figures 9.10 and 9.11, and the workings of the model are explained below.

Each diagram shows the case of a firm which is representative of the group. In figure 9.11 competition from within the group is shown by the two demand curves *dd* and *DD*. The former depicts the firm's perceived demand curve, i.e. the demand curve as perceived by the firm's decision-makers in the dim light of their ignorance about rivals' behaviour. The curve *DD* shows the path

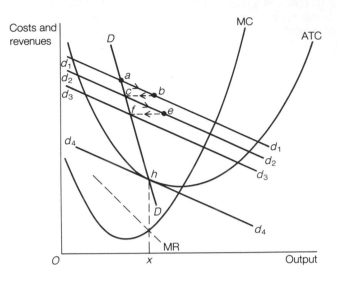

Figure 9.10

that the firm's sales actually do follow when all other firms in the group act in concert; i.e. when the markets dominate the individual seller. Since the decision-maker is considering a product which, although differentiated from, is similar to, the products of other firms in the group, the perceived response to price cuts is shown by *dd* which is more elastic than the actual one *DD* which takes account of the other firms following suit. Thus, suppose the decision-maker is at position *a* – a move to *b* offers an increase in profit by

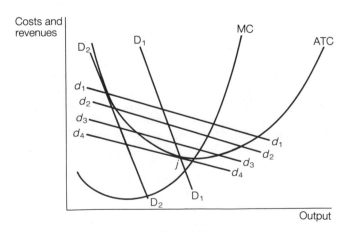

Figure 9.11

lowering price but as rivals follow suit d_1d_1 shifts downwards and c is the position actually obtained by the representative firm. From c a move to e looks profitable but, again, as rivals follow the price cut the position actually achieved is f as d_2d_2 slides down to position d_3d_3. This process of *ex-post* adjustment continues until the *ex-ante* expectation makes further price-cutting inappropriate – when point h is reached and output Ox is produced (d_4d_4).

Figure 9.11 shows the same starting point at a, but allows for freedom of entry in response to profits. As firms move in, DD is shifted left while the processes of internal adjustment (i.e. competition within the group) continue as before. Thus, $D'D'$ shifts to tangency with average costs at position D_2D_2 and the curve dd adjusts downwards until position d_4d_4 is established at which *ex-ante* expectations are of costs just being covered at j but from which *ex-post* reality will mean losses as dd slides further down D_2D_2 when rivals follow suit. In this situation firms will begin to leave the group until the DD curve shifts rightwards to intersect the average cost curve at j. The equilibrium at j is a stable one since only normal profit is being earned.

It would appear that, whether the observer concentrates on competition within the group or competition from without, the model predicts that the firm will operate with excess capacity; i.e. will not be operating at the point of average minimum cost, when in the equilibrium position for price and output.

Reaction to the excess capacity prediction is mixed in the literature on the economics of the firm. One source of criticism which has received a lot of attention is that of Kaldor (1960), which argues that new entrants to a group would not affect each member's sales equally; there would not be an equal spread of competition, and therefore the concept of a monopolistically competitive group has little meaning. This criticism is closely linked with one put forward by Demsetz (1964), that the reason why excess capacity emerges in the model is that the demand curve is sloping downwards, and that the demand curve slopes downwards because of product differentiation. Hence we should not draw any welfare implications from the model – in particular we should not compare such an equilibrium with one obtaining under perfect competition. It has also been suggested that a firm would not base price on short-run demand but would try to take into account long-run demand (Andrews and Brunner, 1975). Finally, it has been argued that excess capacity conditions could not persist because firms would combine to eliminate it (Dewey, 1969).

All the criticisms seem to relate, in part at least, to the concept of the 'group', which seems to be a shaky concept in theory and of very little use as an operational guide. The 'group' can be defined only in terms of the closeness of substitutes; but how is this to be defined? Presumably goods in a group are identified by a high (positive) cross-price elasticity of demand between various commodity combinations. But how high is 'high'? Indeed, identifying the group by measuring cross-price elasticities between 'adjacent' commodities extends its range to the whole economy, indeed, the world economy! (Triffin, 1940).

Yet the concept of monopolistic competition stubbornly refuses to disappear from the literature of economics because (a) it reinforces predictions about how an individual enterprise's behaviour will be circumscribed by the size of the 'group' in which the enterprise is located, and (b) it suggests that economists must spread their net much wider than price if they are to capture all of the independent variables relevant to the firm's revenue function. The first point, about group size, is clear from the analysis of figures 9.10 and 9.11, where the firm's perceived demand curve is actually dominated by market forces. Moreover, in one sense the influence of large numbers offers the means of qualifying the criticism arrived at in the excess capacity prediction. As an industry or group all firms together might gain from spare capacity being eliminated, but if there is free entry to the group then the problem is exacerbated if outsiders would be attracted by the gains accruing from a reconstruction of the industry. In other words, each firm hopes that other firms will 'help' the industry, and that other firms will contribute towards the reconstruction of the industry.

The second point relating to the non-price variables is the fact that the individual firm in such a market faces an incentive to reduce the uncertainty surrounding sales; i.e. to reduce the elasticity in the demand curve for the (branded) product. One way to achieve this is to undertake product advertising. Again a 'free-rider' problem arises to the extent that all firms in a group of closely related products will benefit from the selling outlays of any individual enterprise. Paradoxically, a firm may also find that increased advertising to resist potential entrants would actually increase their chances of successful entry because it increases the size of the market as well as drawing attention not to the advertising firm's product but to the (desirable properties of) buying a product with the same general benefits from some other firm. In other words the gains from 'informative advertising' may be very difficult to capture by the individual firm, and the larger the group, i.e. the less differentiated the individual product, the less likely it is that an individual firm will spend resources on informative or 'non-specific' advertising. Rather each firm will want to increase 'consumer identity' and will be tempted to engage in 'persuasive selling'.

To show the effects of advertising we depict the firm as facing three strategic variables – output, price and selling outlay (advertising). For any level of output the price which the firm can obtain depends upon the level of expenditure on advertising and other forms of selling behaviour. The analysis of how these three variables interact to influence the firm's behaviour has two interesting implications, one of which is of direct relevance to issues discussed in this chapter: (a) sales promotion may be preferred to price cutting as a means of expanding demand for a firm's product, and (b) when a firm in monopolistic competition undertakes advertising activities, excess capacity is no longer inevitable (Demsetz, 1964). However, since we devote the next chapter to questions of product policy it is best, perhaps, to refrain from analysing the effects of selling outlays until then; and so we return to the question of excess capacity in monopolistic competition as part of our discussion in chapter 10. But we end this discussion with the observation of Stigler who in 1953 severely criticized monopolistic competition theory but conceded in 1959 that non-price competition was important.

Oligopoly

Oligopoly is a market situation in which each firm is conscious that its actions are likely to provoke responses from other firms. Thus if A cuts his price then B might follow suit, and C and D might also be forced into similar conjectural behaviour in order to protect their markets. Conjectural interdependence therefore leads to indeterminacy in the sense that additional information (which may be non-economic in character) may be needed to provide a solution to the problem of price and output determination. As Edward Mason (1957) observed: 'Oligopoly is the passport to institutional economics.' Of course the problem of oligopoly may be non-existent, or an artificial problem created by the law. Recognition of interdependence may lead to collusion and a monopoly solution might result, with the only crucial issue being the determination of profit shares. But if the law prevents collusion, prevents the tendency towards monopoly in industries characterized by economies of scale, then an oligopoly problem may exist, and if the enforcement of a collusive agreement is difficult then, again, a problem of oligopoly may exist (Vickers, 1985).

Our discussion of oligopoly pricing and output policy will therefore proceed as follows:

1 An examination of game theory as a framework for the analysis of oligopoly situations.
2 Analysis of non-collusive solutions to the oligopoly problem posed by Cournot, Bertrand and Stackleberg (and with passing reference to the Chamberlin model which we have discussed in the previous section).
3 An examination of collusive oligopoly solution such as price leadership and market sharing.
4 An analysis of contestable markets as a solution to the oligopoly problem.
5 A consideration of oligopoly as a fix-price market situation.

Game Theory

The essence of the problem of conjectural interdependence is captured rigorously in the theory of games, a development in mathematics which was adopted quickly by economists (Hurwicz, 1945). The basic idea of this model is to represent oligopolistic rivals as players in a game in which the stakes are profits or market shares. Each player follows a strategy, by which to enjoy a pay-off within the confines of the rules of the game (market structures, legal controls, etc.).

Zero Sum Game

The simplest version is that of a *zero sum game* involving two players, in which the amount won by one player is exactly equal to the amount lost by the other.

Table 9.2. Pay-off matrix

| | B's strategies | | | |
A's strategies	B_1	B_2	B_3	Row minima
A_1	30	20	40	20
A_2	10	15	30	10
Column maxima	30	20	40	

Each player's strategy is based on consideration of the range of possibilities permitted by the other player. To see this in action consider the simple game depicted in table 9.2. The figures in the various boxes in table 9.2 can be thought of as possible profits for A or possible (equal) losses for B from a particular strategy in the market place, e.g. a lowering of price or an increase in advertising expenditures, etc. This particular game contains two strategies for A and three for B and proceeds as follows. If A chooses A_1 and B chooses, say, B_3, then A gains 40 and B losses 40; if A adopts A_2 while B adopts B_1 the corresponding gains and losses are 10; and so on.

What should A and B do to win the game, i.e. what is the optimal strategy for each firm? In this very simple version of the theory the optima are strictly determined. For example if A is allowed to choose first and A_2 is chosen, firm B would respond by choosing B_1 because this would minimize the loss which B must face given that A is allowed to choose his strategy. If A chooses A_1 then B chooses B_2. Now if the participants have perfect knowledge (to keep things simple) of all the possibilities in the matrix then A will realize that B is always going to retaliate in a way which will minimize losses (i.e. minimize A's gains). A will choose A_1, therefore, since the smallest gain to be made then is 20 (when B chooses B_2). In other words, A concentrates on the row minima to find the best strategy. For B it is a similar story – B will aim for the minimum loss, i.e. the column maxima provide the guide and B would look to strategy B_2. A adopts a 'maximin' policy while B's policy is one of 'minimax'.

Non-zero sum games
Chess and draughts are examples of zero sum games but most economic situations are non-zero (sometimes called variable sum games) in which the players have a choice of mutually beneficial actions, some of which may maximize society's welfare.

Prisoner's dilemma
The prisoner's dilemma is an example of a non-zero sum game. Two men are arrested on a suspicion of murder. Without a confession from one or both prisoners the most that either can be charged with is 'loitering with intent'. In order to obtain the maximum sentences the police interrogator has them locked in separate cells. The strategies facing the prisoners are now as follows.

If neither confesses then both will be convicted of the minor offence. If both confess they will be given long sentences but their cooperation will be taken into account and they will not be given maximum penalties. Finally, if one confesses and the other does not, then the former will be set free and the latter will receive the maximum sentence.

Table 9.3. Pay-off matrix for the prisoner's dilemma

		Prisoner 2	
		Does not confess	Confesses
Prisoner 1	Does not confess	(3,3)	(0,10)
	Confesses	(10,0)	(3,3)

Table 9.3 shows the pay-offs facing each prisoner. If prisoner 1 confesses then he will get a pay-off of 10 which is the value he places on his freedom, whilst prisoner 2 receives the maximum sentence (a pay-off of 0). Similarly, if prisoner 2 confesses he receives a pay-off of 10 and prisoner 1 gets a pay-off of 0. If both do not confess then they will each receive a pay-off of 3. Finally, we observe that if both confess they will receive a pay-off of 3.

What Table 9.3 indicates is that it is in the interests of both prisoners to confess, and that that decision is also the one that each prisoner would make if he knew what the other prisoner intended to do. This outcome is known as the *Nash equilibrium* (Nash, 1950); that is, it is the outcome to a game in which, given knowledge of all other players' decisions, each player is maximizing his pay-off and has, therefore, no incentive to change his decision. The Nash equilibrium need not be Pareto optimal, which would be the outcome with the property that nobody could be made better off without making anyone else worse off.

The aim here is not to undertake any comprehensive critique of game theory. It might be said that, despite over 40 years of development and the emergence of complicated games involving mixed and random strategies, and the assignment of probabilities, game theory remains unable to cope satisfactorily with the enormous complexities of real-world situations of oligopoly (Shubik, 1959). What must be said in its favour, and this is why we include this brief excursion into the model, is that game theory more than any other approach underlines the essentially conjectural nature of the oligopoly situation.

Non-collusive Oligopoly

The Cournot model

In 1836 Cournot suggested a solution to the problem of non-collusive duopoly – that is, a situation in which there are two sellers – on the assumption that each producer can take the other firm's output as given. In 1883 Bertrand produced an alternative model in which it is assumed that each firm takes the other firm's price as given, and it has been argued that, since firms tend to set a price and allow the market to decide how much will be bought, the Bertrand model is realistic. For many purposes, however, such as the possibility that other firms will enter the market, it may be more realistic to assume existing firms will maintain their existing output because they may find it difficult to adjust their capacity. We shall therefore persist with the Cournot model.

Cournot's model also continues to have an analytical appeal for contemporary economists because, in a very simple analytical framework, it captures the essence of the problem of conjectural interdependence. In its simplest form the model can be erected on the following assumptions.

1   There are two firms, A and B, in the market and the product of each is identical to that of the other.
2   The cost curves of the two firms are identical and, to simplify matters, each firm operates under constant zero cost of production.
3   There are complete barriers to entry to the industry.
4   The demand curve for the product is linear.
5   Each firm acts independently of the other, i.e. there is no collusion.
6   Each firm assumes that, once chosen, rival output will remain unchanged (conjectural variations are zero).

Consider, now, A and B taking it in turns to produce. Let A choose output first – on the assumption that B's output will remain at zero units per time period. Thus in figure 9.12, which represents the possibilities for the duopoly, A perceives OC to be the potential market opportunity when marginal cost is

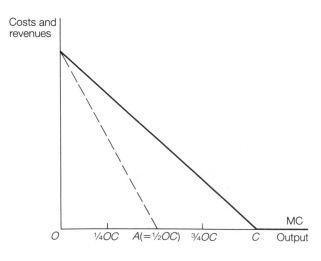

Figure 9.12

[1] If $p = a - bx$, then the revenue $R = p \cdot x = ax - bx^2$; hence MR $= dR/dx = a - 2bx$, i.e. the slope of the marginal revenue function is twice that of the demand function.

zero. A will decide to produce OA which is one-half of OC since the demand curve is a straight line.[1]

B now chooses – on the assumption that A's output will always be OA ($=\frac{1}{2}OC$); i.e. B perceives the *potential market* as one-half of the original market and decides to produce one-half of this potential amount; i.e. $\frac{1}{2}(\frac{1}{2}OC) = \frac{1}{4}OC$. A will now reconsider. Since B is producing $\frac{1}{4}OC$ and is expected to be doing so, A will perceive the potential market as diminished by the amount $\frac{1}{4}OC$, leaving $\frac{3}{4}OC$. Of this amount A will again intend to produce one-half, i.e. $\frac{1}{2}(OC - \frac{1}{4}OC) = \frac{3}{8}OC$. However, if A is producing $\frac{3}{8}OC$, B's perception of the potential market alters to one of $\frac{5}{8}OC$, of which B will intend to produce one-half, i.e. $\frac{5}{16}$, and so on.

Clearly, taking alternative starting points for each firm, the size of the output produced by each firm will 'grow' in the following series:

A's output $= OC(\frac{1}{2} - \frac{1}{8} - \frac{1}{32} - \frac{1}{128} - \dots) = \frac{1}{3}$ at the limit.

B's output $= OC(\frac{1}{4} + \frac{1}{16} + \frac{1}{64} + \frac{1}{256} + \dots) = \frac{1}{3}$ at the limit.

In other words, as a result of their myopic, uncooperative behaviour each producer ends up with one-third of the market and one-third is 'lost'.

Showing the movement towards equilibrium as describing two geometric progressions is useful because it clearly underlines the waste of potential output when the firms ignore collusion. But the equilibrium process itself is more clearly depicted by a technique developed by von Stackleberg in the early thirties (see Fellner, 1947 or Friedman, 1977), and termed the 'reaction function'. Given the assumptions of conjectural variations – A will maintain a chosen output level whatever level is decided by B and vice-versa – we can plot for each firm a set of optimum responses to all possible output levels set by the rival. Figure 9.13 shows the two reaction functions.

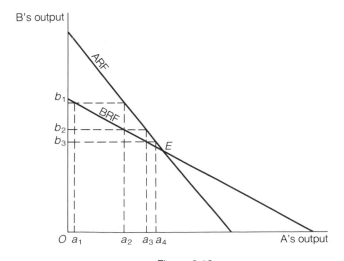

Figure 9.13

In figure 9.13 A's reaction function (ARF) is more steeply inclined than B's (BRF). Suppose that A chooses a_1 – B assumes that A will always produce a_1 and decides to produce b_1. However, if B were to produce $b_1 A$ would decide to produce a_2 which, in turn, would induce B to produce b_2 and then a further reaction from A of producing a_3 – and so on. It is clear from the diagram that the processes of action and reaction push the 'system' towards a stable equilibrium at E.

Using the calculus, a simple route to the equilibrium is found as follows:

1   assume two firms producing outputs q_1 and q_2;
2   assume each firm faces constant zero costs: $mc = ac = 0$;
3   assume a linear (market) demand function: $p = a - bQ$; where p represents market price and Q represents market quantity so that $Q = q_1 + q_2$;
4   assume zero conjectural variations, i.e. duopolist 1 treats q_2 as a constant while duopolist 2 treats q_1 as a constant.

$$\text{Hence: } TR_1 = pq_1 = aq_1 - bq_1^2 - bq_1q_2$$
$$TR_2 = pq_2 = aq_2 - bq_2^2 - bq_1q_2$$

For profit maximization $MR = 0$ (since $mc = 0$)

(1) $MR_1 = \dfrac{d(pq_1)}{dq_1} = a - 2bq_1 - bq^2$ ⎫
                                                          ⎬ simultaneous equations
(2) $MR_2 = \dfrac{d(pq_2)}{dq_2} = a - bq_1 - 2bq^2$ ⎭

The solution yields $q_1 + q_2 = 2a/3b$; $\therefore q_1 = q_2 = \frac{1}{3}$

Bertrand model

In the current Cournot model each firm takes its rival's output as given. Bertrand suggested that, instead of taking output as given, rivals might take each other's price as given. The change in assumption has been accepted as reflecting the shift from flex-price to fix-price situations, although the Cournot model may still be useful in analysing situations where a new entrant assumes that an existing firm will maintain its output. However, the significant difference between the models is that Bertrand's duopolists may charge the competitive price whereas Cournot's duopolists will not. The reason for this is that if each Bertrand firm has enough capacity to fulfil the entire market demand then each firm may undercut the other until the competitive price is reached. If firms have limited capacity then the possibilities of a price war with price oscillating between the minima set by the capacity of one firm could occur. This price war was analysed by Edgeworth (1925).

Stackleberg model
The Cournot model is an example of a follower–follower model; each firm follows the behaviour of the other firm. An alternative hypothesis is that each firm assumes itself to be the leader, and the other is the follower. Suppose A knows B's reaction function and that B does not follow A's lead, then A will produce the monopoly output and B will produce that output which will maximize its profits. But if each firm decides to be a leader then each firm will attempt to produce the monopoly output and each will be disappointed to discover that the price will fall to zero because their combined outputs will be equal to the competitive output. If each reverts to being a follower then the Cournot equilibrium will be attained. The situation is therefore unstable because each firm can perceive the benefits of being a leader.

The kinked oligopoly demand curve
In the Cournot model each firm takes the other firm's behaviour as given, and in the Stackleberg model one firm may accept the lead of the other firm. A third possibility is that one firm believes that other firms may follow some price increases but not other. Thus in figure 9.14 the firm believes that other firms will follow its price reductions but not its price increases – its demand curve is highly inelastic below the prevailing price P and highly elastic above the price P. Hence the demand curve is kinked at the prevailing price and the corresponding marginal revenue curve exhibits a marked discontinuity at the equilibrium output of Ox. In figure 9.15 the firm believes that other firms will follow its price increases but not its price decreases; this model has been applied to inflationary conditions (Efroymson, 1943).

There is at least one interesting prediction to be made from the kinked demand curve model – if the marginal cost curve passes through the range of the discontinuity in the marginal revenue curve then marginal costs can alter without inducing a change in price. We shall pursue this point later in the

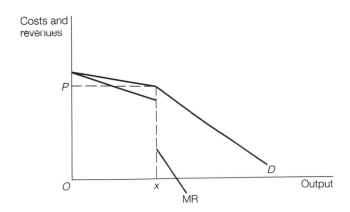

Figure 9.14

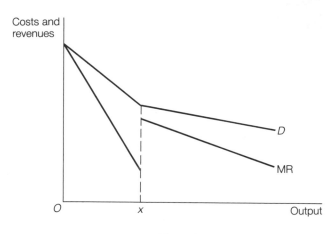

Figure 9.15

chapter. Whatever is said at that stage, of course, will depend upon one's acceptance of the model. For example, Stigler (1947) found that the kinked demand curve model did not provide a good explanation of price movements in the cigarette industry (considered to be an oligopoly) since rivals tended to match each other's price increases as well as price cuts. Such behaviour smacks of collusion in some form which, of course, rules out the kinked demand curve since each firm would have knowledge of rivals' reactions to price changes.

Consistent conjectures equilibrium
The oligopoly models which we have examined are extremely sensitive to the behavioural assumptions they possess. Even when identical assumptions are made about cost and demand conditions, different models can predict every price between marginal cost and monopoly price. Thus the Cournot model assumes that each firm maximizes its profits given the quantity of output of the other firm, and it predicts that the mark-up declines as the number of firms increases. In the Bertrand model each firm maximizes profits given the price of the other firm, and the theory predicts marginal cost pricing even in duopoly situations. Which theory is correct would seem therefore to depend upon empirical evidence. However, there have been recent attempts to resolve the problem logically by placing additional behavioural assumptions upon firms. Each firm, in addition to being rational in its behaviour, is assumed to attempt to equate its conjecture about its rival with the reaction function. This is the essence of what has become known as 'consistent conjectures',and it plays a part in oligopoly theory analogous to that played by rational expectations in macroeconomics. The equating of a firm's conjecture with the rival's reaction function (that is, with his actual behaviour) gives rise to a consistent conjectures equilibrium. The implications of consistent conjectures is, however, still in its infancy. It has been applied in a static context and it will be interesting to see how useful it is in dynamic situations involving the

possibility of investment. Furthermore, there are other areas of oligopoly behaviour to which it has still to be applied, such as advertising.

Collusive Behaviour

Conjectural interdependence suggests that some form of collusion will take place, involving rivals in the oligopolistic industry. Agreement among firms regarding prices and outputs may be formal, supported by clearly defined rules, or informal, even tacit, with some pattern of behaviour being repeated by every firm. One example of the latter, discussed already, is the Stackleberg model in which leader/follower roles are acted out. We can extend the idea now into a general concept of price leadership where one firm sets the price and the other firms always follow. The price leader may be somehow dominant (bigger, more efficient or whatever) or its sales pattern may be a very good indicator of industry trends (sometimes called the 'barometric firm'). Figures 9.16(a) and (b) show a simple price/follower model.

In figure 9.16(a) DD represents the market demand curve while CD_A represents A's 'conjectural demand curve' constructed on the basis of B's follower reactions to prices set by A as leader. The curves MC_B and AVC_B have their usual meanings and apply to firm B, while MC_A relates to firm A. The aim of the model is to resolve the difficulty over conjectural inter-dependence by deriving the demand curve CD_A. The derivation is based on the fact that, given the agreement about a leader/follower relationship, firm B, as follower, becomes a *price-taker* at each price set by A.

Hence, looking at figure 9.16(a), B would satisfy all of the market demand (P_1a) at a price of OP_1 set by A. At the lower price of OP_2, set by A, B would produce P_2b leaving bc for A to produce. At the lower price of OP_3, B would produce P_3d leaving de for A; and so on. At price OP_5, B is just covering costs, leaving the whole of the market to A at a price which is only infinitesimally lower than OP_5. Figure 9.16(b) traces out the corresponding conjectural

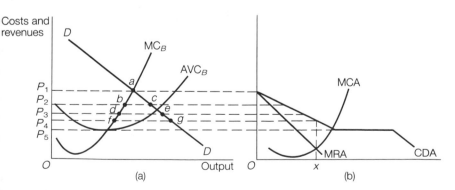

Figure 9.16   (a) Price follower; (b) price leader.

demand curve for A (CDA). Now, being the leader, A's marketing decision-maker will choose a price which maximizes A's profits – price OP_4 – leaving B to do the best it can with quantity P_4f while A produces Ox ($=fg$) units.

In this way the economist is able to perceive a determinate solution to the analytical problems created by conjectural interdependence. However, despite predicting a price and output for each firm the model does not guarantee security for all firms because the whole process depends upon A's willingness to continue as leader. There are, of course, several reasons why A might want B to survive in the same market: the existence of a rival might keep managers on their toes; without B firm A is a monopolist and liable to government control etc. Nevertheless, firm B might seek to obtain more security than is permitted under the informal agreement of the price leadership model.

However, it does not follow that formal agreements among oligopolists guarantee lifetime security for all parties to the agreement. Consider for example, the cases of (a) the market sharing agreement, and (b) the cartel or joint profit maximizing agreement.

Market sharing

Consider duopolists A and B selling a homogeneous product. A's production costs are lower than B's. The two firms agree formally to share their market in the ratio 2 : 1 in A's favour. Having split the market in this way each firm then goes its own way and tries to maximize profits, i.e. each firm equates marginal cost with marginal revenue. Figure 9.17 shows the results. The market demand curve is shown by DD while the demand curves facing each of the firms A and B are D_A and D_B respectively. The slope of D_A is two-thirds that of DD while D_B's slope is one-third that of DD. Aiming to maximize profits A would want to produce and sell OQ_A at a price of OP_A while B would aim for a combination of OQ_B/OP_B. Herein lies a problem – the product is homogeneous yet the firms want to set different prices. Nor is the problem easy to solve – a single price must be charged, and whenever it is set there is the danger that one firm, or both, will try to increase market share. Once a single price is established, e.g. OP_c, each firm becomes a price-taker and wants to equate marginal cost with price in order to maximize profits. In other words, to produce and sell more than the proportion designated by the agreement. If the firm is unable to sell its increased share immediately, the output can be stored, perhaps, with a view to capturing more of the market at a later date. It may be the case, then, that a rigorous set of penalties may have to accompany any market sharing agreement.

The cartel

The cartel represents the most formal of collusive agreements; each member of the cartel surrenders its own identity in the search for maximum group profits. Taking the duopoly again, then, both firms will seek to agree upon that price which will enable both of them to maximize their profit, i.e. to earn more profit than would be possible without collusion. Thus the monopoly solution is chosen – that output which would be sold if the two firms were to merge and form a single firm, producing in two separate plants with differing costs of production. The solution is shown in figure 9.18.

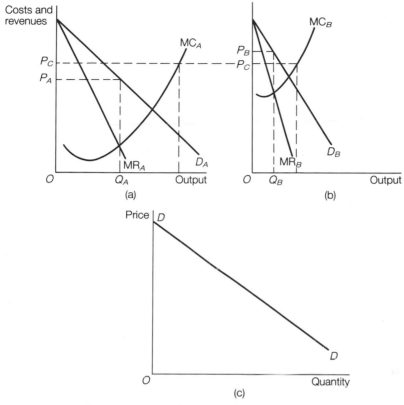

Figure 9.17   (a) Firm *A*; (b) firm *B*; (c) market.

Together the two firms produce that output which equates marginal cost with marginal revenue, and the output is so distributed between the two firms that marginal costs are equalized. However, as it stands this model offers no more security to each firm than the market sharing arrangement. Again, note that since the cartel price is fixed by agreement (i.e. by output level being fixed and the price being determined accordingly) each firm faces an incentive to equate marginal cost with price, and even if firms were prepared to adhere to the agreement in the short run there is no guarantee that the agreement will continue to be honoured over the longer run. Expectations may induce a firm to stockpile in anticipation of a future price war. To safeguard the interests of the cartel over the longer run, then, it may be necessary to extend the range of agreements. One possibility might lie in a pooling arrangement, whereby joint profits enter a central fund out of which each firm draws a share not less than the revenue that might be expected from acting independently of the cartel; another might be a quota agreement to ensure that individual firms do not overproduce. Of course, to enforce such agreements certain penalties may

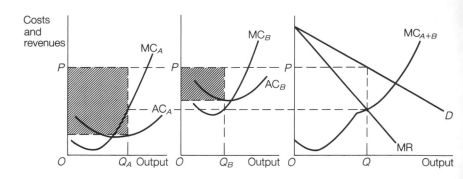

Figure 9.18   (a) Firm *A*; (b) firm *B*; (c) cartel.

be needed again as punishment for breaking the agreement, and it is unlikely that surrendering autonomy to this degree will have a wide appeal unless the rewards are handsome and obvious. A summary of the conditions which need to prevail in order that a collusive agreement can be policed successfully might be useful at this point:

1   the number of firms to be monitored must be small;
2   there must be no random or erratic shifts of customers from one firm to another so that each firm can take constancy of its market share as an indication that other firms are enforcing the agreement;
3   product heterogeneity must be relatively unimportant so as to prevent customers switching brands;
4   market demand must be relatively inelastic;
5   there must be barriers to entry.

Conditions 1 to 4 emerge clearly from a brief excursion into oligopoly theory, but condition 5 requires further thought.

Barriers to Entry

In the light of our previous discussions it would appear that established firms have a choice of three policies: (1) accept the newcomer's output and adjust one's own output accordingly; (2) attempt to lead or dictate a strategy; or (3) secure a joint profit-maximizing policy. The choice of these policies might then be dictated by the nature of the rival's cost and profit functions and the nature of the capital market which would influence each side to hold out for a particular policy.

There may, however, be barriers to entry. A newcomer may have to be of a certain size (achieve economies of scale) before entry is feasible. Hence, an established firm could set a price which attempted to take into account the economies of scale which an entrant must achieve and the nature of the market demand curve. This is the nature of the entry, limit-pricing policy which we encountered in the Bhagwati model of chapter 4; but note: there are qualifications. First, if there is more than one established firm then there may be difficulties in obtaining an agreed policy. Second, it may pay an established firm to permit entry but at a rate which allows the established firm to maximize the present value of its profit stream. Third, the limit-pricing policy may not convince a potential entrant: it may lack credibility. Credible threats, effective entry barriers, may therefore take the form of planned reserve capacity which can be brought into use quickly, advertising and branding policies.

The outcome of any entry-preventing programme depends partly upon who has the first move and what is the likely sequence of events as rivals react to each other's policies. The advantages of having the first move would seem to lie with the established firm because it is familiar with the market. But before examining the possible sequence of events following from a first move it may be useful to examine market structures in which established firms may have no advantage.

Contestable Markets

There may be situations in which no entry-deterring strategies can be pursued by an established firm, nor may it be possible to formulate a post-entry equilibrium. Indeed, if all markets are perfectly contestable then the oligopoly problem disappears.

A perfectly contestable market may be defined as one where: (1) all firms have access to the same technology; (2) the technology may have scale economics which give rise to fixed costs but not to sunk costs; (3) established firms cannot change prices instantly (they may fear a loss of goodwill from customers who conclude that they have been overcharged in the past); but (4) customers can respond instantly to price differentials. Consider, for example, an airline which operates a flight from London to Edinburgh. Although it may be the only company operating on that route, it may not have a monopoly position if a company operating a plane on the London to Paris route can easily switch its plane on to the London to Edinburgh route. What we observe in this case is that both companies have incurred fixed costs in the form of planes but those planes are not specific (or sunk in) to particular routes. As an alternative example we may consider chemical companies, which can be capable of producing a variety of products from a wide range of processes. Chemical firms may therefore obtain economies in scope in their operations. Threat of cross-entry from one market or industry to another may therefore force a firm to act as if its demand curve were highly elastic and to charge a price equal to marginal cost even though it is apparently the only firm in the market. Theory of contestable markets has two further implications. First, if markets are contestable then concentration ratios will be misleading because they will fail to capture the threat of potential entry from a hit-and-run raider who is lurking in another industry. Second, in seeking to control monopolies the state should attempt to convert situations where sunk costs exist into situations where only fixed costs obtain.

Sequential (Perfect) Equilibrium

So far we have been concerned with analysing the behaviour of oligopolists in the short run, with behaviour in one period. However, we want to know also what happens in the long run. In other words, is the equilibrium obtained in one period sustainable in the long run? This is the subject matter of sequential (often called perfect) equilibrium. Consider, for example, figure 9.19, taken from Dixit (1982), which is a two-stage game between an established monopolist and a prospective entrant. In the first stage the entrant has to decide whether or not to enter the market. If he stays out the monopolist earns monopoly profits P_m. If he enters the monopolist has to decide whether to fight, in which case each gets profits P_w, or whether to share the market with each getting P_d. In the game tree in the diagram the pay-offs at each stage are shown, and it is assumed that $P_m > P_d > 0 > P_w$; that is, monopoly profits are superior to duopoly profits whilst a price war is mutually destructive.

The problem then is to determine the strategies at each stage which might give rise to a long-run equilibrium. Thus the threat of a price war cannot be part of a perfect equilibrium because the entrant knows that the incumbent's optimal response is sharing; $P_d > 0 > P_w$. Hence sharing is the outcome in the perfect equilibrium and a price war may not constitute a credible threat. But if the established firm makes a prior irrevocable commitment, such as investing in spare capacity, then he may incur cost C and affect the outcome if $P_w > P_d - C$. Of course much depends upon the costs which are likely to be incurred by an entrant, and this is where the theory of contestable markets becomes relevant. If an outsider does not have to incur sunk costs, but can readily switch capacity from one market to another, then the long-run equilibrium may reveal one firm in the market which does not, and cannot, obtain monopoly profits. The analysis of sequential equilibria depends upon solving the problem backwards and, as such, it has links with dynamic programming, which are discussed in chapter 12.

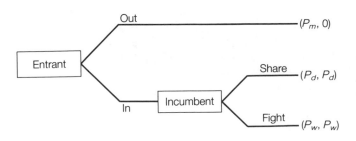

Figure 9.19

Bibliography and References

Andrews, P. W. S. (1949) *Manufacturing Business*. London: Macmillan.
Andrews, P. W. S. (1964) *On Competition and Economic Theory*. London: Macmillan.
Andrews, P. W. S. and Sayers, R. S. (eds) (1951) *Oxford Studies in the Price Mechanism*. Oxford: Oxford University Press.
Andrews, P. W. S. and Brunner, E. (1975) *Studies in Pricing*. London: Macmillan.
Bertrand, J. (1983) Review of Cournot, *Journal des Savants*, 499–508.
Bhagwati, J. N. (1970) 'Oligopoly theory, entry prevention and growth', *Oxford Economic Papers*, 22, 297–310.
Breshnahan, T. (1981) 'Duopoly models with consistent conjectures', *American Economic Review*, 71, 934–45.
Brunner, E. (1952) 'Competition and the theory of the firm', *Economia Internazionale*, 5, 509–26, 727–59.
Chamberlin, E. W. (1933) *The Theory of Monopolistic Competition*. Cambridge Mass.: Harvard University Press.
Clarke, R. and Davies, S. W. (1982) 'Market structure and price–cost margins', *Economica*, 93, 182–92.
Coase, R. H. (1946) 'Monopoly pricing with interrelated costs and demands', *Economica*, 13, 278–94.
Cournot, A. A. (1927) *Researches into the Mathematical Principles of the Theory of Wealth*. New York: Macmillan (reprint).
Cowling, K. and Waterson, M. (1976) 'Price–cost margins and market structure', *Economica*, 43, 267–74.
Davidson, P. (1972) *Money in the Real World*. London: Macmillan.
Demsetz, H. (1964) 'The welfare and empirical implications of monopolistic competition', *Economic Journal*, 74, 623–41.
Dewey, D. (1969) *The Theory of Imperfect Competition: A Radical Reconstruction*. New York: Columbia University Press.
Dixit, A. (1982) 'Recent developments in oligopoly theory', *American Economic Review*, 72, 12–17.
Edgeworth, F. (1925) *Papers Relating to Political Economy*. London: Macmillan.
Efroymson, P. (1943) 'A note on the kinked demand curve', *American Economic Review*, 3, 98–109.
Fellner, W. J. (1947) *Competition Among the Few*. New York: Alfred Knopf.
Friedman, J. W. (1977) *Oligopoly and the Theory of Games*. Amsterdam: North Holland.
Friedman, M. (1953) *Essays in Positive Economics*. Chicago: University of Chicago Press.
Godley, R. and Nordhaus, W. D. (1972) 'Pricing in the trade cycle', *Economic Journal*, 82, 853–82.
Hall, R. L. and Hitch, C. J. (1939) 'Price theory and business behaviour', *Oxford Economic Papers*; reprinted in Andrews and Sayers (1951).
Hicks, J. R. (1939) *Value and Capital*. Oxford: Oxford University Press.
Hurwicz, L. (1945) 'The theory of games: review article', *American Economic Review*, 35, 907–25.
Jefferys, J. B. (1950) *Retail Trading in Great Britain*. London: National Institute of Economic and Social Research.
Kaldor, N. (1960) *Essays on Value and Distribution*. London: Duckworth.
Keynes, J. M. (1936) *The General Theory of Employment, Interest and Money*. London: Macmillan.

Liebenstein, H. (1978) *General X-Efficiency Theory and Economic Development*. London: Oxford University Press.

Lyons, B. R. (1981) 'Price–cost margins, market structure and international trade'. In D. Currie et al. (eds.) *Microeconomic Analysis*. London: Croom Helm.

Machlup, F. (1952) *The Economics of Sellers' Competition*. Baltimore: Johns Hopkins Press.

Marshall, A. (1920) *Principles of Economics*, 8th edn. London: Macmillan.

Marshall, A. (1923) *Industry and Trade*. London: Macmillan.

Mason, E. (1957) *Economic Concentration and the Monopoly Problem*. Cambridge, Mass.: Harvard University Press.

Nash, J. (1950) 'The bargaining problem', *Econometrica*, 18, 155–62.

Pigou, A. C. (1928) *Economics of Welfare*. London: Macmillan.

Salop, S. and Stiglitz, J. E. (1977) 'Bargains and ripoffs: imperfect information and monopolistically competitive price dispersion', *Review of Economic Studies*, 44, 493–510.

Scott Jr, F. A. and Morrell, S. O. (1985) 'Two-part pricing for a multi-product monopolist', *Economic Enquiry*, 24, 295–307.

Shubik, M. (1959) *Strategy and Market Structure*. New York: John Wiley.

Stackleberg, H. (1952) *The Theory of the Market Economy*. Oxford: Oxford University Press.

Stigler, G. J. (1939) 'Production and distribution in the short run', *Journal of Political Economy*, 47, 305–27.

Stigler, G. J. (1947) 'The kinky oligopoly demand curve and rigid prices', *Journal of Political Economy*, 55, 432–49.

Stigler, G. J. (1949) *Five Lectures on Economic Problems*. London: Longmans.

Stigler, G. J. (1964) 'A theory of oligopoly', *Journal of Political Economy*, 72, 44–61.

Stiglitz, J. (1976) 'Monopoly and the rate of extraction of exhaustible resources', *Journal of Political Economy*, 66, 655–61.

Triffin, R. (1940) *Monopolistic Competition and General Equilibrium Theory*. Cambridge Mass.: Harvard University Press.

Varian, H. R. (1980) 'A model of sales', *American Economic Review*, 70, 651–9.

Vickers, J. (1985) 'Strategic competition among the few – some recent developments in the economics of industry', *Oxford Review of Economic Policy*, 1, 39–62.

Yamey, B. S. (1984) 'The economic performance of futures trading', *Three Banks Reviews*, 141, 33–43.

10 Product Policy

Product competition is always present and can be more important than price competition. Such an assertion is based on the reason that trade involves the exchange of property rights and those property rights must be clearly defined in law. Thus one firm can make a product closely resembling one made by another, so that customers may regard the two goods as nearly equivalent, but it is not permitted to make an *exact* copy of another firm's product and claim it is exactly the same as that of the other firm. Therefore product differentiation and product competition is always present. Without product differentiation firms would lose their identity and have no incentive to offer customers something different. Competition therefore occurs by firms offering goods with new characteristics, or with new combinations of characteristics, on terms that customers may find more attractive than existing combinations. Hence competition can exist without perfect substitutes. A firm may not face an infinitely elastic demand for its product at a given price, and it may find that it has to lower the price of its product in order to sell more – but it can also face vigorous and persistent challenges from innovators.

Products are extremely difficult to analyse. Some attributes may be capable of measurement and separately valued, and it is possible to think of commodities as multi-dimensional. But not all characteristics are measurable and some goods may be a mix of measurable and non-measurable attributes. Commodities may be classified, therefore, in terms of the ease of assessing their attributes. Thus, we may have:

1 *Search goods*, whose qualities can be assessed by simple inspection once they have been located in the market. Such goods may be frequent purchases and have a low price, both of which make inspection and experimentation comparatively cheap.
2 *Experience goods*, whose qualities cannot be assessed until after purchase and consumption.
3 *Credence goods*, whose qualities may not be assessable even after purchase. Such goods comprise such things as medical surgery and legal contracts, and are covered by qualities standards imposed, often, by self-regulating professions.

Judging the attributes of goods creates problems for consumers, but especially for management. If consumers cannot assess the characteristics of goods then they may not buy them. Management must therefore strive to persuade consumers to buy goods in terms of their method of presentation of goods, advertising outlays, etc.

Product Innovation and Product Life Cycle

Of particular importance to management is the likely impact which a new product launch will have on the market. Conjectures about the effects may be summarized in a product diffusion or product life cycle curve which shows the time path of sales. Initially sales are low, and then climb rapidly to reach a peak at some time in the future; thereafter sales stagnate or decline. The diffusion curve is neither a demand curve nor a supply curve, but a locus which traces out the interaction of market demand and supply over time. On the one hand the curve traces out the rate at which new consumers learn about, or are infected by, a new commodity. The curve, therefore, can be regarded as embodying a learning or epidemiological process whose determinants include the price of the product, the incomes of untapped members of the market, the expected utility which those would-be consumers expect from buying the product (which will in turn be influenced by the utility which they think existing consumers are getting). On the other hand, the path of the diffusion process will be influenced by the ability of the firm to supply enough of the product to meet demand. As its market expands the firm may find that it is having to attract resources from other firms, and in order to do so it may have to bid up factor prices and increase its costs. Profitability might therefore be expected to decline as costs rise. Furthermore, the greater the initial success of the firm the more likely it is to encourage imitators. The supply of substitutes from other firms might therefore be expected to increase.

Product Diffusion and Optimal Marketing Strategy

The sales of some consumer durable goods tend to be heavily influenced by the information passed from a user to a potential buyer; they are 'experience goods'. For such goods the optimal marketing strategy may be a low price combined with heavy advertising in the first period in order to persuade a large number of households to buy the good and hope that they will infect a large number in the second period.

Brand Share and the Importance of Being First

A marketing manager will seek to establish that share of the market for a commodity which will maximize revenue, and the simplest method of analysing commodity competition is to envisage each commodity as occupying some 'space' in the market; that is commodity competition is viewed as analogous to geographical competition. The alternative procedure is to dissect the characteristics of products and then to pronounce those commodities which have many characteristics in common to be close substitutes. Thus the two approaches need not be competitive, but can be complementary if it is accepted that location may be a characteristic.

We begin with the geographical analogy as pioneered by Hotelling (1929). In figure 10.1 consumers are strung out along a road AB and a firm has to decide where to locate itself. It chooses the mid-point C. If then a second firm enters the market it can locate itself anywhere, but will find it most profitable to go as close as possible to the first firm e.g. D or E, rather than F. The conclusion is that commodity competition takes the form of imitation.

Figure 10.1

The model, however, slurs over the point that pioneering brands may retain a considerable share of the market even though they may appear to be subject to considerable competition from imitators. In other words, the model ignores the point that not all characteristics may be observable before purchase. There may therefore be a distinction between *experience goods* – those whose characteristics cannot be assessed until after purchase and sometimes may require repeated purchase in order to reach a final verdict – and *search goods* which, once located, have characteristics that can be assessed by casual inspection. The problem of assessing the qualities of goods has three implications. First, if characteristics cannot easily be identified then it may be difficult to make price comparisons. Thus some people argue for *unit pricing* on the grounds that consumers would then be able to judge the value of goods. However, the fact that milk is sold by the pint or litre may tell the consumer nothing about its butter-fat content. Second, the fact that goods can only be evaluated after purchase means that the simple entry models of Cournot and Bertrand, which we discussed earlier, may provide no clue as to the likely success of a potential entrant. Third, experience of a good may be a more important entry barrier than any other form of sales promotion conducted by an established firm.

Commodity Discrimination

In addition to seeking a market for one commodity with given attributes, a firm may seek also to split the market into segments in order to practise commodity discrimination. This strategy is analogous to price discrimination (Adams and Yellen, 1976) but with the advantage that it may be more easy and profitable to practise. Price discrimination with a homogeneous product often encounters the problem that consumers may find it easy to switch markets. A firm may therefore choose to pursue one of three commodity strategies:

1   Sell two or more commodities separately and attempt to obtain a monopoly profit on each (see the earlier discussion of the multi-product firm and pricing policy).
2   Sell two or more commodities in a package, such as a holiday tour. This is the *pure bundling strategy*.
3   Sell two or more commodities separately and as a package at a set of prices which attempts to maximize profits. This is the *mixed bundling strategy* used by, for example, restaurants when they offer table d'hôte and à la carte menus, and by car firms which offer various models and also the accessories which enable a car to be transformed into a higher-priced model.

In figure 10.2 the price of commodity A is measured along the horizontal axis and the price of B is measured along the vertical axis. If the firm set minimum prices of P_A^* and P_B^* on the commodities then perpendiculars divide the graph into four zones:

1   In zone 1 the reservation price of customers for each of the goods is above the minimum prices set by the firm and both goods are bought. This is the zone of pure monopoly strategy.
2   In zone 2 consumers' reservation prices are above the firm's maximum price for good A but below the price for good B and so only A will be bought.
3   In zone 3 consumers' reservation prices are below the firm's reservation prices for A and B and neither good will be bought.
4   In zone 4 customers will buy only good B and not good A.

If instead the firm adopts a pure bundling strategy then consumers are sorted into two groups: those who are willing and able to buy the bundle and those who are not.

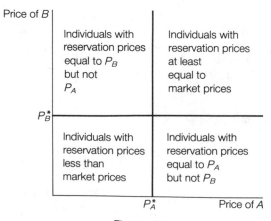

Figure 10.2

In figure 10.3 the slope of the line XX measures the package prices; consumers in zone 1 buy the good and those in zone 2 do not. If the firm adopts a mixed bundling strategy, however, then consumers are divided into four groups as in figure 10.4. Consumers in zone OP_2LMP_1 buy neither good, those in zone P_1MT buy only good B, consumers in zone P_2LS buy only good A and, finally, consumers in zone SLMT buy the package of A and B. Because the price of the package is below the sum of the prices of each component, consumers derive more consumer surplus than they would if they were to buy them separately. As to why some consumers prefer to buy only one good, we may observe that some do not want soup or a pudding with their meal. Which strategy is adopted by a firm will, however, depend upon which promises the greater profits.

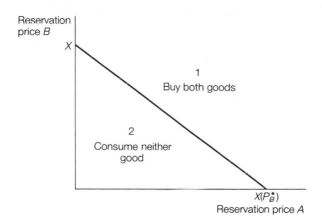

Figure 10.3

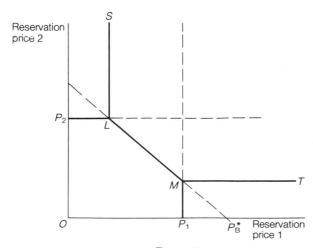

Figure 10.4

Durability of Goods

The durability of a good (Leibowitz, 1982) raises three interesting questions:

1 Does market structure dictate the durability of goods? In other words, do monopolists suppress durability?
2 Should durable goods be sold or leased on a rental basis?
3 What effect does the emergence of a second-hand market for used goods have on the pricing policy for new goods?

The first question is of general interest but has obvious links with the third question. The price of new cars may be influenced by the prices obtained for second-hand cars and it may be argued that it is in the interests of manufacturers of new goods to eliminate second-hand markets by lowering the durability of goods.

A simple approach to the first question is provided by figure 10.5, where it is assumed that the average and marginal costs of producing cars are constant, and that it costs less to produce cars which will have a physical life of 10 years, AC_d, than cars which will last 5 years, AC_n. Hence both competitive firms and monopolists would produce the more durable cars if such a policy would minimize costs. The outputs of a competitive industry and a monopolist would, of course, differ; the competitive industry would produce OQ_C and the monopolist would produce OQ_M; durability is independent of market structure in all cases where average cost curves do not intersect.

The question of sale versus lease turns on the distinction between production costs and maintenance costs. Under a sales policy a firm would be responsible

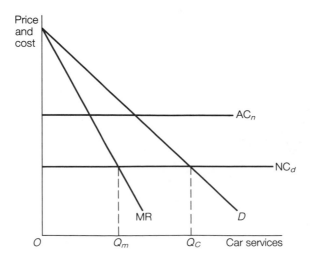

Figure 10.5

for production costs whilst consumers would undertake maintenance. Under a rent policy a firm would undertake both production and maintenance and consumers would have no control over the durability of goods. Because a sales policy does allow consumers some freedom to determine the length of life of assets it could be that firms might prefer rental policies to sales policies. Under perfect competition, however, firms are unable to dictate pricing policy even though it would be in the interest of each firm to switch to leasing. But a monopolist could move to a rental policy.

The effect of a second-hand market upon a firm's profits depends upon the strength of demand in the second-hand market. If no second-hand market existed some consumers would switch their demands to the new goods market, but how much switching occurred would depend upon the degree of substitutability between new and used goods (cross-price elasticity of demand). Thus, in figure 10.6 we assume that a commodity lasts for two periods, that at the end of the first period each unit of the commodity becomes a used good, that there is no discount rate, and that there are no costs in operating the second-hand market. If consumers place the same (rental) value on the commodity in each period then the demand curves are identical ($D_1 = D_2$) and total demand is given by the curve D_V which is the vertical summation of the demands in each period. By vertically adding the demand curves it is assumed that the cost of providing the secondary market is zero, i.e. increases in durability can be made without cost. In effect, durable goods are treated as if they were public goods and and the demands by one group cannot affect the demands by others.

Now if the second-hand market is eliminated and goods in period 1 are perfect substitutes for goods in period 2 then second period demand will switch to the first period and the first period demand curve will become D_f, which is the horizontal summation of D_1 and D_2 demand curves. If first period

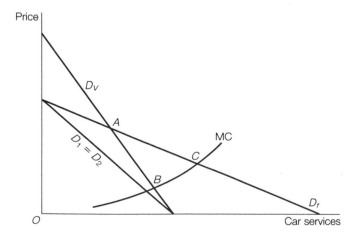

Figure 10.6

goods were not perfect substitutes then the new demand curve would lie below D_f. At point A the two demand curves D_V and D_f intersect (new and used goods are substitutes). To the left of A producers are better off with a second-hand market because it allows them to sell new goods at a higher price. To the right of A producers would be better off without a second-hand market. If MC is the supply curve of a competitive industry then equilibrium will be at B when a secondary market exists and at C when no secondary market exists.

Advertising Policy

The purpose of advertising is to provide information and to persuade customers to buy a commodity; but advertising expenditures cannot be divorced from pricing policy (and hence market structure) as well as the nature of the commodity and location. The assessment of the effects of advertising therefore depend upon the isolation of the effects of other variables.

Market Structures

Monopoly
The simplest analysis of the effects of advertising occurs in the case of the monopolist. In figure 10.7 the initial demand curve is AB, and at price OP the firm sells OQ and its revenue (neglecting costs) is $OP.OQ$. The effect of advertising is to shift the demand curve to CD and, assuming price remains unchanged, revenue increases to $OP.OQ_1$. But the shift of the demand curve also changes the own-price elasticity of demand. The elasticity of the demand curve AB is given by the ratio $OP : OB$ and the elasticity of the new demand

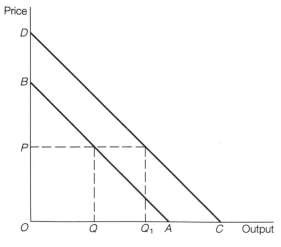

Figure 10.7

CD is *OP* : *OD*. Since the latter ratio is smaller than the former, advertising has reduced the price elasticity of demand at every price. Hence it would be possible for the firm to raise the price until it operated on the elastic section of its demand curve.

The analysis presented in figure 10.7 depends upon the assumption that the demand curve is linear. If the demand curve were non-linear then it would be possible for advertising to leave the price elasticity unchanged.

The Optimal Price–Advertising Decision

The preceding analysis suggests that associated with each level of advertising expenditure there will be a different demand curve and a different price, that the optimal price decision will involve the equating of the marginal revenue from advertising with the marginal revenue from price changes, and that the respective revenue increments will in turn depend upon the elasticity of sales with respect to advertising and the own-price elasticity of demand. We shall now outline two treatments of these issues. The first is a geometric analysis by Boulding (1955), and the second approach by Dorfman and Steiner (1954) which arrives at similar conclusions to Boulding, but uses the calculus.

Boulding's analysis
The firm adjusts to three strategic variables – output, price and selling 'outlay' (advertising). For any level of output, the price which the firm can obtain *depends* upon the level of expenditure on advertising and other forms of selling behaviour. Generally speaking, the more advertising the higher the price that can be obtained, subject to eventually diminishing returns.

When we consider the interaction of all the variables at once we see two interesting implications for non-perfect markets:

1   sales promotion may be preferred to price cutting
2   excess capacity is not inevitable under monopolistic competition.

(1)   To demonstrate this we use Boulding's analysis which makes use of contour lines. We can construct a sales contour by plotting, for each level of output, all those combinations of price (*p*) and total selling cost (TSC) which would enable the seller to sell that output. We would expect, of course, that the higher the selling cost the higher the price that can be obtained – as we said earlier – which suggests that the selling map looks something like figure 10.8.

As an example, consider a contour like S_{40} which shows all these combinations of price and selling cost which enable the firm to sell 40 units of output. Of course, such contours are merely guidelines – they do not show the means of choosing the *best* combination of price and selling cost. To help us find this we need some sort of revenue contour which will show us combinations of price and selling cost which will yield a given revenue, as in figure 10.9. These contours again show diminishing returns – as both price and selling costs are increased, revenue increases, but at a decreasing rate until, eventually, some saturation point is reached and revenues actually begin

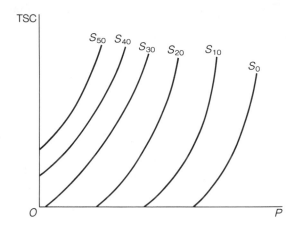

Figure 10.8

to fall, and to maintain the same level of revenue both selling costs and price can be reduced. As we can seen from the diagram there is one combination of selling costs and price which maximises revenue – point X. For any level of revenue less than this it is possible to combine the same price with a higher or lower selling cost, or the same selling costs with a higher or lower price.

If we now put the two diagrams together we can combine an objective of maximizing revenues with the constraints provided by the sales lines. Thus, whenever a sales line touches a revenue line the tangency point shows the best way of selling that quantity of output shown by the sales line in figure 10.10. Thus point Z shows the best way of selling 30 units of output,

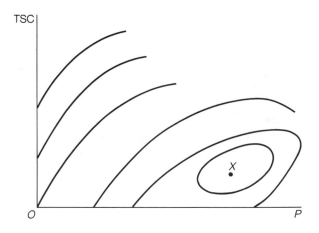

Figure 10.9

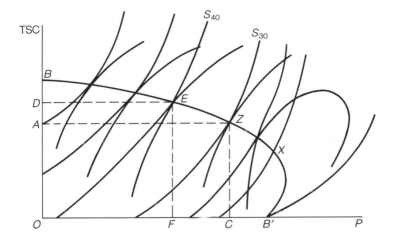

Figure 10.10

i.e. the best way (to maximize revenue) of selling output 30 is to combine a selling cost of $CZ(=OA)$ with a price $OC(=A^2)$; BB' is therefore the optimum selling line, or marketing strategy line. If BB' is steep the best way to raise sales would be to raise selling costs a lot and reduce price a little; if BB' is relatively flat then the price reduction must be large relative to the increase in selling costs, e.g. to increase sales to 40 from 30 means a reduction in price of FC and an increase in costs of AD. If we take extreme cases, e.g. BB' vertical beyond X and horizontal towards B, then in the former case the best way to raise sales would be to increase selling costs without lowering price, while in the latter the best thing to do is to lower price and leave selling costs unchanged. When the curve bends backwards as between X and B' output can be expanded only by a combination of sales promotion (selling costs) and price reductions.

Thus we can see why firms in a monopolistically competitive market might prefer to promote sales (incur selling costs) rather than cut price. The most profitable combination of price and selling costs must, in the above case, lie between B' and X since this is the only range in which total revenue increases as sales increase – if sales are pushed left of X total (sales) revenue actually decreases. We can see also that within this range BB' is fairly steep; therefore in this range of output, where the most profitable position is going to lie, it may well pay to concentrate upon sales promotion rather than engage in price-cutting. The more general conclusion from the whole analysis is that the best way of expanding sales as a rule is likely to be some combination of sales promotion and price-cutting rather than a reliance on either one alone.

(2)   We can now use BB' on the more conventional diagram representing optimum behaviour for the firm – as we move along BB' we observe the price

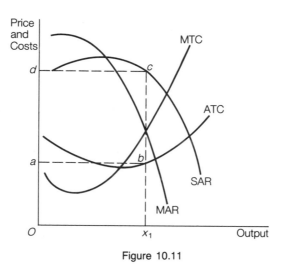

Figure 10.11

at which outputs can be sold, at some given level of advertising outlay; hence we can therefore derive from BB' an average revenue curve, adjusted to take account of advertising outlays at each possible price (SAR). SAR represents the average revenue curve when advertising is taken into account (BB' shows price/selling outlay and output, therefore from it we can derive output per combination of price and selling outlay). MAR is marginal to SAR. APC is the curve of average production costs, ASC represents average selling costs and ATC represents average total costs. Profits are maximized at output Ox, where MAR = MTC and profit equals *abcd* (figure 10.11).

Let us now allow for freedom of entry in response to these supernormal profits. Firms will enter the market until these surpluses are removed – when SAR : ATC as in figure 10.12. As firms come in this will reduce the prices which can be obtained for any level of output and therefore push SAR downwards. It may also push *up* ASC as firms meet the increased competition with more advertising. Thus SAR and ATC are pushed together. But note that SAR = ATC does not mean *necessarily* that average *production* costs are not minimized, i.e. there is no *a priori* reason for excess capacity to exist (Demsetz, 1964).

The Dorfman-Steiner theorem

This theorem applies the neoclassical rules of profit maximization to a single product firm which faces selling outlays as well as product price as a strategic variable in the marketing sphere of its operations. The firm is assumed to purchase advertising messages, and expenditure on such messages enters the

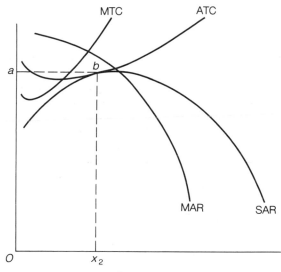

Figure 10.12

demand function for the firm's product as A; using P for price and Q for quantity the demand function is presented as:

$$Q = Q(A,P)$$

and it is assumed that $\dfrac{\partial Q}{\partial A} > 0$ and $\dfrac{\partial Q}{\partial P} < 0$ (10.1)

The firm's profit function is written as:

$$\pi = PQ(A,P) - C[Q(A,P)] - A \qquad (10.2)$$

where C represents production costs.

Differentiating the profit function with respect to both P and A and setting the result equal to zero in order to fulfil the profit maximizing condition yields:

$$\frac{\partial \pi}{\partial P} = Q + P\left(\frac{\partial Q}{\partial P}\right) - \left[\left(\frac{dC}{dQ}\right)\left(\frac{\partial Q}{\partial P}\right)\right] = 0 \qquad (10.3)$$

and

$$\frac{\partial \pi}{\partial A} = P\frac{\partial Q}{\partial A} - \left[\left(\frac{dC}{dQ}\right)\left(\frac{\partial Q}{\partial A}\right)\right] - 1 = 0 \qquad (10.4)$$

(10.3) tells the firm that, for any level of A, price should be set to equate marginal cost with marginal revenue. Rearranging (10.3) yields

$$\frac{P - \dfrac{dC}{dQ}}{P} = \frac{1}{\eta p} \tag{10.5}$$

In other words, the degree of monopoly equals the reciprocal of the price elasticity of demand (ηp).

Condition (10.4) presents the optimum level of advertising expenditure for any price; the firm should spend on advertising until the marginal revenue product of such expenditure, $P(\partial Q/\partial A)$, equals the marginal cost of such expenditure, which, in turn, is determined by the expenditure on one extra unit of advertising plus the extra production cost created by the increased output (demand) which follows the marginal increase in advertising, (dc/dQ) $(\partial Q/\partial A)$. Finally, the Dorfman–Steiner theorem defines the advertising elasticity of demand (the degree of response of product demand with respect to advertising) as $\eta_A = (A/Q)\,(\partial Q/\partial A)$. We can make use of this presently; first rearrange (10.4) and multiply by A/PQ:

$$\frac{A}{Q}\left[\frac{\partial Q}{\partial A}\left(\frac{P - \dfrac{dC}{dQ}}{P}\right)\right] = \frac{A}{PQ} \tag{10.6}$$

which, given (10.5), can be expressed as

$$\frac{A}{PQ} = \frac{\eta_A}{\eta p} \tag{10.7}$$

(10.7) gives the basic Dorfman–Steiner result that the ratio of advertising expenditure to sales should be equal to the ratio of the advertising elasticity of demand to the price elasticity of demand, if profits are to be maximized.

Advertising as a Capital Good

Instead of considering advertising as having a once-and-for-all effect we may regard it as a capital good which gives rise to a stream of returns over time. Thus advertising may exert a persistent effect upon the behaviour of consumers, and it may lead to secondary effects through the influence of the purchases of consumers who were affected by advertising causing other consumers to alter their spending plans. Hence a firm has to consider the optimal amount of goodwill, G (advertising capital), to create. Hence there is a dynamic analogue to the Dorfman–Steiner condition

$$\frac{G}{S} = \frac{\eta_Q}{\eta_P(r + \delta)} \tag{10.8}$$

where r is the discount rate and δ is the depreciation rate. In terms of the previous discussion we may observe that

$$A = \dot{G} + \delta G \qquad (10.9)$$

that is, current advertising is equal to the change in the capital stock (net investment $\dot{G}$) plus the amount which has to be spent in order to maintain the existing stock of goodwill. Hence we can translate equation 10.8 into the terms of A/S by multiplying through by A/S.

$$\frac{A}{S} = \frac{\eta_A}{\eta_P(r + \delta)} \qquad (10.10)$$

because $\delta Q/\delta C = \delta Q/\delta A$.

One problem with this formulation is that it ignores any long-lasting effects of price changes.

Oligopoly

If the market structure is oligopolistic then the optimal price–advertising policy depends upon the presence or absence of collusion. If there is collusion then the appropriate policy is that laid down by the Dorfman–Steiner condition except that that condition must be interpreted at the industry level rather than the firm level. If there is no collusion then the optimal policy depends upon the expected response of other firms. Thus if firms assume that they are in a Cournot situation then the optimal policy is that laid down by the Dorfman–Steiner condition because each firm expects no response from others. If they do expect a response then expectations of increased revenue from either advertising or price reductions will be reduced.

Alternative Theories of the Firm

So far we have assumed that firms attempt to maximize profits, but if there were a divorce of ownership from control then alternative advertising policies might be pursued. Thus a sales-maximizing firm might have a higher level of advertising and sales than a profit-maximizing firm.

Rules-of-thumb Advertising Decisions

The theories we have discussed suggest that management should arrive at its optimal advertising budget by setting the ratio of its expenditure on advertising to sales equal to the ratio of its advertising elasticity to its price elasticity of demand. But surveys suggest firms adopt the practice of making advertising budgets a fixed percentage of sales. If, however, the two elasticities are constant then the rule-of-thumb may be a sensible policy. A constant percentage of sales is therefore analogous to the constant mark-up to determine price, and in the case of established goods the two elasticities may be constant. Furthermore, the available evidence does suggest that firms are prepared to alter their percentage, especially for new products, as market conditions alter. Thus we may conclude, as we did in the case of pricing policies, that rule-of-thumb business practices are not incompatible with the economists' analysis of decision-making.

The Nature of the Product

So far we have considered the interrelations of price and advertising expenditures. Now we must examine the interactions of advertising and the nature of the product (Stigler, 1961). Empirical evidence suggests that advertising outlays tend to be concentrated upon a narrow range of products. The explanation for this concentration of advertising expenditure may be in the frequency of purchase of goods. In the case of foodstuffs, such as sugar and salt, regular purchases mean that consumers are well-informed about the qualities of goods. Hence there is little resort to, or demand for, advertising. But frequency of purchase is influenced by whether or not the population of customers is constantly changing. If the number of potential customers undergoes no change from period to period then the market in each period can be divided into those who are informed as a result of advertising in a previous period and those who did not receive the information previously, or who having received it then forget the message. Advertising in each period would then be directed towards the two groups of uninformed but potential customers. In the case of goods subject to regular purchase there would, of course, be few or none who were uninformed.

In a market which is subject to entry and exit of potential consumers then the information problem becomes more complicated. However, in order to simplify the analysis we shall assume that the potential market size is N and that a proportion C of these consumers is reached when the advertising level is A, thus $C = f(A)$. In addition we shall also assume that a proportion b are new consumers who are entering the market for the first time, or are consumers who have forgotten the information they received in the previous period. Thus we have the following sequence:

First period CN consumers informed.
Second period $C(1-b)N$ first period consumers still informed.
CbN new consumers informed.
$CN(1 - C)(1 - b)$ first period consumers who were not informed in the first period and who did not leave the market but become informed in the second period.
Hence

$$CN[1 + (1 + b)(1 - C)] \qquad (10.11)$$

is the total number of consumers informed in the second period.

In the kth period this becomes

$$CN[1 + (1 - b)(1 - C) + \ldots (1 - b)^{k-1}(1 - C)^{k-1}] \qquad (10.12)$$

for which a large number of periods approximates to

$$\frac{C}{1 - (1 - C)(1 - b)} N = \lambda N \qquad (10.13)$$

where λ is the proportion of the potential market who is informed and is a function of both C and b. The point that emerges from the final equation is that as turnover increases then the value of investment expenditures on advertising diminishes rapidly. There is no cumulative effect of advertising because there are too many new customers who were not previously aware of the product, and too many old customers who have forgotten what was the message.

The nature of the product cannot, however, be divorced from price and from market structure. In the case of high-priced products which consumers buy at infrequent intervals, advertising may be ineffective because consumers may prefer to invest in the acquisition of knowledge about goods. In contrast, low-priced goods may be associated with considerable advertising expenditure. Finally, we should remember Pigou's dictum: the economist should not tell the brewer how to do his job; although beer is frequently purchased, brewers still advertise in order to differentiate their products.

Optimum Price–Quality Combination

Search goods, experience goods and credence goods are different kinds of goods, but we can also distinguish within those categories between different qualities of goods. By 'quality' is meant any aspect of a product, including the services included in the contract of sale, which influences the demand curve. However, quality changes differ from advertising changes because they enter into variable costs. Each quality will have a definite average cost but there may be several different qualities with the same average cost curve. However, profit maximization will dictate only that quality which has the most favourable demand curve will be adopted. Hence we assume that quality can be improved only by raising the average cost curve, and that quality improvement means any alteration in quality which shifts both the average cost curve *and* the demand curve. Given that every quality is associated with a given cost and demand curve it follows that we can derive the determination of the optimum combination of price and quality along the lines of either Boulding's graphical analysis or Dorfman and Steiner's use of the calculus.

Empirical Studies of the Advertising Decision

The theories we have analysed suggest that advertising is expected to change quantity demanded at a particular price. Hence the simplest way of assessing

Table 10.1. Estimated price and advertising elasticities and advertising to sales ratios for selected goods, UK

	Advertising elasticity (1)	Price elasticity (2)	Ratio (1 : 2) (3)	Advertising sales ratio (4)	Ratio (3 : 4) (5)
Cars	0.19	−1.95	0.096	0.007	13.7
Tractors	0.49	−3.29	0.148	0.0136	10.88
Margarine	0.59	−4.3	0.138	0.098	1.41
Coffee	0.14	−0.2	0.678	0.162	4.15
Toothpaste	0.24	−1.98	0.12	0.153	0.78

Source: Cowling (1972).

the effects of advertising is to estimate the demand curve for an advertised product. Table 10.1 shows the estimated price and advertising to sales ratios for selected UK products. The estimated advertising elasticities are all positive but less than unity, suggesting that firms operate in the range where there are diminishing returns to advertising. The own-price elasticities are all greater than 1, which suggests that firms operate on the elastic sections of their demand curves. Column 4 shows the advertising sales ratios, and according to the Dorfman–Steiner theorem these ratios should be equal to their respective ratios of advertising elasticities to own-price ratios. Column 5 therefore indicates the extent to which the actual advertising expenditures were optimal. Cowling suggests that for non-durable goods there was little divergence between actual and optimal, but in the case of non-durable goods the discrepancies may have been due to peculiar features of durable goods markets, such as the introduction of new models, and the fact that advertising may affect the timing of purchase rather than the amount spent on such goods.

Empirical Studies of the Effects of Advertising

The basic problem in assessing the effects of advertising is to determine how demand elasticities are affected by selling outlays. On the theoretical plane there exist two schools of thought. One school suggests that advertising increases demand elasticities by making consumers more aware of the existence of goods and providing them with information by which to make comparisons. Hence advertising lowers prices and may increase short-run profits, but its overall effect is to increase competition. The other school maintains that advertising creates brand loyalties, reduces competition and enables firms to increase their profits. The problem at the theoretical level is the lack of an adequate transmission mechanism which links advertising to prices, and competition which does not rely upon the presence of other factors whose importance may be greater than that of mere advertising.

Thus buyers may have a preference for products which they have previously sampled as compared with new products, so there may be 'an element of asymmetry between new and established firms which is due to the different degrees of experience that consumers have with specific products' (Comanor and Wilson, 1974). Mere quantitative estimates of advertising expenditure may not, therefore, tell us anything about the way in which consumers respond to the messages of different firms.

Price Elasticities

Jean-Jacques Lambin (1976) estimated the price elasticities of demand for various branded goods and then regressed the absolute value of the direct price elasticity alternatively on two variables representing advertising intensity. The first was the volume of brand advertising expenditure per head and the second was the advertising shares of individual brands. In both cases the estimated regression coefficients were negative, which suggested that increased advertising was associated with less elastic demand curves. However the direction of causation may run from demand to advertising as well as from advertising to sales. In other words, as the Dorfman–Steiner condition emphasizes, the optimal level of advertising depends on demand conditions facing the firm. Lambin, however, found no systematic relationship between advertising and sales.

Two studies by Nickell and Metcalfe (1978) and Morris (1979) analysed the relationship between the own-brands of supermarkets and manufacturers' brands, both of which are usually sold in supermarkets. The hypothesis was that own-brands were priced at competitive levels and that any mark-up of proprietary brands could be attributed to concentration and advertising; the more monopolistic was the supplying of industry the more likely would it be for a mark-up to obtain, and the more advertising manufacturers conducted the greater the profits. Support for the hypothesis was found, although Morris noted that no attempt was made to include expenditures on salesmen and other forms of sales promotion undertaken by manufacturers.

The most interesting study of the effects of advertising upon prices was that conducted by Lee Benham (1972), who found that the average price of eye-glasses in the USA in 1963, in states where advertising was completely banned, was \$37.48, whereas the price was \$17.98 in states which allowed advertising. Since the qualities of spectacles – comfort, vision etc. – are easy to test by inspection, Benham's study suggests some attempt should be made to distinguish the effects of advertising upon the demands for different types of product.

Profitability

Because of the difficulties of directly estimating price elasticities recourse is sometimes made to the relationship between advertising and profitability.

There are two major difficulties with such an approach. First, there is the problem that variations in profits may be due to variations in the amount of risk to which different firms are exposed. The second problem is that accounting rates of profit may not be unbiased estimates of the appropriate internal rates of return. Although advertising outlays may be seen as an investment in goodwill most firms do not treat advertising expenditures as an investment, but charge them as outlays in the year in which they are incurred, and no allowance is made for future profit prospects. Hence the book value of assets may be understated because no adjustment is made to take into account the increase in the value of assets resulting from advertising. The problem is further complicated by the fact that not all advertising may be new or net advertising, and some portion may be designed to maintain the existing stock of goodwill intact. Various attempts have been made to deal with the problem of advertising as a capital good but none have been wholly satisfactory. Some writers (Clarke, 1976) have suggested that the effects of advertising are short-term, between 3 and 15 months. Block (1974), however, has stated that when advertising is amortized the observed relationship between advertising and profitability is no longer statistically significant. Comanor and Wilson (1974) have, however, argued that Block's results arise from the use of low depreciation rates in computing advertising capital, and the problem of the relationship between advertising and profitability is still unresolved.

Conclusions on Advertising Policy

Although the empirical work on the effects of advertising does not lead to firm conclusions, it is possible to assert that the theory does appear to pick out the crucial variables in the decision-making process, and the lack of satisfactory tests of the theory stem from data problems rather than weaknesses of the theory. We have, of course, considered only some of the studies of the effects of advertising. We have omitted the wider issues of the effects on consumer sovereignty and the efficient allocation of resources – but these are issues of public policy which will be examined later.

Bibliography and References

Adams, W. J. and Yellen, J. (1976) 'Commodity bundling and the burden of monopoly', *Quarterly Journal of Economics*, 90, 475–98.

Akerlof, G. (1970) 'The market for "lemons" : quality uncertainty and the market mechanism', *Quarterly Journal of Economics*, 84, 488–500.

Benham, L. (1972) 'The effect of advertising on the price of eyeglasses', *Journal of Law and Economics*, 15, 337–52.

Block, H. (1974) 'Advertising and profitability: a reappraisal', *Journal of Political Economy*, 82, 267–86.

Boulding, K. (1955) *Economic Analysis*, 3rd edn. London: Hamish Hamilton.

Butters, G. R. (1976) 'A survey of advertising and market structure', *American Economic Review*, 66, 392–7.

Clarke, D. G. (1976) 'Economic measurement of the duration of advertising effect on sales', *Journal of Marketing Research*, 13, 345–57.

Comanor, W. S. and Wilson, T. A. (1974) *Advertising and Market Power*. Cambridge, Mass.: Harvard University Press.

Cowling, K. (1972) *Market Structure and Business Behaviour*. London, Gray Mills.

Demsetz, H. (1964) 'The welfare and empirical implications of monopolistic competition', *Economic Journal*, 74, 623–41.

Dorfman, R. and Steiner, P. O. (1954) 'Optimal advertising and optimal quality', *American Economic Review*, 44, 826–36.

Hotelling, H. (1929) 'Stability in competition', *Economic Journal*, 39, 41–57.

Lambin, J. J. (1976) *Advertising, Competition and Market Conduct in Oligopoly over Time*. Amsterdam: North Holland.

Leibowitz, S. J. (1982) 'Durability, market structure and new–used goods models', *American Economic Review*, 72, 816–24.

Morris, D. (1979) 'The strategy of own brands', *European Journal of Marketing*, 13, 59–80.

Nickell, S. and Metcalfe, D. (1978) 'Monopolistic industries and monopoly pricing, or are Kelloggs cornflakes overpriced?', *Economic Journal*, 88, 254–68.

Shaked, A. and Sutton, J. (1982) 'Relaxing price competition through product-differentiation', *Review of Economic Studies*, 49, 3–13.

Stigler, G. J. (1961) 'The economics of information', *Journal of Political Economy*, 69, 213–85.

11 Distribution Policy

Location, Distribution and Internal Marketing

Distribution policy is concerned with the following questions. Where should a firm be located? Should it be located near its sources of factors of production or near its consumers? Should it locate itself near its rivals or should it be located near or next to firms producing complementary goods? Should a firm do its own marketing, should it introduce franchising, or should it integrate successive stages of production so that it substitutes internal marketing for external marketing? These are some of the issues which we shall consider in this chapter.

Consumers versus Factors of Production

The relative pull of factor markets and consumers markets will exert an influence on the location of a firm. The traditional examples were the location of steel works near to sources of coal and iron because they were costly to transport, whereas the final products had a high value added relative to transport costs. The introduction of electricity and the grid transformed this pattern and enabled many firms to move nearer to their customers. Hence, since the Industrial Revolution, we have had a shift of industries towards the south of England and this has been intensified by the rise in importance of the European market and the decline of markets in the Commonwealth.

Homogeneous Goods

Our earlier treatment of products in terms of characteristics (chapter 8) enables us to consider brand shares in terms of the 'distance' of one product from another; that is, in terms of location policy. We considered a more formal treatment of location in terms of the Hotelling model in chapter 10.

The Hotelling model of duopoly behaviour is extremely simple but carries strong results, by suggesting that imitative behaviour is the optimal policy. The model assumes no transport costs, inelastic demand and only two firms; and when an attempt is made to relax the assumptions the predictions break down. When a third firm is introduced it will be located nearer one firm than the other. The result will be a leap-frogging outwards. Hence different locations, different products, may be the optimal policy.

Heterogeneous Goods: Central Place Theory

It follows from the previous section that the more interesting questions arise when firms sell different products. Should a butcher locate himself next to a candlemaker? Or should a butcher sell candlesticks? We do observe town centres containing clusters of shops selling different things; and we do observe shops selling a mix of goods. The explanation seems to lie in the costs of shopping which customers incur, economies of scale and store capacity. Shoppers who combine a trip to, say, the butcher's with a trip to the baker's can economize on the time costs of shopping. Hence firms wishing to maximize profits will find it advantageous to offer a mix of goods.

But which goods should a shop offer? The obvious answer is those goods which have relatively inelastic demands, and the analysis would then follow our previous discussion of multi-product firms. What should be the policy, though, if goods which have low demand elasticities have a low turnover, and if store capacity is limited? Then the opportunity cost of space becomes important, and this is influenced by: (1) the rate of sales per unit of time; and (2) the absolute profit per unit of product. Elasticity of demand enters into the picture only through its influence on profit per unit of product. If, however, economies of scale prevail, then it may pay to specialize, but also to locate oneself next to other specialist firms.

Central places can, however, give rise to excess capacity of the Chamberlin type for two reasons. First, a central place economy is an approximation to a space-less economy. Second, a central place has the characteristics of a public good in the sense that the costs of entry for a newcomer may be less than the costs he imposes on others. A newcomer will gain from the agglomeration of existing shops and customers without having to contribute much to that agglomeration. The existence of excess profits will therefore tend to attract outsiders and force a contraction in the sales of existing shops. Thus there will be too many shops selling too small an output to be efficient; there will be too much congestion and only if a local authority introduces licences, zoning schemes, or a tax scheme, will shops become efficient. Hence we need to consider some of the wider aspects of distribution policy.

Distribution Policy

Distribution policy is concerned with the appropriate channels through which goods are marketed. It comprises:

1 Franchising – a firm may sell its goods through independent retailers but seek to bind those firms through exclusive agreements.
2 Internal marketing – a firm may merge two activities and transferred goods may move between departments.
3 Channel conflict – a firm may be faced with the problem of choosing the most efficient set of marketing channels.

Franchising

A manufacturer has a choice between several distribution policies:

1   sell its output to wholesalers and/or retailers and either fix the retail price (resale price maintenance) or leave the retailers to determine their own selling price;
2   integrate forward or conduct its own distribution;
3   attempt to control the inputs of firms downstream (input tying, quantity forcing) ;
4   impose on retailers a royalty based upon output;
5   impose a lump sum fee upon retailers for the exclusive right to sell.

In the first case a manufacturer permits a retailer to fix his own price in order to give the retailer an incentive to promote his product. A retailer would not be willing to engage in advertising if the resulting profits were captured by the manufacturer. Nor would a retailer be willing to promote a commodity if there were a spillover of sales to other retailers. Hence the retailer might insist upon a guaranteed sales territory. In turn a manufacturer might insist upon the retailer accepting a minimum quantity in order to prevent his good being used as a loss leader. Cases 4 and 5 also involve possible differences between manufacturers and retailers in estimating demand. If the manufacturer were certain about the demand for his good, then he might fix a lump sum fee; but a retailer would be willing to pay a lump sum only if he obtained guarantees about product quality and the absence of competition. If the manufacturer were uncertain about demand then he might opt for a royalty based on output or sales, or combine a lump sum entrance fee with a sales royalty.

Franchising might be preferable to vertical integration if there are likely to be managerial diseconomies associated with attempting to control a large number of retail outlets; and if the manufacturer can impose a maximum retail price then he might be able to force the retailer to expand his sales.

The Internal Marketing of Goods

So far we have concentrated upon external marketing of goods by firms to other firms or households. However, a firm may decide to produce a good for its own use rather than purchase it from, or sell it to, another firm or household. Integration by administration, instead of integration by the market or by cooperation (long-term, implicit contracts), can take one of three forms:

1   vertical integration, in which successive stages of production are linked by administrative decisions;
2   horizontal integration, in which several units performing the same operation are tied together by administration;
3   diversification or conglomerate integration, in which units producing unrelated products and using different processes are administratively combined.

A study by Utton (1977) of the extent of diversification among the 200 largest UK firms in 1968 revealed that 31 firms in the food, drink and tobacco group employed 62.9 per cent of their workers in those activities, whereas the 13 textile firms employed only 38.1 per cent of their workers in those activities. Most firms, however, tended to diversify into closely related activities rather than indulge in wide diversification. There may be an element of risk-spreading in conglomerate integration but most diversification seems to have been influenced by complementarity and substitutability in processes and products. The most striking example is, of course, chemicals, where the versatility of the processes and products makes them close substitutes for other goods, and this explains the spread into textiles and food. But the view of conglomerate firms with tentacles stretching into every industry is misleading. For the efficient integration of activities by administration it is important to have shadow prices for goods bought and sold between departments or plants. These shadow prices can be provided by marketing management. Thus, whether A should be bought or sold through the market by firm X to firm Y, or whether A should be produced in department L for use in department M depends upon a comparison of the prices of the goods. This is partly a problem of production (of how cheaply A can be produced) and partly a problem of marketing (what are the prices in the market for A?). To understand why activities might be integrated it is necessary to consider the advantages and disadvantages of integration in terms of productive efficiency. To understand what shadow prices should be established it is necessary to understand the marketing alternatives. We shall therefore conduct our analysis as follows:

1   An examination of the advantages of vertical integration, as compared with use of market, inventory holding or long-term contracts.
2   A discussion of the principles for pricing goods produced in one department or plant which are used in production in another plant; this is known as *transfer pricing*.
3   An examination of the advantages of horizontal integration and the pricing of common services; this is essentially the problem of multi-product pricing considered earlier.
4   An examination of the advantages of conglomerate integration and the pricing of common services; this involves problems similar to those considered under headings 1–3.

Vertical Integration

Vertical integration, which may be defined as the integration by administration of successive stages of production, can be forward or backward depending upon whether it is upstream or downstream towards the final consumer. Thus a steelworks which buys an engineering firm will be carrying out *forward integration*, whereas a steelworks which bought a blast furnace would be undertaking *backward integration*. Vertical integration may take place in monopolistic, competitive or oligopolistic situations and we have therefore the following combinations (which for simplicity exclude those involving oligopoly):

(a) monopoly seller and monopsony buyer;
(b) monopoly seller and competitive buyer;
(c) competitive seller and monopoly buyer;
(d) competitive seller and competitive buyer.

Monopoly buying and selling
Bilateral monopoly can provide an inducement to integration, although it may
be difficult to say much about the method of determining the transfer price.

Monopoly selling and competitive buying
The existence of a wedge between the monopolist's market price and the
marginal cost provides a necessary but not sufficient condition for a competitive
buyer to integrate backward either by buying the monopolist's firm or by
establishing one's own production unit. It is only a necessary condition because
a great deal will depend upon the respective scales of operation of the
monopolist and the competitive firm. Thus suppose, as in figure 11.1, the
costs of producing Q are given by MC and ATC respectively and the demand
for Q is OQ_1; if the firm chooses to produce OQ_1 its unit cost will be OC.
Now, if the price were OP then vertical integration would be irrational unless
it could produce OQ_2 and sell Q_1Q_2 on the open market.

The problem of disposing of surplus output suggests that it may be more
advantageous for the competitive buyers collectively to purchase the monopoly
firm or to offer it, by means of a long-term contract, a lump sum equal to
monopoly rent provided that it sells to them at marginal cost. If such a contract
could be arranged then it might be possible for the sellers to expand output
at the lower cost, then lower product price and obtain greater profits.

Whether such a policy would be feasible and would lead to a fall in product
price depends upon the following factors:

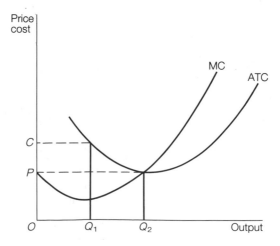

Figure 11.1

1 the ability of numerous buyers to combine to establish such a contract;
2 the elasticity of substitution between the monopoly input and other inputs;
3 the elasticity of supply of complementary factors;
4 the price elasticity of demand for the final product; and
5 the possibility of economies of scale.

The problem with numerous buyers is that an inability to reach a collective agreement for all may leave some of them in the position of being free-riders if surplus output has to be sold on the open market. If the ease of substituting the input, which is now reduced in price, is low, then there may be no gains from integration or establishing a lump sum subsidy contract. Thus in the limiting case, where factors of production are used in fixed proportions, no expansion of output and lowering of final product price will take place – although there may be a possible increase in profits to the firms. If the elasticity of supply of complementary factors is low then a similar problem can arise; the expansion of output at lower cost will be checked by the inability to obtain complementary inputs at low prices. Finally, the ability to change factor proportions, lower costs, and expand output and sales, will be reduced if the final product elasticity of demand is low. Although the demand curve facing a competitive firm is infinitely elastic, the market demand curve facing all competitive firms will have a lower elasticity, and its magnitude will dictate the ability to expand sales at a lower price.

Instead of taking the case of competitive firms integrating backwards we could have analysed the example of a monopolist integrating forward into a competitive market. The analysis is similar and the cases are symmetrical. The monopolist could sell to his competitive outlets, but whether output will be greater, price lower and profits higher will depend upon the magnitude of the various elasticities and their interaction.

Finally, we may observe that the analysis of integration when monopoly is present is further complicated by the possibilities of economies of scale being obtained as a result of the expansion of outputs. With a greater planned volume of output then there could be a reorganization of methods of working, which could lead to lower costs.

Competitive sellers and monopsony buyers
Similar considerations to those which we have outlined in the case of monopoly selling and competitive buying apply to those situations where competitive sellers are confronted by a monopoly buyer. Competitive firms would find it advantageous to integrate forward in order to capture the monopsony rent which the buyer obtains. However, there is no advantage to a monopsony buyer integrating backward when the sellers are competitive.

Competitive buyers and sellers
Examples of vertical integration when monopoly is present are straightforward, but leave unexplained those instances of vertical integration where both factor and product markets are competitive. Typical explanations run in terms of technological and geographical factors. Thus blast furnaces and steel furnaces

may be integrated in order to conserve heat, and some spinning mills may be integrated with weaving sheds because it is costly to transport yarns which are heavy and bulky. However, not all steel is made with pig iron, and much is made with scrap. Hence there may be no technological reason for integration. Furthermore there is the problem of reconciling the optimum sizes of units at different stages of production. For example, in order to be efficient a cotton spinning mill may need to concentrate upon a narrow range of yarn counts; technological economies of scale may dominate others. In contrast a weaving shed may be forced to combine a variety of yarns in order to produce marketable cloths; marketing economies may dominate other possible economies. Hence the pursuit of optimum size at each stage may result in units which are not balanced with each other, and there would be a problem of disposing of surplus at one stage and purchase on the open market at another stage.

Commodity uncertainty and *price uncertainty* may be reasons why competitive firms engage in vertical integration. Although industrial buyers may be more knowledgeable about commodities than are domestic buyers, and it may be more advantageous for firms to set up specialist purchasing departments, there are many instances where quality control may not be possible without direct intervention. Thus woollen spinning and weaving may be integrated, whereas worsted spinning and weaving may not because a woollen manufacturer will need to know the amount of shoddy (reclaimed wool) in his yarn, whereas a worsted manufacturer can more easily assess the quality of 'tops'.

Commodity uncertainty can account for forward integration as well as backward integration. A manufacturer may enter into distribution because he feels that wholesalers and retailers do not promote his goods effectively. Forward integration has to be compared with the alternatives of:

1   re-defining the nature of the commodity by branding, packaging and advertising;
2   long-term contracts.

Price uncertainty can arise where demand and supply are subject to unforeseen fluctuations. Under normal conditions price will convey information and screen buyers and sellers, but if there is an unexpected increase in demand the price mechanism may be suspended or work fitfully. Rationing by price may be replaced by rationing on the basis of loyal and regular customers being served first, the establishment of queues and tied sales, or chance in the form of 'first come, first served'. The possibilities of disruption in supply can vary over time and between different commodities. Thus a firm may be inclined to integrate into the production or control of those commodities which form a large percentage of its total costs. However, this proposition needs to be qualified in the light of the elasticity of the demand for its own product, the elasticity of substitution between inputs, and the elasticity of supply of substitutes. Although an input may be a large percentage of total costs, and therefore any increase in its price will give rise to a large increase in final product price, it may be possible to pass on the cost increase if product demand elasticity is low, or it may be possible to substitute other inputs if the elasticity of substitution is high and the elasticity of supply of substitutes is high. However, it may be more important to have direct control over an input which forms a small proportion of total costs if there are no effective substitutes.

A more fruitful distinction is between capital and variable inputs. A variable input is one whose supply curve is highly elastic, whereas a capital input is one with a low supply elasticity. In the case of a variable input the average and marginal costs of production may tend to equal market price, and there is no advantage for a firm in integrating variable inputs; integration merely substitutes an uncertain future marginal cost of producing the input for an equally uncertain future market price of that input. In contrast, changes in the demand for a capital input, whose supply elasticity is low, can give rise to rents which may be appropriated by the buyer if he integrates backward. What a firm does, therefore, is to replace an uncertain future price by a known cost representing the amortization of the initial purchase price for a capital good; that is, a firm can purchase a capital good and then set aside in each future period an amount which can be used to pay off the debt. These regular payments are compared with conjectured payments for the input on the open market. Hence the gain from integration will be greater the larger is the element of rent in the price of an input, and the larger the variance in the future price of the input, subject to the elasticity of substitution between inputs and the elasticity of final product demand.

Inventories, Cooperation and Long-term Contracts

Instead of integrating successive stages of production it may be more sensible to hold stocks, enter into long-term contracts with sellers or buyers, or form cooperative, quasi-contractual arrangements. The decision as to the appropriate method of ensuring availability of supplies or demands may therefore depend upon attitudes to risk. Thus, if there is a risk that a buyer or seller may renege on a contract then merger may be preferable.

Vertical Integration and Transfer Pricing

Merger may solve some problems but pose others. For example, there is the problem of determining the prices at which goods may be transferred from one department or plant to another, to 'clear' the internal market.

Transfer Pricing with an Open Market

Where there exists an outside market to which a department can sell, or from which a department can buy, then the rule governing the internal transfer price would seem to be unambiguous – the internal price must be equal to the open market price. Sometimes, however, the open market price is not obvious. There may be two possible open market prices, for example, when transport costs arise through differences in the locations of firms or when the outside market is monopolistically determined and the integrated firm must somehow determine a competitive transfer price which will maximize the profits of the firm, provide an incentive for departmental managers to be efficient and to truthfully reveal their supply and demand schedules to head office, and provide a guide to investment decisions and the allocation of resources within the firm.

Differences between Buying and Selling Price

In figure 11.2 we illustrate the derivation of the optimal transfer pricing policy when a competitive market exists. Thus, taking the case of an integrated firm consisting of a manufacturing division and a distribution division, we assume that the manufacturing division's marginal cost is MCM and that the outside market price is OP. The curve NMR is derived by subtracting the marginal costs of the distribution division from the distribution division's receipts for all sales levels; NMR is therefore the distribution division's net marginal revenue curve. Given the information contained in figure 11.2 the manufacturing division should produce OQ, the output at which marginal cost is equal to the outside market price.

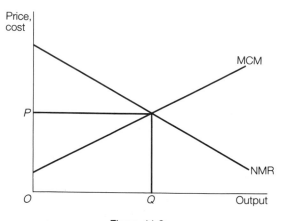

Figure 11.2

Now let us suppose that there is a difference between the buying and selling price because of transport and selling costs. In figure 11.3 the buying price is above the selling price. The distribution division's effective net marginal revenue curve is LMN and the manufacturing division's marginal cost curve is ABC. These intersect at Q_1. Hence the manufacturing division should produce Q_1, supply Q_2 to the distributive division and sell $Q_1 - Q_2$ on the outside market. In other words, headquarters should instruct the manufacturing division to supply its distributive division with all demands at price P_s (the selling price) lest the manufacturing division attempt to increase its profits by charging prices closer to the buying price P_b.

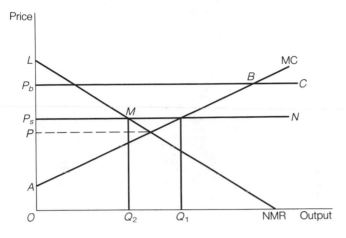

Figure 11.3

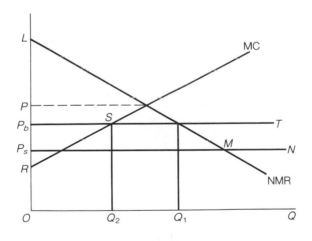

Figure 11.4

In figure 11.4 the marginal cost and net marginal revenue curves intersect above the buying price. The firm's effective marginal revenue curve is *LMN* and its marginal cost curve is *RST*. The profit-maximizing output is Q_1. The manufacturing division should produce Q_2 where its marginal cost is equal to the buying price P_b and the distributive division should buy in from the outside the balance $Q_1 - Q_2$. Hence the distributive division must accept the output that the manufacturing division wishes to supply at the buying price P_b.

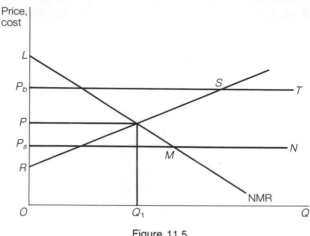

Figure 11.5

Finally, in figure 11.5 the marginal cost and marginal revenue curves intersect between the buying and selling prices. The optimal transfer price is OP, and neither division should trade on the outside market. This case is equivalent to the case where there is no outside market which was analysed in figure 11.2.

Transfer Pricing when there is no External Market

Difficulties can arise when there is no outside market and the problem for head office becomes one of getting both divisions to reveal truthfully their demand and supply schedules. Without the pressure of an outside market there is a temptation for the manufacturing division to inflate its costs through inefficiency. The solution lies in the use of incentives to reveal the truth, and in the degree of autonomy given to the divisions.

Transfer Quotas

So far we have assumed that the task of head office is to determine transfer prices, but many head offices find it more advantageous to determine the quantities to be transferred. Indeed, given the problem of determining the cost as well as the demand schedules for various divisions it is not obvious why controllers should attempt to determine prices rather than quantities. If it has to determine both demand and cost schedules then it is a matter of indifference whether transfer prices or transfer quotas are determined, because the determination of one implies the determination of the other. What has to be assessed, therefore, are the relative advantages of prices or quantities.

One clue to the possible preference for price or quantity lies in the nature of most demand and supply schedules. If production functions are characterized by the existence of fixed proportions between inputs, with the result that cost curves are horizontal, then changes in transfer prices will have little or no effect upon substitution between inputs and the subsequent rates of output. If production functions at different stages of production are characterized by rigid coefficients then some factor demand curves will admit no substitutes. The only relevance of factor prices would be where input combinations were rigid but the proportions varied between firms, then transfer prices based upon the existence of different proportions and different costs between firms might obtain. In contrast, where production functions exhibit substitutability between factors then transfer prices may be a more efficient method of allocating resources than transfer quotas.

Horizontal Integration

Horizontal integration covers a variety of situations:

1   Integration of plants covering the same product where integration can yield no technical economies of scale but can yield managerial, financial, marketing or risk-spreading economies and may also yield monopoly power.
2   Integration of two or more products as a result of jointness in production; for example, mutton and wool, beef and hides.
3   Integration of two or more products as a result of jointness or interrelatedness in demand; for example, fruit gums and pastilles, articles of clothing, foodstuffs.
4   Integration of two or more products as a result of jointness in costs and demands – a composite of 2 and 3.

The internal pricing problem posed by horizontal integration is how to price the use of common services; how, for example, to charge each department or plant for its use of head office services. The problem was resolved in our earlier discussion of the multi-product firm by stipulating that each product manager should be told to maximize his profits and then overheads would be covered out of total revenue. In other words the internal transfer pricing problem was resolved by pursuing the optimal external pricing problem. The snag with this suggestion, however, is that departmental managers can give the impression of maximizing profits whilst being inefficient. Hence the need for efficiency audits and for external efficiency checks. The tendency, therefore, to allocate some portion of overheads to particular goods or departments may be an attempt to find out what charges the departments can bear. There may be a problem in games strategy, of trying to get departments to reveal their 'true' revenues and costs.

Conglomerate Integration

In the case of conglomerates the pricing rules for transfer between vertically integrated processes and the rules for pricing common services apply.

Multinational Corporations

As in the case of vertically and horizontally integrated processes multinational corporations can apply similar pricing policies. There are, however, particular issues arising from different tax and subsidy regimes which will be dealt with in chapter 15.

Profit Centres

Internal pricing problems can be viewed as one aspect of the general problem of assessing the efficiency of various departments and plants when they make investment and pricing decisions. Accountancy textbooks suggest various methods of determining divisional performance, and what we have attempted to do is to indicate the contribution which economics can make to the search for solutions.

Channel Conflict: Optimizing the Distribution Network

In addition to the decisions concerning the choice of price, product, selling outlays and location, management has to consider the most efficient channels of distribution. For example, management may have a choice between one or more selling outlets: own retail outlets, franchising, exports. The standard decision rule is to equate the marginal revenues from the various outlets with the marginal costs of those outlets. More sophisticated approaches have, however, been applied; for example, Corstjens and Doyle (1979) used sigmoidal geometric programming in order to obtain a general solution which incorporated sales volume, channels available, price elasticities of demand associated with each outlet, cross-price elasticities of demand, economies of scale, capacity constraints and any system constraint imposed by the costs of controlling a large number of outlets.

Bibliography and References

Corstjens, M. and Doyle, P. (1979) 'Channel optimization in complex marketing systems', *Management Science*, 25, 1014–25.
Gould, J. R. (1964) 'Internal pricing when there are costs of using an outside market', *Journal of Business*, 37, 61–7.
Hirshleifer, J. (1956) 'On the economics of transfer pricing', *Journal of Business*, 29, 172–84.
Matthewson, G. F. and Winter, P. A. (1984) 'An economic theory of vertical restraints', *Rand Journal of Economics*, 15, 27–38.
Norman, G. (1981) 'Spatial competition and spatial price discrimination', *Review of Economic Studies*, 48, 97–111.
Utton, M. A. (1977) 'Industrial diversification', *Economic Journal*, 87, 96–112.

Warren-Boulton, F. R. (1978) *Vertical Control of Markets: Business and Labor Practices*. Cambridge Mass.: Ballinger.
Waterson, M. (1982) 'Vertical integration, variable proportions and oligopoly', *Economic Journal*, 92, 129–44.

12 Cost and Production Management

Production involves ultimately the creation of utilities and 'cost' refers to the utility attaching to the highest-valued alternative course of action rejected by the decision-maker. Hence this chapter associates production decisions with costs. The chapter is structured as follows.

Cost

1 An examination of the concept of 'opportuntity cost'.
2 The relationship between cost and price in a market economy.
3 The timing of costs and the classification of costs.
4 Joint products and the allocation of costs.
5 Accounting costs and economic costs.
6 The derivation of production functions from costs data.

Production

1 An outline of the standard economic analysis of the production function; this is sometimes called *classical programming*.
2 The use of *linear programming* to solve problems where resources are used in fixed proportions and there may be numerous constraints operating in the short run.
3 A reconsideration of the problems posed by the fact that many activities take place *in time*; that is, they are *time-specific*.
4 *Network analysis* as an approach to the sequencing of production activities.
5 *Dynamic programming* as a means of solving network problems, and its relationship to dynamic versions of classical programming.
6 *Queueing theory* as a means of resolving bottlenecks in sequential operations.
7 *Simulation* as a means of solving apparently intractable problems.
8 *Inventory theory* as a solution to bottlenecks.
9 *Intermittent production*, bottlenecks and costs.

Cost

Cost in economics means opportunity cost, the value placed upon the highest-valued alternative course of action; costs are rejected benefits. If the benefits (net of outlays) derived from a business trip to Paris are estimated at 50 utils and net benefits from going to Stockport are put at 5 utils then the cost of going to Paris is the 5 utils forgone.

Cost and Price

Of course we normally expect to measure costs in terms of the expected money outlays associated with alternative courses of action, and in a market economy which uses money, costs will be measured by the prices which have to be paid in order to carry out chosen activities. Those prices will, in a competitive economy, measure the valuations placed upon resources used by different individuals wishing to carry out different activities. Money prices therefore signal the valuations placed upon resources in various uses.

Durable Goods and the Classification of Costs

There is, however, one large class of goods for which price does not automatically record cost. This class contains durable or capital goods whose services are not instantly consumed. In the case of a capital good the immediate resale price may be as much as 90 per cent of the purchase price, and it is the difference between purchase price and resale price which measures cost, or, to be more precise, *acquisition* cost.

Suppose that a fleet car is bought for £5000 and can be resold immediately for £4500, then the acquisition cost is £500. If the car is kept for a year without using it and can be sold for £4000 then its expected *retention* cost or *depreciation* is not the difference between £5000 and £4000 but the difference between £4500 (acquisition cost) and £4000 discounted to the initial date of purchase, because £4000 one year hence has a lower subjective value than £4000 today.

However, if the car were used we might suppose that its market value at the end of the year would be, say, £3000. The difference between the discounted values of £4000 and £3000 would represent the *operating cost*, although it would be necessary also to add in (appropriately discounted) expenditure on oil, petrol and maintenance. Should the manufacturers bring out a new model at the same time, then resale price of the car might drop to £2000 and the difference between the present values of £3000 and £2000 would measure *obsolescence cost*. Hence we arrive at the cost calculations shown in table 12.1, assuming a 10 per cent discount rate.

The cost components in table 12.1 are often given other names by economists and accountants, although the terminology used by each group can differ because financial accounting tends to use historic costs (see table 12.2).

Table 12.1

	Now (£)	End of 1 year (£)
Expenditures		
Purchase price	5000	May vary between £4000 and £3000 or
Resale price	4500	£2000
Costs		
Acquisition retention	500	(i.e. £5000 minus £4000 both discounted 10 per cent for 1 year)
Operating		(i.e. £4000 minus £3000 both discounted at 10 per cent for 1 year)
Obsolescence		(i.e. £3000 minus £2000 both discounted at 10 per cent for 1 year)

Table 12.2. Cost synonyms

Acquisition cost	Fixed cost Overhead cost Unavoidable cost Supplementary cost	Instantaneous or inescapable forgone benefits
Operating cost	Variable cost Direct cost Prime cost Running cost Retention cost	Avoidable or escapable cost

Byegones are Byegones

The distinction between inescapable and escapable costs is important; because a durable piece of equipment has been acquired its initial cost cannot influence future decisions. The cost of the car was not £5000 but the £500 which could be recouped at resale: £500 measured the cost of the irretrievable decision.

Marginal Cost

Having established a definition of costs in terms of forgone benefits, and drawn a distinction between fixed and variable costs, we are now in a position to explore more thoroughly variable costs – the avoidable costs, the costs which can be avoided at the point of decision-making. What we now require is a concept and means of measuring the cost associated with changing the output programme in response to changing demand or technology. This concept is *marginal cost*, which measures the cost of changing output by one extra unit.

Rate and Volume Changes: Short- and Long-run Decisions

The cost of changing output may vary according to the following factors.

1 Has output to be increased quickly?
2 Is the increase in output temporary or permanent?
3 Has the firm anticipated possible changes in demand?
4 Does an increase in output mean that the outputs of other goods have to be increased?

Rate of output
Suppose we have a firm with given resources and it is faced with a sudden increase in demand. If the increase is considered to be temporary then it may introduce overtime working, double shifts or weekend working, and workers will have to be paid at higher rates of pay. Furthermore, management may be forced to bid up the prices of raw materials, less time may be available for maintenance, and bottlenecks may occur on the shopfloor. Hence anticipated costs may be expected to rise along the curve CC in figure 12.1.

Volume of output
Suppose, however, that the increase in demand has not to be met immediately, or can be expected to be permanent. Management can plan to produce a larger volume of output whilst maintaining a given rate of output by redesigning plant and equipment, and changing the labour force. Cost per unit of output may therefore fall because the firm achieves economies of scale in relation to specific areas of output decision-making, technical economies, managerial

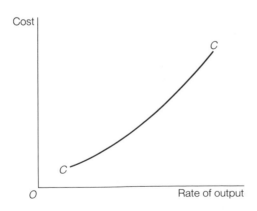

Figure 12.1

economies, financial economies and economies of marketing and risk avoidance.

1 *Technical.* The commonest economy of scale is that which comes
   from the relationship between the surface area and volume of a
   container, such as a boiler or blast furnace. As the surface area is
   doubled the volume is trebled, and there may be little need for
   stronger building materials.
2 *Risk.* With sampling methods it may be possible to maintain quality
   control without increasing supervisory staff by the same proportion
   as output increases.
3 *Managerial.* It may be possible, by coordination and delegation, to
   increase output without having to increase the managerial staff by
   the same proportion. Managerial economies of scale lay at the bottom
   of the shift from functional to multi-divisional structures which we
   discussed in chapter 5.
4 *Marketing.* By sampling methods it may be possible to acquire large
   amounts of information about consumers and thereby reduce risks.
5 *Financial.* A relatively large enterprise may find it relatively cheaper
   to raise large amounts of cash.
6 *Learning effects.* Another source of cost reductions may be achieved
   through learning effects. Repetition increases speed and dexterity.
   Awkward operations may be filtered out.

The Effects of Volume and Rate on Marginal Cost

Although total costs will rise as volume and rate increase, the effects on
marginal cost can differ. In figure 12.2 marginal costs fall as volume increases
because of economies of scale, because of learning effects. Subsequently they
rise as volume effects are exhausted and bottlenecks are encountered as a
result of the rising rate of throughput. Combining volume and rate effects we
obtain the familiar U-shaped cost curve. Over the falling section volume effects
dominate rate effects; over the rising section rate effects dominate volume
effects (figure 12.2).

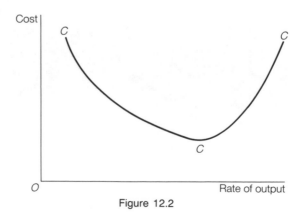

Figure 12.2

Composition of Output (Joint Costs)

So far we have examined the firm's cost function on the assumption that it produces only one good, but most firms are multi-product firms. One reason why firms produce more than one product is that they possess imperfectly divisible assets which are not fully utilized and can therefore be used to produce other goods. Thus even in the classic case of joint production, mutton and wool, once it has been decided to raise sheep it is less costly to use the same sheep to produce wool. What proportions of mutton and wool are produced will, of course, depend upon their relative prices and technology.

Uncertainty

Most empirical studies, however, suggest that cost curves are not U-shaped but L-shaped. Costs fall sharply at low outputs and then tend to be constant or gently declining. Of course we must be on our guard against inferring anything about management's views on costs from empirical studies based upon accounting data. Historic costs are not the same thing as expected costs. Linearity may be introduced by the use of straight-line depreciation, and linear regression is easier than non-linear regression. Nevertheless the persistence of L-shaped empirical cost curves does suggest that some factors may have been overlooked. Some possible omissions are:

1   Indivisibility is not the same thing as fixity. A factor of production such as a factory may be fixed, but it may be divisible: it can be worked in part or whole, on one shift or two shifts. The presence of divisibility may give rise to constant operating costs.
2   Uncertainty may lead to flexibility. If demand is expected to fluctuate between 100 and 200 units no-one will build a plant which has an optimal production of 150 units. Management will attempt to introduce flexibility by having planned reserve capacity. Hence the cost of producing 150 units will be higher than in a plant optimally designed to produce 150, but costs will be considerably lower for output between 100 and 200 units (Stigler, 1939).

Accounting Costs

So far we have dealt with economic cost. Now we must examine accounting costs. In accounting it is possible to distinguish between two branches of enquiry; financial accounting and management accounting. In financial accounting costs are historic costs; they are the costs which have actually been incurred at some point of time. Although attempts have been made to allow for inflation it is still true to say that historic costs retain a strong hold upon the accounting profession and the tax authorities because they have an objective basis; management can defend its actions by reference to the bits of paper which record payments and receipts.

In management accounting, however, there is a more conscious attempt to produce cost concepts which can form the basis for decision-making. This is most apparent in *standard costing* (economists' 'shadow pricing'), where an attempt is made to establish cost standards for various inputs by means of determining a physical standard and selecting an appropriate value to be attached to that physical standard. Standard costs are therefore composed of two components – a quantity and a price. For example, a firm producing plastic tiles may use a standard cost rule of:

(a) 'standard' quantity: 3 kilos of plastic per tile;
(b) 'standard' price: £0.25 kilo of plastic used.

This rule permits an expectation of input costs. However, during the period of production the following data emerge (*ex-post*):

actual production: 5000 tiles;
actual quantity of plastic used: 12,000 kilos;
actual quantity of plastic purchased: 19,000 kilos;
actual price paid per kilo of plastic: £0.35.

According to standard costs 15,000 lb of plastic should have been used and so there was a saving of 3000 lb. However, the purchase price was £0.10 per lb higher than expected. These discrepancies are known as *variances* – quantity variance and price variance – and represent the difference between *ex-ante* cost and *ex-post* cost on outlays. Standard costs can also be estimated for labour, and are usually derived on the basis of work study and the use of incentive payment schemes (discussed in the next chapter on personnel management).

Standard costs may therefore be regarded as an attempt to estimate marginal costs. However, it should be noted that accounting textbooks do not distinguish between the various dimensions of cost which we have analysed, but concentrate upon cost per *volume* of output. They also tend to ignore the time element (present values). Standard cost may therefore be considered to be a shadow price which may undergo considerable modification in the light of actual decision-making.

From Cost Functions to Production Functions

Is it possible to infer the nature of production processes from an examination of cost data? Could a non-specialist member of the Board make an assessment of the working of the production department from the information circulated by the chief accountant? In figure 12.3 we measure the amounts of labour and capital along the axes, and the slope of the line *AB* measures the relative prices of the two factors. The firm can buy *OA* of labour or *OB* of capital with its budget and is observed to buy the amounts given by the coordinates of *E*. If, then, the price of capital falls and the firm's budget is reduced, its purchasing possibilities will lie along *CD*. The firm will not buy combinations along *DE* because they were previously rejected, and therefore will purchase along *CE*. If it purchases the combination given by *F* then *E* and *F* will lie on the firm's production function. By the same procedure of lowering the price of capital

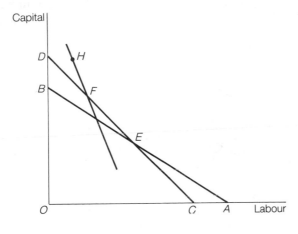

Figure 12.3

and at the same time lowering the firm's budget it may be possible to locate another point such as *H*. The points *E*, *F* and *H* therefore lie on the locus of efficient factor combination to produce a given output.

The Production Function: Classical Programming

The starting point for our analysis is the standard economic analysis of the production function and its use as a means of solving the firm's problem of how to produce efficiently. The approach is sometimes referred to as classical programming because of its use of the calculus as opposed to more modern mathematical techniques. However, we shall begin with a geometrical exposition, and for simplicity of treatment we shall confine the analysis to the case of two factors of production, labour and capital, to produce a commodity *Q*. Thus, we have

$$Q = f(L,K;T) \tag{12.1}$$

where *Q* is the flow of units of the commodity per unit of time. *L* and *K* are the flows of labour and capital services per unit of time, and *T* is the prevailing technology.

The problem of how inputs are transformed into units of output is simplified if it is assumed that there are: (1) constant returns to scale; and (2) diminishing returns to the proportions in which the factors are combined.

Constant Returns to Scale

Textbooks usually define constant returns to scale as occurring when a proportional increase, say *x* per cent, in all inputs leads to the same proportional

(x per cent) increase in output. However, the expression 'returns to scale' is ambiguous. When all inputs are said to increase by x per cent, does this mean an increase of x per cent in the *number* of each input, or an increase of x per cent in the *size* of each input? Clearly there is an important distinction to be made here. For example, if a production process uses a cylinder (e.g. a boiler) which has a surface of y square metres and a volume of z cubic metres, then adding to the process another cylinder with a surface area of y square metres and doubling the number of all other inputs *must* double total volume capacity; if we measure output solely in terms of the cylinders' capacity it must have increased by z cubic metres. Assuming the number of all other inputs is simultaneously increased by the same proportion each time, increasing the number of cylinders should yield:

1   (y) cylinders gives potential volume of z
2   (y) cylinders gives potential volume of $2z$
3   (y) cylinders gives potential volume of $3z$
.
.
.

N (y) cylinders gives potential volume of Nz

Suppose, now, that instead of increasing the *number* of cylinders the production manager increases the *size* of the initial cylinder, e.g. he doubles cylinder size. In this case, then, volume potential of the cylinder will be trebled. If the manager continues to double cylinder size the pattern in table 12.3 will emerge. Increasing the dimensions of the cylinder emphasizes graphically the important distinction between *duplication* and *replication*. When a production process is duplicated the number of inputs is altered; when a process is replicated the dimensions of one or more inputs are altered. There must result always constant returns to duplication, but constant returns to replication is only a special case – increasing or decreasing returns may be experienced. In a world

Table 12.3

	Cylinder size (sq. metres)	Cylinder volume capacity (cu. metres)
1st size	y	z
2nd size	$2y$	$3z$
3rd size	$4y$	$3z(3)$
4th size	$8y$	$3z(3^2)$
5th size	$16y$	$3z(3^3)$
.	.	.
.	.	.
.	.	.
Nth size	Ny	$3z(3N-2)$

of scarce resources replication is the norm, since it is not possible, even in the long run, to duplicate every input: some factor of production remains fixed in supply. It is true, of course, that the longer is the production period the easier it becomes to duplicate production processes, but replication will dominate, either because larger replicas are preferred (they yield increasing returns to scale) or because they are unavoidable (in which case they might yield decreasing returns to scale).

Diminishing Returns to Proportions

The second assumption is that the proportions in which factors can be combined is variable, but that diminishing returns will eventually set in because factors are imperfect substitutes for each other.

The Isoquant Diagram

The assumption of constant returns to scale and diminishing returns to proportions can now be illustrated by means of an isoquant diagram. In figure 12.4 we measure the flows of labour and capital services per unit of time along the horizontal and vertical axes respectively. The curve I_0I_0 represents different factor combinations of labour and capital which will yield the same flow of output per unit of time. The curve I_0I_0 is known as an *isoquant* (equal output curve). With greater inputs of resources a higher level of output than the isoquant I_1I_1 could be attained. The convexity of the isoquant is due to the fact that the resources are imperfect substitutes for each other. As we move round the isoquant it becomes progressively more difficult to substitute one factor for another whilst holding output constant, and the isoquant may eventually curve inwards. Through the points where the isoquant becomes parallel to the axes it is possible to draw loci known as *ridge lines* which divide

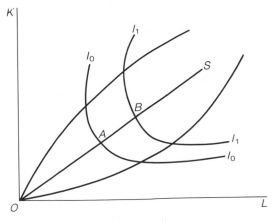

Figure 12.4

the isoquant map into economic and uneconomic regions. Within the economic region an increase in one factor will always lead to increases in output.

The slope of isoquant at any point is known as the *marginal technical rate of substitution* (MTRS) of one factor for another while holding output constant. From MTRS it is possible to derive a more general measure of substitution, *the elasticity of substitution*, which is independent of the units in which factors are measured. The elasticity of substitution is defined as the proportionate change in the amount of a factor employed, divided by the proportionate change in the marginal productivities of factors. Under competitive conditions factor prices measure marginal productivities; hence we can substitute factor prices for marginal productivities in the previous expression.

In figure 12.4 constant returns to scale is indicated by the fact that the two distances, *OA* and *AB*, along the ray *OS* would be equal. Constant returns to scale also means that the slopes of the isoquants at *A* and *B* would also be equal. Hence a knowlege of the whole production function can be inferred from a knowledge of the first isoquant.

Engineering Production Functions

Although the isoquant appears to be an abstract concept, empirical production functions exhibiting the properties of isoquants can be obtained from data in a few industries, notably oil refining, electrical supply and agriculture and an example is shown in figure 12.5. Engineering production functions (Wibe, 1984) do, however, differ from the economist's production function in a few important respects. First they are not derived from considering all possible

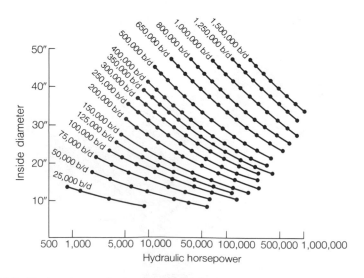

Figure 12.5 Engineering production function for the transportation of crude oil by pipeline (in barrels of 42 US gallons per day). (*Source*: Pearl and Enos, 1975.)

factor combinations. What the engineer does is to examine all combinations within the expected range of relevant factor prices. The information most comparable to the production function of the economist exists usually in the scientific formulae to be found in engineering textbooks. But the engineer seldom bothers with those factor combinations which lie outside the possible range of factor prices because search cost would become prohibitive. The second feature to observe about engineering functions is that they usually omit labour as an input on the grounds that it is difficult to control the heterogeneity of labour. Hence engineering functions apply to partial processes or plant activities rather than operations of firms. Given the restrictions on the availability of data, however, what they do suggest is that stages of increasing and then decreasing returns may occur, and that the range over which constant returns to scale prevail may be limited. It is, of course, possible that such conclusions are inherent in the processes observed because they lend themselves to a doubling of inputs leading to a cubing of output.

The Combination of Factors: the Single-Product Case

The two assumptions of constant returns to scale and diminishing returns to proportions form the basis of the neoclassical economic approach to production; they enable the optimal input combinations to be deduced, and they enable unambiguous statements about the relationship between the marginal products of factors, the demands for factors and the rewards of factors to be made.

Consider first the problem of the optimal combination of factors. In figure 12.6 we assume that management has a budget which will enable it to buy either OL of labour services or OM of capital services or some combination lying within the area bounded by the triangle OLM. What the slope of LM does is to define the ratio of factor prices, and in seeking to maximize output,

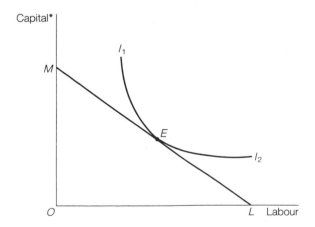

Figure 12.6

given its budget and relative factor prices, management will seek to attain the highest isoquant available, which is I_2I_2 at E. At E the marginal technical rate of substitution of labour for capital, as measured by the slope of the isoquant, will be equal to the ratio of factor prices as measured by the slope of AB. Hence the condition for optimally combining factors is that:

$$\text{MTRS}_{LK} = \frac{P_L}{P_K} \tag{12.2}$$

where MTRS is the marginal technical rate of substitution, P is the price of a factor, and L and K refer to labour and capital.

Demand for Factors of Production

Given the optimality condition it is possible to indicate how the demand for labour and capital will respond as the prices of the factors varies. In figure 12.7 the firm is initially in equilibrium at E. Now, the rental price of capital services is allowed to fall and the firm could purchase OC of capital or OA of labour services or any combination along AC. If at the same time we reduce the firm's budget, so that it could still produce the initial level of output, then the firm would move along the isoquant I_0I_0 from E to F. The move from E to F is known as the *substitution effect* induced by the change in factor prices, and the extent of movement is governed not only by the change in factor prices but also by the elasticity of substitution between those factors.

The relationship between the MTRS and marginal products can be derived directly from the isoquant. Since output remains constant along any given isoquant, the loss of output from any small reduction in the use of one input must be matched exactly by the extra output resulting from a small increase in use of the other input. Hence, where the inputs are L and K and output is x, we may use the calculus to write

$$dL \cdot \frac{\delta x}{\delta L} - dK \cdot \frac{\delta x}{\delta k} = 0 \tag{12.3}$$

$$dL \cdot \frac{\delta x}{\delta L} = dK \cdot \frac{\delta x}{\delta k} \tag{12.4}$$

$$\frac{dL}{dk} = \frac{\delta x}{\delta k} \bigg/ \frac{\delta x}{\delta L} \tag{12.5}$$

In other words the slope of the isoquant (dL/dk) or marginal rate of technical substitution, is derived as the ratio of the two marginal products, ($\delta x/\delta k$) and ($\delta x/\delta L$). It should be clear now why the ridge lines, referred to earlier, mark the boundaries of substitution – the lines pass through all those points where the marginal product of an input is zero.

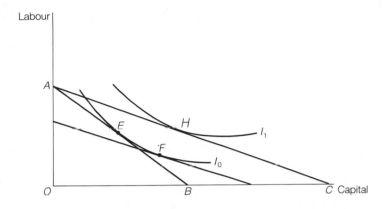

Figure 12.7

Optimization and the Lagrangean Multiplier

So far we have relied mainly on geometry for demonstrating optimality, but for most purposes it is more convenient to use the calculus. Thus, suppose we write a production function as

$$Q = f(L,K) = 2LK \tag{12.6}$$

In this multiplicative form the function indicates that labour and capital are interdependent – the marginal product of labour depends not only upon the amount of labour employed but also upon the amount of capital used. If the production function were of an additive form ($Q = L + K$) a linear programming solution would be adopted – linear programming is discussed later.

Now, suppose that management wants to maximize output but faces a budget constraint of 100 (spending power) and relative prices of 2 per unit of labour and 10 per unit of capital. The optimizing problem can be written as

Maximize $Q = f(L,K) = 2LK$ (12.7)

Subject to $2L + 10K = 100$ (12.8)

or $100 - 2L - 10K = 0$ (12.9)

The solution to the problem is found by using the *Lagrangean multiplier*, λ, to form the expression

$$Q\lambda = 2LK + \lambda(100 - 2L - 10K) \tag{12.10}$$

The problem contains three unknowns; using the first-order conditions for constrained maxima we can find three equations:

$$\frac{\partial Q\lambda}{\partial L} = 2K - 2 = 0 \tag{12.11}$$

$$\frac{\partial Q\lambda}{\partial K} = 2L - 10 = 0 \tag{12.12}$$

$$\frac{\partial Q\lambda}{\partial \lambda} = 100 - 2L - 10K = 0 \tag{12.13}$$

Solving simultaneously yields $L = 25$, $K = 5$ and $\lambda = 5$. Hence, given the prevailing budget constraint the manager should employ 25 units of labour and 5 units of capital.

Although λ appears a trick to solve a constrained maximization problem when the calculus would otherwise be inoperable, it does have an economic meaning. In the above example if the budget constraint were relaxed by 1 unit from 100 to 101, then output would increase by 5 units to 255. In other words, λ is the marginal cost of increasing output by 5 units. If there were more than one constraint then it would be possible to add more Lagrangean multipliers – λ_2, λ_3 ... λ_n.

Dynamic Programming

So far we have looked at the optimal production decision in a static context with instantaneous or timeless flows of inputs or outputs. However, management is also interested in the long-run or dynamic production decision, when the capital stock may be varied. We shall encounter this problem again in the chapter on investment and finance; there we shall use a comparative statics approach and compare successive equilibria when adjustment costs have had to be undertaken. The question arises, however: is there a numerical technique analogous to the calculus of the static approach? The answer is yes! But the mathematics is slightly more complicated and involves the calculus of variations. We shall confine our attention to sketching out the approach and indicating the economic issues.

The dynamic problem facing management is to choose the time paths for the decision variables, output and investment (increased capacity), so as to maximize the present value of the earnings stream subject to a production function where constraints can be varied over time, but only if costs are incurred.

The Optimal Combination of Products

The optimal combination of products is obtained by equating the ratios of the marginal revenues with the ratios of their respective marginal costs. A detailed discussion of the problems encountered when demands and cost are inter-related was given in chapter 9.

The Allocation of Resources in Multi-plant and Shift-working Firms

So far we have concentrated upon two problems:

1 the efficient allocation of resources to the production of one com-modity;
2 the efficient allocation of resources to the production of two com-modities.

The next step is to extend the analysis to the case of allocating resources to the production of one commodity when two or more plants are capable of producing the same good, and to the case where a firm can produce one good from the same plant, but on different shifts. A necessary, but not sufficient, condition for optimal allocation is that there is equality of marginal costs between plants or shifts. However, a great deal depends upon whether the plants or shifts are operating on the rising portion of their marginal cost curves, or the falling portions of their marginal cost curves, or some combination of rising and falling marginal costs. For simplicity we shall confine the analysis to a firm owning two plants, and consider three possible cases:

1 both plants operate on the rising portions of their marginal cost curves;
2 both plants operate on the falling portions of their marginal cost curves;
3 one plant operates on the rising portion of the marginal cost curve and the other operates on the falling portion of its marginal cost curve.

We can illustrate the cases by means of figure 12.8. In case 1 both plants are producing at Q with marginal costs AQ_1. Now, if the first plant reduces its

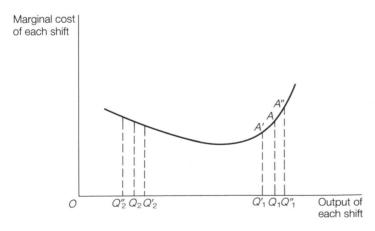

Figure 12.8

output to Q' and the second plant increases its output to Q'', whilst total output remains constant, then costs will rise by the difference between $A''Q''_1$ and $A'Q'_1$. Because the former is greater than the latter costs will rise, and so equality of marginal costs is a necessary consideration for the optimal allocation of output between the plants in case 1.

In case 2 both plants are operating at Q_2. If one plant expands output to Q'_2 and the other contracts to Q''_2, whilst total output remains constant, costs will fall. Hence equality of marginal costs is not a sufficient condition for optimal allocation. In case 3 we assume one plant produces Q_1 and the other produces Q_2, and that marginal cost rises more steeply around Q_1 than it falls around Q_2. In this case reducing the output of the first plant and increasing the output of the second plant causes the costs of the second plant to be greater than that of the first plant. Hence the result depends upon the slopes of the marginal cost curves.

Linear Programming

The standard economic treatment of production assumes that resources can be varied in innumerable ways, and then considers which combination should be adopted when factor and product prices are given. An alternative problem is to consider what should be produced, given that resources can be combined only in fixed proportions and factor and product prices are given. The two ways of looking at the production problem may be regarded as complementary; in the beginning all factor combinations may be possible, and in the long run all combinations are variable, but in the short run factor combinations may be fixed (unless we permit extensive subcontracting). The flexible versus fixed way of looking at the production problem is sometimes referred to as the *putty–clay* distinction. In figure 12.9 the isoquant I_0I_0 indicates all factor combinations

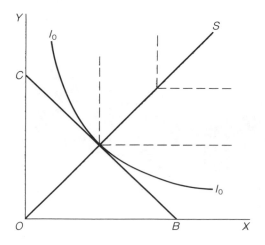

Figure 12.9

capable of producing a given output of A; this is the putty situation when everything is malleable. Now suppose factor prices are given by the slope of BC. Management chooses the combination at L and thereby commits resources. Following the decision we are in the clay situation, in which the scale of output may be varied but factor proportions may not. Hence 'isoquants' along the ray OS appear to exhibit right angles.

One Product, Many Processes

Suppose, as in figure 12.10 that it is possible to produce commodity Q by three processes A, B and C. Each process exhibits constant returns to scale in the sense that it can be replicated, and each process uses factors X and Y in fixed proportions but the proportions differ, with A being X-intensive and C being Y-intensive. Furthermore, let us assume that 100 units of Q can be produced if process A is used at scale L, or if process B is used at scale M, or if process C is used at scale N. Joining points, L, M and N yields an isoquant which is a locus of equal outputs produced by different processes. Moreover the different processes can be used in combination to produce the same output as a single process. Thus $100Q$ can be produced by process A at scale L or process B at scale M or process A at scale S plus process B at scale T. The points S and T are obtained by drawing RS and RT parallel to OL and OM respectively. Thus many of the insights obtained from the standard production analysis carry over to this particular case of linear analysis. The marginal technical rate of substitution becomes transformed into a marginal technical rate of substitution between processes.

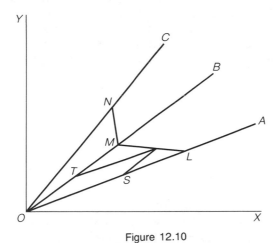

Figure 12.10

Many Products, Fixed Capacity

The single commodity produced by different processes does not pose many analytical problems because it still assumes that factors are freely available.

More difficult issues arise when a firm is a multi-product firm, its processes embody fixed proportions and the capacity of each process is given. Consider the case of a biscuit manufacturer who can produce two varieties of biscuits, A and B. For each type of biscuit he requires labour and capital in different proportions, but uses the same amounts of raw materials. Hence, neglecting raw materials we can depict the two production processes as in figure 12.11; that is, rays OA and OB exhibit constant returns to scale but different fixed factor proportions.

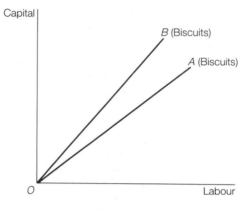

Figure 12.11

An excellent numerical example of the linear programming problem is presented by Bell and Todaro (1969); we reproduce their example below, altering their products (bananas and maize) to varieties of biscuits.

Suppose that the profit on a packet of A is 5 and on B biscuits is 2. Furthermore, let us suppose that a packet of A biscuits requires 6 machine-hours, 4 man-hours and 1 unit of raw materials, whilst B biscuits require 5 machine-hours, 4 man-hours and 1 unit of raw materials. Given that management seeks to maximize profits we can set up the problem as follows:

$$
\begin{aligned}
\text{Maximize} \quad & Q = 10A + 4B & (12.14) \\
\text{Subject to} \quad & 6A + 5B \leq L & (12.15) \\
& 3A + 1B \leq K & (12.16) \\
& 2A + 4B \leq R & (12.17) \\
& A \geq 0 & (12.18) \\
& B \geq 0 & (12.19)
\end{aligned}
$$

where (12.14) is the objective function to be maximized and (12.15 – 12.19) are the constraints upon production, labour inputs represented by L, capital by K and raw materials by R. Thus the total amounts of labour, capital and raw materials cannot exceed the total amounts available – but can, of course, be less.

With a given amount of machine-hours of 360 we can draw the constraint line MN. No more A or B can be produced beyond MN; what the machinery constraint does is to permit the production of 120 packets of A or 360 packets of B or some combination along the line MN. Similarly the labour constraint of 900 unit permits the production of 150 packets of A or 180 packets of B or some combination along the line PR. Finally the materials constraint of 600 units allows the production of 300 B or some combination along the line ST. Given all three constraints management can only operate within the bounded area $TKLM$, and $TKLM$ is the production possibility curve of the firm; it corresponds to the smooth production possibility frontier obtained when two goods can be produced by two processes which can employ factors in variable proportions (figure 12.12).

We can introduce a price line EF which has a slope equal to the ratio of the two product prices. To find the profit-maximizing output combination of A and B we move the price line outwards until it intersects the furthest point on the production frontier. In figure 12.12 this is given by L. What we observe about L is the materials constraint is irrelevant since L lies inside the materials boundary, and only labour and machinery are fully utilized. Since labour and machines are fully utilized the constraints become equalities rather than inequalities

$$6A + 5B = 900 \qquad\qquad (12.20)$$

$$3A + 2B = 360 \qquad\qquad (12.21)$$

which yields $A = 100$ and $B = 60$ as the optimum product mix.

Clearly the solution has been found by solving for A and B in a set of simultaneous equations. In this case the task has been exceedingly simple because the constraints have been equalities. Where this is not the case a solution can be more difficult to find, although the complication involves no more than the introduction of an additional variable. The newcomer to the

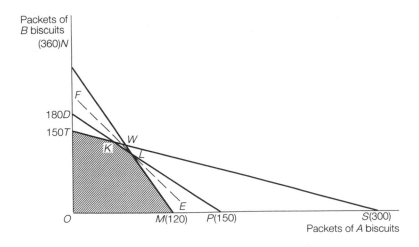

Figure 12.12

equation is known as a *slack variable*, referring to units of resource which are left over, unused or 'slack'. Thus, in the above problem $S_1 = L - 12A - 10B$ tells us that the available labour L is either used up in the production of A (at a rate of 12 per unit) or in the production of B (at a rate of 10 per unit) *or* is not used up; i.e. it remains slack. By introducing the slack variable, inequalities in the equation are transformed into equalities. In the above example we could transform (12.15 − 12.17) into:

$$6A + 5B + S_L = 900 \tag{12.22}$$
$$3A + 1B + S_K = 360 \tag{12.23}$$
$$2A + 4B + S_R = 600 \tag{12.24}$$

We shall make considerable use of the slack variable presently; for the time being we can note that two issues emerge clearly from our simple graphical analysis:

1   Where the number of constraints exceeds the number of choice variables then at least one constraint will not be fully utilized. Thus, at L there are unused raw materials, at K there are unused machines and at T only materials are fully utilized. As a general rule the sum of positive choice variables and positive slack variables must equal the number of constraints in any problem. Solutions will then normally exist at corner points (such as O, T, K, L and M). At L in our example A, B and S_M are positive whilst S_K and S_L are zero, and at O all slack variables are positive whilst the choice variables are zero.
2   The procedure reveals which constraints are the limiting factors once an optimal solution has been reached.

The Simplex Method of Solving Linear Programming Problems

Linear programming problems are capable of graphical solution when there are only two choice variables, but when more than two are involved the simplex method is the means by which a solution is found. To understand this method we begin by defining three types of solution:

1   *A feasible solution* is one which violates none of the constraints of the problem. In figure 12.12 any point in the shaded area is a feasible solution.
2   A *basic solution* is one in which the number of non-zero variables is equal to, or less than, the number of constraint equations.
3   The *optimal solution* is the feasible and basic solution which maximizes or minimizes (if the objective is to minimize cost) the objective function.

The simplex method is an informed trial-and-error procedure. In terms of figure 12.12 a starting point is selected which is both basic and a feasible solution. Usually the origin is taken as a starting point. The next step is to move along an axis to find another solution which is both basic and feasible by assuming that A or B has a positive value and one of the slack variables is zero. Thus, moving along the horizontal axis towards M, which is both basic and feasible, either P or S may be encountered, and a check will indicate that neither is feasible. An attempt must be made to make one of the other slack variables zero. Thus at M, $B = C$ and $S_K = 0$ whilst A, S_L and S_M are positive. Once M is reached the next step is to move along MN by making both A and B positive, but either S_L or S_M zero. The simplex procedure should lead to trying S_L first and reaching L rather than W, but any mistake will be revealed by a feasibility check. From L it is possible to proceed to other points and check to see whether they are both basic and feasible solutions which also raise the value of the objective function (if profits are to be maximized), or reduce the value of the objective function (if costs are to be minimized). Once a point is reached which reduces the value of the objective function in a maximizing problem then the previous solution will be found to be have been optimal.

Now that we have outlined the simplex method we can use it to solve the problem of maximizing the varieties of biscuits. The first step is to transform all inequalities into equalities by introducing a slack variable – S_L, S_K and S_M – for each of the three constraints. This is done because the simplex procedure is merely a method of solving a set of simultaneous linear equations. Note that slack variables perform a similar role to the Lagrangean multiplier in classical programming.

Our linear programming problem is therefore as follows:

$$\text{Maximize } Q = 5A + 2B \tag{12.25}$$
$$\text{Subject to:} \quad 6A + 5B + S_L = 900 \tag{12.26}$$
$$3A + 1B + S_K = 360 \tag{12.27}$$
$$2A + 4B + S_M = 600 \tag{12.28}$$

$$\text{where } A > 0; \ B > 0; \ S_L > 0; \ S_K > 0; \ S_M > 0 \tag{12.29}$$

Step 1
The first step is to write the objective function and constraints in matrix form as follows:

	A	B
$Q\,(=)\quad 0$	$+5$	$+2$
$S_L\,(=)\,900$	-6	-5
$S_K(=)\,360$	-3	-1
$S_M\,(=)\,600$	-2	-4

The total amount of labour available is 900, and what is not used in the production of A (6 units are needed to produce $1A$) or B (10 units) is left over as slack and is equal to some amount of S_L. Thus if the optimal combination were $90A$ and $50B$ then $6(90) + 5(50) = 790$ units of labour would be required, and there would be 110 units idle. A similar procedure would reveal slack in the other resources.

In all the solutions which are both basic and feasible (and the optimal solution must be one of these) the number of positive variables must equal the number of constraints, or the number of variables with a value zero must equal the number of choice variables, which in our case is two. Hence, writing the equations in matrix form starts the procedure at the origin where profit is zero and all resources are unused. The variables at the top of the matrix will therefore always take on zero value and those on the left will take on the value given in the next column of figures.

Step 2
The next step is to proceed along one of the boundaries to try another solution which is both basic and feasible. Since we can move along either boundary we make our decision by choosing the variable in the column which shows the highest profit per unit of output. Thus since the profit on A is 5 and on B is 2, we try positive values of A.

Step 3
The next step is to choose which slack variable to make zero. In other words which constraint will we first encounter as we move along the horizontal axis? What we are looking for is the condition which defines one of the three solutions as feasible. To discover this we divide each total amount of slack in the first column of the matrix by the number of units of each which are used up in producing one unit of A in the second column. Thus we have enough labour to produce 150A (900 ÷ 6), and enough capital and labour to produce 120A and 300B respectively. Hence the first bottleneck encountered is the capital constraint and so S_K is set equal to zero as A becomes positive.

Step 4
The procedure outlined in the previous paragraph, of choosing the column and row of the matrix to be interchanged, defined the *pivot element* of the matrix. The pivot element defined by steps 2 and 3 is -3 in column 2, row 3 and we indicate it by an asterisk. Steps 2, 3 and 4 result in the following matrix:

MATRIX 1

	(1)	(2)	(3)	(4)	
		Step 2		*Step 3*	
		A	B	(1) ÷ (2)	
Q (=)	0	+5	+2		
S_L(=)	900	−6	−5	150	
S_K(=)	360	−3*	−1	120	←(*Step 4*)
S_M(=)	600	−2	−4	300	

Step 5
Finally the matrix is rewritten to make $S_K = 0$ and A positive. This results in a new set of equations which defined point P in figure 12.12. In the matrix A and S_K change places and the new equation or third row becomes

$$A = \frac{360}{3} - \frac{1}{3}S_K - \frac{1}{3}B$$

If S_K and B are both zero the amount of A produced is equal to the total amount of machinery available divided by the number of units of machinery used up in the production of each unit of A produced (360 ÷ 3). Although S_K and B are zero in this second basic and feasible solution we have to allow for positive values, and so from 360/3 we subtract $1/3S_K$ and $1/3B$ because each idle unit of machinery implies that $1/3A$ is not produced and $1/3B$ requires 1 unit of machinery. Hence, we substitute the new equation for A in the original equation.

$$Q = 0 + 5\left(\frac{360}{3} - \frac{1}{3}S_K - \frac{1}{3}B\right) + 2B$$

$$S_L = 900 - 6\left(\frac{360}{3} - \frac{1}{3}S_K - \frac{1}{3}B\right) - 5B$$

$$S_M = 600 - 2\left(\frac{360}{3} - \frac{1}{3}S_K - \frac{1}{3}B\right) - 4B$$

which simplify to

$$Q = \frac{5 \times 360}{3} - \frac{5}{3}S_K + \left(\frac{3 \times 2 - 5 \times 1}{3}\right)B$$

$$S_L = \frac{900 \times 3 - 360 \times 6}{3} - 2S_K - \left(\frac{3 \times 5 - 6 \times 1}{3}\right)B$$

$$S_M = \frac{600 \times 3 - 360 \times 2}{3} + \frac{2}{3}S_K - \left(\frac{4 \times 3 - 2 \times 1}{3}\right)B$$

Given the equation for A the new matrix becomes:

MATRIX 2

	Column 1	Column 2	Column 3
Q (=)	$\dfrac{5 \times 360}{3}$	$- \dfrac{5}{3}$	$+ \dfrac{3 \times 2 - 5 \times 1}{3}$
S_L (=)	$\dfrac{900 \times 3 - 360 \times 6}{3}$	$+ 2$	$- \dfrac{3 \times 5 - 6 \times 1}{3}$
A (=)	$\dfrac{360}{3}$	$- \dfrac{1}{3}$	$- \dfrac{1}{3}$
S_M (=)	$\dfrac{600 \times 3 - 360 \times 2}{3}$	$+ \dfrac{2}{3}$	$- \dfrac{4 \times 3 - 2 \times 1}{3}$

Thus, we have a set of equations in matrix form which can be solved simultaneously to yield values for Q, A, S_L and S_M for point L. What the new matrix reveals is the set of rules for determining the values of the elements of the matrices as we work through them using the simplex method.

1   The pivot element of the old matrix is replaced by its reciprocal.
2   The other terms in the old pivot row (row three) are formed in the new matrix by dividing the corresponding old elements by the old pivot with the sign unchanged.
3   Other terms in the old pivot column are formed in the new matrix by dividing the corresponding elements by the old pivot (sign unchanged).
4   All other terms in the new matrix are formed by dividing the value of the 'cross product', as specified below, by the value of the pivot. The cross product is the old element times the pivot minus the product of the old elements in a comparable position to these two terms in the old matrix. In other words, if we are seeking to replace the element in the *ith* row and *jth* column of the old matrix (denoted by a_{ij}) by the one which will be located in the same position in the new matrix (denoted by a_{ij}^1) where the pivot (which as we see from rules 2 and 3 can never be located in the same row or column as the element being replaced) is located in row r and column s and is denoted as a_{rs} ($r = i$; $s = j$). Hence, we can use the formula

$$a_{ij}^1 = \frac{a_{ij} \times a_{rs} - a_{rj} \times a_{is}}{a_{32}}$$

Thus, to replace 900 in the second row and the first column of the new matrix we have

$$a_{21}^1 = \frac{(900)\,(-3) \,-\, (360)(-6)}{-3}$$

To replace -4 in the fourth row of the third column, we have:

$$a_{43}^1 = \frac{a_{43} \times a_{32} - a_{33} \times a_{42}}{a_{32}}$$

which yields

$$a_{43}^1 = \frac{(-4)\,(-3) - (-1)\,(-2)}{-3}$$

These rules are derived from the principles of matrix algebra; their derivation lies outside the scope of this book and is not essential for a minimum appreciation of the simplex procedure.

An examination of matrix 2 reveals that one of the elements of the profit row is still positive, which indicates that profits can be increased by making that variable (B) non-zero. Hence we seek a pivot and move along the boundary given by the machinery constraint.

MATRIX 2

	Column 1	Column 2	Column 3	Step 2 Column 3	Step 3 Column 1 ÷ Column 3	
		S_M	S_L		
Q (=)	600	$-\dfrac{5}{3}$	$+\dfrac{1}{3}$		
S_L(=)	180	$+\ 2$	$-\ 3^*$	60	←Step 4
A (=)	120	$-\dfrac{1}{3}$	$-\dfrac{1}{3}$	360	
S_M(=)	360	$+\dfrac{2}{3}$	$-\dfrac{10}{3}$	180	

What the pivot does is to tell us that it is the labour slack variable which should be exchanged for B; that is, we move to L in figure 12.12. The next step is to use the rules to form a new matrix.

MATRIX 3

	Column 1	Column 2	Column 3
		S_M	S_L
Q (=)	620	$-\dfrac{13}{9}$	$-\dfrac{1}{9}$
B (=)	60	$+\dfrac{2}{3}$	$-\dfrac{1}{3}$
A (=)	100	$-\dfrac{5}{9}$	$+\dfrac{1}{9}$
S_M(=)	160	$-\dfrac{14}{9}$	$+\dfrac{10}{9}$

Profit has been increased from 60 when $120A$ and no B were produced at point P in figure 12.12 to 620 with $100A$ and $60B$ produced. This is the profit-maximizing output combination of A and B and can be checked by substituting the values of A and B into the objective function $Q = 5A + 2B$. Moreover, we know the optimal solution has been reached because both the variable elements of the profit equation are negative; no further substitution from the row variables below the profit equation can be made for the column variables to increase profit.

The Dual in Linear Programming

To every linear programming problem there corresponds a dual problem involving the same technical coefficients but different variables. If the primary problem is one of maximizing profits then the dual is the minimization of costs, and vice-versa. (We may therefore speak of the primal and the dual problems of programming.)

In the primal problem the task is to find the outputs of good which would maximize profits given product prices, flows of inputs and production functions. The dual problem would be the attempt to find factor prices which would impute the entire revenue to the factors in accordance with the values of their contributions. Hence, if the primary task is to maximize the value of output then the dual problem is one of computing the shadow prices for factors of production given the assumption that the total value of output is paid to those resources.

If we return to our biscuit manufacturing problem then the relationship between the primal and dual problems can be set out as follows:

$$
\begin{array}{ll}
\textit{Primal} & \textit{Dual} \\
\text{Maximize } Q = 5A + 2B & \text{Minimize } C = 900F_L + 360\ F_K \quad (12.30) \\
\text{Subject to: } \quad 6A + 5B < 900 & \text{Subject to: } 6F_L + 3F_K - 2F_M > 5 \quad (12.31) \\
\qquad\qquad 3A + 1B < 360 & \qquad\qquad 5F_L + 1F_K + 4F_M > 2 \quad (12.32) \\
\qquad\qquad 2A + 4B < 600 & \qquad\qquad F_L, F_K, F_M > 0 \qquad\qquad (12.33) \\
\qquad\qquad A, B > 0 &
\end{array}
$$

In the dual problem the implied factor prices are F_L, F_K and F_M respectively. What we first observe in the dual is the importance of the constraints; thus it takes 6 units of labour, 3 units of capital and 2 units of materials to make a unit of A and so the imputed cost per unit of A ($6F_L + 3F_K + 2F_M$) must be not less than the profit on a unit of A – which is given as 5 in the primal problem – if total profit is to be imputed to the factors of production. Similar reasoning applies to the unit cost of B.

What happens if some of the resources are not used? If an additional unit of the surplus factor, materials, were introduced total output would remain constant. The marginal product and price of materials would be zero. In the case of the other two factors the imputed prices can be derived from the solution to the primal problem given in matrix 3 as:

$$S_M(=) \ 160 \ + \ \frac{14}{9} \ + \ \frac{10}{9}$$

$$P\,(=)\,620 \ - \ \frac{13}{9} \ - \ \frac{1}{9}$$

$$B\,(=)\ \ 60 \ - \ \frac{2}{3} \ - \ \frac{1}{3}$$

$$A\,(=)\,100 \ + \ \frac{5}{9} \ + \ \frac{1}{9}$$

The first row indicates that if 1 unit of capital were made idle total profits would fall by 13/9, and if 1 unit of capital were added then profits would rise by 13/9. If 1 unit of labour were added then profits would rise by 1/9. Because the functions are linear then average and marginal profits are equal. Hence the shares attributable to each factor can be calculated as capital equals 520 (360 × 13/9) and labour equals 100 (900 × 1/9).

The optimal solution to the dual problem is a by-product of the solution to the primal problem, and the optimal solution to the dual problem is given as a by-product of the solution to the dual problem. Thus using the simplex method to solve the dual we obtain the following matrix:

	S_{QB}	S_{QD}	F_M
F_K	13/9	2/3	5/9	14/9
F_L	1/9	1/3	−1/9	−10/9
C	620	60	100	160

The existence of symmetry between primal and dual means not only that we can simultaneously solve the problems of optimal outputs and factor prices but that we can also decide upon our method of solution.

The Problem of Time

In our discussions of optimizing production time entered the analysis in a particular way. In classical programming output and inputs were considered to be flows per unit of time, and in effect we were dealing with instantaneous time. When we introduced disturbances we distinguished between the short run and the long run – between 'today' and 'tomorrow'; but tomorrow was similar to today except for a changed level of inputs and output. The analysis was essentially timeless. Yet some activities are time-specific, they take place in *time* (Georgescu-Roegen, 1980). This is most obvious in the case of agriculture, where reaping cannot take place before sowing and some resources, such as labour, must remain idle between sowing and reaping. In agriculture activities take place sequentially.

The contrast between agriculture and manufacturing is striking, and probably accounts for the way in which economists have usually handled production problems. In manufacturing the processes can be operated in parallel, with the result that idleness of resources is minimized. Thus it is possible to see all the components of a car being simultaneously produced, and it is possible to see cars in various stages of production. Released from dependence upon solar energy, manufacturing could rearrange in parallel activities which were previously operated in sequence. The impetus to re-arrangement was also accelerated by the expansion of markets; hence Adam Smith's dictum: the division of labour is limited by the extent of the market.

The ability of firms to arrange processes in parallel is a major source of increasing returns, and is quite distinct from that associated with the volume effects which we noted in the earlier section on constant returns to scale. By splitting off processes and arranging them in parallel it is possible to obtain the maximum benefit of the division of labour in terms of dexterity and increased speed (figure 12.13).

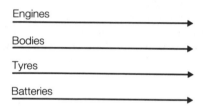

Figure 12.13   Parallel processes in car production.

However, not all manufacturing processes are operated in parallel and we observe often large amounts of capital equipment lying idle for considerable periods. Thus many factories lie idle at night and at the weekends. In these cases it is apparent that it is labour costs – the reluctance of labour to work unsocial hours – which accounts for the idleness of capital equipment; and it is the reluctance of households to vary their time patterns of consumption which accounts for the idleness of some plant and the problems of peak and off-peak production in industries such as electricity supply generation. Costs may, in fact, be the determining factor. It might be possible to produce tomatoes at the South Pole if households were willing to cover the cost.

In subsequent sections we shall examine some of the production problems which the timing of activities creates.

Network Analysis

Of course not all factory production permits all processes to be operated in parallel. In many factories there is a mixture of sequential and parallel processes. Thus the production of a book requires the writing of a manuscript, copy-editing, selection of a book size and format, printing, advertising and delivery of book to the retail outlets. Some of these activities cannot be done before others are completed; copy-editing requires the prior provision of a manuscript. Other activities, however, can go on independently of each other. Hence the task becomes one of finding the optimal mix of sequential and parallel activities.

Confining our attention to the production of a book we can reduce the various activities to the following:

A	writing and submission of manuscript	(24)
B	copy-editing	(2)
C	printing	(6)
D	advertising and sales promotion	(4)
E	delivery to retailers	(1)

where the figures in parentheses indicate the length of time which must elapse before that activity is completed. The problem then is to determine the optimal, or critical, time path. In a strict sequential procedure we would have:

$$A + B + C + D + E = 24 + 2 + 6 + 4 + 1 = 37$$

However, *D*, advertising and sales promotion, can be conducted whilst copy-editing and printing are being undertaken. Hence the optimal production time sequence is:

$$24 + 2 + 6 + 1 = 33$$

In deriving critical paths there are two problems to be avoided: *looping* and *dangling*. Looping refers to the situation where events go back on themselves. Thus in figure 12.14, 6 should not go back to 4. Dangling is the situation where an event does not lead to a further event, nor is it the final event. In figure 12.15, 6 does not lead to 7.

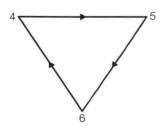

Figure 12.14

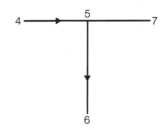

Figure 12.15

Network analysis attempts to set out the logical relationships between activities and it is capable of extension in various ways. Some of the obvious extensions are as follows:

1 The times taken for events to be completed can be treated in probabilistic terms and not in a deterministic manner. Thus the time taken for activity A may be an average of 24 with a standard deviation of 2. Interpretation in a probabilistic manner leads to a link with *decision rules*, where an event may have more than one outcome and where each outcome dictates a different sequence of events.
2 Costs can be imputed to the various routes which allow not only for the opportunity cost of time but also for the costs of other inputs.

The Transportation Problems

Suppose a firm has four factories which serve three markets. The factories have the folowing volume capacities:

A	26
B	32
C	30
D	20
	108

And the demands in each market are:

X	34
Y	36
Z	38
	108

whilst the transport costs per unit to each market are:

		Factory		
	A	B	C	D
Markets X	16	18	12	6
Y	12	22	10	20
Z	6	16	14	18

Given the above information there is a network of 12 possible routes from factories to markets (figure 12.16). The problem is to minimize transport costs. By rearranging the order of factories and markets it is possible to arrive at figure 2.17, which indicates the least cost network. Thus factory A supplies all its output to market X, and B supplies 8 units to complete the demand in X and so on. A network approach to transportation problems is an alternative solution to the linear programming approach encountered above.

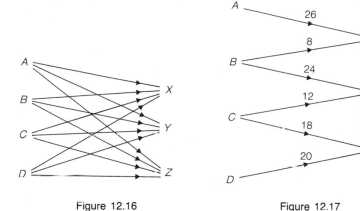

Figure 12.16   Figure 12.17

Dynamic Programming

Sometimes it is simpler to find the optimum policy for the last stage of a sequence and then work backwards. Consider figure 12.18, which represents a complex network involving the shipment of goods from A to K via many possible routes. Thus it is possible to go to B, C, or D and from those points it is possible to go to E, F or G and so on. Figure 12.18 indicates all the possible routes and the costs associated with each route. A solution by dynamic programming would be possible. Suppose the cargo has reached either H or J, then there are no alternatives to choose from. Hence we can consider the previous stage. From E the cargo could have moved along EHK or EJK, and since EHK is cheaper than EJK the latter will be rejected. A similar procedure can be carried out for the other stages.

The solution to the problem we have posed in figure 12.18 is analogous to the classical optimization approach we adopted earlier. What we did earlier was to postulate a terminal date and then compute the discounted values of output and inputs. In figure 12.18 we know the terminal date and the values to be discounted.

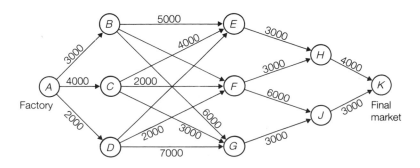

Figure 12.18

Queueing Theory

Queues are ubiquitous; they are not only a production problem; they appear also in marketing and personnel decisions. Airports 'stack' planes in the sky in order to control landings. Hospitals have waiting lists. Customers queue at bus stops and in supermarkets. In factories waiting lines may develop in production scheduling. Batch production may dictate that orders are held in storage until an optimal batch has been accumulated. Queues could, of course be eliminated if prices were perfectly flexible, but price flexibility might be costly.

Poisson Process

Queueing problems can be extremely complex, and the only solution may be simulation. However, it is often worthwhile considering the possibility that a queueing problem can be described by a Poisson distribution. We shall therefore consider a simple queueing problem with the following properties:

1   infinite population of customers or orders;
2   variable arrivals;
3   no simultaneous arrivals;
4   single service channel;
5   single queue, infinite capacity;
6   first come, first served queue discipline;
7   variable service times.

Ignoring an initial period when a service is first established and orders may arrive erratically, we may consider a situation where a steady state has been attained. The arrival of orders may be random but may be described by a Poisson distribution. A Poisson distribution is a discrete probability distribution and is given by

$$f(x) = \frac{\lambda \, x_e^{-\lambda}}{x!} \tag{12.34}$$

where λ is the mean arrival rate and x is any specific number of arrivals. Thus, if $\lambda = 8$ then the probability of $x = 5$ in 1 hour is

$$f(6) = \frac{8^5 \, e^{-8}}{5!} = \frac{32768 \times 0.0003}{120} = 0.082 \tag{12.35}$$

Poisson distributions can be derived for different values of the mean arrival rate, and an important feature of the Poisson distribution is that the standard deviation is the square root of the mean; the Poisson distribution is therefore a single-parameter distribution.

Although arrivals may be random and described by a Poisson distribution, service times may not be random, but may be predetermined as in the case of, for example, steel bars which must be drilled in three places. However, there are also situations where service times may be random; some customers may require more service than others and the time taken to service an order is independent of the time taken to service the preceding order. Inter-arrival times may therefore be described by a negative exponential distribution which is a Poisson distribution when the data are transformed to arrival rates.

Given that arrival rates and service times can be described by a Poisson distribution it is possible to derive the following formula for the simple queueing problem.

1   The degree of utilization of a service facility

$$U = \frac{\lambda}{\mu} \tag{12.36}$$

where U is the degree of utilization, λ is the mean arrival rate and μ is the average service rate.

2   The average number of customers or orders in:

(a) the system $= \dfrac{U}{1-U}$ $\tag{12.37}$

   where system refers to customers in the queue plus those being serviced.

(b) queue $= \dfrac{U^2}{1-U}$ $\tag{12.38}$

(c) queue when a queue actually exists $=$

$$\frac{1}{1-U} \tag{12.39}$$

3   The average time an order or customer is in the

(a) system $= \dfrac{1}{\mu - \lambda}$ $\tag{12.40}$

(b) queue $= \dfrac{U}{\mu - \lambda}$ $\tag{12.41}$

Some simple examples will now clarify the use of the formula.

If a simple queue has an arrival rate of 6 people and a service rate of 10 people per minute, then the degree of capacity utilization is 0.6. The probability of a person having to wait in a queue is 0.6.

The average number of people in:

the system is 1.5
the queue is 1.8
the queue when a queue exists is 2.5.

The average time a person or order is in:

the system is 0.25 minute
the queue is 0.15 minute.

(Note that if an individual waits on average 0.15 minute to reach a service point which takes on average 0.1 minute to serve him then the total time in the system is 0.25 minute.)

Simulation

The simple model can be extended by, for example, introducing more than one channel or alternative distributions. However, many queueing problems do not admit of solution by queueing models, and approximate solutions may have to be sought by numerical experiment.

Consider the problem of a garage proprietor who has one petrol pump and is considering whether to install additional pumps. It is assumed that he makes a 2-hour record of the distribution of time between arrivals of motorists and assigns the time intervals probabilities as in table 12.4. The next step is to

Table 12.4. Distribution of time between arrivals

Time interval (m)	Probability	Time interval (m)	Probability
1	0.11	17	0.02
2	0.10	18	0.02
3	0.09	19	0.02
4	0.07	20	0.02
5	0.05	21	0.02
6	0.04	22	0.02
7	0.03	23	0.02
8	0.03	24	0.02
9	0.03	25	0.02
10	0.03	26	0.02
11	0.03	27	0.02
12	0.03	28	0.02
13	0.20	29	0.01
14	0.20	30	0.01
15	0.20	31	0.01
16	0.20	32	0.01

Table 12.5. Random numbers

24	63	39	21	20	44	65	97	38	22	85	24	28
65	76	59	29	97	68	60	71	74	57	25	91	38
66	59	83	62	64	11	12	67	16	90	82	19	00
42	53	61	23	08	77	11	43	47	03	50	37	
67	54	13	58	18	24	76	15	54	55	95	52	
71	74	60	47	21	29	68	02	02	37	03	31	

compute the long-run probability distribution of arrivals, and to obtain that distribution we shall use figures obtained from random number tables (table 12.5). Next we assign random numbers to the time intervals (table 12.6). Thus, figures 00–10 are assigned to the time interval of 1 minute, 11 is assigned to 2 minutes and so on. The first random number is 24 and according to table 12.6 corresponds to 3 minutes. If the garage opens at 9.00 a.m. then the first arrival is expected at 9.05 a.m. The next random number is 63 and this corresponds to 12 minutes, so the second arrival will be expected to arrive at 9.17 a.m. Hence it would be possible to construct a distribution of car arrivals and, given an assumption about the average service time, derive an estimate of queue length and the average time a motorist is in the queue. A final step would be to make appropriate assumptions about the cost of an extra pump attendant.

Table 12.6. Assignment of random numbers to time intervals

Time interval	Random number	Time interval	Random number
1	00–10	17	72, 73
2	11–20	18	74, 75
3	21–29	19	76, 77
4	30	20	78, 79
5	37	21	80, 81
6	42	22	82, 83
7	46	23	84, 85
8	49	24	86, 87
9	52	25	88, 89
10	55	26	90, 91
11	58	27	92, 93
12	61	28	94, 95
13	64, 65	29	96
14	66, 67	30	97
15	68, 69	31	98
16	70, 71	32	99

Inventory Control

Inventories are the mirror-image of queues. The alternative to loss of goodwill through queues and dissatisfied customers going elsewhere is to hold stocks. Such stocks may take the form of finished goods, spare parts or workers and materials. But holding stocks is costly. What then determines the optimal level of stock? Suppose a manufacturer expects to sell some fixed amount, Q^*, of his product during the next 12 months at a given price, and on the assumption that demand is not subject to seasonal fluctuations. Clearly he has several possible inventory policies he can pursue: he can build up his stock at the beginning of the year and then allow it to run down throughout the year; or he can begin the year with some stock and then deliver extra quantities throughout the year from his manufacturing departments.

Suppose that he begins the year with the entire estimated stock of 1000 units and runs it down through the year to zero, then his average stockholding will be 500. Alternatively, suppose that he places two orders for stock during the year so that his average stock is 250. Then by placing more orders he can reduce his inventory level. Although a smaller inventory lowers carrying costs (storage space), it does raise re-ordering costs. Hence the optimal inventory level will be determined by the balancing of savings in storage costs against increases in re-ordering costs.

To find the optimum inventory level which minimizes the sum of carrying and re-ordering costs we shall begin by examining carrying costs. If the whole of the inventory were delivered at the beginning of the year and then run down to zero then the average inventory level would be

$$\frac{D + 0}{2} = \frac{D}{2} \tag{12.42}$$

where D is the size of the (initial) delivery. If the carrying cost per unit is k then the average carrying cost would be $kD/2$.

Turning to the re-ordering costs we can observe that if 1000 units are to be sold and 250 units are delivered in each delivery, then there would need to be $4 = 1000/250$ deliveries in the year.

If the cost per delivery consists of a fixed charge and a cost per units carried then we have an expression such as $a^* + b^*D$ where a^* and b^* are the relevant costs.

The total reordering cost is therefore the number of deliveries multiplied by the cost per delivery

$$\frac{(a^* + b^*D)Q^*}{D} = \frac{a^*Q^*}{D} + \frac{b^*Q^*D}{D} = \frac{a^*Q^*}{D} + b^*Q^* \tag{12.43}$$

The total cost of the inventory is therefore the sum of the carrying cost and the re-ordering cost

$$C = \frac{k*D}{2} + \frac{a*Q*}{D} + b*Q* \tag{12.44}$$

In order to find the optimal value of D which minimizes the total inventory cost we differentiate C with respect to D, set the derivative equal to zero and solve for D:

$$\frac{dC}{dD} = \frac{k*}{2} - \frac{a*Q*}{D^2} = C \tag{12.45}$$

or $$\frac{k*}{2} = \frac{a*Q*}{D^2} \tag{12.46}$$

Multiplying both sides by $2D^2/k*$ we obtain:

$$D^2 = \frac{2a*Q*}{k*}$$

hence: $$D = \sqrt{\frac{2a*Q*}{k*}} \tag{12.47}$$

The analysis which we have conducted so far has been based upon Baumol (1972). Baumol pioneered the use of inventory analysis in the determination of optimal holdings of money for transaction purposes. The square root formula suggests that there are economies of scale in holding stocks: as the level of sales goes up then the level of stocks should not be increased in proportion. However, before we jump to the conclusion that businessmen who make stocks a constant percentage of sales are wrong, we should note that we have made no allowance for uncertainty, for holding precautionary balances. The rules-of-thumb which are often used may be misleading but in the face of uncertainty they may be the only possible procedure. Inventory cycles constitute one of the unresolved area of macroeconomic analysis and policy.

Bibliography and References

Arvan, L. and Moses, L. N. (1982) 'Inventory investment and the theory of the firm', *American Economic Review*, 12, 186–93.
Baumol, W. J. (1972) *Economic Analysis and Operations Research*. New York: Prentice Hall.
Bell, P. W. and Todaro, M. (1969) *Economic Theory*. Oxford: Oxford University Press.
Downie, J. (1958) *The Competitive Process*. London: Duckworth.

Farrell, M. J. (1957) 'The measurement of productive efficiency', *Journal of the Royal Statistical Society*, series A, 120, 253–90.

Forsund, F. R. and Hjalmarsson, L. (1979) 'Generalized Farrell measures of efficiency: an application to milk processing in Swedish dairy plants', *Economic Journal*, 89, pp. 294–314.

Georgescu-Roegen, N. (1966) *Analytical Economics*. Cambridge Mass.: Harvard University Press.

Georgescu-Roegen, N. (1976) *Energy and Economic Myths*. London: Pergamon Press.

Hillier, F. S. and Lieberman, G. (1980) *Introduction to Operations Research*. London: Holden Day.

Lewis, W. A. (1978) *Growth and Fluctuations 1870–1913*. London: Allen & Unwin.

Menderhausen, H. (1938) 'On the significance of Professor Douglas's production function', *Econometrica*, 6, 143–53.

Mulligan, J. E. (1965) 'Basic optimization techniques – a brief survey', *Journal of Industrial Engineering*, 16, 192–7.

Nadiri, M. I. (1981) 'Production'. In K. J. Arrow and M. J. Intrilligator (eds), *Handbook of Mathematical Economics*, vol. 2. Amsterdam: North Holland.

Page, D. and Bombach, G. (1959) *A Comparison of National Output and Productivity in the UK and US*. Paris: OEEC.

Pearl, D. J. and Enos, J. L. (1975) 'Engineering production functions', *Journal of Industrial Economics*, 24, 55–73.

Stigler, G. J. (1939) 'Production and distribution in the short run', *Journal of Political Economy*, 47, 305–27.

Wibe, S. (1984) 'Engineering production functions: a survey', *Economica*, 51, 401–11.

13 Personnel Management

Personnel management is concerned with the development of a highly motivated and efficient labour force. In the pursuit of this objective management has to take into account the possibilities presented by the external labour market and the gains which can be achieved through coordination and control within the firm. The external labour market offers both possibilities and constraints. The constraints are the size and composition of the working population, social and cultural values, legal restrictions on the form and content of employment contracts, and the rules laid down by trade unions and employers' associations, all of which confront management with industrial relations choices.

Given an awareness of the changing economic and legal structure surrounding industrial relations we can consider the problems confronting managers as follows:

1 The hiring of labour and the modifications which might be necessary to make the marginal productivity doctrine operative.
2 What are the factors which might influence the motivation of workers and cause variations in labour supply?
3 What are the goals of trade unions and how do they affect the determination of wages under collective bargaining?
4 What factors affect the content of employment wage contracts?
5 What are the effects of trade unions?
6 How might labour markets interact, and how might unemployment arise in such markets?

Hiring Labour: Marginal Productivity

Within the neoclassical framework personnel decisions involve no more than choosing that quantity of labour which equates the marginal cost of employing labour with the marginal benefit to the firm from that employment. This marginal benefit is simply the monetary value of labour's marginal (physical) product, while the marginal cost of employment to the firm is the cost of hiring an additional unit of labour, which may or may not equal the wage rate, depending on the state of competition in the labour market (plus any social security taxes which the state may impose and pension contributions which the firm may incur). Transforming marginal physical products into monetary values, usually termed 'marginal revenue products' requires knowledge of the revenue received by the enterprise from additional units of output – marginal revenue; under monopoly conditions this marginal revenue will diminish as output rises, while under conditions of perfect competition each individual unit of output will sell for the same price as all previous units.

The factors determining the demand for labour can be illustrated either by the output-substitution approach or by a simple marginal productivity approach. Figure 13.1 shows the amounts of product Q which can be produced by differing amounts of labour and capital. The isoquants Q_1, Q_2 and Q_3 are equal output curves – along each curve output remains constant as the proportions of the two factors are varied. If the firm's budget permits buying either OL of labour or OK of capital then factor prices are indicated by the slope of KL and the firm's optimum combination of capital and labour is given by the tangency between the factor price line and the highest attainable isoquant, at point a, that is:

$$MRTS_{LK} = P_K/P_L \qquad (13.1)$$

where $MRTS_{LK}$ is the marginal technical rate of substitution of capital for labour as denoted by the curvature of the isoquant, and P_K/P_L is the ratio of factor prices denoted by the slope of LK.

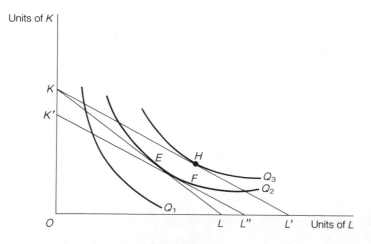

Figure 13.1

Suppose then that the wage falls and the price line moves from KL to KL'. The firm's move to a new output–factor combination can be broken down into: (1) a substitution effect and (2) an output effect. The substitution effect is indicated by reducing the firm's budget but retaining the new prices so that the firm can move along $K'L''$ until it reaches F. The move from E to F is the *substitution effect* and is determined by the ease of substituting labour for capital. The move from *F* to *H* is the *output effect* and is determined by the extent of the reduction in costs and the elasticity of the product demand curve.

In the standard treatment of factor demand it is assumed that all factors are 'normal factors' and there are no inferior factors or Giffen factors. Inferior factors are conceivable; as the sale of operations rises a firm may switch from manual typewriters to electric typewriters and eventually word-processors. Giffen factors have tended to be ruled out in the theory of factor pricing on the grounds that the firm can always borrow to finance its purchases of inputs. Of course in principle there is no reason why the theory of household behaviour should not assume that consumers have ready access to borrowing; indeed when household purchase of 'consumer durables' is analysed, borrowing is assumed to be an important element in the budget constraint. However the traditional, utility-based, consumer behaviour concentrated on the more mundane 'bread-and-butter' commodities, purchased not on credit, but out of wage income. Allowing for borrowing, then, as a common element in the budget constraint, suggests that if a firm keeps quantity x of capital, rather than quantity $x + 1$, before a fall in the wage rate (rise in the relative price of capital) it will not buy more capital after a fall in the wage rate.

Turning now to the marginal productivity approach to factor pricing, the optimal labour hiring rate can be determined on the basis of the following assumptions.

1   The enterprise has perfect knowledge about both the factor and product markets.
2   All employees and potential employees have perfect knowledge of prevailing conditions in the labour market.
3   There is freedom of movement into and out of labour markets.
4   Labour's marginal product can be identified and represented by a smooth, continuous relationship between output changes and number of labour units employed.

Given these conditions it becomes a simple task to identify the profit-maximizing employment rate for any given enterprise. Broadly, as in output markets, it is possible to distinguish between price-takers and price-makers. When the employer's demand is so insignificant, relative to the total market demand, that it cannot influence labour's market price (wage), the employer can obtain all the labour he wants at the going wage rate – *as if* the supply of labour to the firm is *perfectly elastic*. On the other hand if the employer is the sole buyer of labour, a *monopsonist*, then he faces an upward-sloping labour supply curve and the marginal cost of employing labour is greater than labour's supply price. Figures 13.2 and 13.3 and show the two market situations.

In figure 13.2(b) D_L represents the market demand curve for labour, and S_L represents the supply curve to the market. Figure 13.2(a) and (b) together underline the fact that under perfectly competitive conditions the individual buyer of labour must accept the wage as determined in the market. Given this situation the employer hires labour units until labour's marginal revenue product (shown along the MRP curve) is equal to the market wage: ON_1

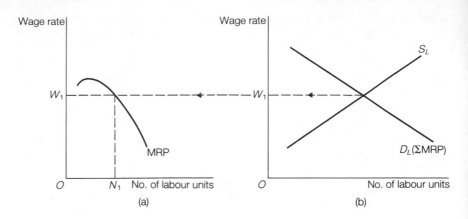

Figure 13.2   (a) Firm; (b) market

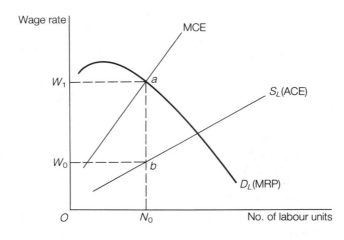

Figure 13.3

labour units are employed at a wage rate of OW_1. The picture in figure 13.3 differs by virtue of the upward-sloping supply curve. As the sole buyer of labour the monopsonist does not face a perfectly elastic supply curve of labour at the going wage; rather he faces the market supply curve, which means that the wage, the price of labour, is now determined by the employment decision of the monopsonist. In the diagram MRP again represents labour's marginal revenue product; the S_L curve shows labour's willingness to work at various wage rates and, as such, it represents the employers' average cost of employment (ACE) curve (cost per worker). It follows that the employer will not consider the labour supply curve as his guide to how many labour units to employ; rather he will look to a curve which shows the *marginal* cost of employment. Because the supply curve slopes upwards from left to right, the marginal cost of employment curve (MCE) must follow the same direction, but at a steeper rate. Thus, where MRP intersects MCE, at point a, determines the number of labour units to employ per period, ON_0. However, to obtain ON_0 the employer is not obliged to pay a wage of OW_0 because this number of labour units are willing to to work for a wage (cost per unit) of OW_0. Consequently the best outcome for the employer is where the marginal benefit from employment equals the marginal cost of that employment, but labour receives a wage which is less than marginal (revenue) product.

The fact that the monopsonist hirer of labour prefers to pay a wage which is less than labour's marginal product suggests that a unionized labour force might succeed in obtaining a higher wage rate without putting any union members out of work. Clearly the range of rates lies between OW_0 and OW_n (a to b) in figure 13.3, and the chosen rate will depend upon the relative bargaining strengths of the two sides. Our earlier assumptions did, of course, rule out unionization; nevertheless the point can well be appreciated here and now; we shall return to the question of trade unions later in this chapter.

Another case worth mentioning now is that of oligopsony where buyers' competition takes the form of following wage increases but not wage cuts. In this case the supply curve of labour (average cost of employment) is kinked at the prevailing wage with a relatively inelastic segment for higher wages (where other buyers follow suit) and a relatively elastic segment for lower wages (where other buyers do not respond). This means that the marginal cost of employment curve is discontinuous at that level of employment which coincides with the kink. Consequently a whole range of marginal revenue product curves can be consistent with only one hiring decision. In figure 13.4 this range of discontinuity is shown as a b and the level of employment, ON, would result from either marginal revenue products MRP, or any other such curve up to the limit of MRP_n.

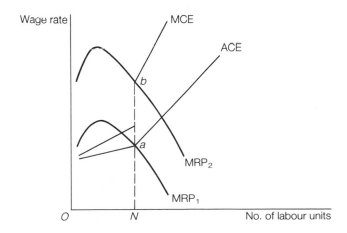

Figure 13.4

Ex-ante and Ex-post Demand

The analysis so far has been based upon the usual *ceteris paribus* assumption. If we are concerned primarily with the short run this assumption does not prove an unusual restriction, since we are then concerned with the firm's intentions – its expected or intended demand for inputs. As we consider the longer run, however, we must allow that intentions may not be carried out as other decision variables change. In the case of a single firm's demand for an input, decisions may be altered over time as the productivity of inputs changes and as other firms adjust to changes in market conditions.

Let us consider a small sample of possibilities. Suppose, for example, that we consider a buyer of labour who is a price-taker in both factor and product markets and that labour and capital (the only other variable input) are quite independent of each other in their effects on total productivity. As the price of labour falls the employer will buy more labour units, and since this does not affect the marginal productivity of capital the actual amount of labour purchased will always be the same as what the firm intends to buy, as long as the buying is done in isolation from other employers. However, in a price-taker market the lower price of labour will be on offer to all employers and as they all increase their employment of labour, the resulting increase in final outputs will lower product price and shift the (*ex-ante*) marginal revenue product curve to the left. Thus, in terms of figure 13.2, reproduced as figure 13.5, as the wage rate falls from OW_1 to OW_0, the actual employment of labour expands only to ON_2 rather than ON_3, as originally intended, because the actual marginal revenue product curve turns out to be MRP′

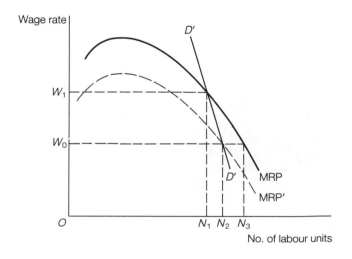

Figure 13.5

rather than the expected MRP. If we repeat this line of reasoning for all possible wage rate charges then the *ex-post* demand for labour follows the steeper relationship shown by $D'D'$.

Suppose now that labour and capital are interdependent in that an increase in employment of labour affects the marginal (revenue) product of capital. It is an interesting point that the demand for labour now becomes more elastic, regardless of whether the two inputs have a complementary or an anti-complementary relationship. If the two inputs are complements an increase in labour employed raises the marginal product of capital which, in turn, leads to more capital being employed, and hence an increase in the marginal product of labour. Complementarity should, of course, be treated broadly and can embrace potential recruits and the existing workforce. The industrial psychologist's preoccupation with whether X will 'fit in' can therefore be incorporated in the marginal productivity principle. If the relationship between the inputs is anticomplementary then less of an input increases the marginal product of the other. Hence a fall in the wage rate induces an increase in the amount of labour employed, which lowers capital's marginal product and reduces the amount of capital employed. However, this reduction, in turn, raises the marginal product of labour. Thus in each case the marginal product of labour curve shifts to the right during the adjustment process and the export labour demand curve is more elastic than the marginal revenue product curve. (Redraw figure 13.5 for the case of interdependent factors.)

So far we have assumed that the firm is attempting to maximize profits. It is, however, conceivable that a firm may be an output-maximizer. Such a firm would exhibit greater fluctuations in its demand for labour than a profit-maximizing firm as the wage varies.

The simple exposition of factor demand therefore yields a checklist of factors which determine hiring decisions:

1 What is the firm's objective? Profits or sales?
2 What is the nature of the labour market? Competitive, oligopsonistic or monopsonistic? Unionized or non-unionized?
3 What is the nature of the product market? Competitive, oligopolistic or monopolistic?
4 How easy is it to substitute between factors of production?

However, the simple theory of the demand for labour which we have experienced leaves a lot of issues not discussed. It says nothing about ignorance and uncertainty. It does not say how an employer assesses the efficiency of workers before they are employed. It does not say anything about how an employer finds workers. It says nothing about the supply of labour and yet supply, as well as demand, conditions are crucial in determining wages and allocating labour. Nor does the theory of the demand for labour have much to say about the internal operations of labour markets. Trade unions are also ignored. The law relating to employment is overlooked. In a nutshell, the theory needs amplification before it can be usable by personnel managers. Fortunately many of the recent advances in economic theory provide many of the significant insights; but we begin with the problem of defining the job.

Job Evaluation

The tasks of the personnel manager involve his interaction with marketing, production and financial managers. 'Marketing' dictates the types of goods to be produced; 'production' determines how they are to be produced; 'financial management' attempts to cost the production of those goods, and the problem for personnel managers is to find the workers to do the jobs at the wages which financial considerations suggest to be feasible. Hence the first task is to have a clear idea of the nature of the jobs.

This is not an easy question to resolve. In some instances managers may have little idea of what is the nature of a job, and it then becomes a problem of finding a suitable person to fill a vaguely defined job. The obvious jobs that fit into this category are those associated with entrepreneurship, with coping with uncertainty.

Setting aside extremely complicated jobs which may defy description, however, we can consider *job evaluation* which attempts to provide a systematic and detailed analysis of the content of jobs which can be presented formally as distinct from an informal, ad hoc, treatment. At one pole job evaluation may take the form of simply ranking all jobs in terms of overall content. At the other pole there may be an attempt to dissect jobs into their components – skill, mental and physical requirements, etc. – and then award points to each component. The points awarded for each element in a job are then aggregated to obtain the total score for a job and the scores for different jobs are then compared. The process of awarding points and then aggregating them is, of course, open to criticism on the grounds that the various components of a job are 'qualities', and it is absurd to attempt to add them together. Hence the only way to tackle the problem is to see what the market is prepared to pay for those bundles of characteristics. However, this criticism overlooks the point that the rankings of jobs obtained by job evaluation are tied to the market by the selection of certain key jobs which have recognizable market counterparts, and the market rates for these key jobs are then used to interpolate or extrapolate the pay for jobs which may have no recognizable market counterparts. This is an important point to consider when firms are operating job hierarchies and on-the-job training in specific skills. In such circumstances only jobs at ports of entry may have market counterparts. Job evaluation has also become important since the 1970s because firms have had to adapt to a changed economic climate in which traditional skills and their associated market rates have become anachronisms. In contrast, the Japanese system of lifetime employment, job rotation, joint consultation and weaker trade unions has led to a greater emphasis on personal selection – selecting able people to perform a variety of jobs, many of which may not exist at the time of appointment.

Search Policy

Given some basic knowledge of the jobs which have to be filled we can now consider the optimal hiring strategies available to employers. Because knowledge of workers' abilities is not easily ascertained, managements pursue a variety of strategies for obtaining the most efficient workers. Thus they can either set a high wage and attempt to cream the market; advertise, or use the services of trade unions, private employment agencies or government job centres; ask their existing employees to recommend someone; indulge in intensive or extensive interviewing; use strategies which make workers transfer information about themselves through signalling and self-selection procedures; or accumulate information through hiring and on-the-job training.

Because there are many methods of obtaining workers, an optimum strategy for managers to pursue would be to equate the ratios of the marginal products of their employees with the marginal costs of the different procedures used to hire them:

$$\frac{MP_1}{\Delta w} = \frac{MP_2}{MC_2} = \cdots \frac{MP_n}{MC_n} \tag{13.2}$$

where MP is the marginal product of employees hired by procedures 1, 2, 3 ... n, Δw is the change in the starting wage (the market creaming strategy), and MC_2, MC_3 ... Mc_n are the marginal costs of hiring labour by methods other than simply raising the wage.

Screening, Filtering and Discrimination

The search rule set out in the previous section presupposes that management knows the productivities of workers and, confronted by the complexities of selecting efficient workers, management may fall back upon proxy indicators such as sex, age, marital status, race, education, etc. Thus, in the past, men may have been preferred to women on the basis that men tended to have had more work experience, were more adaptable, and had already been better sorted and graded both by the education system and previous work experience.

The use of such indicators is similar to the practice of fixing a high starting rate. Thus, in figure 13.6 we assume that there are two groups of workers with different educational qualifications (and presumably abilities). As a result

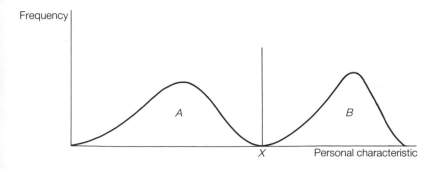

Figure 13.6

of placing the hiring standard at X, group A are discriminated against. This form of discrimination arises from lack of information and not from prejudice; it would disappear if workers in group A offered to work for lower wages than those in group B and if employers believed that it would be worth taking the risk of hiring them at the lower wage. But the problem could be exacerbated if governments attempted to impose equal pay or employment quotas for minority groups.

Signalling and Human Capital Theory

There is a link between employers' filtering techniques and workers' investment decisions. If workers think that employers are using particular screening devices then they will invest in acquiring those indicators. Hence there will be *self-selection.*

Although human capital theory can be applied to both employers' and workers' investment decisions, a distinction needs to be made between general skills and specific skills (Becker, 1964). General skills are those which are relevant to many jobs in many industries, whereas specific skills apply to one firm or industry. Because of their widespread saleability and the inability of employers to own workers, it will be workers who will invest in general skills. Specific skills will tend to be paid for by the employers, but because of the problem of protecting their investment employers will have to pay wages which will control the level of labour turnover.

Information Networks: Casual and Regular Trades and Trust

The problem of finding good workers (or good employers) accounts for the emergence of information-gathering institutions in the labour market. The existence of vacancies may be transmitted by the existing workforce to friends, by local union branches, newspapers and job centres. Because information, once released, becomes a public good, various methods are taken to ensure that it is paid for. Thus the most valuable information is not despatched through government employment centres and, historically, skilled workers have shunned such information sources and relied upon friends. Differences in information networks enable us to classify external labour markets as either *casual* or *regular* (Hicks, 1963). Casual markets are characterized by a relative absence of skills, high labour turnover, little capital equipment, piece-rate wage systems and simple managerial control systems. They may be further subdivided into those characterized by demand instability and those exhibiting supply instabililty. Demand instability may give rise to a pool of idle labour if the peaks of individual employers' demands do not coincide. Dock labour markets in the past tended to display this state of affairs. A worker who failed to get a job with one employer on a particular day might find that all the jobs had been filled once he resumed his search; and although some workers accepted the lifestyle offered by docks markets, there has been a tendency to replace casual hirings by permanent employment. Harvest labour markets also tend to exhibit demand instability, but the problem of unemployment may be eased by migration to another area.

Supply instability is usually characteristic of markets for services. The total demand for taxi-drivers and waitresses may be constant, but customers may trade with different suppliers. Indeed, many aspects of retailing exhibit this form of supply instability and casual market trading.

The regular trades are characterized by investment in skills, often specific, low labour turnover and a tendency for long-term explicit or implicit contracts to be stabilized. Such contracts permit considerable investment in trust and fairness, and these developments not only reinforce the cash-nexus, but also serve to insulate the employment contract from disturbances in the external labour market.

Hiring Standards and Dual Labour Markets

Indicators are known as 'hiring standards' and their use will vary with the state of the external labour market (McCormick, 1959). If the labour market is tight then job specifications will be revised downwards and hiring standards will be consequently lowered. If the labour market is slack, then hiring standards will be raised. Variations in the level of demand throughout the economy can therefore serve to determine the sizes of the casual and regular trades – or, to use an alternative terminology, the 'primary' and 'secondary' labour markets. As the general level of demand rises shortages will be experienced in the primary market and there will be a tendency to suck in workers from the secondary market. How this is achieved will vary according to the relative costs of different production processes and the extent of controls, especially union controls, on the use of labour in the regular trades. Thus employers faced with acute shortages of skilled labour will not compete against each other for scarce skilled workers but may attempt to substitute unskilled and semi-skilled workers drawn from the secondary market. They may do this by dilution; that is, reorganizing jobs so that scarce skilled workers are kept on key jobs, such as maintenance, whilst semi-skilled workers are put on repetitive jobs. When general demand falls then movement from the secondary labour market will slow down. In the sixties there was little evidence of a secondary market in the sense that it was impossible to move upwards into the primary market; in the eighties the boundary has become clearer.

Internal Promotion versus Outside Hiring

Many firms operate with internal labour markets because they can then create a highly motivated labour force and reduce search and training costs. However, there must still be a check against the relative costs of promoting internally as against recruiting from the outside. The decision rule therefore becomes one of comparing the net present value from training an internal recruit against the costs of outside recruitment. Since the oil price rises of the 1970s and the sharp rises in the fixed costs of hiring labour (such as national insurance contributions, holiday pay, unionism, etc.) many firms have pursued a policy of subcontracting work or using part-time and temporary workers. In all these cases it is still essential to compare the relative costs of alternative methods of hiring labour.

Labour and Plant Utilization: Inventories of Goods, Machines and Men

In our discussion of investment in chapter 9 we mentioned plant utilization but did not go into much detail as to its implications. Machines were assumed to work the appropriate number of hours; but the provision of skills and the question of who pays for them provide an introduction to the problems of plant and labour utilization. Empirical evidence points to the following phenomena which require explanation:

1   the tendency for plant and machinery to be idle for considerable periods, especially at night, weekends and during the summer months;
2   the tendency for output to fluctuate more than employment over the course of the trade cycle;
3   the tendency for output to fluctuate less than inventories of goods;
4   the tendency for money wages to be inflexible downwards.

The four stylized facts involve long- and short-run decisions by consumers, employers and workers. Specifically the economic problem over the long run is to reconcile the preferences of consumers and producers. In the short run there may be fluctuations, anticipated or otherwise, in consumers' demands, and the problem is to determine whether these variations should be met by changes in current output, changes in the levels of stocks (including stock-outs) or raising price to ration available supplies. But we began with the long-run problem of shift working.

Shift Working

A striking feature of the British economy has been the low level of plant utilization. Most machinery is idle at weekends and even night work is not frequent. The problem of low levels of plant utilization was commented upon by the National Board for Prices and Incomes report on overtime and shift working in the late sixties. The main determinants of shift working appear to be the following factors:

1   the capital intensity of production;
2   the wage–rental ratio;
3   the size of the shift premium;
4   the elasticity of substitution between capital and labour.

The prevailing state of technology may determine the potential capital intensity of production and incline a firm towards greater capital utilization. However, whether shift working will be adopted may depend upon the size of the shift premium. If workers dislike the disruption of family life which shift working can produce, then they may demand a prohibitive shift premium. Hence we can describe a wage–plant utilization curve whose elasticity will be determined by the ease of substituting capital for labour. These economic factors may underscore any legislation which forbids, for example, the employment of women and young persons.

Overtime and Short-time Working, and Stocks

The tendency for output to fluctuate more than employment over the course of the business cycle has been well documented and its causes have been attributed to the costs of hiring and training labour. Thus within the production function we must distinguish between the number of employees and the hours they work. (We have also noted that we should distinguish the number of machines and their degree of utilization; we should note also the intensity with which employees work.) What is then observed in time series analysis is that the numbers employed fluctuate less than hours worked and output. If we start from a situation at the lower turning point of the cycle with a given number of employees, then the early stages of the upswing are characterized by a reduction in idle time and a greater utilization of plant and equipment, with the result that output increases and real and money wages may rise together. In the later stages of the upswing bottlenecks may occur and more labour may be employed, overtime working may be introduced and productivity may decline; real and money wages may therefore move in opposite directions. With the collapse of the boom, output and hours will fall, but productivity can fall also if the numbers employed are not reduced; real and money wages may therefore continue to move in opposite directions.

Oi (1962) has attempted to explain the phenomenon of labour hoarding in recessions by an extension of human capital theory. Thus the costs of employing labour may be written as follows.

$$C = W_t (1 - r)^{-t} + H + K \tag{13.3}$$

where the first term on the right-hand side is the sum of discounted wage payments, and H and K are hiring and training costs respectively.

The discounted marginal revenue product stream is

$$\text{MRP} = (\text{VMP} + \Delta\text{VMP}) (L + r)^{-t} \tag{13.4}$$

where VMP is the value of the worker's marginal product and ΔVMP is the addition due to training.

Profit-maximizing requires that the discounted cost of an additional worker is just equal to his discounted revenue:

$$H + K = (\text{VMP} + \Delta\text{VMP} - W_t)\,(1 - r)^{-t} \tag{13.5}$$

with periodic rent

$$R = \frac{H + K}{(1 - r)^{-t}} \tag{13.6}$$

Hence a worker will be laid off only if his period rent falls below the value of marginal product. If the value of the marginal product falls below the rent, then the firm will find that it pays to dispense with workers to save on current costs, i.e. wage payments. But as long as workers are bringing in some rent, it pays to retain them because the costs of hiring workers when the boom begins will include a new outlay on hiring and training costs.

Labour hoarding, however, will not be practised if employers know that they can temporarily dismiss workers with the knowledge that they will return when demand picks up. Temporary lay-offs may be possible when there is a probability that workers will return when demand picks up. Temporary lay-offs may be possible when there are state unemployment benefits available and there are no alternative jobs. However, the impact of unemployment benefits needs to be set against the effects of variations in State insurance contributions, which may raise the fixed costs of hiring labour and therefore reduce the incentives to dismiss workers.

Labour hoarding represents one possible response to changing demand conditions. Another possibility is to keep labour fully employed by manufacturing for stock during slack periods. Whether that is feasible depends upon the relative costs of holding stocks.

Finally we should note that when firms operate job hierarchies dismissals may take the form of displacements, and job enlargement may take place as skilled workers take on unskilled functions as well as their own customary jobs.

Labour Absenteeism

Not only may a firm simultaneously determine its wages and labour turnover, it may also determine its wages and absenteeism. In figure 13.7 we measure a worker's demand for absences (leisure) in the top half of the diagram. He will equate his demand for absences with the opportunity cost of those absences; that is, at wage OC he will demand OQ absences. In the bottom half of the diagram we measure the disutility to the employer of those absences; that is, his demand to reduce absences. When OQ absences occur the disutility to the employer is QB, and since QB is greater than QA, it would be profitable to the employer to increase the cost to the worker of absences either by threats or bribes, which shift the cost to OC_1 where OQ_1 absences are produced and

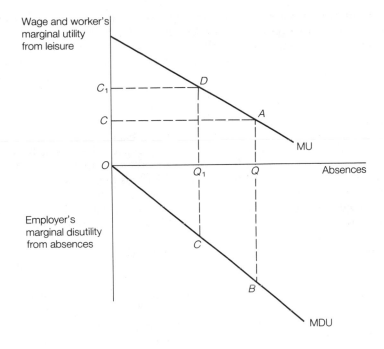

Figure 13.7

marginal costs and benefits are equal ($Q_1C = Q_1D$). Thus absences of OQ_1 might be described as 'Pareto optimal'.

The notion of Pareto optimal absenteeism seems to accord with evidence that employers and employees are often unconcerned about absences. Despite the fact that most employers are not discriminating monopsonists, and have to pay a standard wage negotiated with a union, a process of self-selection takes place which ensures optimality: at this wage only those willing to offer a given number of hours will offer their services. Hence absenteeism within the labour force may exhibit little variance; there may be a group norm. Absenteeism tells us nothing, therefore, about job satisfaction. Indeed if transactions costs preclude an employer negotiating with each employee a standard wage, we may witness the simultaneity of absenteeism and overtime working as a result of which income-preferers and leisure-preferers obtain their optimal wage–leisure combination.

Motivation and Labour Supply

So far we have concentrated upon hiring labour on the assumption that the wage and conditions of labour supply were given. But wages are determined by both supply and demand, and managers need to know something about the conditions of supply before determining optimal hiring policies. Thus two questions which might present themselves to managers attempting to cope with labour shortages might be the following. What might be the effect of an increase in wages upon the existing labour force? Will an increase in wages attract new entrants?

The starting point is the need for some theory of motivation, and we shall use the theory of utility as modified by the concept of a hierarchy of wants (Georgescu-Roegen, 1966). An individual is assumed to have a hierarchy of wants. Basic wants will comprise such things as food and shelter. Lower-order wants may comprise such things as status and prestige. Goods which satisfy one want cannot be used to satisfy another want, although there may be some goods which can satisfy more than one want. What this implies is that a person may have more than one set of indifference curves. Each set of indifference curves will embrace those goods which can satisfy a particular want, and another set of indifference curves will need to be drawn to denote the satisfaction of another want.

With this qualification in mind we can now consider the effect of a wage increase upon the supply of labour. If an employer increases the wage offered to a worker then there will be income and substitution effects operating upon each individual's work–leisure decision. The substitution effect will work in the direction of making him offer more units of labour services. The income effect can, however, work in the direction of making him offer more or fewer units of labour. Which will be the strongest influence cannot be determined *a priori*, but must be settled by reference to empirical evidence, although it might be possible to reduce the adverse effects of a wage increase by a discriminatory wage policy in which successive units of labour are bought at higher prices.

The motivation theory based upon income and substitution effects can be applied to units of labour supply whether measured in terms of heads, hours of work or effort. Before describing some of the empirical evidence it may be useful to consider two other issues. First, although we have concentrated upon the concept of a wage, it should not be interpreted in a narrow sense. Labour economics has always allowed individuals to consume at work as well as at home. Hence the wage may include non-monetary elements, such as pleasant working conditions. Second, theory concentrates upon the benefits from work (income) as compared with the benefits from leisure. In the older literature, however, stress was placed upon the utility and disutility associated with work. This approach fell into disfavour because of the difficulties of treating disutility as negative utility, and because it was assumed that an individual started with a stock of assets and was not entirely dependent upon wages for income. An approach which uses the notion of disutility is that put forward by Herzberg (1959). He distinguished between *motivators* which gave rise to job satisfaction and *hygiene* factors which might promote dissatisfaction. However, his theory has aroused considerable controversy among psychologists (Wall and Stephenson, 1970).

Following the excursus of the previous chapter we can now describe the empirical evidence on labour supply which has been confined to the heads and hours dimensions. In the case of adult males it is assumed that they are faced with a choice between income and leisure, and that the supply curve, whether measured in terms of heads or hours, is probably inelastic with respect to the wage. In the case of married women it is assumed that there is a three-fold choice beween market work, house work and leisure, and that choice is influenced by the relative wages of husband and wife, household labour-saving technology, divorce rates, and number of spacing of children. In the case of young workers decisions are influenced by the relative wages of older and younger workers, parental incomes and subsidies to full-time education. These studies do not of course deal with the movement between jobs in response to changes in relative wages, which we shall discuss after analysing trade unions.

Methods of Wage Determination: Unions and Collective Bargaining

The analyses of labour demand and supply have both been conducted on the assumption that the wage was given. As such both theories are compatible with any theory of wage determination. However, it is customary to think of wages as being fixed by collective bargaining and to attach particular significance to the behaviour of trade unions. Moreover, the economic analysis of trade unions is rendered difficult because they do not supply their members with property rights which can be bought and sold. Hence the analogy with other non-profit organizations and, of course, with workers' cooperatives.

The absence of property rights leaves unanswered the question: 'What are the goals of a union?' If all members count equally, as in the political sphere, then it is possible to have cyclic majorities; that is, if three members, A, B and C rank three policies X, Y and Z differently, then all three policies will receive an equal number of votes. Without some method of measuring the preferences of members there is no way of determining the goals of a union. We do not know, for example, whether the goals include the current employed membership only or the unemployed or future generations of members. In the economics literature resort is sometimes made to a median voter. This leads to an explanation of wage rigidity as follows. If the demand for labour rises then the existing members will not allow in new entrants because that would imply a redistribution of income from them to the new entrants. If the demand for labour falls then the median member would vote against wage reductions because that would mean a redistribution of income to recent recruits. But how does the median member cope with the possibility that he may become unemployed?

In the industrial relations literature some of these problems are tackled by explicitly recognizing the political nature of a union. Thus in Ross's theory (1948) the conflict between rank and file is influenced by the wages obtained by workers in other unions: 'the orbits of coercive comparison'. In Turner's analysis (1962) a distinction is drawn between closed and open unions. In closed unions membership is restricted through such devices as apprenticeships and heavy investment in human capital, and because of their considerable investment members exercise control over union affairs through the practice of periodic elections of lay officials. In the open unions the shifting membership of unskilled and semi-skilled members are led by full-time officials usually elected for life. However, the full-time officials are held in check by breakaway unions, rival unions and unofficial strikes. Turner also drew attention to the different wage policies of closed and open unions, and the fact that there could be alternating phases of closed and open unions.

The economic analysis of unions has, however, tended to run behind the industrial relations literature and has chosen to analyse models in which a union is either a monopolist or is attempting an all-or-nothing contract (Pencavel, 1985). Both models can be fitted into an industrial relations contract as follows. Initially a union may attempt to set the wage and allow the employer to determine the numbers to be employed. This policy is not pursued because the union is a monopolist, but as a self-selection device to determine those who are eligible to form a union. Initially, skills are not known, and have to be determined by what workers are earning rather than by setting skill standards to dictate a wage (Turner, 1962). It is, of course, possible that a union could then move to pressing a monopoly advantage which would yield a once-for-all gain to the current members. The gain would then be preserved by such devices as apprenticeships and low wages for trainees – such devices would be the methods by which future members paid for their union gains. But once a union has achieved the power to set the wage then it may move to set the labour supply by means of an all-or-nothing contract. When such contracts are in operation the management may attempt to obtain flexibility by challenging union manning rules. In figure 13.8 three possibilities are illustrated. First, the union may attempt to obtain wage OW_1 which yields the maximum average net product. Second the union may have some trade-off between wages and employment such as is given by wage OW_2. Third, the union may seek wage OW_3 and employment W_3L.

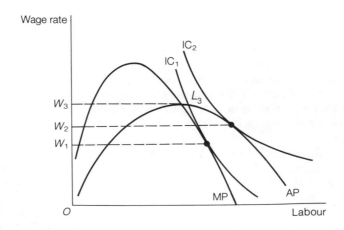

Figure 13.8

Methods of Enforcement

Consider the following problem. An employer may not know in advance the productivity of a worker, nor what his sales (value productivity) will be. But he must offer the worker a contract which will overcome his current work–leisure preference. On the other hand, a worker may not know what his productivity will be, or if he does he may be reluctant to disclose it in advance of a contract. Hence a contract may be for two periods. In the first period, the probationary period, the employer is able to assess the productivity of the worker. The second period begins with the renewal of the contract or its variation, and in this period there may be opportunities for cheating or reneging. Thus at the end of the first period the employer may attempt to drive down wages, not on the grounds that the worker's productivity is lower than expected, but because trade is bad (that is, value productivity low) and the worker may have difficulties in obtaining information on the state of trade, except by striking or quitting and seeking another job.

Strikes

The standard theory of strikes is due to Hicks (1963). A union seeks a wage OW to which the employer replies with a lower offer OW_1. A strike ensues. The union is then envisaged as having a resistance curve which slopes downward over time from its initial claim. The employer is thought of as being guided by a concession curve which slopes upward. Now if both sides were knowledgeable, seasoned bargainers, they would have some idea of the location of each other's sticking points. Hence a strike would be an accident and cheating would be exceptional, rather than common occurrences. However, there are occasions when unusual circumstances destroy the fund of common knowledge possessed by both sides. Hence the curves may not be foreseeable and both sides may attempt to conceal their sticking points. A strike may therefore be the only means of forcing a rival to reveal the position of his resistance or concession curve.

Let us now list some insights into strike activity from various studies.

1 The thesis that the larger the plant the greater is the probability of strike activity is still a matter of debate. The argument is that the more workers are congregated in a particular plant the greater is the probability of differences of opinion leading to conflict; this is a variant of the accident thesis. However, official statistics do not cover small plants, and the incidence of strikes appears to decline as plants become very large. This may indicate that medium-sized plants lack well-established grievance procedures (Revans, 1958; Turner et al., 1971; McCormick, 1979).

2 The importance of grievance procedures may explain the sharp rise in small strikes in the 1940s through to the 1960s, when there was a shift from industry-wide collective bargaining to a greater reliance

on plant-level bargaining. During the 1970s there was a growth in the number of shop stewards, a formalization of grievance machinery and a decline in the number of small strikes.

3   The frequency of strikes is associated with changes in real wages, relative wages, unemployment and incomes policies. This suggests that abrupt changes in information may cause negotiators to misjudge the situation.

4   Some industries appear to be strike-prone, e.g. coal mining, vehicles and port transport. Since some of these industries have exhibited high strike frequency under private as well as public ownership the causes of strike-proneness may have to be sought elsewhere. In coal mining the immobility of miners may be the cause of strikes. Strikes and labour turnover may be alternative responses to unforeseen changes in demand.

5   There is evidence that some regions are more strike-prone than others.

6   Most strikes occur in a few plants in a few regions, which suggests that wide sweeping changes in legislation may be less efficient than the use of a group of specialist conciliators.

7   There is some evidence that international differences in strike activity are an important factor in determining the ease of adjustment of different economies to disturbances.

Third-party Intervention

Strikes may be one way of resolving differences; there may be other methods. A strike may be considered to be the only means of locating the concession and resistance curves. However, there might be situations in which a third party can assist in finding a settlement without open warfare. Third-party intervention may take the form of conciliation, mediation or arbitration. The function of the conciliator is passive – he merely brings the disputants together and allows them to find their own solution. The mediator suggests possible solutions which both parties may have overlooked. The arbitrator makes an award which is binding upon both parties.

Third-party intervention may enable one side to make a concession without appearing to be weak. A union leader may have threatened a strike without having assessed the consequences; he may be new, raw and inexperienced. The third party may then be blamed for the forced retreat. But as we have noted, not all strikes are accidents. The strike may be inevitable and desirable.

Wage Contracts, Salary Contracts and Profit-sharing Schemes

Problems of enforcing contracts may dictate the method of wage payment. In this section we shall consider wage contracts, salary contracts and profit-sharing schemes. In a subsequent section we shall examine piece-rate and time-rate contracts and jousts. We shall now examine the following factors.

1   the degree of risk-averseness of employers and workers;
2   the ease of access to information of employers and workers;
3   the work–leisure preferences of workers;
4   the effects of unemployment benefits;
5   the methods and costs of enforcing contracts;
6   the transactions costs associated with hiring, training and dismissing workers.

For ease of exposition we shall distinguish between (1) wage contracts, (2) salary contracts, and (3) profit-sharing contracts.

Under a wage contract management may offer workers a fixed reward and no job security if workers are no more risk-averse than they are, if unemployment benefits exist, if workers are easy to replace, and if workers are willing to accept the bunching of spells of enforced leisure.

If workers are extremely risk-averse then they will prefer salary contracts in which they are guaranteed a fixed reward and guaranteed employment. Whether management will offer such a contract will depend upon its attitude to risk and its ability to spread risk through the capital market. It may, of course, offer such contracts to specific groups whose contribution to total costs is small and whose replacement costs are high. But the expression 'salary contract' should not be construed as applying solely to white-collar workers; it may be a contract offered to some manual workers.

A profit-sharing contract is one which guarantees employment but not rewards, and is likely to be acceptable where workers can exercise some form of control over decision-making. Indeed it is noticeable that despite government tax concessions to profit-sharing schemes, workers tend to sell their shares very quickly and lose tax benefits. Such behaviour may be influenced by rising share prices, but it does suggest that unions might profitably buy up their members' shares or advance loans against them.

Indexation: an Automatic Profit-sharing Scheme

Employment contracts normally stipulate a monetary reward that is fixed in nominal terms. Workers would, however, prefer a wage which is fixed in real terms; in other words a wage which measures some bundle of consumer goods. Management, on the other hand, would prefer to fix a wage in terms of their own product – that is, a wage which is linked to the selling price of their product. Because of these differences of opinion there is seldom an explicit statement of the real wage measured by the nominal wage mentioned in the contract. Of course, some notion of a real wage is in the minds of the employer and employee, but it is only in periods of severe inflation, when governments underwrite the contract, that explicit indexation of the wage to an index of retail prices becomes common. In normal circumstances changes in the real wage are usually the subject of contract renegotiation. However, Keynes's dictum still applies in Britain; there is no way in which the worker can determine his real wage. It would, of course, be desirable to have some flexibility in wages in order to combat unemployment and inflation. Such *automaticity* need not take the form of an explicit rule; the gold standard operated without a written constitution and the profit-sharing schemes of the Japanese do not appear to have any clear form of indexation. But the bloody parturition of the British worker seems to make such schemes unattainable.

Time-rates, Piece-rates and Jousts

Contracts for service are for products, whereas employment contracts are either for units of time or products. The distinction in employment contracts may, however, be more apparent than real. Most time-rates imply an output and most piece-rates imply some period of production. The distinction between time-rates and piece-rates does, in fact, tend to turn upon whether output can be measured, and what form supervision must take in order to get workers to reveal their preferences and also to measure the quality of output. If tasks are divisible and outputs can be measured, then payment by product or piece will be used; supervision will take the form of monitoring the quality of output and ensuring a constant flow of materials and the absence of extraneous interruptions to a worker's performance. Management's task is essentially that of the consumer – checking the quality of output. If the tasks are not divisible then an all-in contract will be used and management's task will be to monitor the effort of the worker as well as the quality of the product.

An obvious disadvantage of time-rates is that there is no link between payment and output; if pay is doubled then output might not be doubled; hence the attraction of piece-rates. But simple piece-rates have the disadvantage that they do not compensate for the rising cost of effort. Hence the attraction of premium bonus schemes in which the bonus rises as output rises, although at a diminishing rate in order to correct for faulty rate-fixing and learning effects.

Piece-rates became popular around the turn of the century and were associated with the pioneers of scientific management, such as F. W. Taylor. They were used extensively in the First and Second World Wars but declined in popularity in the 1950s in America, and in Britain in the 1960s. Their wartime popularity was undoubtedly due to shortages of labour for monitoring, the influx of women who were less disposed to challenge wage systems, and the existence of numerous repetitive jobs. Their postwar decline owed a great deal to the dissemination of the writings of industrial sociologists, such as Roy (1950) in America and Lupton (1963) in Britain. There was also the impact of that great work, *Management and the Worker*, by Roethlisberger and Dickson. The import of these and other investigations may be summarized as follows:

1 The assumption that workers are interested only in money may be false.
2 The assumption that effort can be harnessed by an incentive scheme may be false.
3 There may be no connection between effort and output.
4 Workers will resent rate-cutting by managers intent on capturing some of the gains from learning-by-doing.
5 If there are too many interruptions, workers may take steps to stabilize their earnings by insisting on lieu-rates which convert piece-rates into time-rates.

6 The spread of the shop steward system as a means of protecting workers against the vagaries of piece-rate systems may mean that production becomes subcontracted and management loses control of the shopfloor.

However, there has been a revival of interest in piece-rates since the mid-seventies. One factor responsible for this revival has been the effect of successive incomes policies which have prevented managers granting time-rate increases. A second factor, most noticeable in the coal industry, has been the failure of time-rates to increase productivity, and the tendency for national time-rate negotiations to develop into political confrontations.

Piece-rates may be usable where output can be measured and quality control presents no serious problems; time-rates may be used where supervision costs are low. There are difficulties, however, in the case of managerial staffs whose output is not easily measurable and for whom an attempt to put a time dimension on work may also be tricky. Abraham and Medof (1980) found that human capital theory did not seem to explain the salary differences between workers in two firms; and it is common for the pay of a manager to double when he is promoted even though there is no apparent doubling of productivity. Managing directors do not suddenly become twice as efficient as their seconds-in-command.

Two explanations have been put forward for the apparent differences in salary rankings. First, there is the obvious point that a manager is paid not only on the basis of his productivity, but also on the basis of that of his subordinates. Hence the higher up the managerial ladder a person is, the more subordinates he will have under him. Second, the economic problem is not to find out who is best at a job absolutely (whatever 'absolute' may mean), but to find out who is is best relative to others. All that one is trying to do is to find out who is the best managing director given that there is no obvious way of assessing abilities. Hence the problem is resolved by establishing prizes of such magnitude that many will take part in the race. Although the idea of a tournament has been applied only to managing directors, it can be generalized. Thus the earnings of barristers obtained under contracts of service may exhibit great disparities because success breeds disproportionately greater rewards.

The Effects of Unions

A problem with assessing the effects of unions is the dearth of good studies of the effects of unions on productivity and wage costs.

Wages

Given the nature of the employer's demand curve, a union may increase wages without reducing employment. If there is unemployment then the unemployed may drift into the unorganized sector and there depress wages. Hence we need to consider the spillover effects of unions. We also need to consider whether the union wage effect should be measured in terms of hourly or weekly earnings. Since a union may comprise both income-preferers and leisure-preferers a measurement in terms of weekly earnings or wage rates might not capture any gains resulting from a reduction in hours worked.

Finally we need to take account of the quality of the available statistical information. In Britain there have been no studies of the effects of individual unions, and given the very high union density it is difficult to obtain information on non-union wages. We do, however, have data on the proportion of workers covered by collective agreements at national and local level. Of course such data may overlook the possibility that non-union workers may be paid union wages as a result of employers attempting to keep unions out of their factories, or because of some arbitration award based upon comparability. There is also the problem that the union wage effect is obtained as a residual after attempting to isolate the effects of age, sex, education, race, etc. on wages, and frequently information on other variables is not available. Bearing in mind these qualifications, various studies suggest a range of estimates of unionism which suggest that national agreements may yield a differential ranging from zero to 10 per cent and that local agreements give much higher differentials (Parsley, 1980).

Finally, we may note that some studies suggest that unions reduce the dispersion of wages within occupations but preserve inter-occupational and inter-industry wage differentials (Routh, 1980).

Productivity

Even if union members obtain a wage differential over non-unionists, it is still possible that wage costs remain unchanged, or fall. The rejection of the simple union-as-a-monopoly thesis of figure 13.8 stems from the problems of formulating contracts for idiosyncratic exchanges (see Addison and Barnett, 1982). What unions may do is to substitute Voice (negotiation and threat of strike) for Exit (labour turnover). A bit of time spent in negotiating may cost less than that incurred in replacing workers. There has only been one attempt, by Pencavel (1978), to analyse this problem in Britain. Using admittedly limited data he suggested that unions in the coal industry did not obtain a differential over the non-union wage but that they did reduce output in the period 1900–13. Of course this raises the question: why did the workers join unions? The answers might lie in such factors as reduced accident rates and increased leisure. In America there have been several studies which suggest that unions can raise productivity, and the source of increased productivity has been sought in the market conditions (competitive or monopolistic) surrounding firms.

Bibliography and References

Abraham, K. G. and Medof, J. L. (1980) 'Experience, performance and earnings', *Quarterly Journal of Economics*, 95, 703–35.

Addison, J. T. and Barnett, H. A. (1982) 'The impact of unions on productivity', *British Journal of Industrial Relations*, 20, 145–62.

Addison, J. T. and Siebert, W. J. (1982) 'Are strikes accidents? ', *Economic Journal*, 92, 387–402.

Allen, S. G. (1984) 'Unionized construction workers are more productive', *Quarterly Journal of Economics*, 98, 251–74.

Baumol, W. J. (1982) *Contestable Markets and the Theory of Industry*. New York: Harcourt Brace.

Becker, G. S. (1964) *Human Capital*. New York: Columbia University Press.

Brannen, P. J. et al. *Worker Directors*. London: Hutchinson.

Brown, W. A. (1981) *The Changing Contours of Industrial Relations*. Oxford: Blackwell.

Buchanan, J. M. and Stubblebine, C. (1962) 'Externality', *Economica*, 29, 371–84.

Craig, J. C., Rubery, J., Tarling, R. and Wilkinson, F. (1982) *Labour Market Structure, Industrial Organization and Low Pay*. Cambridge: Cambridge University Press.

Dertouzos, J. N. and Pencavel, J. H. (1980) 'Wage and employment determination under trade unions: the international typographical union', *Journal of Political Economy*, 89, 1162–81.

Dunlop, J. T. (1950) *Wage Determination under Trade Unions*. New York: Macmillan.

Flanders, A. (1970) *Management and Unions*. London: Faber.

Freeman, R. (1976) 'Individual mobility and union voice in the labour market', *American Economic Review*, 66, 361–8.

Georgescu-Roegen, N. (1966) *Analytical Economics*. Cambridge, Mass.: Harvard University Press.

Hackman, J. R. and Hackman, G. R. (1980) *Work Design*. New York: Addison Wesley.

Herzberg, F., Mausner, B. and Snyderman, B. B. (1959) *The Motivation to Work*. New York: Wiley.

Hicks, J. R. (1963) *The Theory of Wages*, 2nd edn. London: Macmillan.

Keynes, J. M. (1936) *The General Theory of Employment, Interest and Money*. London: Macmillan.

Lazcar, E. and Rosen, S. (1981) 'Rank order tournaments as optimal labor contracts', *Journal of Political Economy*, 89, 841–64.

Lazear, E. and Moore, R. L. (1984) 'Incentives, productivity and labor contracts', *Quarterly Journal of Economics*, 98, 275–96.

Lerner, A. P. (1980) *An Anti-Inflation Plan*. New York: Harcourt Brace.

Lewis, W. A. (1978) *Growth and Fluctuations 1870–1913*. London: Allen & Unwin.

Lupton, T. (1963) *On the Shop Floor*. London: Oxford University Press.

McCormick, B. J. (1959) 'Labor hiring policies and monopolistic competition theory', *Quarterly Journal of Economics*, 78, 607–18.

McCormick, B. J. (1979) *Industrial Relations in the Coal Industry*. London: Macmillan.

McGrath, P. (1959) 'Democracy in overalls: the futile quest for trade union democracy', *Industrial and Labor Relations Review*, 12, 503–42.

Meade, J. E. (1964) *Efficiency, Equality and the Ownership of Property*. London: Allen & Unwin.

Meade, J. E. (1981) *Stagflation*, Vol. 1: *Wage Fixing*. London: Allen & Unwin.

Oi, W. (1962) 'Labor as a quasi-fixed factor', *Journal of Political Economy*, 70, 538–55.

Parsley, C. J. (1980) 'Labor unions and wages: a survey', *Journal of Economic Literature*, 18, 1–31.

Pencavel, J. (1985) 'Wages and employment under trade unionism: microeconomic models and macroeconomic applications', *Scandinavian Journal of Economics*, 87, 197–225.

Reddaway, W. I. B. (1959) 'Wage, flexibility and the distribution of labour, *Lloyds Bank Review*, 53, 32–48.

Reder, M. W. and Neuman, S. R. (1983) 'Conflict and contract: the case of strikes', *Journal of Political Economy*, 88, 867–86.

Revans, R. (1958) 'Human relations, management and size'. In E. M. Hugh Jones (ed.), *Human Relations and Modern Management*. Amsterdam: North Holland.

Roethlisberger, F. and Dickson, W. J. (1939) *Management and the Worker*. Cambridge, Mass.: Harvard University Press.

Ross, A. M. (1948) *The Theory of Trade Union Wage Policy*. Berkeley: University of California Press.

Routh, G. (1980) *Occupation and Pay*, 2nd edn. London: Macmillan.

Roy, A. D. (1950) 'Efficiency and "the fix" : informal group relations in a piecework machine shop', *American Journal of Sociology*, 60, 255–66.

Salter, W. E. G. (1966) *Productivity and Technical Change*. Cambridge: Cambridge University Press.

Sampson, A. A. (1983) 'Employment policy in a model with a rational trade union', *Economic Journal*, 93, 297–311.

Shorey, J. (1980) 'An analysis of quits using industry turnover data', *Economic Journal*, 90, 821–37.

Slichter, S. H. (1937) *Unions and Industrial Management*. New York: Brookings Institution.

Smith, C. F. B. (1978) *Strikes in Britain: A Research Study of Industrial Stoppages in the United Kingdom*. Department of Employment Manpower Papers 15. London: HMSO.

Turner, H. A. (1962) *Trade Union Growth, Structure and Policy*. London: Allen & Unwin.

Turner, H. A. and Roberts, G. (1971) *Management Characteristics and Labour Conflict*. Cambridge: Cambridge University Press.

Turvey, R. (ed.) (1952) *Wages Policy under Full Employment*. London: Hodge.

Wall, T. D. and Stephenson, G. M. (1970) 'Herzberg's two-factor theory of job attitudes: a critical evaluation and some fresh evidence', *Industrial Relations Journal*, 2, 41–65.

Webb, S. and Webb, B. (1902) *Industrial Democracy*. London: Longmans.

Wells, W. (1982) *The Relative Pay and Employment of Young Persons*. Research Paper, London, Department of Employment.

Wood, J. C. (1984) *The Place of Law in Industrial Relations – A Fresh Look*. Brighton: Institute of Manpower Studies, University of Sussex.

Wragg, J. and Robertson, B. (1979) *Postwar Trends in Employment, Productivity and Output, Labour Costs and Prices by Industry in the United Kingdom*. Research Paper No. 4, London, Department of Employment.

14 Investment and Financial Management

Introduction

Investment and financial management is concerned with the cycle of decisions underlying the balance sheet. Decisions are made as to the most profitable investment opportunities, and in order to realize them management borrows by issuing liabilities. When income is realized then payments are made to shareholders. In terms of the balance sheet the investment decisions involve capital projects, such as plant and machinery, and working capital, such as raw materials; the financial decisions concern the capital structure (equities and debt) and dividend policy. But although the subject matter can be expressed in terms of the balance sheet, the analysis of investment and financial decisions has shifted away from accounting concepts and towards a thorough grounding in economic theory. The reason for this revolution is that the main innovations have been embedded in a general equilibrium framework encompassing the markets for all assets available at all periods of time and in all states of (uncertainty) nature. Such an approach has considerable advantages in enabling the technical impedimenta of economics to be transferrred into the relatively underdeveloped area of finance; but it can have limitations. A general equilibrium framework tends to presuppose some central coordination of all activity, some grand auction, and seems to leave little scope for money. Why hold money when it is possible to hold a government debt which yields interest? Although the main developments in financial theory transfer easily from a barter to a money economy, cash management has only a shadowy part to play in most expositions. It is these issues which dictate the following structure to this chapter.

1 The changing nature of the financial system is briefly discussed.
2 The individual's consumption–savings decision for one period is analysed. The separation principle, which enables the decisions of households and firms to be isolated whilst allowing both to optimize, is also stressed.
3 The analysis of the two-period situation is then discussed in terms of a choice between two risk-free government bonds. To speak of risk-free assets may, of course, be misleading. Governments may not default on their interest payments, nor may they default on the repayment of premiums, but if they allow the value of money to change, then they may renege on the real value of interest payments

and premiums. However, in order to proceed with the analysis, we shall ignore these problems. The notion of a default-free asset is useful in financial theory because it provides a step towards the analysis of uncertainty. What the two-period decision analysis enables us to do is to distinguish current and forward interest rates and to consider the use of forward rates to determine the present values (prices) of the future income streams associated with various assets. Finally, the derivation of forward rates enables us to comment on the term structure of interest rates.

4   The next step in the analysis is to consider share valuation when there are riskless dividends. This is another simplification but it does enables us to move from the case of a bond with a limited life to the analysis of a share with an infinite life but which can be sold on any occasion by a shareholder with a limited time horizon.

5   Having considered the valuation of bonds and shares and the derivation of present values we move to discuss investment decisions and their relationship to share values. This involves an examination of various investment decision rules.

6   We introduce risk and consider the relationship between risk and return and portfolio policies.

7   We then turn to the question of dividend policy and the appropriate gearing (debt–equity) ratio for a firm.

8   The efficient markets and options markets literature are briefly mentioned.

9   Finally, we consider money and the requirements of short-term financing.

Financial and Money Markets

The workings of financial and money markets can now be described as follows. Firms borrow from households in order to purchase resources and their borrowing takes place through the issue of securities which promise to pay a return based upon the expected profitability of investment projects. Firms in the private sector borrow through the capital market, through the issues of shares or claims. Most large British firms rely upon retained profits as a source of funds. However these funds are the income of shareholders, and can influence share prices and the values of firms. If a firm ploughs back profits the real value of the firm will rise, and if there is no appropriate adjustment in share prices then a take-over bid may occur. Hence share prices tend to reflect not only the value of dividends but also the capital gains which may accrue from the change in the underlying value of the firm's assets.

Within the capital market a distinction can be drawn between the new issue market and the stock exchange. In the new issue market firms can raise additional finance through the issue of new shares. The stock market enables shareholders to buy and sell existing shares; it provides them with liquidity. In addition to the new issue market and the stock market there are the unlisted securities market (USM) and the options market, both of which are recent developments. The USM enables small and new firms which cannot afford a 'listing' in the new issue market to raise funds. The options market enables individuals and institutions to buy and sell assets at a specified price on or before a specified date; it therefore represents an extension of the idea of a futures market to the financial market.

Banks also play a part in the workings of the capital market, and a distinction is sometimes drawn between market-oriented and bank-oriented financial systems. Thus it is suggested that the West German and Japanese financial systems are bank-oriented because banks form the main channel through which savings flow from households to firms. In contrast the British system is regarded as market-oriented because the banks played a relatively small part in the finance of British industry. British firms tend to raise their long-term capital from households via the capital market, whereas German and Japanese firms tend to raise their finance from households via banks. Reliance upon the banking system is usually regarded as the sign of an immature financial system, but this could be a wrong conclusion to draw. British banks were active in the Industrial Revolution but their subsequent departure from the industrial scene may have been due to the emergence of the Empire – a diversion which was not essential to American banks because of the large amount of internal profitable investment opportunities, nor to the Germans and Japanese with their limited overseas possessions. Moreover, the use of bank finance and the importance of debt finance in Japan and Germany may have more to do with the willingness of their workforces to shoulder some of the risks normally associated with equity shareholders in Britain and America. We should not too readily divorce the workings of the capital market from the operations of the labour market.

Of course the notion that British firms tend to raise their capital from households via the market slurs over the point that the flow of savings reaches firms via many institutions, notably pension funds and finance houses. Individual shareholding tends to be relatively unimportant when compared with institutional shareholding, and it has attracted considerable comment and criticism on the grounds that pension fund managers tend to be cautious and do not provide sufficient risk capital.

However, the financial system in the UK has been undergoing changes in recent decades. The first thing to note is the considerable growth of the industry; in 1965 it accounted for 6.7 per cent of gross domestic product, by 1982 it had risen to 9.6 per cent (Rybczynski, 1982). The second feature is the trend towards concentration and conglomeration in the provision of financial services as a result of mergers and amalgamations. Over the past 20 years there have been mergers between banks and hire purchase companies, and between building societies and life assurance companies. The third feature has been the internationalization of the finance industry as a result of British firms setting up overseas subsidiaries and foreign firms establishing branches in Britain. This world-wide integration of the financial system has been induced by the expansion of world trade. The fourth factor deserving of comment is the removal of restrictions upon the activities of financial institutions. Thus building societies have been moving in the direction of providing banking services, and the commercial banks have been providing housing finance. In 1986 came the move to deregulate the stock market.

Governments play an important part in the financial system, not least because financial theory has tended to develop on the assumption that there exists a riskless asset provided by governments which can be used to provide the basis of a set of forward prices, but also the platform from which risky assets can be evaluated. In the absence of state-owned income-yielding assets, governments must raise finance from the private sector. This they can do by printing money, borrowing or taxing. Whilst an optimal amount of money is needed for the efficient operation of an economy, and governments can earn seigniorage on the supply of that money, the financial requirements of governments usually exceed that which can be obtained by printing the optimal amount of money. Unfortunately, printing more money can be inflationary and be an implicit tax on the community; hence the resort to borrowing and taxing. The essence of borrowing is to borrow and to build up income-yielding assets which can be used to pay off the future interest payments. But if lenders assume that they will have to pay taxes in the future in order to cover the interest payments, then they may reduce their other spending and the government's intentions could be thwarted. The subject of government debt has always been controversial and in recent years it has been suggested that governments should cut down their expenditure in order to avoid creating tax disincentives.

Finally we should note the importance of international finance. The vast expansion of international trade since the end of the Second World War, and the emergence of multinational corporations, has resulted in an expansion of the international capital market and the need to integrate into financial theory the effects of exchange rate adjustments.

The Individual's One-period Consumption–Savings Decision

Figure 14.1 presents in a simplified form the one-period, consumption–savings decision for an individual. The production possibility curve AB shows the productive nature of investment decisions. Initially the individual has OA goods and their total investment could yield OB goods in period 1. The concave shape of the production possibility curve reflects diminishing returns to investment. Thus investing AC will yield OL in the second period and an equal tranche of investment, FE ($=AC$) will yield MY which is less than OL. The individual's investment decision will be influenced not only by the production possibility curve but also by his preference for present as opposed to future income as indicated by his indifference curves, $I_0 \ldots I_n$. His optimal consumption–savings decision will be indicated by the tangency of the production possibility curve and the highest attainable indifference curve. The slope of the line WW', which is tangent to the production possibility curve and the indifference curve I_1, measures the interest rate which is the means of comparing or translating present income into future income (figure 14.2).

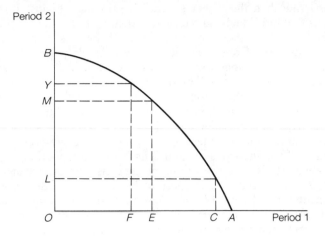

Figure 14.1

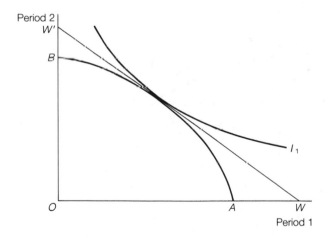

Figure 14.2

The Separation Principle

Firms attempt to maximize the utilities of their owners, but how can they do that when preferences may not be observable and individuals differ in their preferences? The answer lies in the workings of the capital market. If the capital market is perfect in the sense that the borrowing rate is identical to the lending rate then the Fisher separation principle obtains (Fisher, 1965). This means that individuals can delegate investment decisions to the managers of the firms of which they are the owners. As long as managers choose to invest until the rate of return on the least favourable project is equal to the market rate of interest they will maximize the owners' utility functions. This result is shown in figure 14.3. The optimal investment/production decision is P_0P_1 which maximizes the present value of the owners' wealth. This decision is independent of the owners' preferences for present and future consumption. Given the manager's decision then the owners can borrow or lend along the capital market line in order to satisfy their time preferences pattern of consumption. Thus individuals 1 and 2 have the same wealth, but individual 1 borrows against his future wealth to increase his current consumption whilst individual 2 is prepared to lend more of his wealth in order to increase his future consumption. Figure 14.3 also illustrates the *unanimity principle*, which states that if shareholders were asked at a shareholders' meeting to vote on their most preferred production decision they would be unanimous in their preference. Hence managers need not worry about attempting to make decisions which reconcile shareholders' preferences.

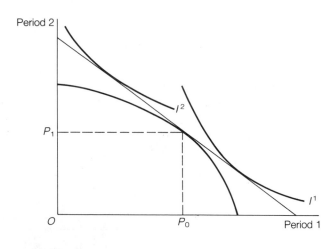

Figure 14.3

Two-period Consumption–Savings Decision

We shall now extend our analysis to consider two-period consumption–savings decisions, and the possibility of government bonds of different maturities. This allows for the possibility of an individual switching from holding a 1-year bond in the first period and then buying a 2-year bond and holding it for the second period *or* buying the two-year bond and holding it until redemption. Despite the fact that there is no risk of the government defaulting, an individual's

Table 14.1

	Today's price	Redemption period	
Time	0	1	2
1-year bond	95	100	
2-year bond	85		100

choice can be complicated by the fact that he has to consider: (1) the current or spot rate of interest; (2) the forward rate of interest which is his best predictor of the spot rate of interest at the end of the first period; (3) governments pay interest as a percentage of the face value of bonds and not as a percentage of the actual price paid for bonds; (4) the maturity of a bond, which is the length of time until the bond is redeemed, because governments repay some capital as well as interest in each period and this can affect comparison between the returns on bonds of differing maturities; and (5) the duration of a bond, which is the length of time to maturity weighted by the present value of each payment relative to the total value of the bond. These issues we shall now explore.

Suppose an individual has a choice between purchasing a bond which matures in 1 year and rewards its holder with £100, and another bond which matures in 2 years and also gives its holder £100. Let us also assume that the prices asked for the bonds are: 1-year bond £95, 2-year bond £85. We can indicate his problem as shown in table 14.1. The current or spot interest rate on the 1-year bond can be calculated as follows:

$$95(1+r) - 100 \tag{14.1}$$
$$r = \quad 5.3 \text{ per cent} \tag{14.2}$$

In other words the individual can expect at time 0 to receive, in time 1, 5.3 per cent for holding the 1-year bond until maturity, and this spot rate of interest is determined by the price of the bond. An alternative way of expressing the above result is to say that the present value of a bond paying £100, 1 year hence when the rate of interest is 5.3 per cent is 95; that is, 100 discounted at 5.3 per cent for one period would be equivalent to a current sum of 95.

Yield to Maturity

The 2-year spot rate is also determined by the price of a 2-year bond as follows:

$$85(1+r)^2 = 100 \tag{14.3}$$
$$r = \quad 8.5 \text{ per cent} \tag{14.4}$$

What we have done in this case is to calculate the single rate of interest which, if compounded, a bank would have to offer in order for a deposit of 85 to grow to 100 at the end of 2 years. This is sometimes known as the *yield to maturity* or *internal rate of return* (more correctly rate of return).

Forward Rates

The interest rate need not be the same in each period, however. In the case of the 1-year bond the interest rate is 5.3 per cent and this gives an implied forward rate of:

$$1.053(1 + r)85 = 100 \qquad (14.5)$$

$$r = 11.73 \qquad (14.6)$$

In other words the forward rate for year 2 is the interest rate for money loaned 1 year hence and paid back 2 years hence. The important point to note at this stage, however, is that the forward rate is not synonymous with the spot rate which will prevail 1 year hence; that is, the rate for 1-year loans which will prevail 1 year hence. However, it will be the best predictor of that spot rate in the sense that if the forward rate diverged from the expected spot rate, then investors would switch from holding one set of bonds to holding the other.

Present Value

Given the forward rates determined in the market it is possible to derive the present value of any investment offering future payments with certainty. Thus if r_1 is today's spot rate on 1-year loan maturing in a year, and r_2 is the forward rate on a 1-year loan maturing in 2 years, then r_3, r_4 ... r_n will be the forward rates on 1-year loans maturing in 3, 4...n years hence. Therefore we can calculate that P pounds will grow to F pounds if P and F satisfy the following equation:

$$(1 + r_1)(1 + r_2) \ldots (1 + r_n)P = F \qquad (14.7)$$

and from this equation we can find the present value of any future sum which obtains n years in the future

$$P = \frac{F_n}{(1 + r)^n} \qquad (14.8)$$

The denominator in equation (13.8) is the discount factor which converts future values into present values; it enables us to value a riskless bond which gives more than one payment. In effect a bond which provides more than one payment is a bundle of bonds, each of which provides only one payment.

Coupon Rates

Most government bonds pay interest which is expressed as a percentage of the face value of the bond. In other words they have a non-zero interest rate which is known as the coupon rate, and this means that the calculations of spot rates and forward rates must be modified to take account of the difference between nominal and actual bond prices.

Maturity and Duration

Maturity refers to the number of years which must elapse before a bond is redeemed. However, most government bonds pay a part of the principal along with the interest in each period. Hence comparisons of bonds of different maturities can be difficult. To overcome this problem a bond's duration is calculated as a weighted average of the time prior to payments using the relative present values as weights. Bonds of similar duration will react in similar ways to changes in interest rates, unlike bonds of similar maturity but different durations.

Term Structure of Interest Rates

At any point of time riskless securities will be priced according to a set of discount factors and the implied forward rates. But there may be no necessary relationship between these rates. Sometimes long-term interest rates are above short-term interest rates; that is, rates are higher the further into the future is the period to which they apply. At other times short-term rates may be above long-term rates. Hence it is important to know what are the prevailing conditions at any point in time, and one method of depicting the relationship is through a *yield curve* which plots the yield to maturity for bonds against their date of maturity. The yield curve is commonly thought to be upward-sloping with long-term rates above short-term rates, suggesting the strong influence of speculation or market segmentation.

Riskless Equities

So far we have considered how to estimate the present values of default-free bonds having a finite life. Now we must analyse the present values of equities which have an infinite life. Companies may issue liabilities whose chief characteristic is that they confer ownership rights on their holders; that is, they confer an equity. In addition, the return on them is a *residual* which may be paid after all creditors and preferred shareholders have had their claims met. Equities do not have a fixed maturity; their cash payments consist of an indefinite stream of dividends. Hence, the present value of an equity is

$$P = \frac{\text{Dividends}_t}{(1 + r)^t} \qquad (14.9)$$

However, shareholders may not wish to hold equities in perpetuity; they may have limited time horizons and may wish to sell their shares at some point in the future. Hence they will be interested in the future price and the capital gains which they can obtain, as well as the dividends they can earn in the interim. Accordingly, equation (13.9) can be rewritten as follows:

$$P_0 = \frac{\text{Dividend}_1 + P_1}{(1 + r)} \qquad (14.10)$$

where P_0 is the present value of the equity and P_1 is its future price on re-sale.

Present Values, Share Prices and Interest Rates

Why have we devoted so much space to present values, spot and forward rates and yields to maturity? The answer is that a well-developed financial market offers considerable scope to borrowers and lenders to buy and sell claims to future income, and it enables apparently indivisible debt instruments, such as a 5-year bond, to be analysed as if it were a set of 1-year bonds. Comparing different securities, however, requires an investor to note the duration of bonds. Finally, although we have conducted the analysis in terms of the individual investor, the household, it can be applied to firms. Even firms sometimes hold securities and, of course, firms must consider the return they offer other investors when issuing shares.

Capital Budgeting: Alternative Investment Criteria

Now that we have discussed risk-free government bonds and the valuation of riskless dividends we can go on to analyse the problems of capital budgeting or investment decision-making. Share prices will be determined by supply (offers of prospective income) and by demand (the demand for those incomes by households). Investment decisions will also be influenced by share prices since they will determine investment costs.

Payback

The simplest investment criterion is known as *payback*, which states that management should invest as long as the initial outlay on a project is recoverable within a given period. The cut-off point is then determined by the number of years which it takes for the expected cash flows to equal the initial outlay. Such a rule ignores any returns which accrue after the cut-off point, and it ignores also the timing of cash flows. Thus two projects may repay the initial loan in 5 years but one may yield greater returns in the first 2 years than the other, and the excess sums could be reinvested to yield a larger return. However, payback is a popular method of investment appraisal and as a rule-of-thumb it may be a crude method of using multiple discount rates in which the returns from distant years are heavily discounted (i.e. ignored).

Accounting Rate of Return

The accounting rate of return is the average after-tax profit divided by the initial cash outlay. It suffers from the disadvantage of using accounting profits based upon historic costs and not cash flows, and it also ignores the time value of money.

Net Present Value

The most obvious criterion which emerges out of our previous discussion is the net present value, which states that management should invest as long as the present value of investment returns minus the cost of investment is positive:

$$\text{NPV} = \frac{\Sigma R_n}{(1 + i)^n} - \frac{\Sigma C_n}{(1 + i)^n} \geq 0 \qquad (14.11)$$

where R_n is the revenue stream discounted over n years, C_n is the cost stream which is also discounted, and i is the market rate of interest which is used as a discount factor.

Rate of Return

A second criterion which also emerges out of our previous discussion is the rate of return, which states that management should invest as long as the discount rate which makes the future income stream equal to the cost of the project is greater than the market rate of interest. In other words the rate of return is that discount rate which makes the net present value equal to zero:

$$\text{NPV} = \frac{\Sigma R_n}{(1 + r)^n} - \frac{\Sigma C_n}{(1 + r)^n} = 0 \qquad (14.12)$$

where r is the discount rate.

Net Present Value versus Rate of Return

In many situations NPV and RR give the same results. There are, however, some circumstances in which the use of the rate of return can give rise to problems. One such difficulty arises when there are changes in the sign of the cash flow over a project's life. For example, in the case of mining projects there may be reclamation costs towards the end of a project's life. Changes in the sign of cash flows can then give rise to multiple solutions to the rate of return calculation. In the usual case, where there is an initial outlay followed by a cash inflow, there will be only one root or solution to the rate of return equation. In more general cases, however, there can be an alternating sequence of cash flows and inflows, and not only would there be positive solutions but there would also be negative solutions. From the economic point of view only positive solutions need to be considered. When there are multiple solutions the sensible policy should be to use the net present value criterion. Difficulties can also arise in the case of mutually exclusive projects.

Marketing, Production and Investment Decisions

So far we have concentrated upon investment decisions in a financial sense, but we need also to examine the marketing and production aspects of a firm's investment decisions. The interests of the shareholders will be in the maximization of the value of their shares whether that valuation takes the form of dividends and interest or capital gains or a mixture of both. If the valuation rises because of the firm's prosperity, then more finance may become available for investment in the firm. Hence we need to look at the real investment decisions of the firm, and these will be found to rest upon three concepts:

1 the marginal product of capital;
2 the marginal efficiency of investment; and
3 the supply price of capital goods.

The Marginal Product of Capital

Capital may be thought of as a fund of services which are normally embodied in physical things, such as plant and machinery. Although the capital of the firm will normally be considered as plant and machinery, what management is interested in is the flow of services from that stock of equipment, and we can think of a *rental price of capital services* which can be compared with the wage or rental price of labour services per unit of time. This rental price can be determined in the following manner. A firm may have the choice of buying a factory or leasing one. Hence it is possible to derive the costs associated with owning a factory and renting it to onself with the costs of leasing a factory per unit of time. These costs will comprise:

1 the interest that would have to be paid on a loan, or which could be earned on one's own funds;
2 the cost of depreciation;
3 the expected rate of change of price of factories.

The implicit rental price of a factory would therefore be the price of a factory multiplied by its depreciation rate plus the market rate of interest and plus or minus the expected rate of change of price of a factory. Thus if factory prices were expected to rise then there could be a capital gain accruing to the ownership of a factory. The rental price so computed would be a nominal price, and would need to be converted into a real price. As we noted in chapter 6 there has been a considerable controversy in the accounting profession as to the appropriate price deflator with the choice being between a price index of all goods indicating the value of the factory to shareholders and an index of factory prices denoting its value to managers. Whichever deflator is used we would arrive at the following decision rule:

The optimum capital stock is that at which the marginal product of capital (the marginal flow of service) is measured by the real rental price of capital services in the market.

The Marginal Efficiency of Investment and the Supply of Capital Goods

Now let us consider the effect of an increase in the demand for the goods produced by the capital stock. Because it is derived demand the value of the marginal product of capital will rise, and quasi-rents will be earned by the existing capital stock. This will induce an increase in the demand for new capital. The availability of new capital will depend upon supply conditions in the capital goods industry and the demand for capital goods by other firms. The marginal efficiency of investment will also depend upon the adjustment costs associated with incorporating new equipment into existing plant and the organizational structure.

The first factor – the nature of supply conditions in the capital goods industry – is straightforward. The second factor can lead to a divergence between the expected (*ex-ante*) price and the actual (*ex-post*) price of capital goods if the rise in the demand for final goods produced by the capital equipment applies to many firms. The third condition depends upon the managerial costs of reorganizing a firm when new equipment is introduced. Hence we arrive at the following investment decision rule:

Equate the marginal efficiency of investment with the adjustment costs of investment.

This is the essence of Tobin's q theory of investment.

What we should finally observe is the interrelationships of marketing, production and financial decisions. From the marketing department is obtained estimates of the profitability of final goods. From the production department is obtained estimates of the 'physical' productivity of new equipment (saving in time, etc.) and from the finance department is derived estimates of the costs of raising funds and the opportunity cost of one's own funds.

The Responsiveness of Investment to Interest Rate Changes

A question that naturally arises out of the previous discussion is: how responsive is investment to changes in the rate of interest? It is a question which is important not only to the businessman but also to governments accustomed to using variation in nominal interest rates to control spending.

The interest elasticity of investment may be defined as the proportional change in investment due to a proportional change in the interest rate.

$$e(I,r) = \frac{\Delta I/I}{\Delta r/r} = \frac{\Delta I}{\Delta r} \cdot \frac{r}{I} \qquad (14.13)$$

where I is the rate of investment, ΔI is the change in investment, r is the rate of interest and Δr is the rate of change in the interest rate.

According to the analysis developed in the previous section, the interest elasticity of investment is the product of two variables: the elasticity of the demand price for machines with respect to the interest rate and the elasticity of investment with respect to changes in the price of machines.

$$e(I,r) = \frac{\Delta I}{\Delta r} \cdot \frac{r}{I} = \left(\frac{P_k}{\Delta r} \cdot \frac{r}{P_k} \right) \left(\frac{\Delta I}{\Delta P_k} \cdot \frac{P_k}{I} \right) \tag{14.14}$$

The elasticity of supply of capital goods will depend upon cost conditions in those industries. The elasticity of the demand price for machines will depend, amongst other things, upon the expected life of machines. Thus suppose we have two machines which yield identical profits of £100 per period but one machine has a life of 2 years and the other has an infinitely long life. If the interest rate is 5 per cent then the demand price of machines will be

$$\frac{\text{machine 1}}{\text{(short life)}} = \frac{100}{(1.05)} + \frac{100}{(1.05)^2} = £140.24 \tag{14.15}$$

$$\frac{\text{machine 2}}{\text{(long life)}} = \frac{100}{(0.05)} = £2000 \tag{14.16}$$

The solution for a machine of infinite life is obtained by recognizing that such a machine is analogous to a perpetual Consol with a £100 coupon rate. The demand price for a perpetuity with a £100 coupon rate is $1/r$. Hence the demand price for a machine of infinite life with a £100 coupon rate is $1/r$.

Now suppose that the interest rate is raised to 10 per cent. The demand prices for the machines become

$$\text{machine 1} = \frac{100}{(1.10)} + \frac{100}{(1.10)^2} = £140.91 \tag{14.17}$$

$$\text{machine 2} = \frac{100}{(0.10)} = £1000.00 \tag{14.18}$$

Thus a doubling of the interest rate has a very small effect upon the machine with a short life and a large effect upon the machine with a long life. The preceding analysis throws some light upon the alleged insensitivity of investment to changes in the interest rate.

Risk

So far our analysis of investment and financial decisions has been conducted upon the assumption that certainty prevails. Some assets, such as 3-month

Treasury Bills, have a return which can be regarded as absolutely certain; but there are numerous other assets whose income stream may be regarded as uncertain. Hence we need to re-work our analysis in order to incorporate uncertainty. The central concept is the *certainty equivalent* which poses the question: what sum of money would an individual require in order to hold a risky asset instead of a safe asset? Five points should be observed about this question.

1 It involves a comparison between a risky asset and a safe asset, which means that our previous analysis was not an unwarranted detour; although it is possible to re-work the subsequent analysis without recourse to a safe asset, it greatly simplifies the investigation.

2 The concept of a certainty equivalent which can leave an individual indifferent between a safe asset and a risky asset forms a natural stepping-stone from analysing a consumer's indifference map depicting two safe goods.

3 It provides a useful basis for defining *risk-averseness*: an individual is more risk-averse than a second investor if for every portfolio the certainty equivalent end of period wealth is less than or equal to certainty equivalent end of period wealth associated with the same portfolio for the second investor.

4 Although the state preference model of Arrow (1965) and Debreu (1959) and the mean-variance model of Markowitz (1952) have been central to the development of investment analysis, they may be regarded as special cases of the certainty equivalent model.

5 The emphasis upon certainty equivalents means that Knight's (1921) distinction between measurable risk and non-measurable risk (uncertainty) has been ignored; although some economists do concede the importance of the unique event but find that they can say little about decision-making under conditions of pure uncertainty (Brearley and Myers, 1984). The simplest method of coping with pure uncertainty is to find someone who has a successful record in such situations.

Expected Net Present Value

In making the transition from certain to risky situations we could simply assume that individuals attempt to maximize *expected net present value*. Thus consider the three assets listed in table 14.2. *A* and *B* are riskless assets with a probability of 1.0 and if asked to choose between them an investor would choose *B*, which has a greater net present value. But how would an investor choose between *B*, *C* and *D* where *C* and *D* have uncertain returns? If we assume a negative NPV of -6 on *C* then *B* is preferable to *C*; but if we assume a positive value of 30 then *C* is preferable to *B*. Hence we need to take into account the risk associated with each project.

One possibility is to weight each possible outcome by its probability in order to obtain the expected net present value. Thus in the case of project *C* the expected NPV would be

$$0.25\ (-6) + 0.50\ (12) + 0.25\ (30) = 7$$

and applying the same procedure to D would give us NPVs for the projects as shown in table 14.3. However, the calculation of the expected NPVs does not give an appropriate decision criterion in most cases, for two reasons: first, it does not tell us how individuals view risk; second, it does not give us an objective measure of risk.

Table 14.2 Distribution of possible outcomes of four different projects

A		B		C		D	
NPV	Probability	NPV	Probability	NPV	Probability	NPV	Probability
9	1.0	10	1.0	−6	0.25	−30	0.1
				12	0.50	0	0.4
				30	0.25	50	0.5

Table 14.3

Projects	Expected NPV
A	9
B	10
C	7
D	22

Utility Theory

Casual observation suggests that the marginal utility of income diminishes as income increases, and that most people are risk-averse and would experience a greater loss of utility from the loss of £100 than from a gain of £100. Most individuals therefore have a utility function which is concave as in figure 14.14. According to the diagram an individual can purchase a 1-year share for £25 whose terminal value has an equal probability of £59 or £11. The individual's utility function is concave and the expected utility from the asset is denoted by C, the point at which the perpendicular from 25 cuts the cord connecting points A and B. The expected utility of C is $0.5U\ (11) + 0.5U\ (59)$, where U stands for utility. Now the utility from £25 is denoted by D which is greater than C. Hence a risk-averse individual would not purchase the option whose expected value is equal to the purchase price because the concavity of the utility function would turn a monetary gain into a monetary loss. Indeed, the individual would be prepared to purchase the share only if he could pay less than, or at the most, P. At P the expected utility from the risky share is just

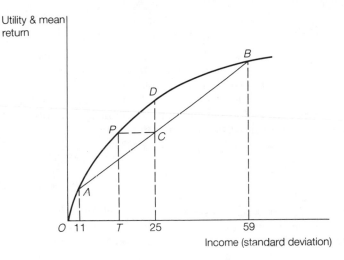

Figure 14.4

equal to the utility from the sum of money forgone in purchasing the share. The distance between T and 25 therefore measures the *risk premium* required to purchase the share, and the amount OT represents the *certainty equivalent* value of the risky option. At prices below T the share is worth buying, and at prices above T it is unattractive.

Now consider table 14.4 where projects A and B have the same degree of risk but differ in their expected utility. The expected utility from A is $0.5U(1000) + 0.5U(2000) = 2.0$, and this corresponds to point A in figure 14.4. Similarly, B indicates the expected utility from B. Since A lies above B we can infer that a risk-averter will prefer A to B irrespective of his degree of risk-aversion. The reason is that risk-averters do not like wide dispersions of outcomes.

Table 14.4

	Investment A			Investment B	
Probability	Profit	Utility	Probability	Profit	Utility
0.5	1000	1.0	0.5	0	0
0.5	2000	3.0	0.5	3000	3.5
Expected net profit	1000			3000	
Expected utility	2.0			1.75	

Measuring Risk

The next step is to introduce a measure of risk associated with the earnings from an asset. Two related measures are frequently used: the variance and the standard deviation. To determine the variance we first calculate the deviation of each expected outcome from the mean expected outcome, then raise it to its second power and multiply the term by the probability of the event. The sum of all these products is the variance:

$$\sigma^2(x) = \sum_{i=1}^{n} P_i (x_i - Ex)^2 \qquad (14.19)$$

where $\sigma^2(x)$ is the variance, x_i is the eventuality and Ex is the expected (mean) outcome. The objection to the variance is that it is in monetary units squared, and it may be preferable to take the computation a stage further and take the square root of the variance in order to obtain the standard deviation. The use of the standard deviation has the advantage of calculation, but it does assume that risk is normally distributed. For example, a security with an expected average return of 10 and a standard deviation of 15 will yield a 68 per cent probability of a return between −5 per cent and 25 per cent. However, the use of the standard deviation cannot handle situations where the distribution of risk is skewed. For example, one asset might offer a 90 per cent chance of 4 and a 10 per cent chance of 14 with a mean value of 5 and a standard deviation of 3, whereas another asset might offer a 90 per cent chance of 6 and a 10 per cent of −4 with again a mean value of 5 and a standard deviation of 3. What has been called the mean variance theory implies that an investor might be indifferent between the two assets, although the man in the street might think one more risky than the other.

Portfolio Analysis

Putting aside the problems of skew we can now consider the behaviour of an individual attempting to maximize his earnings and minimize his risk through diversification. In other words we shall examine the extent to which an individual can minimize his risk by holding a *portfolio* of assets. Before we can analyse the effects of diversification it is important to note that diversification cannot remove the risk attaching to all assets. It cannot remove the risk associated with the fact that *all shares* are subject to fluctuations arising from macroeconomic disturbances. What diversification might do is to reduce the risks which are specific to particular firms and industries. Therefore an individual is concerned with the degree to which the returns on different assets are correlated.

In table 14.5 we assume that an individual holds 70 per cent of his portfolio in X shares and 30 per cent in Y shares. We also assume that there are four possible states of the world: A, B, C and D with different probabilities of

Table 14.5

State of world (1)	Probability (2)	Percentage return on X (3)	Percentage return on Y (4)	0.7 × (3) + 0.4 × (4) Percentage return on portfolio (5)
A	0.10	5.0	−3.0	2.3
B	0.30	7.0	5.0	6.9
C	0.40	−3.0	2.0	−1.3
D	0.20	12.0	15.0	14.4

occurrence. Hence if A occurs then the return on X will be 5 per cent and −3 per cent on Y and the return on the portfolio, which is a weighted average of the proportions in which X and Y will be held, is 2.3 per cent.

However, an individual who is risk-averse will be interested in the average return, given all possible states of the world and the associated risks attaching to shares. The expected mean return will be 5.57 per cent which is derived from averaging the returns in the table. The average risk is derived from averaging the variances.

A Diagrammatic Analysis

In figure 14.5 the mean and standard deviation of two shares A and B are denoted by the coordinates of A and B. The shaded segment shows the set of portfolio of A and B. Only the solid upper curve of the segment will contain efficient combinations. Thus, P is superior to P' because it yields a higher return for the same degree of risk. The minimum degree of risk is at C and as we move from C to B the expected return increases and the degree of risk also increases. As we move from C to B the proportions in which the two securities are held changes, and the degree of correlation between the two returns will determine the degree of curvature of the segment between C and B. Thus, if the returns were perfectly correlated ($R = +1$) then the curvature between A and B would reduce to a straight line, and as the correlation coefficient falls the curve bulges out farther and farther to the left.

The next step is to introduce the indifference curves of a risk-averter (figure 14.6). These curves will slope upwards from left to right, indicating that an investor must be compensated for higher risk by being offered a higher expected return. Combining the portfolio set with the investor's indifference map suggests that he would move to a point of tangency between the portfolio set and his highest attainable indifference curve. However, if we ignore inflation and introduce a riskless asset, such as money or Treasury Bills, and the possibility of borrowing or lending at the riskless interest rate r_1 then an

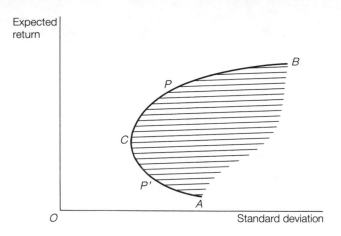

Figure 14.5

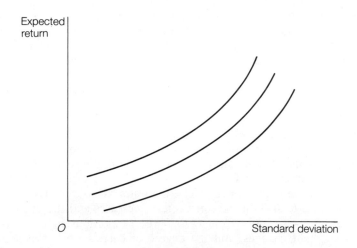

Figure 14.6

increase in utility might be achieved. Thus, in figure 14.7 a risk-preferer might go beyond M and borrow in order to reach P and an extreme risk-averter might lend at the riskless rate in order to reach S.

Capital Asset Pricing Model

We must now extend the analysis beyond the individual to that of the market as a whole. To simplify the discussion we shall assume that all investors share

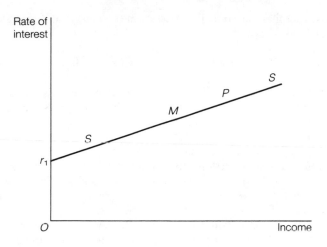

Figure 14.7

the same expectations about future asset prices but differ in their attitudes to risk.

In figure 14.8 the opportunity set and price line describe the risk and return opportunities which confront everyone. Each individual therefore reaches a different equilibrium position on the price line because of his attitude to risk. For example, suppose that we have three investors in the market and that A has £100,000, B has £50,000 and C has £10,000. These investors will allocate their wealth between the risk-free asset and the portfolio of risky assets; and because the individuals have homogeneous price expectations the allocation of M will be the same for all investors; they cannot do better than the portfolio M although the amounts that they purchase may differ.

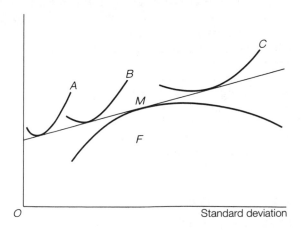

Figure 14.8

Suppose that there are only three assets in the market and that the allocation of the portfolio M is:

$$a_1(M) = 0.3 \qquad a_2(M) = 0.5 \qquad a_3(M) = 0.2$$

Now let A be extremely risk-averse, B be somewhat less risk-averse and C be least risk-averse; then the allocations of the three investors between the risk-free asset and the portfolio of risky assets might be as shown in table 14.6. Thus, in the table, C is a risk-preferer and has, in effect, borrowed to increase his holding of the portfolio of risky assets.

Given the wealth and portfolio allocations of the three individuals then their allocations of wealth to the risky assets will be as shown in table 14.7.

Investor A will allocate 30 per cent of his wealth in the portfolio M (£50,000) to the purchase of asset 1, 50 per cent to the purchase of asset 2 and 20 per cent to asset 3. B and C will also allocate 30 per cent of their wealth to the purchase of asset 1. In aggregate they hold assets in the same proportions as in the portfolio, but they hold differing absolute amounts. Thus, C, the risk-preferer borrows in order to increase his holdings of risky assets.

The final step is to analyse the conditions for equilibrium in the pricing of individual assets and this requires an investigation of the relationship between the means and standard deviations of individual assets and those of the portfolios. Thus consider an individual asset, such as F in figure 14.8 and the portfolio M which also includes F. The portfolio is subject to less risk than F because of the effects of diversification. There is a limit, however, to the amount of risk that can be eliminated and the residual risk, or unsystematic risk, may be due to general factors such as booms and slumps. Therefore those assets whose returns fluctuate more than the portfolio will have lower prices, and those which fluctuate less will have higher prices. The relationship between the systematic risk of an asset and the unsystematic risk of the portfolio is measured by the *beta coefficient*. Since the market portfolio is correlated with itself its beta coefficient is 1 and movements in the market portfolio are usually measured by movements in the *Financial Times* Index of Share Prices. Individual assets may, of course, have betas greater or less than 1.

The usefulness of this approach is, however, dependent upon the ease with which conclusions can be drawn from a two-period model. In effect there may not be unique betas but a family of betas because we have to consider a multi-period decision-making process. Hence the measured betas may be highly unstable because they are an average of many betas whose properties are ignored. Hence from a measured beta it may not be possible to infer anything about the movement to equilibrium following a disturbance because there may be as many paths to equilibrium as there are betas.

Capital Budgeting and the Separation Principle Again

Portfolio analysis and the capital asset pricing model serve to amplify our previous discussion of capital budgeting and the separation principle. In so far

Table 14.6

Investor	Risk-free asset	Risky assets
A	50	50
B	30	70
C	−20	120

Table 14.7

Investor	Wealth invested in (£)		
	Asset 1	Asset 2	Asset 3
A	15,000	25,000	10,000
B	10,500	17,500	7000
C	29,100	48,500	19,400

as investors can diversify, then the inclusion of risk into our discussion of finance makes no appreciable difference to the conclusions concerning the behaviour of the individual investor and the behaviour of management under conditions of certainty.

As long as investors can diversify and use the capital market to obtain an optimal time pattern of consumption then management should not pursue diversification unless they can increase the net present values of the firms for which they are responsible. This has implications not only for investments which are intended to increase the internal growth of the firm but also for merger decisions. Hence the appropriate discount rate for investment projects is obtained by taking the risk-free interest rate and adding to it the risk premium given by the estimate of the beta coefficient. The beta coefficient will reflect both the financial risk and the business risk to which the firm is exposed. Whenever a firm borrows it increases the beta and the expected return of its stock. Therefore to calculate the firm's cost of capital it is necessary to adjust the beta of the asset to remove the effect of financial risk. The residual risk is the business risk of a particular project and not the average business risk on all projects which should be used to discount cash flows.

Dividend Policy

In a famous article Miller and Modigliani (1961) suggested that a firm's dividend policy might have no effect on the value of the firm. This thesis was contrary to the usual view that increasing dividends would increase the value of the firm. Their reasoning was as follows. If a firm's investment and borrowing were given then any attempt to increase the dividends must come through issuing more shares. However, these new shares will be bought only if investors think that they are going to obtain a return on them. Therefore there must be a transfer of wealth from old to new shareholders. The new investors get shares which are worth less than before the dividend change was announced, and the old investors suffer a loss on their shares. Dividend policy is therefore irrelevant and makes an arbitrary distinction between earnings which accrue as dividends and earnings which accrue as capital gains. Dividend policy should therefore be a by-product of investment and borrowing decisions.

The trouble with the Modigliani–Miller thesis is that it does not tell us why firms pay dividends. Why do they not let all dividends accrue as capital gains? Presumably the answer is that although capital markets are efficient, they are not costless. Buying and selling shares involves individuals in transactions costs, and because assets may not be divisible then those costs could be considerable. Therefore small investors might prefer dividends. A second explanation could be that because of the separation of ownership from management and the limitations of accounting data, managers need to communicate their views on expected earnings through the payment of dividends which are intended to be stable for lengthy periods. However, given that taxes imposed upon dividends are considerable, the costs of transmitting information to shareholders by means of dividends seem to be extraordinarily high. Thus a third explanation might be found in the existence of different types of investors, and also the existence of uncertainty. Some investors might prefer no dividends because dividend payments would be subject to taxation, whereas other individuals or institutions, such as charities, might prefer dividends. Hence in a world of certainty there would be market segmentation and specialization. Some individuals would invest only with firms which paid no dividends, and some would invest only with firms which paid dividends. Uncertainty tends to make each firm's return appear to be both unique and uncertain, and investors will wish to diversify their investment. Therefore a firm which wished to maximize the value of its share price could do so by attracting both types of investor, and this would require paying out some fraction of earnings as dividends.

Cost of Debt and Capital Structure

So far we have paid little attention to the methods of financing projects. Implicitly we have assumed that all projects were financed through the issue of equities. Now we shall consider the difference that debt financing can make to a firm. By debt financing we mean that management raises finance through the issue of shares which guarantee a fixed return which must be paid before equity-owners receive their dividends. The mix of securities issued by a firm is known as its capital structure, and it can take a variety of forms.

The question is: does the capital structure of a firm matter? Is it possible to reduce the cost of capital by varying the mix of risky and riskless securities? One possibility is that increasing the amount of debt increases the financial risk of the firm as opposed to the business risk. Business risk refers to the risk attaching to the sale of the products, whereas financial risk refers to the variability in the expected level of dividends and the expectation that debt-holders will be paid in full. As the amount of debt increases then the financial risk of equity-holders might be expected to increase. Thus we might suppose that an initial issue of debt might lower the cost of capital because debt-holders would accept a lower return than equity-holders; but as the amount of debt increased then the amount of expected income committed to debt-holders would increase and so would the risks of insolvency. Hence the average cost of capital might be expected to fall and then increase as the gearing ratio (the ratio of debt to equity) increased.

However, Modigliani and Miller have suggested that for firms in the same risk class (i.e. the same expected income) the cost of capital is independent of the gearing ratio. Their theory rests upon the assumption that capital markets are efficient markets in which assets are substitutes and in which investors are able to purchase and hold any combination of assets. Hence investors can adopt or undo any gearing ratio chosen by a firm, and by changing the prices of debt and equity can equalize their returns. Thus, if a firm were to attempt to increase its debt–equity ratio beyond that which was acceptable to investors (given their preferences and the returns on the assets) then investors would switch between debt and equities and in doing so cause their prices to alter. The simplest case to consider is the zero risk class under perfect competition in which investors would be indifferent between debt and equities. If then the degree of risk can be represented by a linear function in which probabilities are attached to different degrees of risk then intuitively the result derived from the zero risk class continues to hold. The Modigliani and Miller thesis rests upon the following assumption:

1 Firms are in the same risk class.
2 The investment decisions of firms are given.
3 Individuals can borrow and lend at the same interest rate as firms.
4 There is no risk of bankruptcy.
5 There is no corporation tax which allows the deduction of interest from the payments of a geared firm.

Of the five assumptions the fourth and fifth are the most interesting. The fifth assumption suggests that in the presence of discriminatory taxation firms should adopt extremely geared capital structures. However, we do not observe such positions, and one reason for their absence may be the fear of bankruptcy. Only Japanese and German firms have been able to adopt high gearing ratios because their workers have been prepared to act as equity-holders. But note: bankruptcy seldom means the physical destruction of assets. They are usually acquired by other firms and therefore the implications of bankruptcy may be less restrictive than would appear at first sight. Finally we should note that the existence of asymmetry in the distribution of information in the capital market may incline managers to issue some debt in order to convince investors that they are working hard. In other words, debt issue is a form of bond, not about income, but about managerial effort.

Efficient Capital Markets

So far we have ignored the problem of whether capital markets are efficient. The belief in efficient capital markets stems from evidence that stock markets exhibit a random walk (Cootner, 1964). If today's prices bear no relationship to yesterday's prices then markets have no memories, and it becomes impossible to use past prices to predict future prices. All information is contained in present prices, and as we observed in chapter 2 an investor could use a pin to select a share from a list of share prices because current prices would be reflecting underlying values. But what is meant by the statement that prices reflect all available information? We can distinguish three hypotheses:

1   a strong hypothesis based on the information available;
2   a semi-strong thesis based upon all published information;
3   a weak thesis based upon price movements.

The available evidence, as surveyed by Fama (1970), suggests that the strong thesis cannot be sustained; *a priori* it might require a complete set of markets in all contingent claims. Furthermore, there is some evidence that in the timing of both purchases and sales, insiders (company personnel) enjoy and gain an advantage over outside investors. There is, however, support for the semi-strong hypothesis, and the evidence of random walks does suggest that the weak hypothesis can be rejected.

Options

In recent decades the market in securities has been widened by the development of options. An option enables its holder to buy or sell an asset at some time in the future. Thus, in the case of a *put* option the holder has the opportunity to sell an option at a fixed price within a given period, whilst the holder of a *call* option has the opportunity of purchasing an asset at a fixed price within a given period, and a *warrant* is similar to a call option. Option markets are therefore organized futures markets comparable to those existing for some primary commodities. But what determines the price of an option? Three factors would seem to be important.

1   The ratio of the asset price to the exercise price is crucial because the less the holder is asked to pay the better is his return.
2   A market rate of interest is important because an option is a free loan and the value of that loan increases with the rate of interest and the period of maturity to the option.
3   The worth of an option varies with the degree of risk attaching to the future value of the underlying share. If the asset price is expected

to fall below the exercise price then the holder would not exercise the option. If it rises above the exercise price then a profit can be expected. Black and Scholes (1973) have incorporated these factors into an option valuation formula.

Short-term Financing

So far we have concentrated upon medium- and long-term financing decisions, and on situations where finance is usually raised through the issue of shares. Now we must turn to the problems of short-term finance. The distinction between short- and long-term does, as we indicated in the introduction, depend upon a firm's market situation. In the case of heavy industries much finance for short-term needs may have to be financed through the issue of shares. Nevertheless a division can usually be drawn in practice.

Short-term financing is normally achieved through the use of money or trade credit. Some economists regard credit as money, whereas others prefer to restrict the definition of money. The distinction may be a fine one. Money is usually defined as anything which is generally acceptable as a medium of exchange, and is taken to comprise cash (notes and coins) issues by the monetary authority and bank credit issued by commercial banks. The question therefore arises: is trade credit similar to bank credit? If a bank has idle cash reserves and lends on the basis of those reserves is that comparable to firm A lending to firm B by not demanding immediate repayment for goods? Or, over the whole economy, does trade credit cancel out? Is trade credit merely a means of increasing the velocity circulation of existing money? The answers to these questions are not obvious and reflect the tendency of theory to run behind changes in monetary institutions and practices, and the problems created by the instability of credit. There is, however, a tendency not to accept trade credit as money because of its lack of general acceptability as a medium of exchange.

The Demand for Money

Two reasons, time and uncertainty, have been advanced for the holding of money. Time should not be confused with the lack of synchronization of the timing of payments and receipts. If there were perfect foresight then all contracts could be arranged at one point of time and no money need be held; there would be only book-keeping entries. Nor are technical factors, such as the fact that workers have to be paid weekly or monthly whereas receipts from a firm's sales may accrue at a much longer interval, a crucial factor. Instead, we must pay regard to the fact that decision-making takes time.

Transactions Motive

There is, however, an opportunity cost of time which is the interest forgone by holding money, and we can establish a simple transactions model for determining the optimal money balance. Suppose, for example, that a firm's receipts occur at 6-month intervals, and its payments, mainly wage payments, occur weekly, then a saw-tooth pattern of income and expenditure will result as shown in figure 14.9. Every 6 months the firm will receive income OY and this would be run down more or less continuously over the 6 months. On average, therefore, the balance held for transactions purposes would be one-half of planned expenditure.

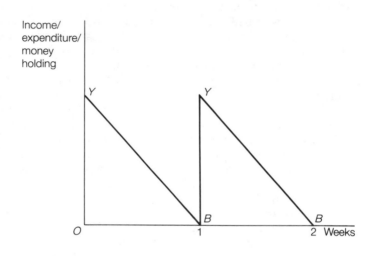

Figure 14.9

Transactions balances are influenced by the timing of payments and receipts, the general price level which measures the purchasing power of money and the rate of interest which measures the opportunity cost of holding money (as opposed to income-yielding assets). Thus expected changes in the price level or the rate of interest could move the YB curve upwards or downwards.

A formal treatment of the optimal transactions balance, pursuing ideas developed in inventory theory, was put forward by Baumol in 1952, and his analysis of inventories was dealt with in the chapter on production management.

Precautionary Motive

The timing of payments and receipts may be variable, however, and cause firms to increase their cash holdings in order to avoid financial embarrassment. An inability to meet creditors may force a firm to borrow at higher interest rates from the banks. Hence in order to avoid the costs of a stock-out, a sudden lack of cash, a firm may increase its money holdings to guard against unforeseen contingencies.

Speculative Motive

Finally, Keynes drew attention to the point that people have in mind some normal or long-term rate of interest and that their money holdings would be regulated by reference to any divergence between the actual rate and the expected normal rate. Hence at extremely low interest rates people would prefer to hold money rather than bonds because a possible rise in the actual rate, towards its long-term rate, would result in capital losses. Keynes's conjecture came in for considerable criticism during the inflation of the 1960s and 1970s, and there was a greater emphasis upon the transactions and precautionary motives. Even amongst Keynesians there has been a tendency to stress not the existence of a highly elastic demand curve for money at low interest rates, but the tendency for the demand curve to shift under the impact of waves of pessimism and optimism.

A Generalized Demand for Money Function

Although we have distinguished three motives for holding money it should not be imagined that firms or households hold money in three separate compartments. They hold money upon which the three motives exert varying degrees of influence. We can therefore bring together the various forces in terms of a generalized demand for money function as follows:

$$Md = f(Y, r, r^e, P, P^e, T) \tag{14.20}$$

where Md is the demand for money, Y is the firm's receipts, r is the prevailing money rate of interest, r^e is the expected rate of interest, P is the prevailing price level, P^e is the expected price level and T is the technology of payments and receipts. Three points should be noted about the equation. First, the expected real rate of interest, $r - P^e$, is incorporated as the relevant opportunity cost of holding money. Second, the inclusion of the technology of exchange provides a link between the utility approach to the demand for money and the production function approach to money holdings. Third, we may observe that the demand for money is a demand for real money balances. Hence, equation (14.20) can be expressed in real terms by dividing through by the price level; and if management considers future interest rates and receipts it is likely to have regard to the future movement of income. Therefore Y can be replaced by the discounted value of future income, W. Thus, the generalized demand for money function provides a link with the firm's objective of maximizing realizable wealth.

Bibliography and References

Arrow, K. J. (1965) *Some Aspects of the Theory of Risk-Bearing*. Helsinki: Yrjo Jahnsson Lectures.

Baumol, W. J. (1952) 'The Transaction Demand for Money: An Inventory Theoretic Approach', *Quarterly Journal of Economics*, 66, 545–56.

Black, F. and Scholes, M. (1973) 'The pricing of options and corporate liabilities', *Journal of Political Economy*, 81, 637–54.

Black, F. and Scholes, M. (1974) 'The effects of dividend yield and dividend policy on common stock prices and returns', *Journal of Financial Economics*, 6, 1–22.

Brearley, R. and Myers, S. (1984) *Principles of Corporate Finance*, 2nd edn. New York: McGraw-Hill.

Cootner, P. H. (1964) *The Changing Character of Stock Market Prices*. Cambridge, Mass.: MIT Press.

Debreu, G. (1959) *Theory of Value*. New York: Wiley.

Fama, E. F. (1970) 'Efficient capital markets: a review of theory and empirical work', *Journal of Finance*, 25, 383–417.

Fisher, I. (1965) *The Theory of Interest*, reprint of 1930 edn. New York: Augustus M. Kelley.

Henfrey, A. W. et al. (1977) 'The UK stock market and the efficient market model; a review', *The Investment Analyst*, 48, 5–24.

Knight, F. H. (1921) *Risk, Uncertainty and Profit*. New York: Houghton Mifflin.

Markowitz, H. (1952) 'Portfolio selection', *Journal of Finance*, 7, 77–91.

Miller, M. H. and Modigliani, F. (1958) 'Some estimates of the cost of capital to the electric utility industry 1954–57', *American Economic Review*, 56, 33–91.

Miller, M. H. and Modigliani, F. (1961) 'Dividend policy, growth and valuation of shares', *Journal of Business*, 34, 411–33.

Modigliani, F. and Miller, M. H. (1958) 'The cost of capital, corporation finance and the theory of investment', *American Economic Review*, 56, 261–97.

Mossin, J. (1973) *Theory of Financial Markets*. Englewood Cliffs, N.J.: Prentice Hall.

Royal Commission on the Distribution of Income and Wealth (chairman Lord Diamond). Report No. 2: *Income from Companies and its Distribution*. London: HMSO, Cmnd. 6172.

Rybczynski, T. (1982) 'Structural changes in the financing of British industry and their implications', *National Westminster Bank Review*, 25–36.

Sharpe, W. (1981) *Investment*. Englewood Cliffs, N.J.: Prentice Hall.

15   Multinational Corporations

A multinational corporation is a firm which owns and operates plants in more than one country. The relationships between plants may take one of three forms.

1   The multinational may own and operate plants producing similar goods – horizontal integration.
2   The multinational may control plants which combine to form a sequence of operations – vertical integration.
3   The multinational may control plants producing diverse and unrelated goods – the firm is a conglomerate.

Scope and Extent of Multinationals

Multinationals are not a new phenomenon. The present-day transnational corporations are descendants of the great trading companies of the seventeenth century, and no doubt it would be possible to extend the lineage back even further. In the nineteenth century multinationals emerged mainly to exploit raw materials in the underdeveloped world. By 1914, 35 per cent of the long-term international debt, some $14 billion, was invested in overseas subsidiaries (Dunning, 1983). The territorial spread of this direct foreign investment was much wider than at present because it included Eastern Europe and China. The major foreign investor was the UK, followed at some distance by USA, Germany and France; and about three-fifths of the investment was in the developing countries.

During the interwar years there was a slowing down of activity, although investment continued, notably in oil production in the Middle East and the Dutch East Indies. The postwar revival witnessed the American domination of foreign investment until the late sixties. It also heralded a shift in the direction and emphasis of investment away from minerals, which were increasingly becoming nationalized, and towards manufacturing. In the final period from the mid-sixties to the early eighties the shares of the USA and UK started to decline and those of West Germany, Japan and Switzerland started to rise. There was also a shift of investment towards Western Europe and the USA and away from the Commonwealth, as well as a marked interest in investment in high-technology and information-intensive industries. Finally there was a movement towards a greater degree of integration of the activities of the multinationals and their subsidiaries, with the result that planning by administration across national boundaries became more noticeable.

Plan of this Chapter

Given the definition of a multinational, the forms which it can adopt and the extent of their activities, we need to ask whether the analysis contained in previous chapters is applicable to such a firm. Thus we seek answers to the following questions.

1   Why does a firm choose to establish subsidiaries in more than one country rather than export from one production centre or permit production under licence of the goods in different countries by indigenous firms? In other words, what strategic considerations might impel a firm to become a multinational?
2   Given the strategic decision, what structural and control problems might emerge and how might they be resolved?
3   What particular marketing decisions arise for a multinational with respect to prices, advertising, and location of production and selling centres?
4   Given the marketing decisions what investment and financial problems may arise?
5   Are there any specific production problems stemming from the international transmission of technology?
6   Are there likely to be specific personnel problems?
7   What political problems may arise from operating in more than one country?

Strategy

Trade Theory

A firm has a choice between exporting goods, permitting them to be produced abroad under licence or establishing subsidiaries in foreign countries. In order to resolve this conflict of choice we shall examine the reasons for foreign trade and the problems which might arise with direct exporting. The standard theory of international trade suggests that countries will export those goods in which they have a comparative advantage, and that this advantage will stem from international differences in factor endowments – countries will export those goods which use their most abundant factor intensively. Therefore trade is a means of overcoming the uneven geographical distribution of resources.

The simple outline of the theory in the previous paragraph assumes that transport costs and tariffs are not impediments to trade, that preferences (tastes) for goods are everywhere the same, and that all countries have the same access to technologies. Consider then the implications of tariffs. If a country prohibits the imports of goods by imposing a tariff or quota then we may expect to find illegal entry of goods or an inflow of resources from abroad. Movements of goods and movements of resources are therefore substitutes. Confronted by a tariff a firm may decide to set up a foreign subsidiary, or issue a licence to produce to a foreign firm, or it may pursue a mixture of the two policies depending upon the impact of tariffs on its costs and whether scale economies are possible. Evidence for an interaction of trade, tariffs and direct foreign investment can be found in the increase of investment by multinationals in Western Europe following the creation of the EEC in the 1960s.

Standard trade theory presents a hypothesis based upon factor endowment and a hypothesis based upon the interconnections of trade, tariffs and foreign investment. However, the theory seems too general and does not appear to come to grips with many features of trade and foreign investment. Thus, a factor endowment theory seems a plausible explanation of trade in primary products but not of trade in manufactures and services, and trade in primary products accounts for only some 35 per cent of world trade. What has to be explained, therefore, is trade in manufactures between countries with rather similar factor endowments. Rehabilitation of the theory has been attempted by suggesting that the theory is a *long-run theory*, and that in the short run differences in tastes and technologies may be expected to prevail. Unfortunately, differences in tastes tend to destroy simple notions of gains from trade which rely upon individuals having stable preference patterns, and trade enables them to move from one indifference curve to another; *trade may destroy old wants and create new ones*.

Differences in technologies have been incorporated into theory by postulating a *product cycle hypothesis*. Thus an advanced industrial country, say the US, pioneers the development of a new process or product. Initially the new idea is developed in the country of origin, but subsequently there will be an attempt to find a cheaper production centre. Hence there will be a move to a country with lower wage costs; in the long run, then, the new technology will be internationally diffused.

Trade theory therefore suggests that capital and know-how will flow from centres of high cost to low cost centres. In other words a capital arbitrage hypothesis is postulated. However, this attempt at resuscitaton of the theory also runs into difficulties.

1   If the problem were simply one of foreign investment then we should expect financial intermediaries to be prominent, but most direct foreign investment seems to be undertaken by non-financial companies.

2   Some countries, such as the UK, are both home bases and hosts for many multinationals. Capital and multinationals appear to move in all directions, and this suggests the implausible hypothesis that national capital markets are not perfect.

3   American capital flows show an outflow of foreign direct investment and an inflow of portfolio capital, which suggests that Americans are risk-preferrers.

4   The theory assumes competitive conditions, which would seem to rule out horizontally integrated multinationals. Under competitive conditions increases in demand are more likely to be met by increases in the number of products rather than by an increase in output by existing producers.

To sum up: there is a grain of truth in trade theory; there is a connection between trade, tariffs, investment and endowments; there is a tendency for trade to occur because of differences in factor rewards; but the theory does not provide sufficient insight into the distribution of foreign direct investment in subsidiaries. Capital may flow because 'other things' are flowing between countries, and it is these other things which we must now examine.

Intangible assets and horizontal integration

Trade theory throws some light upon foreign investment, but for a more rigorous explanation it is necessary to return to the nature of the firm and consider why it is necessary to establish a set of contracts embracing plants in different countries. In chapter 3 we suggested that firms emerge because of the costs of using markets, and that the source of those costs lies in externalities, such as the need to monitor the performances of workers engaged in joint production. An obvious example of an externality which can prompt the creation of a multinational firm is the ownership of 'know-how' about products or processes. A firm may possess superior knowledge but this knowledge has the property of being a public good; once the knowledge has been revealed it may be possible to put it to use at little cost.

Evidence for an association between intangible assets, such as research and advertising, and direct foreign investment by US firms, has been uncovered by Goedde (1978) who found the influence of R and D strongest in engineering, and the influence of advertising strongest in food and chemicals (including pharmaceuticals). Yannopoulos (1983) has drawn attention to the incentive to internalize information in the banking and finance industries where multinationals have been prominent in the past 30 years.

Vertical Integration and Risk

The intangible assets hypothesis provides insights into the reasons for the emergence of horizontally integrated multinationals. It is, however, less useful in explaining the development of vertically integrated firms. However, we can appeal to the arguments developed in chapter 11. Vertical integration by administration can enable investment in trust to take place and ensure availability of supplies. In the banana export trade the perishable nature of the product has required close integration of production, transportation and marketing despite the low technology involved in production (Read, 1981). In the oil industry refineries need to operate at capacity and require a constant flow of crude oil inputs. Storage of crude oil can be costly, and backward integration has developed to ensure supplies.

The product cycle hypothesis also provides a partial basis for integration. Semiconductors may be produced and assembled in Britain or America but labour-intensive operations may be carried out in the Third World. United States tariff laws permit goods which are exported for processing and which are then re-imported to pay duty only on the value added abroad. Hence offshore procurement is extensively practised (Helleiner and Lavergne, 1979).

Conglomerate Integration, Spillovers and Risk

Conglomerate integration may arise in order to spread risks, not only for shareholders, but also for managers and employees. Although shareholders can diversify easily within a country they may find it difficult to diversify in international markets, and this objective may be more easily achieved by companies. Similarly, by spreading risks firms may ensure a higher degree of utilization of managerial skills. Pearce (1983), however, has estimated that the world's leading multinationals have some 22 per cent of their sales outside their main industries, and that the reasons for such diversification lie in technological spillovers, as in the case of chemicals. Evidence to support the risk-spreading hypothesis is, in fact, difficult to obtain, and most studies suggest that rates of return on the market values of firms' equities are still closely tied to the economic conditions in the national home markets (Rugman, 1979; Miller and Pras, 1980).

Structure

The decision to establish plants in other countries raises the question: what is the appropriate company structure to implement strategy and to ensure control and performance? We need therefore to consider the appropriate extensions to the analysis of chapter 5.

Model 1

Decisions to create foreign subsidiaries may be the result of accidents, and the simplest structural change which can usually be made, by a small firm is shown in figure 15.1. The chief executive of the overseas subsidiary reports to the chief executive of the home country with other possible secondary channels of communication between functional managers at home and abroad.

Model 2

In the case of multi-product firms, or firms with more than one overseas unit, a link may be established through the creation of an export or international division with a divisional manager having the same status as domestic product group managers (figure 15.2). Thus Levi Strauss, in the early eighties, had two US groups, Jeansware and Sportsware, and an international group which

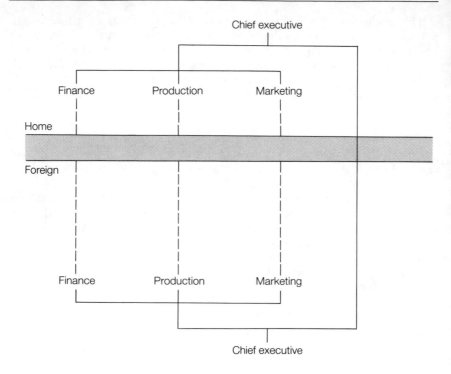

Figure 15.1   Model 1: ——, Direct links; –––, indirect links. (*Source*: Brooke and Remmer, 1970.)

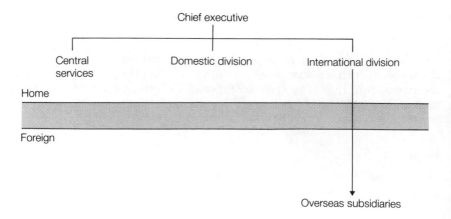

Figure 15.2   Model 2. (*Source*: Brooke and Remmer, 1970.)

looked after overseas interests including the 28 per cent of production provided through independent contractors.

Model 3

Potential conflict between product and international divisions can be overcome by eliminating the latter and directly linking product divisions to overseas subsidiaries. In effect each product division acts as a sponsor of a foreign subsidiary. Thus Courtaulds, which was originally a holding company with 70 largely autonomous subdivisions, switched to a multidivisional structure of five product groups with world-wide responsibilities in 1970. Hewlett Packard has four operating groups with world-wide responsibilities: Electronic Data Production, Electronic Test and Measurement Production, Medical Electronic Equipment, and Analytical Instrumentation. One reason for this type of structure is that it may be much easier to control the returns to intangible assets. Thus Hewlett Packard spends the equivalent of about 10 per cent of its sales revenue on research and development.

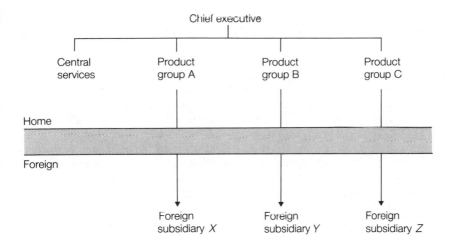

Figure 15.3   Model 3. (*Source*: Brooke and Remmer, 1970.)

Model 3 may arise as a result of domestic growth spilling over into foreign markets or from the acquisition, through merger with foreign competing companies, of new product groups.

Model 4

Model 3, however, does not overcome the basic inertia or unwillingness of domestic-based product divisions to interest themselves in foreign subsidiaries. Hence there may emerge a matrix organization, a combination of product and

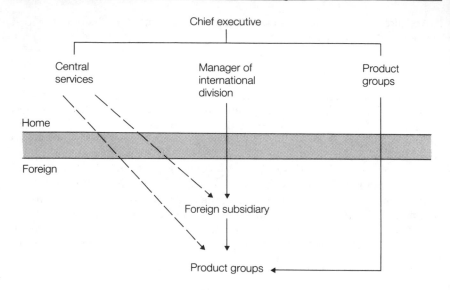

Figure 15.4   Model 4. (*Source*: Brooke and Remmer, 1970.)

geographical management. In 1926 ICI was formed as a result of a merger of four companies. It was a defensive merger and its creation led to a series of cartel arrangements in the UK and Commonwealth. In the late 1940s these cartels began to crumble, and the decision was made to base future strategy upon manufactures of oil-based products as opposed to coal-based derivatives. In the 1960s changes in world conditions led to a decision to enter Europe, and plants were established in Holland and West Germany. In 1977 the thrust of policy was confirmed when ICI divested itself of its metal-using plants and Imperial Metal Industries was formed. By the late 1970s the vast and diverse interests had resulted in the construction of a matrix structure of product policy groups and territorial groups (Pettigrew, 1985). In similar fashion General Motors had introduced a matrix form of management in an endeavour to gain economies of scale and to help develop the first world car and truck.

Marketing

Marketing decisions are deeply embedded in the choice of location for a subsidiary and in its relationship with head office. The product cycle hypothesis emphasizes the importance of purchasing decisions, whilst the imposition of tariffs or export subsidies by host governments draws attention to the determinants of the market for final goods. Furthermore, a firm may be faced with the choice of national or international advertising of goods, and considering the extent to which national markets require product differentiation. Pricing policy is also important because a firm may need to set prices in different markets in order to ensure that consumers cannot easily switch to the cheapest of its outlets.

But what distinguishes the marketing problems of multinationals from their national counterparts is the added emphasis placed upon oligopolistic market structures. Thus placing the firm's decision within the context of a product cycle hypothesis we can distinguish stages of monopoly followed by oligopoly and then competition. Possessed of specific know-how, a firm's decision to establish a subsidiary has the effect of creating a monopoly situation in the host country. This decision is likely to be followed by imitators, however, in order to protect their sales. Thus if A decides not to export to N but to establish a subsidiary, then the effect on B, C and D may be to reduce their sales to N because A now enjoys lower costs. Hence they may follow suit; bunching of direct foreign investment as a result of oligopolistic inter-dependence is therefore likely to occur as rivals follow the lead of an initiating firm.

Market concentration can lead to a bunching of foreign investment, and market concentration can lead to a reduction in foreign competition. Consider the case where a country imposes a tariff in order to protect its home market for nationals. This could lead to a an inflow of foreign investment by multinationals and to a reduction in concentration. The interaction of foreign investment and market concentration may therefore operate in both directions and their effects may need careful analysis.

Production Management

There are three aspects of production management which deserve special attention. First, there is the problem of transmitting new products and processes. Second, in the case of the vertically integrated firm there is the problem of synchronizing sequential processes at arm's length. Third, there is the problem of monitoring productivity and performance.

The diffusion of processes and products involves a choice between leasing rights to foreign-owned firms or establishing subsidiaries. Although the licensees may place restrictions on the licensors there is a risk that licensing may strengthen a rival and enable him to develop modifications which circumvent the initial patent. Leakages of know-how tend to be greatest for products because they can be bought, dismantled and assessed, whereas to copy processes may require a thorough knowledge of shopfloor practices. However, licensing may be inevitable where a firm finds it difficult to obtain local management and a labour force capable of conducting operations. Furthermore, it may be inevitable where there is a long lead time involved in establishing a plant. Thus, Teece (1977) found that the average resource cost of transferring a new technology amounted to 19 per cent of the project.

The transmission of processes also raises the question of whether, especially in the case of subsidiaries in developing countries, the processes should be made more labour-intensive and the machinery employed should be 'last year's vintage'. The objection to such an arrangement is that the markets in replacements may not exist, and it may be more profitable to use the latest techniques and compensate for the initial scarcity of skilled labour by importing it.

Synchronization of processes involves the problems of establishing transfer prices which clear markets, and the use of incentives to promote such clearances. These issues were examined in chapter 10.

Finally there is the problem of assessing the efficiency of multinationals. Comparisons may be difficult because the newcomer has a new product and new processes and carves out a new market. However, this conclusion may stem from the period of observation. If there is a leakage of know-how then the gap between the multinationals and the nationals may diminish, and if other multinationals follow suit and enter a foreign country then the advantages may be short-lived. Short-run analysis may award the prize to the multinational, but in the long run those national firms which survive may be just as efficient as the subsidiaries of multinationals. The gains from risk-spreading may be cancelled out by the costs of internalizing numerous operations in different countries (Lall, 1973; Rugman, 1979).

Labour Markets and Personnel Management

During 1983 Japanese unions expressed disquiet at proposals to build a car factory in Britain because of its effects upon the wages and employment of their members. Similar views had been expressed by American and British trade unions at the export of capital to other countries; and in Britain doubts had been expressed at the wisdom of allowing a Japanese car factory to be built and to permit it to compete against the publicly owned British Leyland. Opposition has also been expressed against the import of cheap textiles from Hong Kong. Hence we must consider the impact of multinationals upon labour markets in home and foreign countries, and we also need to consider the alternative effects of imports.

Home Country

The effect of direct foreign investment by a multinational upon the home-based labour force, and upon labour market conditions generally, is not capable of simple resolution and the results depend upon the nature of the model adopted. The factor endowment theory of trade suggests that a country will export those goods which use its most abundant factor intensively, and that the movement of goods will tend to bring about an equalization of factor rewards. Consider then a situation in which we observe not a movement of goods but an outflow of capital from a capital-abundant country to a labour-abundant country. Intuition suggests that labour's reward will fall in the home country because the real capital stock is lowered. But the outflow of capital will also lower the amount of trade between the two countries and this will have the effect of releasing relatively large amounts of capital from the export industry relative to the proportions used in the domestic import competing industry. Hence the internal adjustment of resources will mitigate some of the effects of the capital outflow. For example, suppose that manufactures are capital-intensive and services are labour-intensive, then an outflow of capital will lower the return to labour in manufactures but the fall in output in manufactures will result in a transfer of resources from manufactures to services. Since services employ relatively more labour than capital any movement of capital from manufactures to services will tend to raise labour's reward. The resulting effect upon the reward to labour will therefore depend upon the amounts of capital that flow abroad and towards the service sector.

However, even if no capital were to flow towards the service sector because it was all exported, the employment and wage effects of the capital outflow might depend upon the mobility of labour and whether the profits earned upon the foreign investment were spent in the service sector. Thus full employment might persist and wages might rise. Favourable wage and employment effects might also result if we abandon the $2 \times 2 \times 2$ model (that is, two goods, two factors and two countries) implicit in the analysis of horizontal integration, and consider the effect of risk reduction in the context of vertical integration. Thus a multinational might integrate forward or backward in order to ensure supplies, and the resulting reduction in risk could ensure greater stability of wages and employment. Of course a great deal depends upon how the international division of labour is carried out. If all skilled jobs go abroad then home-based workers may experience an expansion of employment opportunities but a reduction in relative and absolute wages. The capital which flows abroad may be human capital. The crucial issue therefore may be whether the state can tax the return on foreign investment in order to compensate those who might experience a fall in income from employment.

Foreign Country: Personnel Management and Labour Markets

Because of differences in legal systems, trade union organization and cultural values multinationals may be forced to pursue a decentralized personnel policy. However, to the extent that the multinational has a monopoly of know-how it may be able to stand aloof from the national scene and adopt a distinctive company policy. Thus the British industrial relations system tended in the 1950s to be characterized by industry-wide collective bargaining between employers' associations and federations of trade unions. Yet Ford consistently adopted a company wages policy independently of other employers, and even of governments' incomes policies.

Whether and how a multinational can have any effect upon wages and employment is still debatable. The available evidence is conflicting, and many conclusions can be criticized for a failure to control for industry-mix, size of plant and skill requirements. Thus the competitive model would suggest that there should be no difference between the wages paid by a multinational and those paid by other firms, but that there may be a considerable impact upon employment; if full employment exists and labour is mobile then the establishment of a multinational's subsidiary will, unless it has been acquired by merger, lead to a rise in the demand for labour, and wages will be bid up. Indigenous firms will have to pay the same wages even if they lose some of their employees. Hence there may be no correlation between wages and employment.

However, the competitive model may be inappropriate for the analysis of multinationals which may seek to alter patterns of work organization and industrial relations through the import of know-how and cultural values. Thus at the turn of the century, and through the interwar years, American firms such as Ford pioneered the introduction of scientific management, and in the early sixties Esso (Exxon) productivity bargaining, whereby changes in work practices became the subject of negotiation and the pattern of industrial relations established in the thirties was modified. In recent years Japanese firms in Britain have not introduced the more obvious features of Japanese firms – permanent employment, seniority-based wage systems, lifetime training and group decision-making, but they have emphasized quality, discipline and commitment (White and Trevor, 1983).

This brings us to the final issue: do multinationals achieve a better system of industrial relations than indigenous firms? Resolution of the question tends to founder upon problems of measurement and the availability of evidence. The simplest measure is strike activity. Gennard and Steuer (1971) found that foreign subsidiaries in Britain had fewer strikes than their indigenous competitors in the 1960s, whilst Forsythe (1973) reached the opposite conclusion for Scotland for the same period. The differences in conclusions may stem from differences in industry-mix, size distribution of plants and regional factors. Creigh and Makeham (1978) attempted to control for plant size and differences in labour intensity, and found no significant differences in strike activity between foreign-owned and indigenous plants in manufacturing industry. However, the effect of foreign ownership may also depend upon the period of observation. Buckley and Enderwick (1982) found that in the period 1971–73 foreign-owned plants in Britain had higher strike rates than British-owned plants. This difference stemmed from a variety of factors. First, American-owned plants had a greater strike propensity than British- or EEC-owned plants. Second, differences in strike activity were greater in mechanical engineering, instruments, vehicles, paper and print and other manufacturing industries, whereas British-owned plants had more strikes in food, drink and tobacco, chemicals and oil refining. Third, foreign-owned plants tended to have higher strike rates in the smaller plants. Fourth, foreign-owned plants had more strikes over labour utilization. These findings relate to the period before the first oil price rise, and may suggest that foreign-owned firms were more responsive to changing market conditions than British-owned plants. Thus it is significant that British-owned firms, such as British Leyland, British Steel and the National Coal Board, had higher strike activity in the period after the second oil price rise, and that these disputes were associated with changing managerial attitudes, including the import of foreign managers such as Ian McGregor.

Investment and Finance

In chapter 12 we set out a theory of investment and finance. The question which now arises is: can the analysis of that chapter be extended to the operations of multinationals without serious modification? Do international differences in the tax treatment of corporate income, and the possibility that the international capital market may not be as perfect as national capital markets, mean that a different approach to investment and finance by multinationals is needed?

In chapter 14 it was suggested that management will rank its projects on the basis of their net present values and undertake those which are expected to yield a positive return. Hence we should expect multinationals to appraise investment opportunities on a global basis and choose the least-cost methods of finance irrespective of source. In other words, investment and finance would be centralized. In assessing projects management would also be expected to have regard to the expected or desired levels of sales, the capital–output ratio and the price of output relative to the user cost of capital. Such a model may not apply in circumstances which may be considered to be non-competitive. Hence many investigations of multinationals' investment behaviour have been conducted on an ad hoc basis and using proxy variables.

Boatwright and Renton (1975) investigated changes in multinationals' capital stock moving both into and out of the UK, and found that the neoclassical model based on desired capital stock proved statistically significant. However, the lag structure was not estimated accurately, and the authors assumed a high elasticity of substitution between labour and capital. In another study Goldsbrough (1979) included not only measures of activity in foreign markets, but also international changes in labour costs resulting from exchange rate variations; he concluded that the allocation of funds among industrial countries was directed at producing in the least-cost location.

Taxation

In examining the demand side of the investment decision we paid no attention to the importance of taxation. Yet firms are interested in net income after tax, so what we need to consider now is how taxes influence investment decisions, and whether transfer pricing plays a role in the avoidance of tax.

Most countries impose corporation taxes, and although intended to fall on windfall profits and rent they do in practice also affect the opportunity cost of capital. Whether such taxes fall on the suppliers of capital or the buyers of goods produced with that finance does, of course, depend upon the relevant demand and supply elasticities, and those must be regarded as an empirical issue. However, the subject is further complicated by the possibilities of home and foreign investment and the existence of different tax rates in the two countries. At the margin a multinational is seeking the same return on its investments irrespective of their source, and a tax-neutral system would not distort that choice by making post-tax returns equal.

In practice tax systems need not be neutral, and investment decisions may be considerably influenced by the arrangements for collecting tax employed by the home and foreign countries. We shall therefore consider several possibilities.

1 Suppose the home country imposes no tax but the foreign country imposes a tax on all corporate income irrespective of ownership. In the foreign country tax neutrality prevails because no distinctions are made between domestic and imported savings. In the home country, however, there is a bias in favour of domestic investment and the tax system is not neutral. If the tax positions were reversed then the home country would have a neutral tax system but there would be no tax neutrality in the foreign country.

2 If both countries impose taxes then the net effect would depend upon which country was allowed to impose the first slice of tax, and whether the second country made allowance for the fact that the income had been taxed once. Since it is customary for the host country to take the first slice, then the source country has three possible options: either it can grant complete exemption to foreign-earned income or it can give a credit against taxes paid abroad, or it can allow the foreign tax as a deduction against income taxable at home. Neither of these two latter policies gives tax neutrality with respect to either exports or imports of capital. To what extent neutrality is not observed in practice is a matter of empirical investigation, but it seems doubtful, given the possibilities of retaliation, that massive distortions occur.

Transfer Pricing

Multinationals may manipulate transfer prices between subsidiaries in order to move taxable profits into countries where tax rates are lower. Transfer prices may therefore serve two purposes: first, they may be used to clear internal markets; second, they may be used to circumvent taxes. Whether they are used for the second function depends upon factors which are basically external to the multinational. Thus Lall's study (1973) of the pharmaceutical industry in Colombia found evidence of transfer pricing by multinationals, and argued for a policy by host governments of 'monitoring intrafirm trade and enforcing reasonable transfer prices'. However, the Colombian economy was characterized by exchange controls and effective tax differentials. The effects of transfer pricing can only be assessed indirectly by looking at the overall performance of multinationals and whether or not they earn excess profits over time.

Finance

So far we have dealt with the revenue or demand side of the investment decision. Now we must turn to the supply side. Thus we may consider a multinational as seeking to raise its finance in the cheapest possible manner irrespective of source. But to what extent can the international capital market be treated as an efficient financial market in the sense that the concept was used in chapter 12?

In chapter 14 we discussed the capital asset pricing model which seeks to explain how risk-averse investors, behaving competitively, set prices for financial assets yielding uncertain streams of future income. Asset-holders were envisaged as diversifying their portfolios in order to reduce risk as well as maintaining their return. The risk attaching to a particular asset was assumed to be composed of the risk associated with a particular firm's fortunes and the risks associated with the overall behaviour of the economy. Hence the return on any asset was assumed to be equal to the return on a risk-free asset, such as short-term government bonds, plus a risk premium. The risk premium would be determined by the covariance or correlation between the asset and the aggregate of all assets in the portfolio.

The CAPM attempts to link behaviour in product markets with behaviour in financial markets. It recognizes that there are imperfections in product markets and that there are substantial differences in rates of return on capital assets which can persist for considerable periods. Accordingly it sees compensation for these disparities by adjustments in asset prices in financial markets. Hence it assumes imperfect product markets and perfect financial markets.

The CAPM model has shown some success in explaining stock market behaviour, and the evidence was examined in chapter 13. However, it has been less successful in dealing with the behaviour of non-financial companies. Transactions costs are less important in financial markets. The major problem, however, is whether a model which has been applied to national markets can be extended to international markets where exchange rate variations are present, where differences in accounting procedures may obscure relevant information and where political factors may be pervasive. Hence it is not surprising the analysis of financial decisions by multinationals is a rapidly expanding area of research.

Public Policy

Political attitudes towards multinationals tend to be coloured by the thought that multinationals have replaced colonial domination as the means by which advanced economies extract surpluses from Third World countries. This is known as the 'dependency theory'. However, 'dependence' is an elusive concept to analyse (Lall, 1975; Little, 1983). In an international economy all countries tend to be dependent upon one another. Moreover, a considerable amount of investment by multinationals takes place between advanced countries. Host countries may, in fact, encourage foreign investment as a means of raising income levels, and it may be preferable to foreign aid (which may be too closely tied to issues of global military strategy) and to economic development through trade. Trade may suffer from the disadvantage of freezing a country's comparative advantage. In contrast foreign investment by multinationals may provide new technologies. Of course, we should not ignore the disadvantages. Much investment by multinationals is highly concentrated geographically; it tends to go to countries rich in primary products, or to countries which are already at a high level of economic development.

Bibliography and References

Boatwright, B. D. and Renton, G. A. (1975) 'An analysis of United Kingdom inflows and outflows of direct foreign investment', *Review of Economics and Statistics*, 57, 478–86.
Brooke, M. Z. and Remmer, H. L. (1970) *The Strategy of Multinational Enterprise: Organization and Finance*. New York: Elsevier.
Buckley, P. J. and Enderwick, P. (1985) *The Industrial Relations Practices of Foreign-owned Firms in Britain*. London: Macmillan.
Casson, M. (ed.) (1983) *The Growth of International Business*. London: Allen & Unwin.
Caves, R. E. (1982) *Multinational Enterprise and Economic Analysis*. Cambridge: Cambridge University Press.
Creigh, S. W. and Makeham P. (1978) 'Foreign ownership and strike-proneness: a research note', *British Journal of Industrial Relations*, 16, 369–72.
Dunning, J. H. (1983) 'Changes in the level and structure of international production: the last one hundred years'. In M. Casson (ed.), *The Growth of International Business*. London: Allen & Unwin.
Enderwick, P. (1985) 'Ownership nationality and industrial relations practices', *Industrial Relations Journal*, 16, 50–9.
Forsythe, D. J. C. (1973) 'Foreign-owned firms and labour relations: a regional perspective', *British Journal of Industrial Relations*, 11, 20–8.
Gennard, J. and Steuer, M. (1971) 'The industrial relations of foreign-owned subsidiaries in the United Kingdom', *British Journal of Industrial Relations*, 9, 143–59.
Goedde, A. G. (1978) 'US multinational manufacturing firms: the determinants and effects of foreign investment'. Ph.D. dissertation, Duke University; cited by Caves (1982).
Goldsbrough, D. J. (1979) 'The role of foreign direct investment in the external adjustment process'. *IMF Staff Papers*, 26, 725–54.
Helleiner, G. K. and Lavergne, R. (1979) 'Intra-firm trade and industrial exports to the United States', *Oxford Bulletin of Economics and Statistics*, 41, 297–311.
Helpman, E. (1984) 'A simple theory of international trade with multinational corporations', *Journal of Political Economy*, 92, 451–71.
Lall, S. J. (1973) 'Transfer pricing by multinational manufacturing firms', *Oxford Bulletin of Economics and Statistics*, 35, 179–95.
Lall, S. J. (1975) 'Is "dependence" a useful concept in analysing underdevelopment?', *World Development*, 3, 799–810.
Little, I. D. (1983) *Development Economics*. New York: Basic Books.
Miller, J. C. and Pras, B. (1980) 'The effects of multinational and export diversification on the profit stability of US corporations', *Southern Economic Journal*, 46, 792–805.
Pearce, R. D. (1983) 'Industrial diversification amongst the world's leading multinational enterprises'. In Casson (1983).
Pettigrew, A. (1985) *The Awakening Giant*. Oxford: Blackwell.

Read, R. A. N. (1981) 'Corporate foreign direct investment strategies and trade liberalisation in the Japanese market for bananas, 1960–76', *University of Reading Discussion Papers in International Investment and Business Studies*, no. 60; cited in Casson (1983).

Rugman, A. (1979) *International Diversification and the Multinational Enterprise*. Lexington, Mass.: Lexington Books.

Stopford, J. M., Dunning, J. H. and Haberich, K. O. (1980) *The World Directory of Multinational Enterprises*. London: Macmillan.

Teece, D. J. (1977) 'Technology transfer by multinational firms: the resource cost of transferring technological know-how', *Economic Journal*, 87, 242–61.

White, M. and Trevor, M. (1983) *Under Japanese Management*. London: Heinemann.

Yannopoulos, G. N. (1983) 'The growth of transnational banking'. In Casson (1983).

16　Workers' Cooperatives

Labour-managed firms, or workers' cooperatives as they are sometimes called, are firms in which the members hire capital and raw materials at fixed rates and claim the residual as their income. Thus workers' cooperatives stand the capitalist firm of Alchian and Demsetz on its head. They are not subject to specific outside influences, such as capitalists, although they may be influenced by government policies on taxes, for example. Labour-managed firms may emerge in one of three ways.

1　They may arise in response to a crisis, a bankruptcy of a capitalist firm. During the 1970s many such cooperatives emerged, and were sometimes provided with government and local assistance.
2　Labour-managed firms may be transformations by capitalist owners possessed of idealistic impulses.
3　Workers' cooperatives may start from scratch as idealistic ventures.

The Standard Theory of the LMP

The objective of a capitalist firm is to maximize profits as the difference between income and the payments to labour and raw materials. In the case of a labour cooperative the objective is to maximize the income of the members after making payments to other resource owners. Both may be compared with the entrepreneurial firm in which the entrepreneur makes payments to the other resource owners and claims the residual (in the Alchian and Demsetz firms the entrepreneurial role becomes combined with that of the capitalist). Under competitive conditions there would be no difference in the results produced by the firms, since any differences would be eliminated by movements of resources within each institutional framework. In the long run there would be a tendency for rewards to be measured by marginal products.

In the short run, however, differences may be noted. In the capitalist firm an increase in demand would lead to an increase in output. In the cooperative an increase in demand could lead to a restriction of employment and output. The reason for this curious state of affairs is as follows. Since every member of the cooperative would be eligible for an equal share of the residual, then an increase in employment and output could cause a fall in the average and marginal products of labour. New entrants would be making a contribution equal to their marginal product but would expect to be paid a share based upon the average product of all the members; since the average product is greater than the marginal product then there would have to be a redistribution of income from existing members.

The restriction of output would be of little consequence if there were freedom of entry to the industry. But that would depend upon the nature of the capital market. If there were no capital market and all capital was raised from members then there need be no expansion of output in response to the increase in demand. The conclusions drawn from the short-run model also have implications for long-run behaviour. If members of cooperatives cannot invest in other cooperatives, and when they leave their cooperative are not eligible to income (a pension) then they will try to avoid the risks of putting all their eggs in one basket, and they will be tempted to consume their income. Hence the growth rates of cooperatives will be lower than those of capitalist firms and, indeed, managerial firms. Indeed we reach the startling conclusion that it is the joint stock company which is the ideal socialist firm and the workers' cooperative which is the ideal capitalist firm. A joint stock company system would allow workers to spread their risks and save safely for their old age, and joint stock firms would reap any available economies of scale.

The conclusions which we have drawn from a competitive model also carry over into conditions of monopolistic competition and into conditions of uncertainty (Meade, 1972; Hey, 1981). A capitalist firm will always expand output more than a labour-managed firm.

Crisis Cooperatives

The above line of reasoning helps to throw some light upon the behaviour of cooperatives which have been formed as a result of the collapse of capitalist firms. Initially there is a reduction in the incomes of the members as losses previously borne by capitalists are shared equally among members. The second stage is that cooperatives attempt to restrict employment and output in order to raise the incomes of their members to levels comparable with those of workers in successful capitalist firms. It is the policy of income reduction which causes trade unions to be critical of cooperatives, and many are non-union shops.

Conversion Cooperatives

Many of the criticisms which have been advanced against cooperatives may not apply to conversion cooperatives. Thus the John Lewis Partnership is one of the largest retail firms in Britain and would seem to be obtaining all the economies of scale available to retail undertakings. Similarly the Scott Bader Commonwealth Group has tended to be successful in the chemical industry. The reasons for success would seem to lie in the existence of a sound financial base coupled with an element of paternalism and professional management.

Inegalitarian Cooperatives

The disadvantages of cooperatives might be overcome if they were allowed to pay new entrants a lower income than existing members; for example, in accordance with their marginal products. Such 'inegalitarian cooperatives', as Meade has dubbed them, emerged in Yugoslavia in the 1960s, and of course the effects bear a striking resemblance to the results produced by trade unions which have seniority rules and unequal shares between older and younger members. Such firms do appear to be successful in Japan, where they generate high incomes, high growth rates and full employment. But there can be dangers. As in the case of a trade union, a cooperative which obtains a monopoly position may restrict employment in order to capture any gains for existing members, whilst new members have to pay for those rents by waiting and serving long training periods at low wages.

Government Intervention and Community Support

The disadvantages of cooperatives can be overcome if the government decides to create a capital market and imposes taxes upon firms which restrict output; for example, turnover taxes. In the 1950s the Yugoslav government pursued such a policy, but in the 1960s relaxed its controls in favour of greater autonomy, with the result that the cooperatives restricted employment. A disadvantage of government and community support is that it may delay the adjustment to changed economic circumstances, and in some cases lead to feather-bedding.

The Future of the Cooperatives

Despite the paucity of cooperatives in Western economies there are signs that they may be on the increase as a result of conversions from existing institutions. A considerable proportion of the world's population live in socialist countries, and they have been conducting extensive experiments in workers' participation. Despite the failure of the Great Leap Forward communes there have been signs of a return to considering the role of communes in economic development in China. In Hungary there have been experiments with the use of the market mechanism – implying a decentralization of decision-making. In Sweden there are now experiments with workers' investment funds. Moreover, the success of the Japanese with inegalitarian cooperatives has stimulated experiments elsewhere. Only in Britain does there appear to be a retreat from workers' participation, and yet there are some encouraging signs. In some instances, such as the National Freight Corporation, the privatization of the firm has led to a buy-out by the existing workforce.

Bibliography and References

Hey, J. D. (1981) 'A unified theory of the behaviour of profit-maximizing, labour-managed and joint stock firms operating under uncertainty', *Economic Journal*, 91, 364–74.

Meade, J. E. (1972) 'The theory of labour-managed firms and profit sharing', *Economic Journal*, 82, 402–28.

Vanek, J. (1975) *Self-Management*. London: Penguin Books.

17 Public Enterprise and the Public Regulation of Private Enterprise

Introduction

Public enterprise may mean one of three things:

1 Those industries which are publicly owned but are operated at arm's length from Parliament in order to combine in the most efficient manner sound commercial practices and public responsibility. In this category are to be found the so-called nationalized industries or public corporations which were first established in the late 1940s (e.g. coal, railways).
2 Those activities which are owned and run by the state directly through departments of state (e.g. health, education).
3 Those activities which the state influences through the use of anti-monopoly measures, taxes and subsidies, but which are usually owned and operated in the private sector.

The third category comprises virtually the whole of economic activity and will be dealt with briefly in this chapter.

The Case for State Ownership and Direction

The case for public enterprise rests upon the existence of externalities and indivisibilities whose repercussions cannot be resolved or internalized by any agency other than the state. Health and education confer benefits not only upon the individual but also upon others. A may derive benefits from B's excellent education but be reluctant to hand B the money with which to finance his way through college. B might spend the money on riotous living, sell education vouchers in a black market or be duped by some private institute which offers dubious education certificates. So from altruistic or selfish motives A may be willing to finance B's education only if he can be sure that the product is being well monitored. Similarly, A may feel that the only way to ensure a decent wage for C, who is a coal miner, is to have the coal industry nationalized.

Goods may be classified as private goods or public goods with the dividing line being drawn on the principle of exclusion. If B can exclude A from a good which he has bought then the good is a private good. Public or collective goods are those goods from which exclusion is impossible or difficult. Of course some goods may have mixed characteristics – they may be partly private goods and partly public goods – for example, higher education. Whether it is possible to disentangle the characteristics such that A pays for his private benefits and the state pays for the public benefits will depend upon the costs of distinguishing the relevant characteristics. It may be desirable but it may be also be difficult and inefficient to administer a two-part pricing system.

Externalities are usually associated with indivisibilities. If production units cannot be built upon a small scale then exclusion may be difficult. Half-filled railway carriages, underutilized roads and empty hospitals are all examples of where A might benefit from B's demands. We are, in fact, back with the prisoner's dilemma. If A and B would both benefit from the clearing of a swamp then A might conceal his preferences in the hope that B might pay. Similarly, B might conceal his preferences with the result that the swamp does not get drained. What is required is some mechanism for the revelation of preferences and the only *deus ex machina* might be the state. The market can provide structures only when the indivisibilities are small; and if plant is also replicable then the market can ensure efficiency. Individuals might join a golf club or buy tinned beans from a firm until capacity is exhausted. Would-be consumers, seeing that the golf club is congested or that there are long queues for tinned beans, can go away and join another golf club or buy from another firm. Competition between golf clubs and between tinned beans firms also ensures their efficiency. If, however, indivisibilities are large and only one firm is in the market then that firm might restrict output to cover costs. In those circumstances state monopoly might be preferable to private monopoly.

Strategy

What sort of strategy might a public enterprise pursue? From the Paretian welfare economics of chapter 2 we can derive some suggestions.

Pricing

Paretian welfare economics defines an optimum as a situation from which it is impossible to make someone better off without making someone else worse off. This rule is translated into operational usage by noting that each individual will equate his marginal benefits with his marginal costs, and if both marginal benefits and costs are measured by prices and all individuals face the same prices then an optimum might be attainable. Hence public enterprises should equate their marginal costs with prices on the grounds that consumers should pay a price equal to the cost of supplying them with the last unit. That price will also measure the marginal benefit which they obtain from that commodity.

Unfortunately the marginal cost pricing rule encounters several obstacles. First, if there are unexhausted benefits from a bridge or plant such that marginal cost is below average cost then a marginal cost pricing policy will fail to provide a guide to their replacement; in the jargon of accounting it will not be covering overheads. This difficulty can be overcome by several methods. The state could decide to cover the overheads; but that might lead to a violation of the welfare optimum elsewhere. Taxes on income might discourage people from working; taxes on other goods might distort relative prices and purchases. Also people who do not benefit from a particular state service might object to benefiting others.

The alternative is for the public enterprise to have a two-part tariff. Consumers would be charged a fixed, lump-sum fee in order to consume the service and price per unit of the service consumed. Thus telephones, gas and electricity use two-part tariffs. The two-part tariff reflects the distinction between volume and rate which we mentioned in the chapter on cost and production management, and its use is symmetrical; that is, it can be used for underutilized as well as congested services. For example, in the case of roads a motorist could be charged a fixed fee, the road tax on his car, and a usage tax imposed upon the petrol he uses. Two-part tariffs seem to be perfectly sensible because they enable management to tap the consumer surplus enjoyed by purchasers.

However, any pricing policies can encounter difficulties because of the presence of externalities and imperfections elsewhere in the economy. Thus in some instances the state might not want to charge a price because that would defeat the purposes of public ownership. The most obvious example is medicine, where the state might not wish to deter anyone from coming forward for treatment. In such circumstances there is zero pricing as the most efficient solution; although recent practices have admitted prescription charges and the possibility of charging in-patients for meals and bedrooms. By and large, however, the health service, and to a lesser extent the education service, are based upon allowing 'customers' to come forward, and for doctors and teachers to determine treatment and benefits.

The second objection stems from the possibility that the private sector is riddled with monopoly. Thus if the coal industry sells coal to the electricity industry which, in turn, sells electricity to a monopolistic engineering industry, should coal and electricity be priced at marginal cost? The theory of the second-best suggests not. Instead both coal and electricity should impose a mark-up equal to that charged by the engineering industry in order to make the ratio of marginal costs to prices everywhere equal.

The final objection to marginal cost pricing is one which stems from Austrian economists. According to such writers the marginal cost pricing rule confuses decisions with outcomes. It is only as a result of competition that survivors will be found to be those firms whose marginal costs were covered by the market price. It is impossible to start from a decision to charge a price equal to marginal cost when the market price may not be known; and any attempt to do so may suggest that the firm is a monopolist who may be able to fix both market price and his own marginal cost; he may therefore be inefficient – raising price to cover inflated costs.

The various criticisms of public enterprises and their pricing policies have some effect upon government policy in the 1980s. Profits are now regarded as the index of efficiency and also a means whereby particular undertakings can make a contribution to the general financing of the public sector. Hence the Rayner reforms of the Civil Service and government departments has led to commercial prices for publications of the HMSO. It has also led to steep increases in the prices of gas and electricity. Public sector pricing is therefore being used to implement the Ramsay rule that taxes should be placed on goods in inelastic demand or inelastic supply.

Investment

Welfare economics also provides some guidelines to investment appraisal. Both the net present value rule and the rate of return rule can be used for investment appraisal. However, problems can arise with the measurement of benefits and the appropriate discount rate. There is the problem of measuring social benefits where monetary measures may be difficult to obtain. There is also the question of whether the market rate of interest should be used as a discount factor. Indeed there would seem to be three possible discount rates: (1) use the market rate because that is the best we have got; (2) use a discount rate lower than the market rate because the market rate is influenced by monopoly elements in the market; and (3) use a higher discount rate because public enterprises are subject to less risk than private ventures. In practice there is a tendency to use a discount rate similar to that used by large private firms.

Finance

Most public enterprises are financed either out of taxation or through borrowing. On various occasions there have been proposals to introduce some form of venture capital on which dividends might be paid. The argument is that some public enterprises feel constrained by the Treasury and should be allowed to go to the market. Furthermore, such a scheme might provide a market test of efficiency. Unfortunately problems might arise if the state enterprise ran into financial difficulties. Would the State be prepared to underwrite the losses of private shareholders?

Structure and Control

Public enterprises are operated either as departments of state or as semi-autonomous public corporations. In both cases there are problems of ensuring control and efficiency. The problems stem from the difficulty of defining the public interest. In the 1970s the nationalized industries had their prices held down in order to reduce inflation. As a result they incurred severe losses. In such circumstances the concept of efficiency becomes nebulous.

The Coal Industry and the Energy Sector

Many of the problems confronting public enterprises can be illustrated from the history of the coal industry under nationalization. The coal industry was nationalized for three reasons: first, it was felt to be a way of stabilizing miners' incomes; second, it was thought to be the only method of providing adequate finance and investment; third, it was argued that the coal industry was one of the commanding heights of the economy. All three arguments have been questioned in the 40 years since the industry was nationalized.

The history of the nationalized coal industry can be subdivided into four periods.

1   From 1947 to 1957 there was a coal shortage, but governments did not allow the price of coal to rise in order to ration available supplies and obtain an indicator of how much investment should be undertaken. Instead they physically rationed coal and attempted to expand the industry. The result of physical rationing was to exaggerate the extent of the coal shortage and distort effective planning.

2   From 1957 to 1970 the coal industry was in the doldrums owing to the availability of cheap oil from the Middle East. Successive governments ran the industry down slowly because of the social effects that closures would have on mining communities. In the process miners' wages fell.

3   From 1970 to 1979 the industry enjoyed a minor boom owing to the rise in oil prices. The National Union of Mineworkers fixed wage and employment levels, and the government covered any deficits.

4   From 1979 onwards oil prices tended to depress demand in the world economy and an excess supply of coal occurred. The problem was exacerbated by the expansion of the world supply of fuels induced by the rise in the price of oil. The discovery of British oil and gas became a contributory factor because the demand for them caused a rise in the exchange rate, and American coal became competitive with British coal. The depressed state of British industry caused the Central Electricity Generating Board, in search of ways of cutting costs, to press to be allowed to import cheap coal, and to be relieved of its obligation to use British coal. Indeed, the CEGB went further and suggested that the further supply of base-load electricity should be provided by nuclear power stations, and that coal-fired stations should be used only as standby units. By 1982 it was estimated that excess capacity amounted to some 20 million tonnes of coal. When the Coal Board attempted to close pits a long and bitter strike took place in 1984 and 1985.

The strike raised many issues of policy. What should be the price paid for coal by the CEGB to the NCB? Should the two concerns be treated as one public enterprise for which the transfer price is arbitrary? Should the price be based on the world price? Should the Board's accounting costs based upon historic costs be used as the basis for decisions about pit closures? What should be the optimal rate of contraction of the coal industry? The answers to these questions have still to be found, because they involve the interplay of public interest and commercial efficiency. In an attempt to obtain commercial efficiency the government is experimenting with privatization, but it is not clear that privatization is the solution. Many privatized public enterprises would still be monopolies, and their affairs would still require some form of regulation. Then the danger could arise that the owners of the privatized industry would 'capture' the regulators, which is a state of affairs that has occurred in America.

Transport

Transport is another area where public enterprise has been common. Inland transport was the subject which first exercised welfare economists such as Dupuit. We begin therefore with a consideration of road transport. The case for public ownership rests upon the basic needs of defence and law and order. Assuming that roads are publicly owned, however, how shall their services be charged? The simplest procedure, in the absence of congestion and exhaustion of capacity, would be to set prices equal to zero and recoup expenditure out of general taxation. That policy runs up against the objections which we have discussed earlier. Some roads are, however, subject to congestion. Owing to the presence of externalities, the cost to one person of putting his car on the road is less than the costs he imposes on others. The divergence of private cost from social cost would then suggest the imposition of a tax to equate private cost with social cost. But how should such a tax be administered? The simplest method based on traffic flows might be to impose a petrol tax, tolls on particular stretches of road, or parking meters. But by analogy with the distinction between volume and rate discussed in chapter 12 we might impose a tax on the volume of traffic, such as a lump-sum road tax.

Road traffic comprises private and public transport, and both compete with rail traffic. Historically, railways were regarded as a monopoly by virtue of sole ownership of the track. Hence the introduction of rate regulation. With the development of the internal combustion engine, however, there has emerged a problem of regulating competition between road and rail. Rail frequently complains that road users do not pay their full costs for use of the roads, and for accidents and claims subsidies. But there have been considerable difficulties in applying subsidies. Should they be general in order to allow managerial discretion? Or should they be specific, such as subsidies to commuters? If they are applied to commuters, would they interfere with the location of industry. The political pressure to curb subsidies has probably accounted for the rise in the use of price discrimination by British Rail.

Privatization and Public Regulation

The difficulties of managing private enterprises have led to pressures to sell off and privatize public undertakings. However, privatization does not automatically ensure greater efficiency. Many firms may still be monopolies even if they pass into private hands. Hence the demands for some form of regulation, as in the case of telecommunications. A regulatory body would presumably attempt to set rates so as to achieve a competitive output; but US experience of regulatory bodies suggests that they may be slow to adjust rates in periods of inflation, with the result that regulated bodies incur losses. It has also been the case that the regulated 'capture' the regulators and persuade them to set monopolistic rates.

The Monopoly Problem

The objection to monopoly is that it causes an inefficient allocation of resources; output is less than it would be under competition. The standard analysis has been based upon the structure–conduct–performance paradigm. Structure refers to such things as the number of sellers and the existence of barriers to entry. Conduct covers such issues as price and distribution policies. Finally, performance refers to profitability and technological progress.

In order to assess the structure of an industry it is customary to measure concentration. Various measures have been devised and none is ideal: concentration ratios, Herfindahl indices, the Hannah–Kay index, etc. The concentration ratio, which looks at the percentage of total output produced by a given number of firms, say 5, is arbitrary, whilst the Herfindahl index, which we encountered in chapter 9, imposes considerable problems of data collection. There are also problems of including imports. Above all there are the imponderable issues raised by the theory of contestable markets. There may be only one firm in the industry, but it may be subject to enormous potential competition should it raise its price.

In Britain aggregate concentration appears to have increased from around 22 per cent in 1949 to about 41 per cent in 1968, and thereafter remained constant (Prais, 1976). Between industries Curry and George (1983) found an average concentration ratio in 118 industries of 50.6 per cent concealed some industries with ratios of 90 per cent. Hart and Clarke (1985) found that 85 per cent of the variation in inter-industry concentration ratios could be explained by industry size, economies of scale and the number of plants per firm.

In the light of these problems of measuring concentration it should come as no surprise that the effects of monopoly on performance often appear to be limited. Harberger (1954) estimated that the welfare loss from monopoly was 0.1 per cent of GDP in the USA, which suggested that anti-trust legislation might yield a smaller return than tackling basic inequalities in health and education. His estimate has been criticized for its use of accounting data as a measure of profits and its failure to realize that monopolists will use resources to protect their monopoly positions. In the light of these criticisms Cowling and Mueller (1981) estimated the welfare loss in the USA to be 13.1 per cent and 7.2 per cent in Britain, but these results have, in turn, been criticized by Littlechild (1981), and by Masson and Shaanan (1984). Nor can firmer conclusions be drawn at the industry level. On the one hand some writers have found a positive correlation between concentration and price–cost margins. On the other hand some writers have found no association. The lack of conclusive evidence may have arisen for a variety of reasons such as the use of different periods of observation – which would suggest that the monopoly problem is transitory.

British Policy

The lack of generalizations has much to commend the inherent British pragmatic approach to the monopoly problem, although it may face businessmen with the problem of not knowing what attitude the authorities might take to, for example, a proposed merger. In 1948 a Monopoly Act was passed, and between 1948 and 1956 the Monopolies Commission investigated the problem of dominant firms, such as the British Match Corporation. The outcome of 8 years of investigation, however, was a conclusion that the major problem was the existence of trade associations which imposed restrictive practices. Hence the 1956 Restrictive Trade Practices Act outlawed many such restrictions although some exemptions, 'gateways', were allowed. The effect of the Act was to cause many agreements to be abandoned, but also to promote mergers and secret agreements. The effects therefore led to the passing of the Monopolies and Mergers Act 1965, and to the Competition Act 1980. The latter allowed individual firms to be investigated, and particular practices, such as price discrimination, to be analysed. In addition the Monopolies and Merger Commission was allowed to investigate public enterprises.

Assessing the impact of anti-monopoly policy is rendered difficult by the pragmatic approach. Had Britain adopted the view that monopoly was illegal *per se*, then the increase in concentration noted by Prais might have been averted. But British policy has also been affected by conflicting ideas. In the 1960s, for example, policy was influenced by the feeling that British firms were too small by foreign standards, and were failing to achieve economies of scale. The result had been a tendency to regard monopoly policy as having only a marginal influence upon economic activity.

Bibliography and References

Clarke, R. (1985) *Industrial Economics*. Oxford: Blackwell.

Cowling, K. G. (1982) *Monopoly Capitalism*. London: Macmillan.

Cowling, K. G. and Waterson, M. (1976) 'Price–cost margins and market structure', *Economica*, 43, 267–74.

Cowling, K. and Mueller, D. C. (1981) 'The social costs of monopoly power revisited', *Economic Journal*, 88, 727–48.

Curry, B. and George, K. D. (1983) 'Industrial concentration: a survey', *Journal of Industrial Economics*, 31, 203–55.

Hannah, L. and Kay, J. A. (1977) *Concentration in Modern Industry*. London: Macmillan.

Harberger, A. C. (1954) 'Monopoly and resource allocation', *American Economic Review*, 44, 77–87.

Hart, P. E. and Clarke, R. (1980) *Concentration in British Industry*. Cambridge: Cambridge University Press.

Holterman, S. E. (1973) 'Market structure and economic performance in UK manufacturing industry', *Journal of Industrial Economics*, 22, 119–40.

Littlechild, S. C. (1981) 'Misleading calculation of the social costs of monopoly power', *Economic Journal*, 91, 348–63.

Lyons, B. (1980) 'A new measure of minimum efficient plant size in UK manufacturing industry', *Economica*, 47, 125–32.

Masson, R. T. and Shaanan, J. (1984) 'Social costs of oligopoly and the value of competition', *Economic Journal*, 94, 520–35.

Nickell, S. and Metcalfe, D. (1978) 'Monopolistic industries and monopoly profits, or are Kelloggs cornflakes overpriced? ', *Economic Journal*, 88, 254–68.

Phillips, A. (1976) 'A critique of empirical studies of the relations between market structure and profitability', *Journal of Industrial Economics*, 24, 241–9.

Prais, S. J. (1976) *The Evolution of Giant Firms in Britain*. Cambridge: Cambridge University Press.

Stigler, G. J. (1964) 'A theory of oligopoly', *Journal of Political Economy*, 72, 44–61.

Turvey, R. (1971) *Economic Analysis and Public Enterprises*. London: Allen & Unwin.

Index